American Automobile Association

All-in-One

ROME

AND

SURROUNDINGS

MILL HOUSE® ASSOCIATES

COLLIER BOOKS
MACMILLAN PUBLISHING COMPANY
NEW YORK

Mill House Publishing Ltd.
Monxton Mill, Monxton, SP11 8AW
Hampshire, United Kingdom

Collier Books
Macmillan Publishing Company
866 Third Avenue, New York, NY 10022
Collier Macmillan Canada, Inc.

Library of Congress Cataloging-in-Publication Data
AAA all-in-one. Rome and surroundings / Mill House Associates.
— 1st Collier Books ed.
p. cm.
Includes index.
ISBN 0-02-035123-2
1. Rome (Italy)—Description—1975– —Tours. 2. Rome Region
(Italy)—Description and travel—Tours. I. Mill House Associates.
II. Title: Rome and surroundings.
DC804.A37   1989   88-31586   CIP
914.5′6304928—dc19

Macmillan books are available at special discounts for bulk purchases
for sales promotions, premiums, fund-raising, or educational use.
For details contact:

Special Sales Director
Macmillan Publishing Company
866 Third Avenue
New York, NY 10022

All prices quoted in this book were accurate at the time of
going to press. Sadly, prices are constantly changing. Mill
House Associates apologizes in advance for any inaccuracies
which may occur as a result of this changing world.

First Collier Books Edition 1989
Printed in the United States of America

THE ALL-IN-ONE GUIDE

This book represents a whole new way of looking at travel – one that starts from *your* point of view.

- You have your own particular interests, and you want to know where to find the facts. Until now you had to buy an armful of guidebooks – no more. **All-in-One** covers everything, from castles and museums to boat rides and golf, with the best food, hotels and hotspots en route.

- You want the best at a price you can afford – this book is just that. It's been researched by people who live in the region and know what's good value – **all-in-one** book.

- You're not a packaged tour traveler, so you want non-touristy spots and driving directions. These, too, are included: maps, road and visual references checked out for you. **All-in-one** location when you need it.

- You don't want to have to retrace your steps, so we've built in a unique BUILD-A-TOUR concept which allows you to design your own tours, **all-in-one**.

- You don't want clichés. You *do* want to know where to eat, what's a bargain, what to see when you're on the spot. So we advise you what to choose at that specific restaurant and why this particular hotel has been selected. You have it **all-in-one** and right at hand.

- In golden bygone days, route maps and books were extraneous: you had a friendly, knowledgeable guide at your elbow every step of the way. They were all-in-one experts: so is this **All-in-One** book.

  We hope you'll find it an especially helpful, amusing and comprehensive companion.

Acknowledgements

Editorial Director:	Peter Verstappen
Managing Editor/Senior Writer:	Emma Stanford
Editors:	Kate Truman Tean Mitchell
Writers:	Susan Jewell Patricia Strathern Paul Strathern
Researchers:	Virginia Dahlenburg Valentina Rettordini Suzy Westphal
Art Director:	Robert Mathias
Cartographers:	Nicholas Skelton Kevan Hamman
Indexer:	Helen Norris
Typesetter:	Input Typesetting Woodman Works Durnsford Road Wimbledon SW19 8DR

CONTENTS

How to Use this Guide 7
Everything You Need to Know 9
Rome – A Heritage of History 20
Italian Cuisine 22
Wining Your Way Through Italy 28

ROME

Getting About 35
Top Sights 40
Local Delights 44
Bridges/Gardens/Parks 47
Museums 49
Roman Walking Tours 55
Shopping 73
Restaurants 109
Cafés 118
Hotels 121
Nightspots 131

DAY TRIPS AROUND ROME

Day Trip Diagram 133

Tour 1: Visionary Villas
Route A : Rome – Tivoli 134
Route A1: Tivoli – Palestrina 138
Route A2: One-Day Extension: Tivoli – Subiaco –
Fiuggi – Palestrina 139
Route B : Palestrina – Rome 144
Route C : Palestrina – Frascati 144

Tour 2: The Castelli Romani
Route A : Rome – Frascati – Marino – Nemi – Albano –
Castel Gandolfo 145
Route B : Castel Gandolfo – Rome 152
Route C : Castel Gandolfo – Aprilia (Anzio) 152

Tour 3: Anzio and Antiquities
Route A : Rome – Pratica di Mare – Ardea – Anzio –
Ostia Antica 154
Route B : Ostia Antica – Rome 160
Route C : Ostia Antica – Fregene – Via Aurelia 160

Tour 4: Taking to the Water
Route A : Rome – Ladispoli – Cerveteri – Bracciano –
            Trevignano Romano – Osteria Nuova 163
Route B : Osteria Nuova – Rome 171
Route C : Osteria Nuova – Campagnano – Morlupo 172

Tour 5: Villages with a View
Route A : Rome – Morlupo – Fiano Romano – Ponzano
            Romano – Stz Piana Bella di Montelibretti 173
Route B : Stz Piana Bella de Montelibretti – Rome 177
Route C : Stz Piana Bella de Montelibretti – Tivoli 177

LONGER TOURS

A Longer Tour North to Lower Tuscany and Umbria 179
Route D : Ladispoli – (Civitavecchia) – Tarquinia –
            Orbetello – (Grosseto) – Castiglione Della
            Pescaia 180
Route D1: Castiglione Della Pescaia – Siena 189
Route E : South from Siena to Orvieto 202
Route F : Siena – Cortona – Perugia – Assisi – Spoleto –
            Orvieto 203
Route G : Orvieto – Bolsena – Viterbo – Bracciano –
            Rome 236

A Longer Tour South to Naples and the Amalfi Coast 246
Route H : A Southern Tour: Rome – Anagni – Cassino –
            Capua – Caserta – Naples 247
Route I : Naples – Ercolano – Pompeii – Sorrento –
            Amalfi – Salerno – Naples 279
Route J : Agnano – Pozzuoli – Gaeta – Terracina –
            Circeo – Anzio – Rome 305

Index 320

HOW TO USE THIS GUIDE

This book divides into three distinct sections: Rome; driving tours centered on Rome; and two longer motoring tours which take you north to Siena, returning to Rome by way of Perugia and south to Naples and Salerno via Caserta. With the shorter tours based on Rome you can use our unique Build-a-Tour system. This enables you to link day trips together to form your own tour around Rome lasting two, three, four or more days. You can do this by taking one of the link routes which connect each individual day tour out of Rome. These eliminate the need to return to the capital if you want to stay in the country.

There's a simple classification system which divides each tour into three sections. **Route A** is the outward journey from Rome. At the final point of interest on the tour there is a choice of routes: **Route B** always returns directly to Rome; **Route C** is a link route which connects with Route A of the next tour.

For example, set off on Tour 1, Route A to Tivoli and Palestrina, then connect via Route C (Tour 1) with Frascati (which is on Tour 2). From Frascati you can take Tour 2, around the Castelli Romani, then take Route B back to Rome, or carry on via Route C to Anzio on Tour 3.

The link routes (C) are designed to take you quickly from one area of outstanding appeal to another. Precise details of the round-Rome tours and the links are shown on page 133.

HOTEL CODES

Wherever possible, we've tried to give you a good representative range of hotels, from small, family-run and remarkably reasonable accommodations to rather more elegant and elegantly-priced establishments.

For hotels we've used L-for-lire symbol codes to indicate not only price but also value for money. Broadly speaking, the codes indicate the following prices per double room for one or two people, not including breakfast:

L	$25–40
LL	$40–70
LLL	$70–155+

Prices are further affected by time of year and demand at the particular locale: for example, hotels in all categories tend to be more expensive in towns than in the country.

Precise closing dates for many hotels were unavailable at time of going to press. So if you're traveling out of season and a closing period has been indicated it's best to write ahead.

HOTEL SYMBOLS

For simplicity we've used hotel symbols throughout the guide. These are as follows:

📺	=	TV in room	🍶	=	Mini-bar in room
☎	=	Direct dial telephone	⚲	=	Swimming Pool
		in room	🏌18	=	Golf course
✗	=	Restaurant on	⚬	=	Tennis
		premises	🅿	=	Parking lot
♀	=	Bar on premises			

GENERAL HOTEL DOS AND DONT'S

1. Do reserve your first few days' accommodations before you arrive.

2. Do plan your motoring route a few days in advance then reserve rooms along the way. Citing a credit card will confirm the reservation, but you'll pay even if you don't show up.

3. Don't panic if the hotels on your route are full. Many local Tourist Offices will help you find a room.

4. Never leave valuables lying about in your room or car. Either keep them with you, or make sure they're locked away – either in your room, or the hotel safe.

RESTAURANTS

Again a good selection, from the cheap and cheerful to the expensive but excellent, has been included. We've bent over backwards to avoid the terribly pretentious. Pride of place has been given to restaurants where the welcome is genuinely warm, the food – whatever the price – good value for money and where at least some excellent local dishes are available.

Restaurants are graded as follows for a single meal with wine:

L	$15–35
LL	$35–60
LLL	$60–75

Credit card designations are as for hotels. Above the café/bar level, many restaurants accept them.

CREDIT CARD SYMBOLS

Plastic is a way of life. Here are our symbols for credit cards:

AE	=	American Express
DC	=	Diners Club
MC	=	MasterCard, Access, Eurocard
V	=	Visa, Barclaycard, Carte Bleue

EVERYTHING YOU NEED TO KNOW

PASSPORTS AND VISAS

To get into Italy you will need a current US passport, but no visa is required for a visit of less than three months.

MONEY

Italy's currency unit is the Italian Lire (L), pronounced *leera*. The 50 lire and 100 lire coins are silver, and the 500 lire coin is two-tone with a bronze center and silver rim. Paper money is covered by bills of 1,000, 2,000, 5,000, 10,000, 50,000 and 100,000 lire.

Currency Regulations

You can import into Italy an unlimited amount of money in foreign currency or traveler's checks, but you can only bring in (or take out) a maximum of L200,000. You may be asked to show how much money you're bringing into the country, and how much you're taking out. You're not allowed to leave Italy with more money than you had when you entered the country. You may be asked to provide evidence of any Italian currency you've purchased, so keep the receipts supplied when you change money.

Currency Exchange

While it's a good idea to arrive with some Italian currency, traveler's checks are still the best way to transport cash. Exchange rates for banknotes are notoriously low on both sides of the Atlantic. Major banks such as the Banca Nazionale del Lavoro, the Banco di Roma and the Cassa di Risparmio di Roma (plus numerous smaller ones) all offer exchange facilities. They are generally open Monday to Friday 8:30am–1:30pm and 3pm or 3:30pm–4pm or 4:30pm (closed on public holidays – see pages 11 and 18) with a one- or two-hour lunch break in most provincial areas. The bank rate is set and commission charges, at around 1%, vary little. If there's a specific desk it'll be marked *cambio*.

In larger cities an exchange office or hotel will also exchange cash or traveler's checks. The rate is unfixed, so use them only in an emergency outside banking hours.

Credit Cards

After a slow start, the Italians are finally accepting plastic as inevitable, but cards are still regarded with deep suspicion outside the main tourist areas. Visa is the most widely accepted. Should you lose your credit card, report it immediately on these numbers:

American Express 1678–72000 (24 hr service, toll free)

Diners Club(06) 3213841 MasterCard(06) 479811 Visa(06) 67181

INSURANCE AND HEALTH

Arrange trip cancellation insurance with your travel agent before you pay the full cost of your holiday. In-flight personal and baggage insurance is often covered automatically if you pay for your ticket by credit card. Check this before you assume it applies to you.

You should also take out a comprehensive policy covering you and your belongings for the duration of your visit. Health insurance will cover most treatment costs incurred abroad (read the small print) and can be extended to include emergency repatriation. Dentistry is often excluded from these packages.

If you are involved in an accident in Italy the emergency service telephone numbers are: **Police**: 113, **Highway/Traffic Police**: 55 77 905, **Ambulance** (Italian Red Cross) 5100. The **US Embassy** number in Rome is (06) 46714.

WEATHER

Even in mid-winter it's seldom very cold in and around Rome. A snowfall is definitely a freak event. On the other hand, in mid-August central Italy can be unbearably hot – especially in the cities. At other times expect to find a pleasant warm climate with moderate rainfall. Here's a guide to average temperatures in Rome, which give a good indication of what you can expect over the whole central Italian region.

Average temperature in Rome

Month	°F	°C	Month	°F	°C
January	48	9	July	84	29
February	51	11	August	83	29
March	57	14	September	77	25
April	64	18	October	68	20
May	73	22	November	57	14
June	80	27	December	50	10

POSTAGE

Most main post offices are open Monday to Friday 8:15am–2pm, and Saturday 8:30am–noon. You can send telegrams 24 hours a day by calling 6795530. Current postal rates to the US are: L600 for postcards, L700 for letters up to 20 grams (one sheet of airmail paper in an airmail envelope equals 5 grams), and express letters cost an extra L2,200. Stamps can also be bought at *tabacchi* (tobacconists-cum-newsstands) where you buy postcards.

TELEPHONES

The Italian telephone system can be erratic at the best of times.

You'll find public telephones in all main public places, as well as in most bars and restaurants. Most phones take tokens (*gettone*), though some of the more modern ones now take coins. *Gettone* are obtainable from the token machine beside the phone and cost L100. For help in placing your long-distance calls ask for *telefoni*, and the operator will place your call. The cheapest time to call the US is on Sunday, and between 11pm and 8am on weekdays.

A word of warning: try to avoid calling from your hotel, as many hotels charge excessively for this service. It's often twice, or more, the actual cost of the call. Roman telephone numbers, in common with many outside districts, have numbers with anything from three to seven digits. If you're dialling into a city from outside the area, dial the appropriate area code, which starts with a zero, then the number you require. For example, the area code for Venice is 041, for Florence it's 055.

For international calls to the US dial 001, then your US area code, followed by the number.

NOTE: Don't forget that Italian time is six hours ahead of Eastern Standard Time (that's an hour ahead of Greenwich Mean Time). Italian clocks go forward an hour in spring, and back an hour in the fall. This can lead to confusion for a couple of weeks, as changes in Europe between summer and wintertime rarely coincide with changes in US zones.

OPENING HOURS

Sights
Throughout this book you'll find details of opening hours for all the major attractions we mention. You can generally assume churches will be open from around 9am to 6 or 7pm, though some lock up at lunchtime, close earlier in winter and discourage idle visitors on Sunday morning. Mondays are very quiet on the sightseeing front with most museums and many other sights closed. Regional sites often close from October to May.

Banks
In major centers most banks are open Monday to Friday 8:30am–1:30pm and 3pm or 3:30pm–4pm or 4:30pm. Banks are closed on Saturday but the *cambio* (exchange offices) tend to be open Monday to Saturday, 9am–1:30pm and 4:30pm–8pm.

Shops
Retail stores are usually open 9am–1pm and 3:30pm–7:30pm. This holds true for most food, gift and clothing stores, especially in Rome and larger towns. In villages these hours are likely to vary. In winter, many stores are closed on Monday morning throughout the country. During the summer, they may close for their annual vacation, which can last for anything up to four weeks around

July to August. Many gift shops in tourist regions close during the winter (October to March). Supermarkets are often closed on Saturday afternoon during the summer and Thursday afternoon in the winter.

Tourist Offices
Italian Tourist Offices are a law unto themselves. Even if they state their opening hours clearly on the door, there's no guarantee they'll actually reopen when they say. In large towns, such as Siena and Perugia, the Tourist Office is open year round Monday–Saturday 8:30am–1pm 3:30pm–6:30pm (approx). Saturday is often a half-day however, particularly in winter. Out in the countryside, small town Tourist Offices maintain a distinctly erratic timetable and close down entirely over the winter. They reopen for the summer season between April/May and September. Where we cannot be specific, opening hours are not given. Where they are stated, they're by no means guaranteed.

TIPS ON TIPPING

Naturally, all tips are discretionary, but here's a rough guide to the going rate for good service rendered:
Taxi drivers: 10%.
Washroom attendants: Ignore the L500 in the bowl and pay L200.
Cloakroom attendants: These require a fee, usually between L300–500, depending on the quality of the establishment.
Waiters: Service is always included, though it's still polite to leave something – 7–10% depending on the quality of service.
Wine waiters: Should not be tipped separately, unless in exceptional circumstances.
Cafés and bars: Service is included at the table, but not at the bar. Leave 10%.
Hotel baggage porters: Service is included in the bill, but expect to pay L1,500 for each bag.
Concierge: Depends on how much you use him. If quite a bit, L3,000–5,000 per day is about right.
Airport and other baggage porters: L1,500 per piece is the accepted rate.
Hairdressers and barbers: 10–15% depending on how much their handiwork pleases you.
Theaters and movies: You pay to be shown to your seat even if the theater's empty (L1,000). The ushers have no other salary.
Museum and palazzo guides: Though you've paid for the tour, tip the guide around L3,000 as you leave.
Gas station attendants: If the attendant does anything beyond putting the gas in (washes the windshield, checks the oil, etc.) give him L1,000 or so.
Deckchair attendants: L500–1,000.

SIZING UP

Go to a dozen stores in any city and you'll find variations on the sizing theme, so only an overall conversion is given here. If in doubt, try it on or buy a size larger.

CONVERSION CHART: WOMEN'S CLOTHING

Dresses

US	8	10	12	14	16	18
UK	10	12	14	16	18	20
Continental	38	40	42	44	46	48

Cardigans, sweaters, blouses

US	10	12	14	16	18	20
UK	32	34	36	38	40	42
Continental	38	40	42	44	46	48

Shoes

US	4½	5	5½	6	6½	7	7½	8	8½
UK	3	3½	4	4½	5	5½	6	6½	7
Continental	35½	36	36½	37	37½	38	38½	39	39½

CONVERSION CHART: MEN'S CLOTHING

Clothing sizes

US	34	35	36	37	38	39	40	42
UK	34	35	36	37	38	39	40	42
Continental	34	36	38	40	42	44	46	48

Shirts

US	14	14¼	14½	15	15¼	15¾	16	16½	17	17¼
UK	14	14¼	14½	15	15¼	15¾	16	16½	17	17¼
Continental	35	36	37	38	39	40	41	42	43	44

Shoes

US	6½	7½	8	8½	9½	10½	11	12	12½
UK	6	7	7½	8	9	10	10½	11½	12
Continental	39	40	41	42	43	44	45	46	47

SHOPPING

Theoretically it's possible for you to reclaim VAT (Value Added Tax) on goods purchased in Italy. However, in practice the process is so complicated and involves so many forms, that it isn't worth your while unless you're making a considerable purchase (i.e. one running into hundreds of dollars). When this is the case, the shop where you buy the goods will help with your exemption arrangements.

CUSTOMS

Italian Customs

When you arrive in Italy from the US you're allowed to bring in up to $400-worth of foreign goods – but these must either be gifts or for your personal use. (Also, you can't do this again within 30 days.) Included in this allowance are: 400 cigarettes or 200 cigarillos or 100 cigars or 500 grams of tobacco; two liters of wine or one liter of alcohol more than 22% proof or two liters of alcohol less than 22% proof; 50 grams of perfume plus one liter of toilet water; adults can bring in L75,000-worth of other goods, children under 15 a mere L37,500-worth.

US Customs

Returning home to the good old US of A, you may import $400-worth of foreign goods duty free. This applies to all travelers including babes-in-arms. You must be over 21 to qualify for the allowance of one liter of alcohol, 200 cigarettes and 100 non-Cuban cigars. The cost of these items will be deducted from the $400 allowance. No meat, fish, fruit, plants, seeds, soil or other agricultural products are admitted. Only one bottle of US trade-marked perfume is allowed.

If you mail gifts home, there's a maximum value of $50 per package. Each recipient may receive only one package per day. You can't send perfumes worth more than $5, tobacco or alcohol.

If you already own expensive foreign-made articles such as cameras, personal stereos, jewelry or watches which you intend to travel with, it's a good idea to register them with US Customs before you leave home. It can save a weary couple of hours of explanations upon your return.

MOTORING MADE EASY

Touring by car gives you the freedom to discover the real Italy. There's an extensive network of roadways (over 750,000 miles) ranging from simple tracks to superb *autostrade* (which cover over 3,500 miles). All main cities are linked by fast *autostrade* (toll motorways), and by lesser, toll-free roads. These range from *superstrade* (free highways) through *strade di grande comunicazione* (main roads), *strade di interesse regionale* (regional highways), *strade importanti* (main roads) to *altre strade* (lesser roads).

Documents

Your current US driving license is acceptable throughout Europe. A driving license, passport and a credit card are all you need to hire a car. When renting a car, you'll receive the necessary Green Insurance Card and registration papers as a matter of course. The International Driving Permit (IDP) isn't required in Italy. Your AAA card or the equivalent may come in handy if you need breakdown services in Italy. You should keep all these papers with you: not in the car.

Motorist's vocabulary

Gasoline	*La benzina*
Fill it up	*Il pieno*
I need oil/water/air	*Ho bisogno d'olio/d'acqua/d'aria*
Please wash the car	*Lavi la macchina, per favore*
Where is the garage?	*Dov'é il garage?*
The car doesn't work	*La macchina non funziona*
Motor	*Il motore*
Battery	*La batteria*
Fan belt	*La ventola*
Tire	*Il pneumatico*
Headlight	*Il faro*
Brakes	*I freni*
Gears	*Gli ingranaggi*
Antifreeze	*L'antigelo*
I have right of way	*Ho la precedenza*
One way	*Senso unico*

Roadwork signs:

Detour	*Deviazione*
Roadworks	*Lavore stradali*
Uneven road surface	*Strada dissestata*

The basics

Gas is sold by the liter. One US gallon equals 3.78 liters. At present, gas costs around L1,350 per liter for super.

All distances on maps and on signposts are marked in kilometers. One kilometer is approximately ⅝ths of a mile. Unless otherwise indicated the speed limit in built-up areas is 50kph (just over 37mph). For toll roads (*autostrade*) it's usually 110kph (just over 80mph), while for highways it's 90kph (56mph). Cars on *autostrade* are often checked by camera. If you exceed the limit you can be heavily fined on the spot. You'll also suffer a heavy fine if you're caught driving after you've been drinking heavily; you can even go to jail for six months. Don't drink and drive, even though there's no official alcohol test and no legal level of alcohol you're not permitted to exceed.

Another thing to watch out for is that Italian traffic lights go from green to amber-and-green before turning to red. Use of the horn is forbidden in most built-up areas: you'll see a sign *zona di silenzio* when you enter such areas.

Ambulances, fire engines and all police vehicles have automatic right of way on all public roads.

Use dipped headlights at night in cities. Flashing your headlights has the same meaning as sounding a horn. Yellow headlights are compulsory on Italian cars. Foreign motorists bringing their own car into the country must fix yellow discs to their headlights or cover them with transparent yellow varnish.

Using seat belts is not compulsory but is strongly advised.

The following essential rules are worth remembering:

- Priority is from the right on all traffic circles, but not for traffic coming into a road from side roads.

- Follow all arrows painted on the road when you're in lane. When the arrow indicates turn, you must turn. You'll find, however, that Italians regard this rule as a threat to their freedom of choice and make a point of swapping lanes at every opportunity. This can be particularly alarming on highways.

- Outside built-up areas you're normally allowed to park on the right-hand side of the road. In towns you can park at a *zona disco* for specified periods: purchase the discs for these zones at any gas station.

- After overtaking on a multi-lane highway, you're meant to return to the inner lane or face a heavy on-the-spot fine. The fact that many Italians tend to ignore this rule completely is their concern, not yours.

Breakdowns

If you break down, make sure you try to move your car to a position causing the least obstruction to other road users. Use your hazard lights and display a warning triangle (compulsory in Italy).

There's a motorway network of emergency phone boxes. These connect, via the police, with the ACI (Italian equivalent of the AAA). Or you can call the police (*carabinieri*) for assistance.

If you break down on other roads, ask for help from a local garage. Be sure to check prices before asking anyone to start work on your vehicle. Always obtain car rental company approval before repairwork starts.

Accidents

If you have an accident be sure to swap names, license plate numbers and insurance information with the other party. If anyone is hurt call the police (113) at once. If your car is rented be sure to call the car rental company, preferably in Rome where they're more likely to speak English. Get the names and addresses of any witnesses if possible. If the accident is serious, it's a good idea to take photographs. Should the accident have caused any injuries, you're liable to be held at the police station for three or four hours. If you need an ambulance, dial 5100. This connects you with the Italian Red Cross.

CAR RENTAL

International car rental companies, such as Hertz, Avis and Budget, are at all major airports, such as Fiumicino (Leonardo da Vinci), Ciampino and in most major cities. This is also true of some of the European and larger Italian groups.

To rent a car you'll need a passport, valid driving license and one of the major credit cards such as American Express, Visa, Diners Club or MasterCard. Alternatively, some companies will accept a cash deposit. Terms and conditions on this vary widely so check when inquiring.

Many car rental companies offer better rates if you reserve before you travel to Italy so it's advisable to call them using their toll-free numbers well before you depart. (Some of their special packages must be booked considerably in advance like APEX airline fares.) The key point to bear in mind is that shopping around can save you pots of money.

It's also worth looking into the airlines' joint fly-drive programs. These offer low-cost car rental as an add-on to the basic air fare. Indeed in the off-season, airlines have been known to throw in the car at no extra cost.

Do check with airlines such as Air Canada, Alitalia, Pan Am, TWA and American Airlines to see what they offer in the way of car rental 'bolt-ons'. Again comparative shopping pays.

Other tips to bear in mind
Short-term rentals, generally less than one week, are way more expensive on a per day basis than longer hires. The reason? They try to capture business travelers for maximum rates. As a result you may be better advised to hire for a week even if you're not sure you'll be using the car every day.

The more expensive rates of the major multinationals may actually be cheaper when three other factors are taken into account: the insurance premiums for personal accident insurance and collision damage waiver; gas for the car; and – very importantly – how much free mileage you get. Is the first tank of gas included?

Do insure: the complications of not doing so can waste money and valuable vacation time.

When choosing a car rental company, be sure to ask how extensive their national (or, if crossing a border, international) network is. Also ask if breakdown service by one of the automobile clubs is included. Having your Fiat collapse in Siena when the nearest repair point is Rome is decidedly unromantic.

Once you've found exactly what you want, obtain a reservation order number to avoid confusion when picking up the car, plus written confirmation of your reservation, its length, and the rate.

Car rental offices in Rome
Avis, Via Tiburtina 1231A
Tel: (06) 436961
Budget, Via Sistina 24B
Tel: (06) 461905
Hertz, Viale Leonardo da Vinci 421
Tel: (06) 51711
Maggiore, Viale di Villa Massimo 13
Tel: (06) 866956

Before you start
One car's turn indicators are positioned where another model's windshield wipers are. Murphy's law dictates that in neither case do these accord with your car back home. Consequently, a quiet five minutes spent checking out all the controls in the car rental parking lot represents time amply repaid once under way. Several of the major car rental firms provide magazines or other instructional material which may help. Special tip: inserting the key and starting the car is easy. Given various anti-theft devices (which again vary widely), removing the key can be another matter. Make sure you've mastered this minor but vital maneuver.

Many car rental companies also provide maps. These are a must. Much as we've tried to anticipate your every driving need with clear directions and maps, space dictates that we can't be as graphically detailed as we'd like. A map has other benefits. It shows you what's just off the route which may appeal.

NATIONAL HOLIDAYS

These can result in severe congestion on the roads, when many people return to the country to visit family. So try not to drive on the following days:

New Year's Day	January 1
Epiphany	January 6
Easter Monday	April 4†
Liberation Day	April 25
Labor Day	May 1
Proclamation of the Republic	June 2*
Assumption Day	August 15
All Saints' Day	November 1
Unification Day	November 4*
Immaculate Conception	December 8
Christmas Day	December 25
St Stephen's Day	December 26

† *A moveable feast: same day as back home.*
* *These two days are celebrated on the first Sunday of June and November respectively.*

USEFUL ADDRESSES

In USA & Canada
Italian State Tourist Offices
New York: Suite 1565, 630 Fifth Avenue, NY 10111
Tel: (212) 245 4961
Chicago: Suite 1046, 500 North Michigan Avenue, IL 60611
Tel: (312) 644 0990/1
San Francisco: Suite 801, 360 Post Street, CA 94108
Tel: (415) 392 5266
Montreal: Store 56, Plaza 3, Place Ville Marie, Quebec
Tel: (514) 8667667

In Rome
Tourist Information
ENIT (National Tourist Board), Via Marghera 2
Tel: (06) 4971282
EPT (Provincial Tourist Board), Via Parigi 5
Tel: (06) 461851
There are also information offices at Termini station and Fiumicino (Leonardo da Vinci) airport.
These are normally open 9am–7pm, with some offices closing 1pm–4pm.

Airline Offices
Alitalia, Via Leonida Bissolati 13
Tel: (06) 5456
Pan Am, Via Leonida Bissolati 46
Tel: (06) 4773
TWA, Via Barberini 67
Tel: (06) 47211

Rome Airports Information
Fuimicino:
Flight information
Tel. (06) 60121
Ciampino:
Flight information
Tel. (06) 4694

Churches
Church of Jesus Christ of Latter Day Saints, Via Cimone 95
Rome Baptist Church, Piazza San Lorenzo in Lucina 35
St Paul's American Church, Via Napoli 58
San Silvestro Catholic Church, Piazza San Silvestro 1
Santa Susanna Catholic Church, Via XX Settembre 14

Night Pharmacists
Brienza, Piazza del Risorgimento 44
Tel: (06) 352157
Internazionale, Piazza Barberini 49
Tel: (06) 47211
Piram, Via Nazionale 228
Tel: (06) 460754

Main Post Office
Piazza San Silvestro
Tel: (06) 160
Open: Mon–Fri 8:30am–9pm,
Sat 8am–noon

After hours gas stations
AGIP Lungotevere Ripa 8 (Trastevere)
ESSO Via Anastasio II 268 (Trionfale)
MOBIL Corso di Francia/
   Via di Vigna Stelluti (Flaminio)

24-hour newsstands
Via Vittorio Veneto
Via del Tritone
Piazza Cola di Rienzo

ROME – A HERITAGE OF HISTORY

Saints and sinners, popes and poets, Romeos and rascals, Juliets and jilters – you'll find them all in Rome. Since the legendary founding of Rome by Romulus over 2,700 years ago in 753BC, the city has played host to a cornucopia of colorful characters. After Julius Caesar forgot to look behind him, there was no looking back. Nero fiddled while Rome burned and a succession of emperors fed Christians and other dissidents to the lions. Nor did things improve much when the Christians took over, judging from the record of the Borgia popes. But it wasn't all bad. Roman baths and roads, and the surviving monuments of ancient Rome bear witness to a grandeur and civilizing influence which once extended across Europe from Britain to North Africa. The *Pax Romana* underpinned the greatest empire the ancient world had ever seen. In those days it was said 'all roads lead to Rome.'

With such a daunting history to live up to, it's not surprising that Rome has had its leaner periods through the centuries. Four centuries ago the city was described by a visitor as little more than a haunt of thieves and vagabonds living amongst ruins. Yet not long after this Rome's finest monument, St Peter's, was built. To this day, it remains the greatest church in Christendom, adorned with masterpieces by the geniuses of the Renaissance, such as Michelangelo and Raphael. Today, St Peter's stands in the Vatican City – a state within a city, with its own foreign legations, currency and even its own army: the celebrated Swiss Guards.

The Italians claim their culture is second to none, and most of their best-known artists lived and worked in Rome at some stage in their careers. Virgil, the poet of the Roman Empire and author of the *Aeneid*, lived for many years in and around Rome. Dante, author of the *Divine Comedy* (reckoned by scholars to be the finest of all poems), spent time in the capital. Foreign masters have also flocked to Rome through the centuries, drawn by the magnetic quality of a city whose appeal is unique among the great capitals of the world. Lord Byron misbehaved here, and Goethe fell in love; Keats rhapsodized by the Spanish Steps, and Norwegian playwright Ibsen was once voted the worst-dressed foreign resident in Rome.

Today you won't find many shabbily dressed Romans. The locals pride themselves on their chic and elegance. Stroll past the cafés of the Via Veneto if you want to see what the Roman smart set are wearing today: it's what the world's smart set will be wearing tomorrow.

Rome is no longer the hub of Italy; the commercial and financial center of the country has long since moved north to Milan and Turin, making Italy the world's seventh industrial power. But Rome is still the nation's capital. Its self-importance remains undiminished, as does its lively and easygoing way of life. In Rome, you're less than 20 miles from the beaches of the Mediterranean. Drive east, and within a couple of hours you can be in the lovely unspoilt countryside of the Ernici mountains. Head north, and you come to the historic cities of Siena and Perugia. In nearby Frascati and Orvieto you can sample Italy's finest wines. While south of Rome you can visit one of Italy's more modern historic sites: the beach at Anzio, site of the Allied landings in World War II. There are beautiful lakes both north and south of the city. Overlooking Lake Albano you'll find the Pope's summer residence at Castel Gandolfo, but our favorite is Lake Bracciano to the north. We guarantee you'll find something to suit all tastes in and around Rome.

ITALIAN CUISINE

Italian cooks are not kitchen magicians like the French, working for hours on a sauce that would mystify the most sensitive palate. Instead, they're masters of combining ingredients and condiments in a straightforward manner to bring out the best in each vegetable or meat. Italians bring dedication and a matchless passion to their love of food. In a city of more than two and a half million people, only a handful of Rome's thousands of restaurants are non-Italian. Eating out is entertainment, and a meal can last for hours.

There is no question that pasta is the best known Italian food. But exactly what is it? Simply a dough made from water and semolina, a semi-fine flour ground from the inner kernels of hard durum wheat. With the help of a machine this becomes macaroni, rigatoni or spaghetti. Eggs are added to the dough to make various noodles such as lasagne, tagliatelle and fettuccini.

Rome has always had its earthy side and Roman cuisine reflects this. The cooking in the capital and the surrounding regions of Lazio and the Abruzzi is vigorous and colorful. The highlights of the Roman table are pasta dishes such as *spaghetti all'amatriciana* (tomato sauce highly seasoned with bits of bacon, garlic, red peppers and onions), and *spaghetti alla carbonara* (sauce of beaten egg yolks, oil, black pepper and bacon). *Gnocchi alla romana* is a Thursday-only dish – tiny dumplings of semolina flour smothered in butter and Parmesan cheese.

In addition to local cuisine, Rome also has many restaurants which specialize in other regional Italian dishes. Some to seek out include *polenta*, a flavorful cornmeal mush from the Piedmont area in the north, that dates back to the Etruscans. The Roman Legions conquered the world on a version of this northern speciality. Conquer your appetite with a plate of *polenta con salsicce* (with sausages). From Liguria we get *pesto*: a delicious green pasta sauce made from fresh basil, garlic, olive oil and pecorino cheese.

The Veneto is Italy's rice producing region. *Riso con seppie* (rice cooked in the ink of tiny cuttlefish) is just one exquisite recipe. There's even a rice cake dessert, *torta di riso*.

Emilian cooking has been famous in Europe for centuries, and rightly so. The classic *bolognese* meat and tomato sauce was born in the city of Bologna. Tortellini, tiny doughnut-shaped pasta, often served with a delicious cream sauce, is another local treat.

Tuscan dishes are a reflection of the serenity of its rolling hills. They are savory without being aggressive. This is the land of the white truffle: a gourmet's delight. Steak lovers are in for a memorable feast when they sample the enormous charcoal-broiled *bistecca alla fiorentina*. Game goes well with robust Chianti wine produced in the area and *pappardelle al sugo di lepre* (flat noodles and hare in wine sauce) is a flavorful Tuscan speciality.

Everyone knows that Naples means pizza, but it also means seafood and Italy's best coffee. All over Italy meals end with a tiny cup of espresso. In Rome the house will most likely offer a sambuca, the sweet, aniseed-flavored liqueur from Civitavecchia, just up the coast. It should be served with three coffee beans floating on top to bring good luck and to cut the sweetness. *Buon appetito!*

MENU TRANSLATOR

To help you find your way around Italian menus, here's a menu translator. Just try reading through these ingredients and see if they don't stimulate the taste buds. As there are so many superb dishes to choose from, we suggest you simply mark out the ones that particularly catch your fancy, and then keep your eyes open for them on menus as you travel.

Antipasti	Hors d'oeuvres
acciughe (alici)	anchovies (cured in salt)
antipasto misto	sliced sausages and olives
cozze	mussels
frittata	flat omelette with cooked vegetables, bits of ham, other meats and herbs
frutti di mare; insalata di mare	bits of shellfish and squid in oil and lemon juice dressing, with capers
lumache	snails
melone o fichi con prosciutto	melon or figs with cured, raw ham
ostriche	oysters
pomodori ripieni	tomatoes stuffed with rice
vongole	clams
Minestre e Zuppe	Soups
pasta e fagioli	thick soup with beans and macaroni
stracciatella	broth with beaten eggs, flour and grated Parmesan cheese
zuppa di cozze	mussels cooked in broth; served in their shells
Riso, Risotto	Rice dishes
risotto alla bolognese	rice cooked in sauce of finely chopped beef, bacon, tomatoes, onions, garlic and herbs
risotto alla milanese	flavored with wine, butter, onions, beef marrow and broth

Pasta Asciutta	Pasta in sauce
angolotti	round meat-stuffed pasta
cannelloni	pasta tubes, stuffed with a meat, herb and cheese mixture, smothered in creamy cheese sauce and baked
fettuccine	wide, flat noodles
gnocchi	tiny dumplings of semolina flour or boiled potatoes and flour
lasagne	wide, flat noodles, sometimes green when spinach is added to the flour mixture
linguine	very narrow, flat noodles
paglia e fieno	"straw and hay" – narrow green and white noodles
penne	diagonally-cut macaroni in short lengths
polenta	cornmeal mush, served either fresh and soft or firm and cut
rigatoni	tubes of macaroni cut in short lengths
tortellini	small doughnuts of pasta stuffed with meat and herbs

Sugo	Sauces
all' amatriciana	bacon, tomato, red peppers, onion and garlic sauce
all' arrabbiata	tomato sauce with herbs, cayenne pepper, bits of spicy sausage and bacon
alla bolognese	classic tomato and meat sauce
alla boscaiola	tomato sauce with tuna, anchovy paste and mushrooms
al burro	butter and grated Parmesan
alla carbonara	a blend of olive oil, butter, garlic, Parmesan cheese and beaten egg yolks with diced bacon
alla genovese; al pesto	sauce or paste of fresh basil leaves, garlic, oil, pine nuts and pecorino cheese
alla marinara	capers, black olives, garlic and parsley in olive oil
alla napoletana	highly-flavored tomato sauce
alla pizzaiola	meat juices, garlic, tomato, olive oil, oregano and parsley
alla putanesca	sauce of tomatoes, capers, black olives, garlic and chopped parsley
alla vongole (in bianco)	clam sauce (without tomatoes)

Pizza	**(All with mozzarella and tomato base)**
Capricciosa	usually ham, mushrooms, tomatoes, black olives, anchovies, hard-boiled egg
funghi	mushrooms, oil
Margherita	tomatoes
Napoletana	anchovies, tomatoes
salsicce	sausage slices

Pesce e Frutti di mare	**Fish and Shellfish**
anguilla	eel
aragosta	California-type clawless lobster
baccalà	dried, salt-cured cod, soaked in water to remove salt before cooking
calamari	squid
dentice	Mediterranean flat fish
gamberi; gamberetti	large shrimps; very small shrimps
granchio	crab
mazzancolle	large prawn
merluzzo	cod
ombrina	sea perch
pesce spada	swordfish
polipo	octopus
sogliola	sole
spigola	sea bass
trota	trout

Carne	**Meat**
bistecca alla fiorentina	large rib, T-bone or porterhouse baby beef steak that's oiled, seasoned and charcoal-broiled
bollito misto	boiled beef, chicken, pork sausage, tongue, vegetables, with a green sauce (*salsa verde*, made from anchovies, capers, chopped parsley, dill pickles, garlic, olive oil, onion and vinegar)
coda alla vaccinara	stewed oxtail in sauce of garlic, olive oil, tomatoes and white wine
cotoletta alla milanese	veal cutlet, floured, dipped in beaten egg, rolled in breadcrumbs and Parmesan cheese and fried in butter
alla bolognese	breaded veal cutlet, topped with slice of ham and Parmesan cheese and browned in the oven
lombata (-ina) *ossobuco*	stewed T-bone thick slice of veal shank with a round center bone
pollo alla diavola	chicken, halved and flattened, broiled over coals, often with a touch of cayenne pepper in the basting oil

saltimbocca alla romana	veal thinly sliced, topped with fresh sage leaf and a slice of ham and fried in butter
scaloppine, scaloppa	boneless, thin slice of veal prepared in many ways
trippa alla romana	strips of tripe, cooked in herbal tomato sauce, flavored with mint leaves and grated goat's cheese

Contorni, Verdure e Insalate — **Vegetables and Salads**

carciofi	globe artichokes
alla giudia	trimmed, flattened and deep-fried
alla romana	stuffed with garlic, mint leaves and parsley, cooked in oil and water, or white wine
fritti	quartered hearts dipped in batter and deep-fried
ceci	chick peas or garbanzo beans
cetrioli	cucumbers
fagiolini	green beans
finocchio alla parmigiana	fennel gratin with Parmesan cheese and butter
funghi porcini	variety of large wild mushrooms, served roasted or fried, flavored with garlic
melanzane alla parmigiana	fried slices of eggplant baked in tomato sauce, mozzarella cheese and grated Parmesan
tartufi	truffles

Dolci — **Desserts**

charlotte	whipped cream cake; often liqueur-flavored
crostata	open-faced pie on pastry crust, covered with various fruits and cream filling
millefoglie	a napoleon: layers of thin pastry, whipped cream and custard
monte bianco	whipped cream and chestnut-flavored dessert
semifreddo	moulded whipped cream, ice-cream or custard mixture, sometimes with a bit of cake inside or as a base
St Honoré	light pastry, custard and whipped cream cake, with chestnut-flavored garnishing
zabaglione	creamy dessert, served either warm or cold, made of egg yolks, sugar and flavored with wine, usually Marsala

zuppa inglese	cake soaked in liqueur, filled with vanilla or chocolate cream, topped with whipped cream

General

affumicato	smoked
aglio	garlic
ai ferri; alla griglia	grilled
al forno	baked
all'agro	with oil and vinegar dressing or oil and lemon juice
alla brace	charcoal-broiled
alla casalinga	homemade
a piacere; scelta	of your choice
bollito; lessato	boiled
farcito; ripieno	stuffed
fettini	slices (of meat)
fresco	fresh
ghiacciato	iced or chilled
haché	ground (meat)
piatti espressi/del giorno	dishes of the day
secondo quantita	charged by weight
trifolati	chopped, fried in butter or oil

WHERE TO EAT

Ristoranti These are normally the most elegant places in town. Comfortable surroundings and an extensive menu.

Trattoria Usually a small informal restaurant, often family-run, where you'll find some of Italy's best cooking.

Osteria This is rather more basic, but sometimes these modest establishments can be superb. Be warned, however, that some of the most expensive restaurants are also called *osteria*, reflecting either their humble origins or reverse snobbery.

Pizzeria Many of these serve regular meals as well as the world's best pizzas.

Tavola Calda Italy's closest equivalent to a snack bar, serving delicious short orders, which you eat standing at the bar or sitting on high stools.

WINING YOUR WAY THROUGH ITALY

If you're thirty-something, chances are your introduction to Italian wine was via a wicker-bottomed flask of Chianti at the local "Mom and Pop" Italian restaurant. Italians call this wicker a *fiasco* – appropriate because until relatively recently that's a perfect one word description of the Italian wine scene.

It's not as though wine was new to the Italians. History records that as early as 200bc the Greeks founded colonies here for the express purpose of cultivating the grape. Indeed the Cretans called the country *Enotria* – the land of wine. They had every reason to do so. With its sunny climate and profusion of rich alluvial riverine valleys the whole country is like a custom-designed arbor – every single region has its special wine. In combination they produce more of the stuff than any other nation on earth.

What's more, Italians are prodigious consumers. Their per capita consumption tops 85 liters per year. Eliminate the bambinos and this is an even more staggering figure. This sheer volume is one of the problems. For far too long the emphasis was on quantity rather than quality – too much haste and far too little care was the end result. Last, but hardly least, of the problems was a decidedly *dolce far niente* attitude towards proper labeling of the end product. In the bad old days the poor buyer not only didn't necessarily know where the Chianti came from, there was no guarantee that all the wine in the bottle was from the Chianti region.

It wasn't ever thus. From the Middle Ages up until the end of the Napoleonic wars Tuscan vintners led the world in advanced wine-making techniques. Then the dreaded phylloxera attacked the vines. The disease persisted to a greater or lesser extent right up until the end of World War II.

Italy's favorable climate and soil were partly to blame. These guaranteed that some vines and grapes would always survive. Thus many Italians juggled and compromised to keep production going at the expense of quality. In similar circumstances the French simply didn't permit this. This situation was exacerbated by Italy's natural conditions – over-rich soil and sunny days create an excess of sugar in the grape. Fine wine needs acidity which was often lacking.

There were (and are) other problems. The Italians' attitude towards wine is a major one. Wine, like Italian food, which tends towards the robust rather than the subtle, was taken for granted. Domestically there was no great interest in, or market for, fine wines.

Some of the old estates continued to produce exceptional wines throughout this period but exceptional was the operative word.

In 1963, drowning in a sea of grapes and casting an envious eye at the price France was obtaining for wine exports, Italy finally reacted. A classification system was introduced. Selected regions qualified for DOC classification. The initials stand for *Denominazione di Origine Controllata* – controlled denomination of origin.

Upon initial examination DOC regulations sound like a wonderful consumerist notion because they:
- spell out the amount of grapes that can be grown per hectare.
- specify the quantity of must which can be pressed from these.
- set a minimum alcoholic content.
- define the grape variations that can be used and (sometimes) the maximum proportion of each.
- guarantee the wine has been produced in a specific region.
- often spell out aging and bottling specifications.

These are all laudable goals. There's just one ghastly problem. In all cases these regulations are set by the local wine growers, the appropriate *consorzione*; it's as though they built an asylum and then let the inmates run it. The result is that in some areas far too many grapes are still harvested per hectare, the permitted blend of varieties in selected cases calls for grapes which many experts feel detracts from the end product, while in others, excludes varieties which would be of benefit.

In certain areas the system works perfectly well. In others it doesn't. Some of Italy's most prestigious vintners break the rules, others simply opt out of the system.

More recently the government has issued the DOCG designation, *Denominazione di Origine Controllata Garantita* reserved for wine of high repute. This means that the government guarantees their quality as well as setting maximum bottle size.

The first four wines to attract this honor were *Vino Nobile di Montepulciano* and *Brunello di Montalcino* from two Tuscan mountain villages (25kms apart) and *Barolo* and *Barbaresco* from Piedmont. With the 1984 vintage Tuscany's *Chianti* joined the charmed circle, while in 1987 *Albana di Romagna* from the Emilia-Romagna region was included. This latter entry raised a fair furor amongst many wine experts since the region continues to have excessive grape yield policies and many feel the end product suffers as a result.

So what should you order in this muddled situation? Here are some rules:

1. When in the region sample the region's wines. Sicily seems an unlikely spot for good wine but *Corvo Salapurata* makes a lovely medium dry white and a more-than-passable red. The *Chianti Classico* which comes from the region surrounding the ancient Roman road from Florence to Siena will give the term 'Chianti' a whole new meaning. (you can spot *Classico* by the black cockerel on the label.) Tuscany's two DCOG's are also

good bets but heavy – these wines are aged in wood for 3½ to 5 years, so perhaps best saved for the evening meal.

2. Don't always assume that price equals quality. *Rosso di Montalcino*, at half to a third the price of *Brunello*, is far better value than its more renowned stablemate.

3. Do stop at the first wine tasting museum on your route and sample to see what suits you. These are called *Enoteca*. Some, such as Siena's, offer over 500 choices and are true museums, others are little more than wine stores.

4. Be willing to experiment. In practice this means notice what the locals are imbibing and give it a shot. Odds are you'll be able to order a glass instead of a bottle. It also pays to ask the owner what he'd recommend. When he tells you that his cousin produces a white that would make *Lacrima Cristi* cry he may not be fooling.

5. Don't feel hidebound by convention. Unlike the French the Italians regard wine as fun. If you feel like a *Lambrusco* with your fish no one's going to raise an eyebrow. Indeed the next table may be similarly indulging.

6. A broad rule of thumb (with lots of exceptions) is that as you travel south the whites are sweeter, the reds heavier. Some say the women and men follow suit.

7. If traveling with companions consider ordering different glasses (or half bottles) instead of fixing on one selection. Thus around Rome you might taste test a *Frascati*, versus a *Marino* or a *Colli Albani*. Tasting is both fun and leads to informed judgement – what holidays are all about.

8. Consider buying a pocket guide to Italian wine. Our favorite here is **The Simon & Schuster Pocket Guide to Italian Wine** by Burton Anderson. At $9.95 it'll pay for itself if as a result you miss just one lousy bottle of over-priced wine.

SOME WINE TERMS EXPLAINED

The following brief explanation of common terms should help.

Wine Types

Bianco White
Rosato Rosé
Rosso Red

Wine Tastes/Methods

Dolce	Sweet
Abboccato or Amabile	Both terms literally mean 'soft in the mouth' semi-sweet, i.e. Abboccato is the sweeter of the two
Secco	Dry
Amarco	Bitter
Frizzante	Fizzy, between still and sparkling.

Spumante	Sparkling
Classico	From the heart of the designated DOC region.
Riserva	Aged for a specific period in cask or bottle – but at least for one year.
Vino Vecchio	'Old', in other words one or two years beyond the legal limit. Generally not as old as Riserva
Imbottiglia all' origine	Bottled where it was grown.
Contenuto	Contents in Liters.
Annata	Year of vintage.
Uve	Grapes
Passito	Wine from grapes left longer on the vine to mature.
Profumato	Wine with a strong bouquet.
Superiore	Indicates wine with higher than legally required minimum alcoholic content. Sometimes indicates superior quality – but don't count on it

ROME

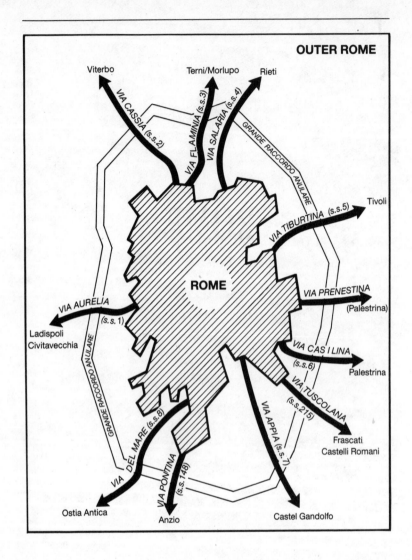

GETTING ABOUT

BUSES

Buses are the best way of getting around the city. There's an efficient network of routes with buses running from about 6am–midnight, and a night service (*notturno*) on main routes. Bus stops are marked *Fermata*. You must buy your ticket before boarding as most buses operate without a conductor. Tickets are sold singly or in booklets of five at most tobacconists and newsstands or at ATAC (Bus Transport Agency) booths. There are weekly tickets for tourists; transport maps are available here as well. Board the bus at the rear door (*salita*) and place your ticket in the machine. You get off the bus by the middle door (*uscita*). It's best to try to avoid using buses during the rush hours – 8am–9am, 1pm–2pm, 4pm–5:30pm and 7pm–8:30pm. Most of the city's population goes to work by bus so crowds and traffic can be overwhelming.

TRAMS

There are still a few trams pottering around Rome. They have the same flat fare as Roman buses. A more relaxing (if slower) method of transport. The *Circolare* is one of the pleasantest routes for a trip around the city and a good way to get your bearings.

SUBWAY

Rome's underground railway system (*metropolitana*) has just two lines. It opens at 5:30am and runs until 11:30pm – not very useful for late-nighters. The original line, Line B, runs from Termini Station through the EUR district to the beach at Ostia – trains are pretty infrequent and stations grubby. The ultra-modern Line A (completed in 1980) runs in two directions from Termini Station; one to the eastern part of the city and one to the west, terminating at Via Ottaviano, just north of St Peter's. It'll also take you to Cinecittà – the Hollywood of Italy. Most newsstands and tobacconists sell books of five to 10 tickets or the monthly ticket. Although major stations have change booths, it's a good idea to keep some coins in your pocket for ticket machines.

TAXIS

Taxis can be picked up at taxi stands or called by phone for a small extra fee. The driver turns the meter on as he leaves the stand to pick you up. Extra charges are also made for services at night, Sundays, public holidays and for each piece of luggage. Use only yellow taxis with meters to avoid disagreements about fares! Travel by taxi is not expensive but try to avoid the rush hours.

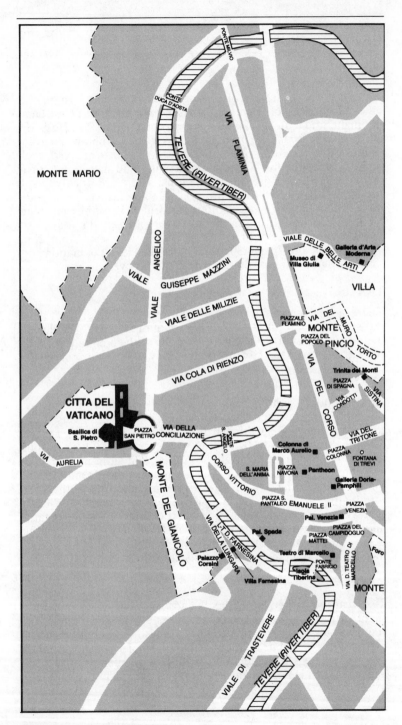

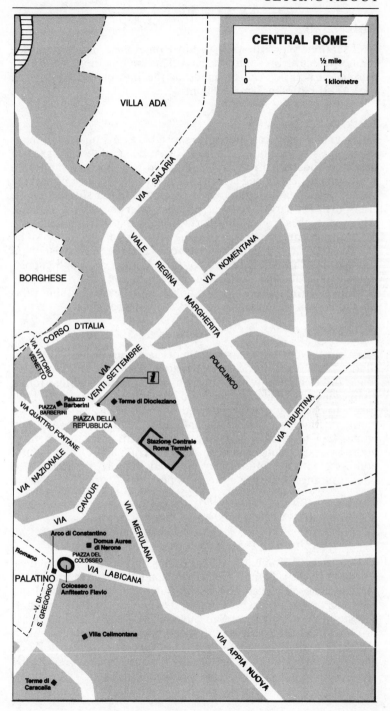

CENTRAL ROME

0 ½ mile
0 1 kilometre

VILLA ADA

VIA SALARIA

VIALE REGINA MARGHERITA

VIA NOMENTANA

BORGHESE

CORSO D'ITALIA

VIA VITTORIO VENETO

VIA VENTI SETTEMBRE

POLICLINICO

Palazzo Barberini

PIAZZA BARBERINI

VIA QUATTRO FONTANE

Terme di Diocleziano

VIA TIBURTINA

PIAZZA DELLA REPUBBLICA

Stazione Centrale Roma Termini

VIA NAZIONALE

VIA CAVOUR

VIA MERULANA

Arco di Constantino

Domus Aurea di Nerone

Romano

PIAZZA DEL COLOSSEO

PALATINO

VIA LABICANA

V. DI S. GREGORIO

Colosseo o Anfiteatro Flavio

Villa Celimontana

VIA APPIA NUOVA

Terme di Caracalla

RAIL

Rail services play little part within Rome itself. Trains are used mainly to leave or enter the city. The main station is *Stazione Termini*. Enquiries can be made at the information office (tel. (06) 4775) between 7am–11:30pm.

CARS

Driving in Rome can be little short of a nightmare. Romans are aggressive behind the wheel, often completely disregarding accepted codes of driving conduct. Add to this the complicated road systems, congested streets and a chronic shortage of parking spaces, and you'll see why we'd recommend you stick to public transport. The largest city car park is under the Villa Borghese, with approaches from Muro Torto. Most inexpensive hotels can't offer any parking space and parking fines tend to be heavy, so be prepared to pay for garaging your car. The speed limit is 50kph (30mph) but this is generally ignored by Roman drivers. Signposting is erratic and misleading, so make sure you map out a route before venturing into the traffic flow. Never leave anything valuable in the car. Even if it is locked away in the trunk.

CAR RENTAL

Cars can be hired at Fiumicino and Ciampino airports, Termini Station and from agencies throughout Rome. Rentals may be made direct or in advance through travel agencies. Most rental charges include basic insurance and breakdown services, but don't forget to check. If you're involved in an accident, call the police at once. Make no statement until they request one. Ask any witness(es) to remain and give a statement. Exchange names, addresses, car details and insurance companies' names and addresses with the other party involved. Report the accident to your insurance company as soon as possible.

Avis, Via Sardegna 38, tel. (06) 4701228
Hertz, Via Sallustiana 28, tel. (06) 463334

BICYCLES

Cycling around Rome is least hazardous on Sundays and holidays when the traffic is lighter. Not recommended for the faint-hearted at other times. You can hire bicycles by the hour or the day from **Biciroma** on the Piazza del Popolo, Piazza di Spagna, Piazza Santi Apostoli or on the Piazza San Silvestro. Cost is L3,000 an hour, or L10,000 for the whole day. For the most pleasurable cycling in Rome, hire a bike in the Borghese Gardens near the Porta Pinciana. They have children's bicycles, too. Great fun at the weekends and you can cycle for hours under the trees.

SCOOTERS

Mopeds and scooters are a favorite way for Romans to get around the city. Again, not a good idea unless you have nerves of steel. To rent a scooter you must be over 21, possess a current driving license and present your passport. Try **Scoot-a-long**, Via Cavour 302 (tel. (06) 6780206).

HORSE-DRAWN CARRIAGES

Horse-drawn carriages (*carrozzelle*) are sadly being nudged out of existence by Roman traffic although it's still a romantic way of seeing the city sights. They may be rented at Via Veneto, Piazza di Spagna, Piazza San Pietro, Trevi Fountain, Colosseum and Termini Station. They are expensive so discuss the fee with the driver in advance. It's possible you may be able to bargain for a lower rate. Try to pick a time when there's less traffic in the city center, or go for a spin through the Villa Borghese gardens.

ON FOOT

Pedestrians beware! Walking is a marvelous way of seeing the city but Roman drivers take little notice of traffic lights and generally ignore pedestrian crossings. Walk when the green sign saying *Avanti* lights up and stop when the red sign says *Alt* – keep your eyes open! Make sure you've got comfortable shoes, preferably rubber soled, as much of Rome is paved with cobblestones, some made from lava. Sadly, Rome is notorious for purse-thieves and pickpockets, so don't carry your wallet in an obvious place. Try to avoid carrying a shoulder-bag or wearing valuables when you are out walking.

GUIDED TOURS

You can hire an authorized guide from **Sindacato Guide Turistiche** at Rampa Mignanelli 12 (tel. (06) 6789842) or the EPT office at Via Parigi 11 (tel. (06) 461851). CIT and other agencies offer tours of varying lengths around Rome's principal sights. The bus company (ATAC) runs sightseeing trips from the information office at Termini Station. There's no commentary but you are given a comprehensive illustrated guide. The two-hour tour takes in all the main sights – a good way to start a visit to the city.

TOP SIGHTS

Arco di Constantino (Arch of Constantine), Piazza del Colosseo
This huge and ornate arch was erected by the Senate in 315AD to honor the Emperor Constantine, "liberator of the city and bringer of peace", after his triumph over Maxentius in the battle of the Milvian Bridge in 312. It is 21m high, 26m wide and 7½m deep, making it the largest of Rome's triumphal arches. Fourth-century Roman sculpture was at a low ebb, so many of the best reliefs are taken from earlier structures and have little to do with Constantine himself. The battle scenes show Trajan's great victories.

Basilica di San Pietro (St Peter's Basilica), Via della Conciliazione, Vatican City
Open: Daily May–Sep 7am–7pm, Oct–Apr 7am–6pm
The basilica dominates Piazza San Pietro flanked by two semi-circular colonnades designed by Bernini. The interior is simply awe-inspiring. You are not immediately aware of its immensity until you approach the bronze Baldacchino rising high above St Peter's throne, and realise the number of chapels which line the aisles. Among the many famous works of art, of particular note is Michelangelo's marble *Pietà*, in the chapel immediately on your right, and the bronze statue of St Peter whose right foot has been kissed by so many faithful over the centuries, it has become quite smooth.

Cappella Sistina (The Sistine Chapel), Vatican Museums, Vatican City
The Sistine Chapel is famed for its paintings by Michelangelo which cover the ceiling, the vault and the wall above the altar. The ceiling alone took Michelangelo four years to paint in acute discomfort (mostly lying down) after which his eyesight was greatly impaired. The Sistine Chapel is one of the most remarkable works of Renaissance art and should not be missed. The paintings are currently (and controversially) being restored and cleaned – a task that will take 10 years to complete.

Colonna di Marco Aurelio (Column of Marcus Aurelius), Piazza Colonna
This magnificent column was erected by the Senate in 180–196 to commemorate Aurelius's triumphs over the Sarmatians, the Quadi and the Marcomanni. It stands 42m high and is almost 4m in diameter. It's constructed from 27 drums of marble from the quarry at Carrara (Michelangelo obtained much of his marble from Carrara too). A spiral relief runs up the column, depicting warlike scenes. A staircase (190 steps) inside gives access to the

platform at the top, where an original statue of Marcus Aurelius was replaced by a bronze of the Apostle Paul in 1589.

Colosseo (Colosseum), Piazza del Colosseo
Open: Mon 9am–1pm, Tues–Sun 9am–1 hr before sunset
Admission: L3,000
You can't miss the Colosseum but do take care crossing the roads to get there. Roman drivers have little regard for pedestrian crossings. The Colosseum is Rome's greatest remaining monument, a third of a mile in circumference. The arch at the entrance was called the Gate of Life, for this is where successful gladiators departed, having fought and won in the arena. The walls in the center were built in the Middle Ages and used as soldiers barracks; they were not part of the original arena. The Colosseum has been restored extensively over the past years and the upper levels can be visited again – the views over Rome are stupendous.

Domus Aurea (Nero's Golden House), Via Labicana 136
Open: Apply to Sovrintendenza Archeologica di Roma, Piazza delle Finanze 1
Tel: (06) 4750181
At first sight these gloomy remains may seem something of a disappointment but Nero's house was legendary for its extravagant beauty in his lifetime. The palace was situated high on a terrace with light and airy rooms. It was called "golden" because the main facade was entirely gilded. Several succeeding emperors destroyed large portions of the palace to accommodate projects of their own but, fortunately, the marvelous domed octagonal hall has survived. You need a lot of imagination to recreate what was once Nero's pleasure palace with its ivory ceilings and built-in scent sprays. But paintings remaining in the underground rooms still inspired Raphael in the 16th century.

Foro Romano (Roman Forum), Via dei Fori Imperiali
Open: Daily Jul–Sep 9am–6pm; Oct–Jun Mon–Sat 9am–1 hr before sunset, Sun 9am–1pm
Admission: L5,000
Situated west of the Colosseum near Palatine Hill, the Roman Forum was the center of political life, justice and business activity in ancient Rome. Today, very little is left of this center of activity but you can still identify the Temple of Saturn with its eight granite columns; the Treasury Department of Rome; the Temple of Vesta, where the Holy Fires burnt day and night, guarded by the Vestal Virgins; and the Basilicas, courts and business centers.

Il Campidoglio (Capitoline Hill), Piazza del Campidoglio
The Campidoglio is built on one of the seven hills of Rome. The lovely little piazza at the top, designed by Michelangelo, is

approached by gentle steps bordered on both sides by grass and oleander trees. Surrounding the piazza are the **Senatorial** and **Conservatory Palaces**, and the **Capitoline Museum**; in the center is a bronze statue of Marcus Aurelius. On Saturdays and Sundays, if you happen to be visiting, you'll see Italian couples lining up to get into the Conservatory Palace, where civil marriages take place. It's great fun to watch the happy couples, the brides dressed in lovely gowns, emerging from the so-called Registry Office.

Il Palatino (Palatine Hill), Via dei Fori Imperiali
Open: Wed–Sat 9am–2 hrs before sunset, Sun 9am–2pm
Closed: Mon–Tues
As the name denotes, this is the hill on which Rome was founded in 753BC. It later became the residential area of Imperial Rome before Rome expanded into the Forum. As you walk down from the hill and through the ruins, you really get the feel of ancient Rome. The hill is also a very enjoyable spot for a picnic. The gardens are a wilderness of shrubs and trees. On the west of the Palatine is the **Lupercal** – the spot where Romulus and Remus were supposed to have been suckled by the wolf.

The Pantheon, Piazza della Rotonda
Open: Mon–Sat 9am–4pm, Sun 9am–1pm
This ancient building is the best preserved Roman temple still standing, built in about 120AD by Hadrian over the ruins of a temple built by Agrippa in 27BC. Under the 16 granite columns at the front of the building are the huge bronze doors which have been opening every day for 2,000 years. The dome inside was, until recently, the largest in the world, and was the inspiration Michelangelo needed for the roof of St Peter's. Buried near the chapels are three Italian kings and the painter, Raphael.

Teatro di Marcello (Marcellus Theater), Via del Teatro di Marcello
This extraordinary building was begun by Julius Caesar in 13BC and completed under Augustus in 11BC. Augustus named it for his son-in-law and nephew Marcellus who would have succeeded Augustus as Emperor had he not died prematurely. The theater is 120m in diameter, capable of containing an audience of 16,000. The remains, although fragmentary, are impressive. Sadly only 12 out of the original 41 arches in each of the two tiers remain. The theater was converted into a fortress and residence during the Middle Ages, then became a palace in the 16th century.

Via Appia Antica (Appian Way) and **Catacombe di San Callisto**
Open: Fri–Wed 8:30am–noon 2:30pm–5:30pm   Closed: Thur
Admission: Catacombs L3,000
The Via Appia Antica – the Old Appian Way – was constructed

in 312BC to link Brindisi in the far south of Italy with Rome. Just outside the city walls, the Appian Way with its ancient catacombs is a must. The most beautiful and famous catacombs are those of St Calixtus. Originally private burial chambers, they were extended to their present size over a period of 300 years. Some 20kms of intricate passages have been explored to date and the total estimate of burials is around 170,000. There's some fascinating ancient graffiti – including early Christian symbols.

To reach the Appian Way take the 118 bus from the Colosseum to the Via Appia Antica stop. This is a great spot for a picnic under the umbrella pines on a sunny day.

LOCAL DELIGHTS

Fontana delle Tartarughe (The Fountain of the Tortoises), Piazza Mattei
A graceful little fountain from the late Renaissance, sculpted by Taddeo Landini. Four naked youths with their feet holding down dolphins and their hands gripping the dolphins' tails, hold up bronze tortoises to the bowl of the fountain. A light-hearted and charming work, legend has it that it was built in just one night.

Fontana del Tritone (Triton Fountain), Piazza Barberini
A masterpiece by Bernini in very realistic style. Four dolphins with open mouths drink the waters while balanced on their tails is a scallop shell holding the seated Triton. Water pours from the conch trumpet he holds to his mouth down his superb torso. Under his sea throne you can see the Barberini bees. Not as famous as the Trevi fountain but not to be missed – this is a great Roman landmark.

Fontana di Trevi (Trevi Fountain), Piazza di Trevi
This truly beautiful fountain is a must for any visitor to Rome. Designed by Leon Battista and Nicola Salvi, it shows Neptune in a chariot drawn by sea horses. The song *Three Coins in a Fountain* was inspired by this fountain. Legend has it that if you toss a coin over your left shoulder into the fountain you'll be sure to return to Rome. In the evening the surrounding piazza buzzes with Italians and tourists alike, in the fine spirit of Italian gaiety. The most famous and spectacular of all the fountains in Rome, it was finally completed in 1762, after a century of planning.

Fontanella delle Api (Fountain of the Bees), Piazza Barberini
Designed by Bernini in 1644, the fountain has three bees (symbol of the Barberini family) spouting thin jets of water into the basin below. Pope Urban VIII (himself a Barberini) had the fountain inscribed as though it has been built in the 22nd year of his pontificate – in fact, it was only the 21st. Superstitious Romans thought this an evil omen and cut away the final "I" of the Roman numerals. As it happened, Urban VIII died eight days before attaining his target.

Isola Tiberina (Tiber Island)
Right in the middle of the rushing waters of the River Tiber, the island is connected to Trastevere and the Cenci district of Rome by two ancient bridges. This peaceful spot has been associated with medicinal matters for thousands of years. The church of St Bartholomew is said to be built on the site of an ancient temple to the god of healing, Aesculapius. The tradition is continued by

the Hospital of the Brothers of St John of God that stands here. There's a tiny piazza too – a haven of peace in the middle of Rome. Walk down the steps to the river and the **Ponte Rotto** – the broken bridge. Its single span, all that remains of the original, has stood isolated in midstream since 1598.

Luna Park EUR

EUR stands for Esposizione Universale di Roma – Mussolini's name for the grounds he set aside for the 1942 World Fair, later cancelled at the outbreak of World War II. Enter EUR along Via Cristoforo Colombo and on the left you'll find Luna Park, a permanent year-round funfair. A terrific roller-coaster, hosts of other rides and stacks of stalls. It's clean and well-organized for maximum fun.

Monumento Nazionale a Vittorio Emanuele II (Victor Emmanuel Monument), Piazza Venezia

This huge landmark is a memorial to the first King of Italy. Known to Romans as "the wedding cake", it's a mountain of white marble in the middle of Rome. It took 26 years to build and the style is nothing but grandiose. Steps lead up to bronze statues representing Thought and Action, then to the Altar to the Nation. The tomb of the Unknown Soldier is on the first level and from the very top there are wonderful views over the whole of Rome. Completed in 1911 it must be the most remarkable memorial ever built.

Piazza Navona

The Piazza Navona is oval in shape, taking its form from the Stadium of Domitian over which it was built. Bernini's fountain of the four rivers – the Nile, the Ganges, the Danube, and the Plate – dominates the center of the piazza. In ancient times chariot races were held here; in the Middle Ages the piazza was flooded and mock naval battles were held. Today, it's a meeting place for Romans and visitors alike. Amateur artists and students display their paintings, sometimes very beautiful, in the hope of a sale. Cafés, restaurants and bars abound.

Sant'Agnese in Agone, Via Santa Maria dell'Anima 30

The king of Baroque, Borromini, created the facade of this church in 1653. His twin towers were probably the inspiration for Sir Christopher Wren's designs for St Paul's Cathedral in London. So the story goes, St Agnes was thrown naked into the stocks after refusing to renounce her faith – the site was then a brothel – but her hair unloosed miraculously to cover her. Remains of the Emperor Domitian's athletics stadium (around 90AD), including mosaics and some of the original sidewalks, lie under the church.

The interior is exquisite, richly adorned with stucco, gilt, and marble pictures by pupils of Bernini on the altars.

Santa Maria in Cosmedin, Piazza Bocca della Verità
A pot-pourri of styles from the sixth to 13th centuries, all restored late last century with great care. Santa Maria in Cosmedin remains one of the most beautiful medieval churches in Rome. There's a charming Romanesque bell tower, and a portico with the famous **Bocca della Verità** (Mouth of Truth). If you put your hand into the mouth and tell a lie, legend says you will lose your hand. An 18th-century tourist was reportedly stung by a scorpion when testing this theory. Perhaps his was merely a white lie.

Scalinata della Trinità dei Monti (Spanish Steps), Piazza di Spagna
This monumental flight of steps connects the Piazza di Spagna to the church of Trinità dei Monti. It was the brainchild of the French minister Cardinal Mazarin and the French gave financial aid to the construction. The steps were built between 1723 and 1726 by Francesco de Sanctis. They have long been a favorite perching place for many of Rome's most colorful and Bohemian visitors, not to mention the azaleas which bloom in spring, transforming the steps into a gorgeous mass of color. At the foot of the steps is the **Boat Fountain** decorated with suns and those industrious Barberini bees. On the right is the house where Keats died in 1821. It's now a small museum to the poet and his friends, Shelley and Byron, and is well worth a visit. At the top of the steps is an imitation Egyptian obelisk and the church of Trinità dei Monti. There's a lovely view of Rome from here.

Villa Farnesina, Via della Lungara
Open: Mon–Sat 9am–1pm Closed: Sun
Admission: L2,000
This Renaissance villa was constructed between 1508–11 by Baldassare Peruzzi. It contains excellent frescoes by Peruzzi, Sodoma, and some particularly fine pieces by Raphael. The villa was built for Agostino Chigi, a Sienese banker who was so rich and ostentatious that when he gave open-air banquets the used silver plates were apparently thrown into the Tiber. (In fact, they dropped into nets specially positioned to catch them.)

BRIDGES/GARDENS/PARKS

Il Gianicolo (The Janiculum), access from Fontana Paola
The park, on the west bank of the Tiber, was laid out in the late
1800s to pay tribute to Italian patriots who fought French troops
here defending Vatican sovereignty over Rome in 1849. Italians
settled in Argentina donated the curious lighthouse which flashes
red-white-green (the colors of Italy's flag). You'll find open-air
puppet shows for children, and, at noon every day, a cannon is
fired from a spot just below the terrace. The view from the terrace
is magnificent.

Pincio Gardens, access from Piazza del Popolo
These charming, rather formal gardens were laid out by the architect Giuseppe Valadier at the beginning of the 19th century. This
was originally the site of the terraced gardens belonging to the
legendary gourmet Lucullus – still celebrated for his elaborate
feasts. The paths in the gardens are lined with white marble busts
of Italian heroes and patriots; some, alas, lacking their noses.

Ponte Fabricio, Piazza di Monte Savello
This is the oldest bridge in Rome and is still in use today, over
2,000 years since it was built. The bridge links Trastevere to the
Tiber Island. It is also known as **The Bridge of the Four Heads**.
The two busts on the parapet represent the double-faced god
Janus who was the Roman god of bridges, doorways and passages.
Over the arches is an inscription that states that the Consul Fabri-
cius built the bridge in 62BC.

Ponte Milvio, Via Flaminia
This bridge was the scene of the famous battle in 312 where
Caesar Maxentius was defeated by Constantine. Constantine was
convinced the Christian god was responsible for his victory and,
in thanks, permitted Christians to worship openly. A bridge has
stood on this site since the second century BC; the present bridge
has been repeatedly rebuilt and restored, especially in the 19th
century when the fortified gate was built.

Ponte Sant'Angelo, Castel Sant'Angelo
This, the most magnificent of Rome's bridges, was built by the
Emperor Hadrian in 136AD and called the *Pons Aelius* after one
of his forenames. The three central arches date from the second
century. Most of the statues of angels lining the bridge were
carved by students of Bernini to his specification. Two were carved
by Bernini himself – the angels holding the crown of thorns and
the scroll. The originals were replaced by copies in the 17th cen-

tury and moved to the church of Sant'Andrea delle Fratte. Cross to the left bank and turn left for a stunning view of St Peter's.

The Vatican Gardens, Vatican City
Open: Mar–Oct Mon–Tues, Thur–Fri from 10am for guided tours
The Vatican gardens may only be visited on a guided tour. It is best to book to avoid disappointment. This can be done at the Vatican information office on the left of St Peter's Basilica as you approach it. The beautifully-kept gardens contain plants from many parts of the world, including oak trees from England, hibiscus and bougainvillea bushes from the tropics. You'll see the Pope's guest house which was once an old fortress and the little amphitheater with frescoes on the ceiling. The deep fountain beside the English garden is one of the few remaining in the old Vatican gardens and is fed with water from Lake Bracciano, north of Rome.

Villa Ada, Via Salaria
This large and pleasant park situated west of the Via Salaria, above the Tiber, was once owned by Italy's royal family. There are two playgrounds, bicycle tracks, a roller skating rink and ponds. In summer, there are frequent music festivals, often featuring ethnic themes. The park also contains the **Catacombs of Priscilla**, where many early Christians are buried. You'll find the oldest known representation of the Virgin and Child here.

Villa Borghese, Porta Pinciana
This 17th-century country estate now has modern roads running through it but, with its tall trees, cool fountains, and panoramic views of Rome, it's still a wonderful place to escape to from the heat of the Roman sun. There's much to see here, so plan a leisurely afternoon. The park, created by Cardinal Scipione Borghese, measures over 6kms in circumference. Be sure not to miss the lake garden where you may like to take a boat out on the water. The **Giardino Zoologico** (open daily 8:30am–sunset) is located in the north-east of the estate. It's quite a small zoo but the kids will love it. There are several monuments scattered about the park, and an artificial lake. The **Piazza di Siena** is where race meetings are held at the beginning of May.

Villa Celimontana, Piazza della Navicella
The main entrance to this park is situated on the western incline of the Celian Hill, which lies between the Baths of Caracalla and the Colosseum. It's a lovely walled park with several ponds and a bicycle racing track. A pleasant place to visit with the children and while away a hot afternoon.

MUSEUMS

Galleria Doria-Pamphili, Palazzo Doria, Via del Corso
Open: Tues, Fri–Sun 10am–1pm Closed: Mon, Wed–Thur
Admission: L2,000
Perhaps the most important collection in the world still owned by
the family who created it. Raphael, Titian, Velasquez, Caravaggio
and others are represented, including many real masterpieces.
The private apartments, which contain original furnishings, can
also be visited. The yellow salon is hung with superb tapestries
made by Gobelins for Louis XV. The *palazzo* itself dates from
1435, but has been added to over the centuries.

Galleria Nazionale d'Arte Antica, Via delle Quattro Fontane 13
Open: Mon–Tues 9am–2pm, Wed–Sat 9am–7pm, Sun 9am–1pm
Admission: L3,000
The National Gallery of Ancient Art holds one of the most
impressive and representative collections of Italian painting from
the 13th to 18th centuries. It contains works by El Greco, Fra
Angelico, Raphael, Caravaggio and other masters. The gallery is
partly housed in the Palazzo Barberini, a Baroque edifice com-
menced by Carlo Maderno in 1625 and completed by Bernini in
1633. There are many fine rooms with beautifully painted ceilings.

Galleria Nazionale d'Arte Moderna, Viale delle Belle Arti 131
Open: Tues–Sat 9am–2pm, Sun 9am–1pm Closed: Mon
Admission: L4,000
The works of the 1881 Italian National Exhibition form the
nucleus of the Modern Art Gallery. It represents the principal
collection of Italian art from the 19th century to the present day.
Umberto Boccioni and Giorgio de Chirico are well represented.
Foreign exhibitors include Henry Moore, Jackson Pollock and
Max Ernst. Interesting temporary exhibitions.

Galleria Spada, Palazzo Spada, Piazza Capodiferro
Open: Mon–Sat 9am–2pm, Sun 9am–1pm
Admission: L2,000
This small but selective gallery exhibits works of art collected by
Cardinal Spada in the 17th century. The bulk of the collection is
dedicated to the late Renaissance masters. It's attractively displayed in salons, still in the original settings. The garden gallery
is famous for its *trompe l'oeil* perspective. You can see it from
the courtyard.

Keats and Shelley Memorial House, Piazza di Spagna 26
Open: Mon–Fri 9am–1pm 3:30pm–6pm Closed: Sat–Sun
Admission: L3,500
These are the rooms once inhabited by the poet John Keats and his friend Joseph Severn. Now it holds an interesting collection of drafts, poems and correspondence relating mainly to Keats, although Shelley and Byron are also represented. An insignificant door with a brass plaque indicates the entrance to this house in which Keats died in 1821. Inside, you feel that little has changed since. A charming little museum, full of ghosts of the past.

Museo Capitolino, Piazza del Campidoglio
Open: Tues–Sat 9am–2pm, Tues & Thur also 5pm–8pm, Sat from
    Apr–Sep 8:30pm–11pm, Sun 9am–1pm Closed: Mon
Admission: L4,000
These museums include the Museo Capitolino, Museo dei Conservatori and the Pinacoteca, Museo Nuovo and Palazzo Senatorio. The Museo Capitolino contains some spectacular sculptures including the famous *Satyr of Praxiteles*, the *Dying Gaul*, busts of Roman emperors and some exquisite mosaics.

Museo Nazionale d'Arte Orientale, Palazzo Brancaccio, Via Merulana 248
Open: Mon–Sat 9am–2pm, also Thur 3:30pm–7pm, Sun 9am–1pm
Admission: L3,000
A growing collection of Oriental art objects augmented by the findings of an Italian archeological institute. The 14 rooms have displays from Iran, China, India, Tibet, Nepal, Thailand, Korea, Afghanistan and Pakistan, ranging from prehistoric times to the present day. Exhibits include paintings, bronzes, sculpture, clothing, ceramics and jewelry.

Museo Nazionale Etrusco, Villa Giulia, Piazza Villa Giulia 9
Open: Tues–Sat 9am–7pm, Sun 9am–1pm Closed: Mon
Admission: L4,000
This superb collection of Etruscan art is housed in the Villa Giulia, built in the 16th century for Pope Julius III. The Etruscans were a highly cultivated and artistic people whose history and achievements were passed over by the Romans. Our knowledge of their civilization is fragmentary, and their language has never been deciphered. Here's a wealth of sculpture, jewelry, glassware, pottery and votive offerings. Most notably, the superb terracotta sarcophagus showing a husband and wife reclining on a sofa – smiling portraits of very real individuals. Don't miss the villa's lovely garden complete with Etruscan temple.

Museo Nazionale Romano, Via E. De Nicola 79, Piazza della Repubblica
Open: Tues–Sat 9:30am–2pm, Sun 9:30am–1pm Closed: Mon
Admission: L4,000

The museum is situated in part of an old Carthusian monastery built over the ruins of the Baths of Diocletian. One of the world's most important archeological museums, it contains a marvelous collection of early Greek and Roman objects. Amongst the principal statues you'll see the Venus of Cyrene, the Ludovisi Throne, the Girl From Antium and the Daughter of Niobe. There's a beautiful garden with a collection of fragments under the oleanders and cypress trees.

VATICAN MUSEUMS

Viale Vaticano, Vatican City
Open: Oct–Jun Mon–Sat 9am–2pm, Jul–Sep Mon–Fri 9am–5pm, Sat 9am–2pm, last Sun of each month 9am–2pm winter, 9am–5pm summer
Admission: L8,000

Appartamento Borgia
These rooms are named for Alexander VI (1492–1503), a somewhat wicked Pope, who took over an entire floor of the palace of Nicholas V as a private residence for himself and his family. Pinturicchio painted the walls and ceilings between 1492 and 1495 with his pupils' help. The *Room of the Saints* is perhaps his finest work.

Biblioteca Apostolica Vaticana
The collection of the Vatican library is the most valuable in the world. The library has been expanded since its foundation in 1450 by Nicholas V and contains (in addition to books printed after the end of the 15th century) about 7,000 incunabula, 80,000 manuscripts and 25,000 hand-written medieval books. The magnificent 70m-long library hall was built by Domenico Fontana.

Cappella di Niccolò V
In the 1100s the chapel probably formed part of a tower which was incorporated into the first papal palace in the 13th century. Consequently this is one of the most ancient parts of the Vatican Palace. Nicholas V converted it into a chapel and commissioned the wonderfully talented Fra Angelico to decorate the interior between 1447 and 1451. Fra Angelico, a Dominican monk, was assisted by Benozzo Gozzoli, both natives of Florence.

Collezione d'Arte Religiosa Moderna
This marvelous collection of modern religious art comprises some

500 sculptures and paintings by a superb selection of artists from around the world. All the works have been donated by the artists themselves, or collectors. The upper level has a gallery devoted to the French painter Rouault, a Chapel of Peace by Giacomo Manzù, works by Chagall, Braque, Kandinsky, Henry Moore, Klee, Gauguin and others. The lower rooms are partially situated beneath the Sistine Chapel; works by Picasso, Villon, Leger and others are displayed here.

Galleria delle Carte Geografiche
The Map Gallery, situated in a 120m-long barrel-vaulted room, is beautifully painted with 16th-century maps of Italy. It contains superb images of all of Italy's regions, including city views and landscapes, plus maps of Malta, Corfu and Avignon. They're a pure delight – full of stormy seas, tossing ships, alive with fantastic creatures and extraordinary detail.

Loggia di Raffaello
By appointment only
In the early 1500s Julius II (1503–13) commissioned Bramante (architect of St Peter's) to design three loggias. When Bramante died in 1514, Leo X (Julius's successor) engaged Raphael to continue with the work. Raphael collaborated with several other artists including Perin del Vaga, Francesco Penni and Giulio Romano. The loggia is sometimes known as "Raphael's Bible" as it contains many scenes from the Old Testament.

Museo Chiaramonti
This museum, founded by Pope Pius VII in the 19th century, was laid out by Canova. It contains a great number of both Roman and Greek works including statuary, urns, vases, portrait busts and sarcophagi. Some of the most notable works are the *Prima Porta Augustus* (discovered in 1863), the *Portrait of a Roman*, the *Penelope* relief (dating from around 450BC) and the *Spear-Carrier* (Doryphorus), a copy from the original by Polycletus.

Museo Gregoriano Egizio
This museum was laid out in 1839 by Father Ungarelli, an Italian Egyptologist. The eight rooms contain statues mainly discovered in the Egyptian temple of Isis, situated in the Campus Martius. In Room III there's a copy of the *Rosetta Stone* (the original is now in the British Museum, London). The Stone dates from 196BC and has inscriptions in hieroglyphics, demotic and Greek. It was this that led the French Egyptologist, Champollion, to decipher hieroglyphics for the first time in 1822.

Museo Gregoriano Etrusco
This Etruscan Museum was founded by Pope Gregory XVI in

1837, and contains objects excavated in southern Etruria. The 18 rooms house one of the finest collections of Etruscan artefacts in the world, representative of both the daily life of the Etruscans and their notion of life after death. The grave goods are exceptional – a golden clasp decorated with ducks and lions, a bronze throne and a medallion with gold leaves are superb examples of Etruscan art.

Museo Gregoriano Profano
Until 1963 the Museum of Pagan Art was housed in the Lateran Palace. The collection was founded by Pope Gregory XVI in the 19th century – he also founded the Etruscan Museum. The modern building in which the museum is now housed was built during this century. The collection mainly comprises Roman sculpture and Roman copies of Greek sculpture.

Museo Missionario Etnologico
The collection, originally displayed in the Palazzo Laterano, was founded in 1926. It was transferred to the Vatican in 1970. This wide-ranging collection comprises artefacts brought back from the various mission fields of the Roman church.

Museo Pio-Clementino
The museum is named after Pius VI (1775–99) and Clement XIV (1769–74), who were mainly responsible for amassing this superb collection of sculpture. Some of the most outstanding exhibits are, a first-century Roman copy of the *Apoxyomenos* by Lysippus (Room X), the second-century Roman copy of the *Apollo Belvedere* by Leochares (Room VIII) and the *Sarcophagus of Constantia* (350–360AD), made from porphyry. Perhaps most famous of all is the Greek masterpiece, the *Laocöon* (Room VIII), disinterred in Nero's Golden House in 1506.

Museo Sacro
The Museum of Sacred Art was particularly favored by Pope Pius XI (1922–39). Its collection mainly comprises pieces discovered during the excavation and exploration of early Christian sites and catacombs in and around Rome. A particularly interesting work is the *Nozze Aldobrandine* (Aldobrandini Wedding), a delightful old fresco discovered in the 1600s.

Pinacoteca
This picture gallery, founded by Pius VI, was later plundered by Napoleon. The pictures are hung in chronological order, dating from the Middle Ages to the present day. Some of the painters represented in the 16 rooms include Fra Angelico, Filippo Lippi, Perugino, Raphael, Leonardo da Vinci, Titian and Caravaggio. The collection of Medieval art is particularly fine.

Stanze di Raffaello

Situated above the Appartamento Borgia, this suite of rooms comprised the official residence of Julius II (1503–13) and succeeding Popes until Gregory XIII (1572–85). In 1508, when Raphael was 26, Julius II commissioned him to decorate the four rooms, a task which occupied him until his death in 1520. The first two chambers, *Stanza della Segnatura* and *Stanza d'Eliodoro* are fully Raphael's work. The increased vitality and rich coloring of the *Stanza d'Eliodoro* was perhaps inspired by the unveiling of Michelangelo's triumphant ceiling frescoes in the Sistine Chapel. The other two rooms were largely the work of Raphael's pupils and assistants.

ROMAN WALKING TOURS

INTRODUCTION

Strolling through Rome is a great way to get the feel of the city and its history – at your own pace. The city is crammed with interest and atmosphere, but don't turn a walk into a marathon. The great news is that when you feel yourself flagging – after a while you'll swear those seven hills are 70 – there's sure to be a bar or café where you can stop off for a drink or a leisurely lunch.

Here are six walks that will give you an insider's insight into Rome's inimitable charms.

ANCIENT ROME STROLL

This is a walk that will take you through a different Rome – the capital of the ancient world. Start at the bottom of **Il Campidoglio**, the Capitoline Hill. Once the religious center of ancient Rome, center of government, and site of the Temple of Jupiter, it's where emperors were crowned after a victory.

From here take . . .

1. The **Cordonata**. These steps were designed by Michelangelo in 1536. At the base are the two fountains of the lions, which spouted wine (one red, the other white) during public festivals 300 years ago. Romans have dubbed them "the whining lions". The medieval steps to the left lead to . . .

2. **Santa Maria d'Aracoeli**, built on the spot where the Emperor Augustus received a vision that described a man "coming from the East who was the son of God". As you head up Michelangelo's stairs near the top on your right is . . .

3. The **Cage of a She-Wolf**, a tribute to the she-wolf that suckled Romulus and Remus, twin founders of Rome. The top of the stairs is guarded by . . .

4. The **Statues of the Dioscuri**, the gods who have always protected Roman armies. The beautiful square at the summit is . . .

5. The **Campidoglio**, also planned by Michelangelo. The angle of the buildings and the small statues at the top give the compact square an appearance of depth and height. In the center of the courtyard is the golden-bronze statue of Marcus Aurelius with a bit of gold remaining on the horse's head. The Romans used to believe that the world would end when the statue "turned" to gold. On the right is . . .

6. The **Palazzo dei Conservatori and Museum** (open Tues–Sat 9am–2pm, Tues & Thur also 5pm–8pm, Sun 9am–1pm, admission L4,000). This Renaissance building contains fabulous frescoes and sculptures. Don't miss the huge statue of Constantine in the courtyard. Directly opposite is . . .

7. The **Museo Capitolino** (open Tues–Sat 9am–2pm, Tues & Thur also 5pm–8pm, Sat also 8:30pm–11pm, Sun 9am–1pm, admission L,4,000). This is one of Italy's truly great museums. When you come out of the back of the square you will find . . .

8. The **Palazzo Senatorio**, which is the town hall and mayor's office. The bell at the top is rung only on really special occasions (about three times each century). The last time it tolled was 1944 when the Allies entered Rome. The fountain in front of the Senate was designed by Michelangelo. The large reclining figures on each side represent the Tiber and Nile rivers, once the boundaries of the Roman Empire. A small, contrasting statue of Minerva was done by the Master's students. Leave the stunning square, exiting right on Via del Campidoglio. Turn left at No 3 for the **Tabularium** (open daily 7am–sunset), the archives building of ancient Rome where the 12 tablets of the Roman Laws were kept. From the middle of the gallery you'll see . . .

9. The **Roman Forum** (open daily Jul–Sep 9am–6pm, Oct–Jun Mon–Sat 9am–1 hr before sunset, Sun 9am–1pm, admission L5,000). This was the center of justice, political life and business activity in the ancient city. Until excavations began in the last century, the Forum was a cattle pasture covered with 20ft of dirt. Although it's difficult to recreate the Forum of old, postcards reconstruct the view as it was 2,000 years ago. You can still identify:
   A. The **Temple of Saturn** with its eight huge granite columns, the ancient Treasury Department.
   B. The **Arch of Severus** built in 203AD to commemorate victory over the Parthians.
   C. The **Temple of Antonius and Faustina** dedicated to Antonius Pius and his wife.
   D. The **Arch of Titus** adorned with scenes from the life of Titus, and his triumphant conquest of Jerusalem.
   E. The **Senate of the Roman Empire**.
   F. The **Temple of Vesta**, where the Holy Fire burned night and day, guarded by the Vestal Virgins.
   G. The **Sacred Way** where triumphal parades took place.
   H. The **Basilicas**, law courts and business centers. To the right of the Forum is . . .

10. **Palatine Hill** (Wed–Sat 9am–2 hrs before sunset, Sun 9am–2pm) where Rome began. The remains of Iron Age huts testify to the antiquity of the site, supporting the Roman legend that Romulus's house was here. The foundations of the city were laid on this site in 753BC. Ancient Rome seems strangely close to these evocative surroundings. Cross the gallery before descending the steps to . . .

11. The **Mamertine Prison** (open daily 9am–12:30pm 2pm–6:30pm, admission free – donations welcome). Situated on the corner, this was the Sing-Sing of the ancient capital; the end of the line for her enemies. It's now the chapel of **San Pietro in Carcero**. St Peter and St Paul were prisoners here until they converted their jailers, creating a spring in the prison to perform baptisms. They were released and later martyred. Turn left when you come out, down Via di Tulliano. On the left you'll see . . .

12. **Caesar's Forum**. It was built by Caesar in 54BC to handle the overflow of business from the original Forum. The tall columns were taken from the Temple of Venus – the goddess of love from whom Caesar claimed to be descended. Cross Via Fori Imperiali, walk across the greenery, and down to your left to . . .

13. **Trajan's Column** in the center of **Trajan's Forum**. Built in 113AD, it shows a detailed inventory of contemporary warfare methods. There are 2,500 characters carved in the column, with St Peter added at the top in 1587. Just off to the right are the Trajan markets, an early version of the department store which housed around 150 different shops in Roman times. Now walk back with the park on your right, the Imperial Forum on your left. You'll pass the spot where . . .

14. **Augustus's Forum** stood. On your left you'll see the columns he erected to celebrate his victory over Antony and Cleopatra. Further down you pass **Nerva's Forum**. Now you may wish to stop for a refreshing drink on the delightful roof terrace of the **Hotel Forum** (off to your left). Or, continue down Via Fori Imperiali. On your right there's . . .

15. The **Basilica of Constantine** (or of Maxentius) from the 4th century AD with its brick walls and high vaults. On the outside walls are four marble maps showing the growth of the Roman Empire. These were erected by Mussolini. A fifth map, which displayed his empire, has been removed. A bit further on the right is . . .

16. The **Temple of Venus and Rome**, which was the largest temple of ancient Rome. It was designed by the Emperor Hadrian who was a gifted architect. You're now in . . .

17. **Piazza del Colosseo**. The large, stone-outlined square in the street was once a monumental statue of Nero, which stood nearly as high as the Colosseum. It's now the site of an archaeological dig excavating the Colosseum's maze of underground tunnels. At the other end of the piazza is . . .

18. The **Arch of Constantine**, built to commemorate the emperor's victory over a rival for the throne. After winning this battle in 312AD Constantine legalized Christianity. In front of the arch is a white circle on the pavement marking the Fountain of the Gladiators. After fights in the Colosseum, gladiators would come here to wash off the blood. Dodge across the piazza to . . .

19. The **Colosseum** (open daily May–Sep 9am–7pm, Oct–Apr 9am–4pm). Completed in 80AD, it's Rome's greatest remaining monument, one-third of a mile in circumference. In midsummer, a silk awning was drawn across the top to provide shade for the 60,000 spectators. Occasionally the arena was flooded; then gladiators fought on floating barges. You enter the stadium through a broad archway: the **Gate of Life**. Victorious gladiators left by this route for their dip in the fountain. Now turn down Via di San Gregorio which runs behind the Arch of Titus. The ruins on the right are palaces that covered the Palatine Hill. At . . .

20. **Number 30** there's another entrance to the Forum. Through the arch you can see the foundations of **Domitian's** private stadium. Further down on the right you walk under the aqueduct that carried water to the palaces. Across the road is . . .

21. **San Gregorio**, the church where the musical saint composed the Gregorian chants. To the left of the church climb the steep, narrow Clivo di Scauro to Via San Paolo della Croce. Continue through the archways to the charming piazza and church of . . .

22. **SS Giovanni e Paolo**, with its unusual apse built by architects from Lombardy. Retrace to Via San Gregorio; then take the first right into Via dei Cerchi. At the intersection glance to your left and you'll see Via delle Terme di Caracalla and the famous . . .

23. **Baths of Caracalla**. That incredibly ugly structure slightly off to your left is the headquarters of the FAO (Food and Agricultural Organization). Now cross Via dei Cerchi. You arrive at . . .

24. The **Circus Maximus** where Romans ran riot with blood-curdling chariot races and only slightly less death-defying horse races. This, the largest stadium ever constructed, held 250,000

fanatical race-goers. On the right you'll see other fascinating ruins as you walk down the enormous Circus. Continue downhill to . . .

25. **Piazza Bocca della Verità** where Romulus and Remus were allegedly found by the she-wolf. Off to the left is the graceful Romanesque tower of . . .

26. **Santa Maria in Cosmedin.** Inside the portico is the **Mouth of Truth,** which has come a long way since it was an ancient Roman drain-cover. Legend has it that if you put an unwary hand in its mouth and tell a lie you've lost that limb for good. Next you'll see . . .

27. The **Temple of Vesta**, exclusive property of those pillars of the community, the Vestal Virgins. To its right is . . .

28. The **Temple of Manly Fortune** dating from 100BC. Young pagan women came here to pray for a good husband. It's worth a try. As you walk towards it off to your right, soaring above the parked cars, you can see the magnificent . . .

29. **Arch of Janus** built by Constantine. Its empty niches were once filled with brightly painted pagan statues. Leave the piazza on Via del Teatro di Marcello. Past No 45 are . . .

30. The **Ruins of a Roman Market**, which sold olive oil and vegetables. Glance to your left at the intersection of Vicolo Jugario and you'll see . . .

31. **Tiber Island** in the middle of the river. This island was the site of a hospital in Roman times and there's still one here today. Two ancient Roman bridges connect the island with the river banks. Continue straight on and you'll see . . .

32. The **Forum Boarium** on the right. The arches are all that remain of this appropriately named pig and cattle market. Across Via del Teatro di Marcello is . . .

33. The **Teatro di Marcello.** The semi-circular building was constructed by Augustus and named after his nephew. The first stone theater in Rome, it was a model for the Colosseum. During the Middle Ages it became a fortress for the powerful Orsini family. The present Count Orsini lives in grand style in the sumptuous apartments at the top. To its right stood . . .

34. The **Temple of Apollo** built by Emperor Augustus. All you can see today are three columns, the sole remains. Continue up Via del Teatro di Marcello. On the left is . . .

35. The **Ancient Jewish Ghetto.** A sprawling jungle of medieval streets and buildings. On your right is Capitoline Hill. Opposite No 18, look up to . . .

36. The **Tarpeian Rock** from which traitors were hurled to their deaths. Across the street is . . .

37. **Caffè del Teatro** where a delicious cappuccino brings you to the end of this walk.

HEART OF ROME RAMBLE

This walk takes you down **La Scalinata di Piazza di Spagna** (Spanish Steps) through the picturesque streets of modern Rome. Start from . . .

1. The **Villa Medici** on Viale Trinità dei Monti (open for guided tours only Wed 9am–1pm, Sun 10am–1pm, admission ʟ4,000). This villa has been the seat of the French Academy in Rome since 1803 when it was bought by Napoleon. The cannonball in the center of the 16th-century Medici fountain has a strange history. It was shot here from Castel Sant'Angelo by Queen Christina of Sweden. There's a small dent in the door of the villa where the missile struck before rolling to its present position. Although the villa is privately-owned you can visit the statue-filled formal gardens. Now walk down to . . .

2. **La Scalinata della Trinità dei Monti** (Spanish Steps) where you have an excellent view of Rome's most famous monuments. If you're lucky enough to be here in April, you'll find the steps lined with hundreds of brightly-colored azaleas in huge terracotta pots. Behind you is the church of **Trinità dei Monti**, constructed in the 16th century during the reign of Charles VII. One of the French churches of Rome, it features a fantastic fresco, *The Deposition*, by Daniele da Volterra. The obelisk in the center of the upper square, brought to Rome in the third century AD, was placed here by Pius VI in 1788. The 137 French-built steps (constructed by Specchi and de Sanctis in 1725), are known by their current name simply because the Spanish Embassy is located here. Walk down the steps past jewelry vendors and painters to the 17th-century . . .

3. **La Barcaccia** (Barcaccia Fountain) constructed by Pietro Bernini, father of the celebrated Gian Lorenzo Bernini. The image of the leaking boat was inspired by the presence of a barge in the same spot when the Tiber flooded in 1598. The water in the fountain is supposed to be some of the sweetest in the city. Take a sip. To the left of the fountain further down Piazza di Spagna is . . .

4. The **Colonna dell'Immacolata Concezione** (Column of Immaculate Conception) topped by a statue of the Virgin Mary. On the day of the Immaculate Conception (Dec 8), the Pope visits the column and a new wreath is placed on Mary's arm. At the far end of the piazza is . . .

5. The **Palazzo della Congregazione di Propaganda Fide** founded by Gregory XV in 1622. The exterior is the work of Bernini (the Younger) and Borromini. Now backtrack towards the steps. At Piazza di Spagna 26 you'll find . . .

6. **Keats's House** (open Mon–Fri 9am–1pm 3:30pm–6pm, admission L2,000). The former home of the English poet is now a museum. Amongst the various documents and memorabilia are souvenirs of fellow ex-patriot writers Shelley and Byron, who lived nearby. Across from the steps you'll find . . .

7. **Via del Babuino** filled with antique shops and galleries. On your left is . . .

8. The **Fontana del Babuino** (Fountain of the Baboon), which was one of the "talking statues" of medieval Rome. When the Romans wished to air a grievance they'd hang a message around the statue's neck. Continue past the Greek Orthodox Church; then turn right on Vicolo dell'Orto di Napoli to . . .

9. **Via Margutta**. For generations this street has been the center of Roman artistic activity. On your immediate right, you'll find the excellent restaurant **Osteria Margutta**, Via Margutta 81. It's just the place for a satisfying meal in comfortable modern surroundings. From the restaurant turn left on Via Margutta, glancing into the many antique stores located on this handsome street. Next, turn left on Vicolo del Babuino to Via del Babuino. Turn right and you'll come to . . .

10. **Piazza del Popolo** located at the foot of **Pincio**, the high hill to your right. The piazza's design evolved over three centuries. Sixtus V erected the obelisk (the second oldest in Rome dating from the 13th century BC) at its center in 1589; four lions lurk at the base. Intended as an impressive entrance into Rome for pilgrims from the north, the piazza was completed between 1816 and 1820. The overall impression is neo-Classic. Carlo Rainaldi designed the twin churches of **Santa Maria dei Miracoli** (1678) (nearest to *Rosati*), and **Santa Maria in Monte Santo** (1675). Bernini worked on the latter, then it was completed by Carlo Fontana who also assisted Rainaldi with Santa Maria dei Miracoli. If you're in need of refreshment, **Rosati's** is the place to relax and watch the world go by. From the piazza take Via del Corso for a spot of window-shopping. Then turn right onto . . .

11. **Via Canova**. At No 6 you'll see a wall covered with busted sculptures and sculptured busts. Carry on to No 24 where you can see contemporary sculptors hard at work. Turn left on Via di Ripetta. You'll see . . .

12. The **Mausoleo di Augusto** (Tomb of Augustus), on your left, begun by the emperor himself in 27BC. Many first-century emperors had their ashes deposited here; the tomb stood until the fifth century when it was sacked by barbarians. On your right is the glassed-in . . .

13. **Ara Pacis** (open Mon–Sat 9am–2pm, Sun 9am–1pm, admission L1,500). The Altar of Peace was built by the Senate during the reign of Augustus as a tribute to the emperor and the peace he brought to the Roman world. Portraits of the Imperial family adorn the altar. Proceed down Via di Ripetta. A left turn onto Via Borghese will bring you to . . .

14. The **Borghese Market** (open Mon–Sat). Here wonderful stalls sell prints, maps, silver and old books. On the left is . . .

15. The **Palazzo Borghese**, a beautiful Renaissance palace called "the harpsichord" by Romans because of its shape. Nip around the corner to Via della Fontanella Borghese for a view of one of Rome's most romantic courtyards. Directly opposite is the highly-recommended restaurant, **La Fontanella**. Now backtrack and turn left into Via della Lupa. A left turn onto Via dei Prefetti takes you to . . .

16. **Il Parlamento** (Parliament Building) where you'll see the Italian Parliament guarded by a colorful militia. Walk past the building; then turn right on Via dell'Impresa. The **Palazzo Chigi**, which houses the senior government offices, will be in front of you on the left. Go to the right of the *palazzo* down a small street and you'll arrive at . . .

17. **Piazza Colonna**, the center of Rome for centuries. In the middle of the piazza, beside the fountain, is the **Column of Marcus Aurelius**, built to commemorate the great general's victories. Don't leave the piazza without peeking into the beautiful courtyard of **No 355**. Cross Via del Corso into the Galleria. You may wish to stop off at **Berardo** for a princely pastry. Exit the Galleria, turning right on Via Maria in Via Lata to Via delle Muratte. A left turn will take you to . . .

18. **Fontana di Trevi** (Trevi Fountain) depicting a magnificent Neptune in a chariot drawn by sea horses. Toss a coin over your left shoulder into the fountain. If you believe the legend, you'll be sure to return to Rome. From the fountain take Via della Stamperia to Via delle Tritone and . . .

19. **Piazza Barberini**. Bernini's fabulous Triton Fountain occupies center stage with the resplendent sea god rising from the depths sounding his conch shell horn. At the end of the walk Via Veneto leads off to your left or, if you wish to return to Piazza di Spagna, you can take a left on Via Due Macelli.

MODERN AND ANCIENT ROME WALK

This Roman stroll, from Piazza della Repubblica to Piazza del Popolo, gives you a taste of the old and the new plus the added attraction of a visit to the beautiful Borghese Gardens. It also covers three of the greatest museums in the world. Starting from . . .

1. **Piazza della Repubblica**. Planned in 1870, the piazza has a lovely Naïad fountain in the center. Traffic is particularly ferocious here, so make your way carefully round to the eastern side where you'll see the remains of the **Baths of Diocletian**. Built in the third century AD, these were the biggest and most beautiful baths in the whole of Rome. The complex boasted libraries, fountains, gardens and concert halls as well as 900 baths. It now houses the **Museo Nazionale Romano** (open Tues–Sat 9:30am–2pm, Sun 9:30am–1pm, admission L4,000). One of the greatest collections of Greek and Roman sculpture in the world, the museum also displays classical Roman paintings and frescoes. Don't miss the **Ludovisi Throne** which dates from the fifth century BC. It's a masterpiece with a sensational relief depicting Aphrodite, the goddess of love. When you leave the museum walk up Via Orlando to . . .

2. **Piazza San Bernardo** with its wonderful fountain. This huge Moses fountain, also called **Fontana dell'Acqua Felice**, was built in 1587. The colossal statue of Moses was called "the most shameful parody of Michelangelo's work in Rome". A criticism that, so legend has it, caused its sculptor Prospero da Brescia to die of grief. Cross over to Via Barberini, which leads to . . .

3. **Piazza Barberini**. Here you'll find the delightful little **Fountain of the Bees**, designed by Bernini in 1644. In the center of the piazza is the famous Triton Fountain, another Bernini masterpiece with its four dolphins supporting Poseidon's half-man, half-fish offspring. On the north side of the square is the beginning of the famous . . .

4. **Via Veneto**, where the "beautiful people" used to gather and the era of *La Dolce Vita* was born. This street is now the center of a smart residential area lined with grand hotels and expensive shops. On the right is the **Palazzo Margherita**, now the American Embassy. Built in 1886, it used to be the home of Queen Margaret, wife of King Umberto I. Continue up Via Veneto – stopping off at the terrace of **Doney's** café on the right for a *cappuccino* and a *corneto* – an Italian croissant. At the top of the street you come to . . .

5. The **Porta Pinciana**, a gateway built in the ancient walls that encircled Rome from the third century AD. This is one of the finest remaining sections of the Aurelian wall. Carry on through the gateway. (Be very careful of the traffic here as it hurtles round in all directions.) Cross Piazzale Brasile to Viale del Museo Borghese. Turn right for . . .

6. The **Borghese Gallery**, a lovely little palace built for Cardinal Borghese in 1613 (open Tues–Sat 9am–2pm, Sun 9am–1pm, closed Mon, admission free). There's a fine collection of works by Bernini here, including the stunning *Rape of Proserpina* statue. Turn down Viale dell'Uccellieria, passing the zoo (open daily 8:30am–sunset). It's not a great zoo so we don't recommend you stop here. Continue on round, turning left into Viale del Giardino. You'll reach a little lake beside its **Temple of Aesculapius**. This is a popular place with Roman families in the summer, both for the shady trees and the rowing boats on the lake. Continue down Viale delle Belle Arti to . . .

7. The **National Gallery of Modern Art** (open: Tues–Sat 9am–2pm, Sun 9pm–1pm, admission L4,000). Built in 1911, the neo-Classical building houses a collection of Italian sculpture and painting from the 19th century to the present day. There are some interesting Futurist exhibits, plus works by Braque and Modigliani among others. Leaving the gallery, continue along Viale delle Belle Arti until you come to . . .

8. The **Villa Giulia**. The villa is now a museum devoted to Etruscan art (open Tues–Sat 9am–2pm, Sun 9am–1pm, admission L4,000). Originally it was the country retreat of Pope Julius III, notorious for his sybaritic lifestyle. The Etruscan collection housed here is spectacular. Don't miss it, especially the decorative vases inspired by the ancient Greeks. Retrace your steps to the Modern Art Gallery. Climb the steps to Viale F. La Guardia; then turn right into Viale delle Magnolie. Walk over the bridge to . . .

9. The **Pincio Gardens**. Try and get here at sunset. The view over Rome is at its most spectacular as the sun sinks over the city. Named for the Pincio family who created a garden on this spot in the fourth century AD, it's one of the loveliest gardens in Rome, with magnificent umbrella pines and palm trees. Sadly, many of the statues of Italian patriots have been daubed with graffiti. Leave the gardens by a path heading downhill beside the terrace to . . .

10. **Piazza del Popolo**, one of the largest squares in Rome. The obelisk was transported from Egypt by Augustus. Erected in 1589, it used to be a landmark for pilgrims visiting the Holy

City. At the end of this walk, why not treat yourself to a *gelato* at **Rosati's**? You'll find this famous Roman ice-cream parlour on the far side of the piazza.

RENAISSANCE ROME I

Here's a walk that explores the romantic world that was Renaissance Rome, plus a variety of other Italian wonders. We start in the **Piazza Venezia** by taking a look at the enormous . . .

1. **Altar of the Nation**. Started in 1885 and completed in 1911, this monument is dedicated to Vittorio Emanuele, the first king of modern Italy (he sits on a horse in the center) and celebrates the country's unification. It's known to Romans either as "the wedding cake" or (more accurately in our opinion) as "the typewriter". The tomb of Italy's Unknown Soldier with an eternal flame is directly in front of the king's statue. Inside the monument are various offices, a police station and water tanks. The ruins on the right are the remains of an *insula* (apartment block) of the first century AD, discovered during Mussolini's excavations of 1927. On the left of the altar is . . .

2. The **Tomb of C Publius Bibulus** (or what remains of it). A fragment of a Roman wall, pierced by a door, stands on the grass. It also dates from the first century BC. This important landmark marks the beginning of Via Flaminia, one of the great consular roads that leads to the Adriatic. To your left is . . .

3. The **Palazzo Venezia** (open Tues–Sat 9am–1:30pm, Sun 9am–12:30pm, admission L4,000). It was the Embassy of the Republic of Venice during the 16th century. Mussolini's office was here. He used to stand on the balcony (above No 3) to deliver his mesmeric speeches to crowds in the square below. Leaving the monument behind, cross the square. At the angle of Via del Corso and Via del Plebiscito, you can see the house where Napoleon's mother lived after the great Bonaparte was sent to St Helena. She used to sit in the enclosed green balcony watching the people pass below. Standing atop a marble platform directing the constant flow of Fiats in and out of the piazza, you'll see the high priest of Roman traffic wardens. He's sometimes referred to as "the ballet master" because of the flamboyant gestures he employs. The entrance to Palazzo Venezia is at Via del Plebiscito 118. The museum houses some smashing Renaissance tapestries and bronzes. From the *palazzo* turn left onto Via del Plebiscito, noting the numerous palaces that once housed Renaissance society. For example . . .

4. The **Palazzo Altieri**, on your right at Via del Plebiscito 49. The coat of arms above the entrance represents Pope Clement X who built the palace in the second half of the 17th century. The papal crown and keys in the design symbolize the Pope, the stars his family. On your left is . . .

5. The **Chiesa del Gesù** (Church of Jesus) which sports the most Baroque decor in Rome. It contains the tomb of St Ignatius Loyola, founder of the Jesuit Order (his body lies in a solid gold casket). The altar of St Ignatius is ornamented with silver, gold and precious gems. Travelers should pause a moment by the "Madonna of the Streets". She'll answer your prayers for a safe journey. A few yards later you'll come to the Largo Argentina where you will find lots of feline friends in . . .

6. The **Republican Forum**, which dates from 300BC but was only discovered in 1926. The temples are known as A, B, C, and D because the experts can't agree on what they actually were. This is where Romans dump unclaimed kittens. Literally hundreds of stray cats live here fed on leftover pasta by volunteer teams of little old ladies. Now return to the corner of Via del Plebiscito and walk through the Largo delle Stimmate on your right to . . .

7. **Via dei Cestari**. The street is blessed with a host of holy haberdashers for nuns and priests. Religious shops sell everything from bishops' brocaded capes to gold goblets. Take a detour into Via dell'Arco della Ciabella on your left where you'll find . . .

8. **Part of a Roman Wall**, which once linked the Pantheon with the Republican Forum. Then continue to Via di Santa Chiara. On this corner you'll find . . .

9. The **Cloister of Santa Chiara**. Sisters in this Rome nunnery are cloistered for life, save at election time when they're let out to vote. Now turn around. In front of you you'll find Piazza Minerva with . . .

10. The **Obelisk Mounted on an Elephant** in the center. This statue, supporting the smallest obelisk in Rome, is by Bernini. Behind it is the bare, 500-year-old facade of . . .

11. **Santa Maria sopra Minerva** (St Mary's over Minerva), built over the Roman temple of Minerva, the goddess of wisdom. The church is Rome's only example of Gothic style architecture. Don't miss Michelangelo's statue *Christ Holding the Cross* (1519). Other treasures include the crystal casket of St Catherine of Siena, Italy's patron saint, frescoes by Filippino Lippi (1489) and the tomb of Fra Angelico. When you come

out of the church continue along Via Minerva to Piazza della Rotonda where you'll see . . .

12. The **Pantheon** (open Mon–Sat 9am–4pm, Sun 9am–1pm, admission free). Built by Hadrian in about 120AD, over the ruins of a temple built by Agrippa in 27BC, the Pantheon is the finest Roman temple in existence. Directly across the piazza is a 600-year-old hotel. Just beyond the Pantheon, leave the piazza on Salita di Crescenzi. Peek into No 30, which contains a most appealing Renaissance Lion-in-the-Clouds. At the top of the street there's a junction with Via della Dogana Vecchia. Straight ahead you can see the back of . . .

13. The **Italian Senate Building**, called Palazzo Madama after Margaret of Austria, the illegitimate daughter of Emperor Charles V. If the guards are armed with light machine guns the Senate is in session. Just to the right of the Senate is . . .

14. **San Luigi dei Francesi** (St Louis of the French). St Louis is the fellow in stone to the left of the entrance holding a sword in one hand and what looks like a bomb in the other. In fact, it's the papal orb. Inside the chapel, which is the French Church in Rome, are three magnificent works by Caravaggio representing scenes from the life of St Matthew. Turn right as you leave, passing between the church and the Senate on Via del Salvatore. This takes you round to the front of the Senate and Corso del Rinascimento. Cross the street diagonally; just to your left turn right into the delightful . . .

15. **Piazza Navona**. This is a wonderful piazza, designed by Bernini for Pope Innocent X. It stands on what once was the site of the stadium where the Emperor Domiziano crucified Christians. Across the piazza to the left is the **Palazzo Doria Pamphili** which Innocent X built for his family. Directly across from you is the church of . . .

16. **Santa Agnese** (St Agnes), built to honor the saint who was martyred here. The magnificent 17th-century Baroque facade was created by Borromini; the ornate interior executed by pupils of Bernini, while he designed the three fountains in the piazza. On the far left is . . .

17. The **Fontana del Moro**, which depicts Neptune struggling with a large fish surrounded by tritons. It is called *Il Moro* (the negro) because the Romans thought the central figure was a black man. At the right end of the piazza is . . .

18. The **Fountain of Neptune**, who's shown struggling with an octopus. The crowning glory is . . .

19. The **Fountain of the Four Rivers**, in the center of the square. The figures represent the main rivers of the four continents

known in those days. The Nile, with the veiled head for Egypt; the Ganges, leaning on a pole for India; the Danube, holding a shield for Europe; and the Plate, holding his hand up in horror for the Americas.

We are going to leave the walk here. Why not drop into the bar **Tre Scalini** for a *tartufo* (rich chocolate ice-cream topped with whipped cream); as close to heaven as you'll ever get for L6,000.

RENAISSANCE ROME II

Here's a walk that combines a classic castle with marvelous markets and palaces as pretty as a picture. Start from . . .

1. The **Piazza Navona**. Walk along the piazza to your right, behind Bernini's *Il Moro* statue. Exit on Via della Cuccagna to Corso Vittorio Emanuele where you'll see . . .

2. The **Piccola Farnesina** directly across the street. This is one of the loveliest small Renaissance palaces in Rome. It houses the **Museo Barracco** which contains the personal collection of the Barone Barracco including early Greek sculpture and Egyptian works. Now turn left and you'll find . . .

3. The **Palace of the Massimo Family** at Corso Vittorio Emanuele 141. The name of this great Roman family was first recorded in the 11th century and their descendants still live in the palace. For centuries the poor were allowed to sleep in the lovely arched porch. You can visit the courtyard with its stunning gilded open gallery. When you come out cross Corso Vittorio Emanuele to . . .

4. **Sant'Andrea della Valle**. This church is built over the former **Teatro di Pompeii** where Caesar was slain. From the church, turn left onto Largo dei Chiavari to Largo del Pallaro where you'll see houses and high rises built in a semi-circle over the seats of the ancient theater. On your right by the church ruins, just before the entrance to the **Teatro dei Satiri** walk through the narrow passageway called Passetto del Biscione. As you emerge you'll be outside a terrific restaurant . . .

5. **Pancrazio**, perhaps the most historic eating place in the world. You can dine among the ancient ruins of the Teatro di Pompeii on the exact spot where Caesar was killed. Just past the restaurant is . . .

6. **Campo dei Fiori**, the liveliest general market in Rome. In the center you'll find a statue of Giordano Bruno, a heretic monk burned to death on this spot in 1600. Take a walk through the market where you can savor marvelous cheeses, sausages and vegetables. At the far end, on the right, you come to Piazza della Cancelleria where you'll see . . .

7. The **Chancellery**. Built between 1438 and 1511, it now houses the Vatican Law Court. Now walk back through the market and exit on Via dei Baullari for . . .

8. The **Palazzo Farnese** (not open to the public). This is considered to be the finest Renaissance palace in Rome, commissioned by Antonio Sangallo who died in 1546, before it was finished. Michelangelo designed the top story; then Giacomo della Porta completed the building (to Michelangelo's design) in 1589. The palace is now the French Embassy with an upper-floor gallery decorated with splendid early 17th-century frescoes. The two fountains in the piazza are baths (made of Egyptian granite) from the **Baths of Caracalla**. Leave the piazza on Via del Mascherone. At the end of the street you'll see . . .

9. **Il Mascherone** (The Mask). This fountain has had the same perplexed expression for over 300 years. Now turn right on Via Giulia, considered the most handsome street in Renaissance Rome. Pausing at No 186, you'll see the beautiful . . .

10. **Gardens of the Farnese Palace**. Then, above No. 185, there's part of a . . .

11. **Bridge** begun by Michelangelo to connect the Farnese Palace with the Villa Farnesina in Trastevere. He got no further than the span across Via Giulia. At Via Giulia 1 is . . .

12. The **Palace of the Falconieri Family**. Built by Borromini in the 17th century, it's now the Hungarian Academy. If the main door's open you can see one of the most beautiful Renaissance fountains in Rome. Continuing down Via Giulia the next sight is . . .

13. The **Carceri Nuove**, at No 52. These prisons, built in 1652 under Innocent X, were considered to be the most solid in Europe as late as 1845. The building now houses the **Criminology Museum**. Walking further you'll find . . .

14. The **Sacchetti Palace** at No 66, which has been the residence of the Sacchetti family for centuries. At the end of this street you enter . . .

15. **Piazza dell'Oro**, the center of Rome's Florentine community in Renaissance times. Above the sacristy of the church, **San Giovanni dei Fiorentini**, is a delightful 15th-century statue of St John the Baptist. Leave the piazza on Via Paola; then cross directly over Corso Vittorio Emanuele to . . .

16. The **Ponte Sant'Angelo**. The bridge is decorated with Bernini's archangels, each of which holds a different symbol of Christ's crucifixion. When you walk across pause at the far end. If

you look up to the left there's a wonderful view of St Peter's. After the bridge you can pay a visit to . . .

17. The **Castel Sant'Angelo** (open Tues–Sat 9am–1pm, Sun 9am–noon, admission L3,000). This was Hadrian's tomb built in 135AD. Converted into a fort during the Middle Ages, the interior contains numerous historical relics. A drink at the bar up top gives you a fascinating view of Rome and Vatican City. Now recross the bridge. At an angle off the street on your left is Via di Panico. Amble along here to Piazza dei Coronari, where you turn left into Via dei Coronari. As you do, you'll instantly come upon . . .

18. **Raphael's House**, at Via dei Coronari 122–123. This ancient home was bought by the artist's executors to provide an income for the upkeep of Raphael's tomb. It does so to this very day. A little further along on your left you'll see the beautiful . . .

19. **Renaissance door** at No 148. The windows flanked by sculpted pilasters and a worn inscription above the door reads: "Regard as your own only what you create". Now, just as you approach Piazzetta di San Simeone, turn right up Via dei Gabrielli to the lovely . . .

20. **Palazzo Taverna** with its ivy-covered walls and rustic fountain. Retrace your steps across the piazzetta to . . .

21. **San Salvatore in Lauro** (enter via No 14). This church possesses a glorious series of Renaissance cloisters. Don't miss the entrancing interior cloister with its fine small fountain. At the end of your walk you may have built up quite an appetite. The answer could well be a meal at the **Osteria dell'Antiquario.**

A pleasant way to get back to the heart of things is to continue along Via dei Coronari to Piazza di Tor di San Guigna.

TRASTEVERE WALK

This great walk takes you across the River Tiber to the lovely area called **Trastevere** – from the Latin *trans Tiberim*, meaning "over the Tiber". Not originally part of Rome, this was where the ancient Etruscan lands began. We start by the river at the . . .

1. **Teatro di Marcello**. Caesar started work on this huge theater and it was finished by Augustus between 13 and 11 BC. Holding over 16,000 spectators it was built of travertine stone from the Tivoli quarry. Two tiers of arches remain, topped by the palace built by the Savelli family in the 16th century. It remains an imposing structure and dominates the riverbank. Cross over Lungotevere dei Cenci to reach . . .

2. The **Ponte Fabricio**, which leads across to Tiber Island. Built in 62BC by Consul Fabricius the bridge is still in use more than 2,000 years later. It's also known as the Bridge of Four Heads – look at the statues on the parapet of the bridge and you'll see why. At the end of the bridge you reach . . .

3. **Tiber Island**, a lovely peaceful little spot in the middle of the river. Legend has it that the outline of the island – shaped like a boat – is that of the vessel that brought Aesculapius, the god of medicine, here from Greece. There's even a mast for this island-boat. Look at the obelisk at the southern tip of the island. St Bartholomew's church now stands on the spot where Aesculapius's temple stood. On your left you'll see the hospital of the "do-good-brothers" – the *Fatebenefratelli*. Continue to stroll from the steps to the square down to the river on your right. Soon you come to . . .

4. The **Ponte Rotto**. Originally called the Aemilian Bridge, it collapsed into the river three times. Only a single arch remains, standing in the middle of the Tiber since 1598. The martyr brothers Simplicius and Faustinius were thrown from the bridge into the swirling river below on Diocletian's orders in the third century AD. Walk back up to the **Ponte Cestio** which takes you over to the far side of the river. Founded in the first century BC, this bridge was reconstructed in the 19th century. On your left you can see the church of **Santa Maria in Cosmedin**; to your right Janiculum Hill and the Lighthouse. Turn left along Lungotevere dell'Anguillara until you come to **Ponte Palatino**, then turn up . . .

5. **Via dei Vascellari**. You are now in Trastevere, the city across the Tiber. It's hardly changed since medieval times; a warren of little narrow streets and tiny piazzas. The people of Trastevere are reputed for their courage and strength. They even claim to be the direct descendants of the ancient Romans, speaking their own local dialect. Continue down this little street to . . .

6. The **Piazza Santa Cecilia** named for the patron saint of music who was martyred here. Saved by a miracle from suffocation in her bathroom – a favorite way of disposing of people in Roman times – she was then condemned to be beheaded. Even this drastic solution was not entirely successful as she lived for three days afterwards. Her church stands on a site dedicated to her name since the fifth century. You'll find it just inside a beautiful flowered courtyard with an ancient tank. The statue below the altar by Stefano Maderno (1599) represents the legend of St Cecilia, while her sarcophagus lies in the crypt. There's a beautiful ninth-century mosaic in typical Roman style in the apse. Continue down Via di San Mich-

ele to Via della Madonna dell'Orto, then to Via Anicia. You'll then reach . . .

7. **Piazza San Francesco d'Assisi.** In the 17th-century church, a marble statue by Bernini commemorates the death of another martyr, Ludovica Albertoni. Continue up Via di San Francesco a Ripa until you come to . . .

8. **Piazza Santa Maria in Trastevere**, a beautiful square with a 12th-century basilica. It was here that a miraculous fountain of oil flowed for a whole day in 38BC. The facade of the basilica is decorated with superb mosaics; inside there's a lovely painting of *The Assumption* by Domenichino dating from the 17th century. The 12th-century mosaics in the chancel represent scenes from the life of the Virgin Mary with great detail and beauty. You can take a break for a coffee or lunch at one of the terraced cafés surrounding the square. The colored facades of these houses are particularly beautiful at sunset. Now head down Vicolo dei Cinque towards the river. You reach **Piazza Trilussa** – named for a famous early 20th-century Trastevere poet who wrote racy verse about Roman life. Although the enormous fountain dates from 1612, it wasn't placed here until the 19th century when the river embankments were built. Turn left, away from the river, down Via Santa Dorotea. Legend has it that Via Santa Dorotea 20, with its beautiful upper-floor window, was the home of Raphael's mistress, La Fornarina. His famous painting of her is in the Barberini Palace. Turn right into Via della Lungara for the entrance to . . .

9. The **Villa Farnesina** (open Mon–Sat 9am–1pm, admission L2,000). This lovely villa houses an extraordinary collection of Renaissance paintings. The wonderful frescoes by Raphael are not to be missed. This country house, set in splendid gardens, was built in 1508 for the banker Agostino Chigi, known as the "Magnificent". Chigi was a great patron of Raphael; he died just a few days after the great painter himself. Head back to Porta Settimiana, then turn right into Via Garibaldi. Cross Via G. Mameli for the steps leading up to the church of . . .

10. **San Pietro in Montorio**. There's a splendid view over Rome from the area in front of the church. To finish your walk you can either continue into the gardens of the **Janiculum**, turning right into Passeggiata del Gianicolo (the best view of Rome is to be had from the top of the hill); or, retrace your steps to Via Dorotea, cross Ponte Sisto and so back into Rome.

SHOPPING

DEPARTMENT STORES

Discount System, Via Viminale 35
Tel: (06) 4746545
Open: Mon 3:30pm–7:30pm, Tues–Sat 9am–1pm
  3:30pm–7:30pm
Credit cards: AE

Not quite a department store, but a huge shop selling all kinds of clothes and accessories at discount prices. It's a bit like Loehmann's – everything is sold at half price or less, and everything comes from the best designers in Italy. Every brand of designer jeans you can imagine is on sale here including Trussardi for men and women. The men's clothes are by Valentino, Missoni and even Armani. For women there is a great choice from Fendi and Krizia among many other famous names. Leather goods, belts and handbags, too – but you'll have to search out the real treasures. The quality is great but the styles may not be to your taste. Well worth a visit or two as stocks change all the time. What is more, your suit by Valentino at half the price you'd pay at a regular store will have its label still in place. Cut price chic – and no one will ever know!

Fendi, Via Borgognona
Tel: (06) 6797643
Open: Mon 4pm–8pm, Tues–Sat 9:30am–1pm 4pm–8pm
Credit cards: AE, DC, MC, V

Eight different Fendi shops on both sides of this street, one of the most famous for fashion in the whole of Rome. These eight shops make up a kind of department store, Roman style. There are handbags and shoes at Nos 4E and 4L; right across the street is the main Fendi shop at No 36. For clothing, go to No 40; luggage is at No 38; everything in fur is at No 39. Everything is Fendi own-label – from pareos and swimming costumes to suitcases and furniture. There is Fendissime, too, for children's clothes. Fendi seems to be taking over the whole street and the window displays are a delight in themselves. It's not all under one roof – but almost.

La Rinascente, Via del Corso
Tel: (06) 6797691
Open: Mon–Sat 9:30am–7:30pm
Credit cards: AE, DC, MC, V

La Rinascente is Italy's biggest department store group. Its own brand name, Elle Erre, offers clothes for men, women and children. The store's system is less sophisticated than in many American shops but you can still find a fair selection of reasonably-priced goods here. There's a particularly good range of outsize clothes under the Elle Erre brand name. Trendy in-house boutique for the under-20s with beachwear and casual clothes, plus a small department that specializes in sailing gear – everything from jackets to deck wear. Good exchange rates if you make your purchases with dollars or traveler's checks.

La del Rinascente, Piazza del Fiume 2
Tel: (06) 841231
Open: Mon–Sat 9:30am–7:30pm
Credit cards: AE, DC, MC, V

This is the other Roman La Rinascente branch, situated in a slightly out-of-the-way district. The store offers the same excellent rates of exchange for shoppers buying with traveler's checks or dollars. Good brand-name clothes, pleasant perfumes and an excellent lingerie department. Plenty of useful goods at attractive prices all under one roof. Well-stocked household appliances and gadgets in the basement. It isn't Bloomingdale's but department stores are not a Roman tradition. City shoppers prefer to choose in specialized small stores, crossing the city to find exactly what they're looking for.

MARKETS

Campo dei Fiori, Piazza Campo dei Fiori
Open: Mon–Sat 6am–2pm

Undoubtedly the most exciting neighborhood food market in Rome. The people are as colorful as the produce which includes great mounds of lemons, tomatoes, strawberries and melons. Even if you're not shopping, do watch the Italians at it – bravura performances from one and all. Take a stroll through the stalls to savor the marvelous cheeses, sausages and fruits. There are some clothes as well – cheap Bermuda shorts in Madras cotton would make a nice souvenir. In the piazza you'll find cafés where you can sit and watch the action over an iced coffee. The imposing statue in the center, rising high above the awnings, is of Giordano Bruno, burnt alive for heresy on this spot in 1600.

Mercato dei Fiori, Via Trionfale
Open: Tues 10am–1pm

The brightest flowers in town come from here, Rome's only flower market. The two-story covered hall is packed with delicious scents. Upstairs, flowers in season; downstairs, giant house plants. Bargaining is not just tolerated, it's expected. Incidentally, chrysanthemums and asters are for funerals only; present them to your hostess and she'll think you're up to no good. If you are a gardener, then this is the place to come and see how the Romans do it.

Piazza Vittorio Emanuele
Open: Mon–Sat 7am–2pm

This, Rome's largest market, entirely covers the huge square and is highly entertaining. It's mostly fruit and vegetables but you can also pick up clothes, furniture and all kinds of household goods. Stalls tend to specialize – one stallkeeper sells nothing but lemons. It's a great place for unusual cheeses and shellfish. You can put together a delicious Roman picnic of prosciutto ham, sausages, cheese and salad without leaving the piazza.

Porta Portese, Ponte Sublicio
Open: Sun 6:30am–1:30pm

Rome's sprawling flea market has booths selling objects of every kind – an occasional original antique, old and new clothes, plus lots more. It's always crowded, so do beware of pickpockets and bad buys. Be prepared to barter (offer about half the stated price) for anything that catches your eye. The stallholders expect and relish it. Really off-beat items appear from time to time, such as a life-size Roman chariot from some studio back lot. Plenty of second-hand books to browse through, plus stalls of 19th-century lace-trimmed nightdresses and linen summer jackets for men. Even if you don't buy, the atmosphere is great, it's well worth strolling through on a Sunday morning.

San Giovanni, Via Sannio
Open: Mon–Sat 8am–1pm

Near the church of San Giovanni in Laterano, the market is a kind of Porta Portese annex, mostly for clothes (terrific leather flying jackets) and all kinds of camping equipment. Many of the clothes are second-hand so you can put together a good 50s or 60s "look" if you search carefully. The prices will be low if you bargain and *do* bargain, it's all part of the fun. You'll find a lot of these same dealers at the Porta Portese flea market on Sunday mornings. This is a favorite market for Roman bargain hunters, but less well known to visitors to the city. Slightly off the beaten track but well worth a visit.

Via Andrea Doria
Open: Tues–Sat 8am–1pm

This is a large and bustling food market where the wares are beautifully displayed in heaps of bright colors and geometric patterns. Stalls tend to specialize less than those of Piazza Vittorio Emanuele but the foodstuffs are of high quality and you can concoct the ideal picnic within minutes. Check the delicatessen stalls (*salumerie*) for delicious smoked sausage, prosciutto hams, and all kinds of lovely cheeses.

Via del Lavatore
Open: Tues–Sat 8am–1pm

A real local small market which has existed on this piazza for hundreds of years. It's just five minutes walk from the Trevi fountain, in a narrow piazza right under the buttressed walls of the Quirinale. This is where the locals come for their fruit, vegetables and fish. The choice is wonderful – from sun-ripened tomatoes to bunches of wild asparagus and great mounds of cherries. The zucchini are sold with their yellow flowers – fritters made with these are a Roman treat. There are several cheap clothes shops here which are good for shirts and colorful beach shoes. Wander round the alleyways that surround the market. There are pleasures to be seen at every corner.

ANTIQUES

Armando Perea, Via del Babuino 118
Tel: (06) 6792069
Open: Mon 4pm–7:30pm, Tues–Sat 10am–1pm 4pm–7:30pm
No credit cards

The Perea family has been dealing in *objets d'art* and bric-à-brac since the early 1900s, so don't be afraid to ask for information about the wares on display. It's a shabby shop piled high with a welter of fascinating items. A total delight for addicted antiques browsers. Etchings, prints, sketches and books are jumbled in with everything else.

Davoli, Via Giulia 168
Tel: (06) 6550097
Open: Mon 4:30pm–7:30pm, Tues–Sat 10am–1pm
   4:30pm–7:30pm
No credit cards

A good selection of *objets d'art* from the 17th century onwards, with a particular leaning towards 18th-century bronzes and paintings both in oils and watercolors. It's a small but sophisticated shop where (for a change) customers are welcome to spend time browsing. Keep an eye out for fine specimens of 18th-century furniture. Friendly, pleasant, English-speaking assistants.

Galleria Borghese, Palazzo Borghese, Via di Ripetta 117
Tel: (06) 6876458
Open: Mon 3:30pm–8pm, Tues–Sat 10am–1pm 3:30pm–8pm,
  Sun 10am–9pm
Credit cards: AE, MC

An enormous antiques showroom in the 16th-century Palazzo Borghese where the stock changes constantly, but is always based on a theme. This can vary from period European furniture to Oriental art, when you'll find everything from huge Chinese vases to wonderful piles of carpets from Afghanistan and Turkey. Half the fun is the elegant surroundings with ornate painted ceilings, candelabra and a delightful garden. Not expensive and well worth a visit.

Galleria Coronari, Via dei Coronari 59
Tel: (06) 6569917
Open: Mon 4:30pm–7:30pm, Tues–Sat 10am–1:30pm
  4:30pm–7:30pm
Credit cards: AE, DC, V

This is an absolutely enchanting shop; tiny (in fact one room) but stuffed with treasures ranging from bric-à-brac to genuine antiques. You'll find 19th-century porcelain dolls, doll houses, jewelry, clocks, watches and mechanical toys alongside genuine and rare *objets d'art*. Prices vary but aren't outrageous.

Galleria Romana, Via Giulia 81
Tel: (06) 6541447
Open: Mon 4pm–7:30pm, Tues–Sat 10am–1pm 4pm–7:30pm
No credit cards

A very sophisticated selection containing some rare and impressive antiques. The gallery comprises two rooms with the accent on fine neo-Classical furniture. You'll also see beautiful 18th-century clocks and marble busts of famous Romans.

Emporio Floreale, Via delle Carrozze 46
Tel: (06) 6780207
Open: Mon 4pm–8pm, Tues–Sat 10am–1pm 4pm–8pm
No credit cards

If you collect Art Nouveau glass, this is the place to come and browse. They specialize in Art Deco too and have a fine collection of both paintings and furniture. English-speaking staff and a friendly welcome. Reasonable prices.

Granmercato Antiquario Babuino, Via del Babuino 150
Tel: (06) 6785903
Open: Mon 4pm–8pm, Tues–Sat 10am–1pm 4pm–8pm
Credit cards: AE, DC, MC, V

A bright modern shop selling lots of silver and silver plate; everything from inkwells to picture frames. They also have a selection of fine Sheffield cutlery, lovely little perfume bottles and miniatures. A treasure trove of reasonably priced and unusual objects, all beautifully displayed. Helpful English-speaking assistants.

Il Cenacolo, Via dei Coronari 187
Tel: (06) 6542260
Open: Mon 4pm–7pm, Tues–Sat 9:30am–1:30pm 4pm–7pm
Credit cards: AE

A rather grand antiques shop beautifully situated on the first floor level of the Palazzo Lancellotti, which dates from the 16th century. Most of the wares are also 16th century and of fine quality. Sculpture, paintings, porcelain and furniture.

Impianti Elettricci, Via delle Carrozze 17A
No telephone
Open: Mon 4:30pm–8pm, Tues–Sat 10am–1:30pm 4:30pm–8pm
No credit cards

A marvelous muddle of 20th-century gadgets crammed into one showroom. Dictaphones from the 1920s, radios from the 1930s, ancient typewriters and Vitaphones (pre-record player disc players), not forgetting "His Master's Voice"-type gramophones. Many are in excellent working order, affordably priced and it's a pleasure simply exploring. Start your collection now.

La Chimera, Via Giulia 122
Tel: (06) 6548354
Open: Mon 4:30pm–8pm, Tues–Sat 10am–1:30pm 4:30pm–8pm
Credit cards: AE

A sophisticated and discriminating store, one of the most up-market on a very smart street, with prices to match. Marvelous 18th- and 19th-century furniture, marble busts and *objets d'art*, all beautifully chosen.

La Chiocciola, Via dei Coronari 185
Tel: (06) 6541954
Open: Mon 4pm–7:30pm, Tues–Sat 10am–1pm 4pm–7:30pm
No credit cards

This charming shop specializes in furniture, some new but mostly antique. Much of the furniture has been beautifully inlaid or decorated with intricate marquetry work. Pieces range from the small to the gigantic. Pleasant service but high prices.

La Gazza Ladra, Via dei Banchi Vecchi 29
Tel: (06) 6541689
Open: Mon 3:30pm–7pm, Tues–Sat 10am–1pm 3:30pm–7pm
No credit cards

A tiny shop that specializes in walking sticks. Lots of rare and beautiful antique sticks here which come from all over Europe. Don't miss the Venetian canes made from glass. There are ivory and ebony sticks too, all beautifully carved. This is a good spot for an unusual memento or gift. The owner is an expert in the field and speaks English.

La Pinacoteca di Via Giulia, Via Giulia 188
Tel: (06) 6564291
Open: Mon 4pm–8pm, Tues–Sat 10am–1:30pm 4pm–8pm
No credit cards

If your passion is 19th-century Italian paintings, you couldn't do better than shop in here. The shop deals only in paintings of this period, particularly works by the Macchiaioli group, who were based in Florence and influenced by the Realist school of French painters. The proprietor has an exhaustive knowledge of the works for sale and is happy to advise. Expensive.

Liberty Deco, Via Giulia 107
Tel: (06) 6542204
Open: Mon 4:30pm–8pm, Tues–Sat 10am–1:30pm 4:30pm–8pm
Credit cards: AE

Plenty of pricey, but marvelous Italian and French furniture from the 1920s; writing desks, tables and chairs. Art Deco is the key-note here and you'll find lots of glassware, ceramics and lamps from this period. Some fine pieces of 50s work too.

Lo Scrittoio, Via dei Coronari 103
Tel: (06) 6875536
Open: Mon 4pm–7:30pm, Tues–Sat 10am–1pm 4pm–7:30pm
No credit cards

This charming shop specializes in desks and nothing but desks. From 18th-century *escritoire* to 19th-century boardroom, all the pieces are in immaculate condition. Prices vary from expensive to very expensive. Friendly service by English-speaking assistants.

Metastasio Casa d'Arte, Via dei Coronari 33
Tel: (06) 657667
Open: Mon 4:30pm–7:30pm, Tues–Sat 10am–1pm
  4:30pm–7:30pm
No credit cards

This store is a work of art in itself with a marvelous beamed ceiling. It specializes in 18th-century French and Italian furniture, much of it with a sea-going flavor; sea-chests, galley tables, benches and casks. All are in superb condition. Nautical prints, paintings and etchings are also on display.

Monetti, Via Giulia 169
Tel: (06) 6877436
Open: Mon 4:30pm–8pm, Tues–Sat 10am–1:30pm 4:30pm–8pm
No credit cards

This little shop specializes in beautiful pieces of Empire furniture in superb condition. You'll also find Italian paintings from the 18th and 19th centuries, and delightful models of many of Rome's top architectural sights as they would have appeared in their original state. Friendly, English-speaking assistants.

1900, Via Vittoria 37
Tel: (06) 6789465
Open: Mon 4:30pm–7:30pm, Tues–Sat 9:30am–1:30pm
  4:30pm–7:30pm
Credit cards: AE, DC

A tiny store, high on the list of Rome's most sophisticated shoppers, specializing in Art Deco and Art Nouveau *objets d'art* and furniture. Every piece is in perfect condition and – as this is the center of fashionable Rome – prices are very high. The friendly and well-informed staff speak English.

Orient, Via Bocca di Leone 4
Tel: (06) 6791801
Open: Mon 4pm–8pm, Tues–Sat 10am–1pm 4pm–8pm
Credit cards: AE, MC, V

This is the place for antique rugs in Rome. They have *kilims* from Samarkand, Anatolia, China and Tibet. Each rug is an individual masterpiece with stories and legends woven into it. Made by nomadic tribes, *kilims* are a popular collector's item. Here, there's a fabulous choice; prices are fairly high.

G. Panatta, Via Francesco Crispi 177
Tel: (06) 6795948
Open: Mon 4pm–8pm, Tues–Sat 10am–1pm 4pm–8pm
Credit cards: AE, MC, V

Lots of lithographs, prints and engravings as well as illustrated 19th-century books. Check out the lovely bookplates, cards and gift-tags decorated with Florentine designs in bright colors. They also sell splendid copies of Etruscan frescoes. The colors are subtle and they would look splendid framed. Reasonable prices.

Quel Qualcosa, Via dei Coronari 110
Tel: (06) 6875358
Open: Mon 4pm–8pm, Tues–Sat 10am–1:30pm 4pm–8pm
Credit cards: AE, DC

A lovely little shop with a tempting selection of new and antique lace – sheets, veils, tablecloths, curtains, collars, cuffs and doilies. There are plenty of other items, mechanical toys, chinaware and antique dolls. Helpful English-speaking staff.

Soligo, Via del Babuino 161
Tel: (06) 3614158
Open: Mon 4pm–8pm, Tues–Sat 10am–1:30pm 4pm–8pm
Credit cards: AE, DC, MC, V

Antiques and memorabilia for the military history enthusiast. Military bits and pieces from all over the world including uniforms, sabers, pistols, shells, portraits, prints, medals and etchings. The staff speak English and are very well-informed.

Studio C + T, Via dei Coronari 187
Tel: (06) 6542260
Open: Mon 4pm–8pm, Tues–Sat 10am–1:30pm 4pm–8pm
No credit cards

This big shop specializes in *objets d'art* from the 16th to 19th centuries. There are some fine Italian paintings and particularly interesting religious artefacts – crucifixes, medallions, etchings and statues. Helpful English-speaking assistants.

Studio Interni, Via dei Coronari 40
Tel: (06) 6897858
Open: Mon 4pm–8pm, Tues–Sat 10am–1:30pm 4pm–8pm
Credit cards: AE, DC

Recommended for top quality Italian glass and silver, mostly from the 18th century. The shop has four large rooms, which it also stocks with heavy 19th-century furniture including desks and commodes imported from England. The staff speak English.

AUCTIONS

Christie's, Palazzo Lancellotti, Piazza Navona 14
Tel: (06) 6564032
Credit cards: AE, DC, MC

Sales by this internationally famous auction house are held at its Roman branch in the Palazzo Lancellotti. The sales are generally held in the evening, starting at 9pm; items are on display during the three days before the sale. Ring to check for details, or call round – the palazzo has an exquisite interior and is well worth a visit.

Finarte, Via Margutta 54
Tel: (06) 6786557
Credit cards: AE, DC, MC

This Italian auction house has regular sales in Rome – either check the listings in *This Week in Rome* or call round for a catalog. The sale room is appropriately situated on a street which, until the 19th century, was full of artists' studios. There are still exhibitions in the galleries here. The company specializes in Italian art and furniture of all periods. Its sales are well worth a visit even if you're not buying.

Sotheby's, Piazza di Spagna 90
Tel: (06) 6781798
Credit cards: AE, DC, MC

The Rome branch of this well-established firm holds regular sales; anything from 18th-century prints to jewelry and furniture. Items are on display for three days before the actual sale, which is usually in the evening. Check by telephone to see if there's an interesting auction coming up. The office is open on Sundays, so you can call in for a catalog. It's right by the Spanish Steps.

BOOKSTORES

Anglo-American Bookshop, Via della Vite 57
Tel: (06) 6795222
Open: Mon 4pm–7pm, Tues–Sun 9:30am–1pm 4pm–7pm
Credit cards: AE

A small bookshop packed with a wide selection of English-language books and all kinds of recent publications. There's another department at Via della Vite 27 which has scientific books and English language magazines.

Books on Italy, Via dei Giubbonari 30
Tel: (06) 6545285
Open: Thur 5pm–7pm or by appointment
No credit cards

A most unusual bookstore housed in an apartment block. A vast collection of books, all in English, covering every aspect of Italy and Italian life. From art and gardens to 19th-century travelers' tales, plus novels set in Italy. Prices vary according to the rarity of the books and there are some great finds for collectors.

The Economy Book Center, Via Torino 136
Tel: (06) 4746877
Open: Mon–Sat 9:30am–7:30pm
Credit cards: AE, DC

This is the place to pick up a novel to relax with on your holiday. A large, well-stocked store with a vast selection of English-language paperbacks. You can also sell your unwanted books here. A good range of guide books to Rome and the rest of Italy. English-speaking staff.

Franco Maria Ricci, Via Borgognona 4D
Tel: (06) 6793466
Open: Mon 4:30pm–7:30pm, Tues–Sat 10am–1:30pm
   4:30pm–7:30pm
Credit cards: AE

Franco Maria Ricci is the name behind the most beautiful and expensive arts magazine in the world: *FMR*. Here you can buy not only the magazine but beautifully printed and produced books illustrated by famous artists. Each one is a superb collector's piece. A good place for beautiful and expensive stationery including diaries, calendars and notebooks.

Giuliana di Cave, Piazza di Pietra 24
Tel: (06) 6780297
Open: Mon 4pm–8pm, Tues–Sat 10am–noon 4pm–8pm
Credit cards: AE, DC, V

A little shop on a beautiful, quiet piazza, it sells antique prints, 19th-century architectural engravings of Rome, plus photographic prints. Lots of second-hand books too, as well as many fine old leather-bound volumes and old guide books. The owner speaks a little English and the welcome is charming.

Il Leuto, Via di Monte Brianzo 86
Tel: (06) 6569269
Open: Mon 4pm–8pm, Tues–Sat 10am–1pm 4pm–8pm
Credit cards: AE, V

This shop is devoted to the performing arts from cinema to dance and theater. It also sells photographs of the ballet and plays, and portraits of actors. Here's the place to find a photograph of your favorite Italian screen goddess or scenes from those fabulous 50s movies. They sell theater tickets as well and the staff are knowledgeable.

Libreria all'Orolgio, Via Governo Vecchio 7
Tel: (06) 6540659
Open: Mon 4pm–7pm, Tues–Sat 9:30am–1pm 4pm–7pm
Credit cards: AE, V

This bookstore specializes in aviation but also has a good collection of books in both Italian and English on dance, theater and the arts. It also stocks lots of hobby books. There is a good collection of all kinds of maps – aeronautical, geographical, nautical and archaeological.

Libreria Antiquaria, Via Sistina 23
Tel: (06) 483826
Open: Mon 4pm–7pm, Tues–Sat 10am–1pm 4pm–7pm
Credit cards: AE, V

As the name suggests, this shop specializes in antique books. Rows and rows of leather-bound volumes on subjects ranging from the natural sciences to travel. There are many illustrated books and, of course, books about Rome in days gone by. Maps, rare and modern, too. A good shop for collectors; browsers are welcome.

Libreria del Fiume, Via del Fiume 6
Tel: (06) 3619204
Open: Mon 4pm–8pm, Tues–Sat 10am–1pm 4pm–8pm
Credit cards: AE, MC

This is a branch of the Italian Touring Club which specializes in good up-to-date maps of Italy and the rest of the world. Lots of good guide books as well, with a wide selection in English. Stop off here for your detailed map of Rome.

Libreria Internazionale, Via Riva di Ripetta 22
Tel: (06) 3612091
Open: Mon 4pm–8pm, Tues–Sat 9am–2pm 4pm–8pm
Credit cards: AE, V

All you ever wanted to know about the sea and sailing. This bookstore has a great collection of nautical books in all languages, including English. They also sell nautical maps which cover the whole world. A fascinating shop for sailors and armchair America's Cup contenders.

Libreria Pileri, Via della Meloira 88
Tel: (06) 310673
Open: Mon 4pm–8pm, Tues–Sat 10am–1pm 4pm–8pm
Credit cards: AE, V

This is not only a bookstore selling old books, it also offers prints and old postcards, engravings and toy soldiers made of lead. A shop for collectors to browse in. Old postcards of Rome make lovely, inexpensive souvenirs of the city.

Libreria San Silvestro, Piazza San Silvestro 27
Tel: (06) 6792824
Open: Mon 4pm–8pm, Tues–Sat 10am–1pm 4pm–8pm
Credit cards: AE, V

The best and biggest selection of art books in town. Many of them are on sale at half their original price. Beautifully printed books from all the great names in art publishing. If you want to know more about Michelangelo, you'll find it here and it won't be expensive.

Lion Bookshop, Via del Babuino 181
Tel: (06) 3605837
Open: Mon–Sat 9am–7:30pm
Credit cards: AE

A first-rate Anglo-American bookstore, devoted exclusively to English and American hardbacks and paperbacks. Everything from best-sellers to guidebooks. You name it, they have it. English-speaking staff and the shop is well laid out. Good selection of travel books on Italy.

Open Door Bookshop, Via della Lungaretta 25
Tel: (06) 5896478
Open: Mon 4pm–8pm, Tues–Sat 10am–1pm 4pm–8pm
Credit cards: AE, V

A fine collection of new and second-hand books in both Italian and English. A nicely laid out bookstore that specializes in the arts, music and all kinds of literature. A good place to browse – as its name suggests – with English-speaking staff to help.

Piazza Borghese
Open: Daily

Open-air market just off the Via del Corso with stalls selling all kinds of books, both new and second-hand. A good place to pick up a cookery book full of Italian dishes to cook back home. Lots of nice inexpensive prints too, with a good choice of views of Ancient Rome and some nice architectural drawings.

Rizzoli, Largo Chigi 15
Tel: (06) 6796641
Open: Mon 4pm–8pm, Tues–Sat 9am–2pm 4:30pm–8pm
Credit cards: AE, V

An international bookstore, large and very well laid out. There is a great section of beautifully produced art books. This is the place to find the definitive volume on Titian or della Francesca. Good section of maps and guides in English, plus modern literature and novels in hardback and paperback. A great shop to browse in, there are all kinds of sections from poetry to cookery.

FOOD SHOPPING

Bernasconi, Largo Argentina 1
Tel: (06) 6548141
Open: Mon–Sat 8:30am–7:30pm
No credit cards

The Bernasconi specialty is the *bombe* – like a doughnut minus the hole, hot and sugary. But this great cake shop, a favorite with Romans, has a huge choice of all kinds of pastries. It's always crowded, and there's a small bar where you can drink a *cappuccino* munching on the cake of your choice.

Castroni, Via Cola di Rienzo 196
Tel: (06) 6874383
Open: Mon–Wed, Fri–Sat 8:30am–8pm Closed: Thur
No credit cards

This is the most popular food store in Rome, with all kinds of very special Italian delicacies. There's a whole range of oils from super virgin Tuscan olive oil to oil flavored with garlic. Black olives, green olives, anything-in-between-olives; delicious Parma ham; pasta galore; truffles and all sorts of exotic items. There are even jars of peanut butter should you get a sudden craving for the taste of home. A store that's a favorite with Romans and visitors alike.

Da Quinta, Via di Tor Millina 15
No telephone
Open: Mon–Sat 10am–10pm
No credit cards

A great place for an ice cream or a sorbet, very close to the Piazza Navona. The flavors are traditional – pistachio and chocolate are both terrific – or try a *crema* – vanilla ice cream. Delicious cones come with a generous helping of different flavors topped with cream. This is real ice cream, Roman style.

Enoteca al Parlamento, Via dei Prefetti 15
Tel: (06) 6795156
Open: Mon–Sat 9am–1pm, 5pm–8pm Closed: Thur am
No credit cards

A very up-market wine dealer, conveniently located near the
Lower House of the Roman parliament. There's a counter serving
glasses of wine or champagne and elegant bar snacks. Some of
the best wines Italy has to offer can be purchased here. Everything
from *brunellos* to *barolos*.

Ercoli, Via della Croce 32
Tel: (06) 6791645
Open: Mon–Sat 9am–1:30pm 5pm–8pm Closed: Thur pm
No credit cards

Ercoli specializes in cold cuts – everything from smoked hams to
salamis. The Parma ham is delicious, as is the stuffed roast pork.
All is beautifully displayed and the choice so wide and tempting
it's hard to decide what to have. If you are planning a picnic in
the nearby Borghese Gardens, then this is the place to stock up.

Franchi, Via Cola di Rienzo 204
Tel: (06) 6874151
Open: Mon–Sat 9am–7:30pm Closed: Thur pm
No credit cards

Absolutely marvelous range of prepared dishes including salads,
quiches, pastas and lobster, plus over a hundred different kinds
of cheeses, from ricotta to mozzarella. Truffles are a speciality
here but, as always, not a bargain. A great place to put together
a delicious al-fresco lunch. The tiny whole artichokes bottled in
olive oil would make a lovely gift.

Moriondo & Gariglio, Via della Pilotta 2
Tel: (06) 6786662
Open: Mon 4pm–7:30pm, Tues–Sat 9:30am–1pm 4pm–7:30pm
No credit cards

This tiny shop, hidden away in a corner of the Piazza Pilotta, is
well worth searching for. The minuscule kitchen in the back of
the store produces some of the best-quality chocolates in the
world. Although expensive, the chocolates are absolutely delicious
– how about some real Roman chocolate-covered cherries for the
folks back home?

Vini e Olii, Via della Croce
No telephone
Open: Mon–Sat 9:30am–7:30pm Closed: Thur pm
No credit cards

This delightful, traditional store is sadly one of the last of its kind in Rome. As the simple name implies, it's a store which sells nothing but wine and oil. The shop's own particular wine is stored in marvelous 18th-century tanks made from marble. The *maestro* offers a huge selection of liqueurs, wines, and, of course, a particularly fine choice of olive oils. The white-aproned staff are smart, courteous and efficient.

GIFTS

Di Cori, Piazza di Spagna 53
Tel: (06) 6784439
Open: Mon 4pm–8pm, Tues–Sat 10am–1pm 4pm–8pm
Credit cards: AE, V

A tiny shop completely crammed with gloves from top to bottom. All kinds of materials are used including wool, cotton and leather. The hides are all of the finest quality and the gloves come in every conceivable color at reasonable prices.

Forma e Memoria, Via di Ripetta 148
Tel: (06) 6547622
Open: Mon 3:30pm–7:30pm, Tues–Sat 10am–1pm
   3:30pm–7:30pm
Credit cards: AE

Lots of lovely, modern Italian glassware and not expensive. They also sell colorful cardboard filing boxes and all kinds of kitchen equipment such as beautiful marble salt and pepper mills. English-speaking staff.

Fratelli Rossetti, Via Borgognona 5A
Tel: (06) 6782676
Open: Mon 4pm–7:30pm, Tues–Sat 10am–7:30pm
Credit cards: AE, DC, MC, V

A tiny shop which stocks the entire range of the brothers Rossetti's beautiful shoes for both men and women. Ultra-elegant designs to flatter anyone's feet in all sorts of colors and leathers. The only problem with footwear as beautiful as this is making the rest of your wardrobe match up!

Gazzelle, Via del Corso 30
Tel: (06) 3614194
Open: Mon 4pm–7:30pm, Tues–Sat 9:30am–1:30pm
  4pm–7:30pm
Credit cards: DC, V

Leather clothes for men and women at low prices. The quality is reasonable and the clothes come in all styles, from black leather mini-skirts to sedate suede jackets. Good flying jackets for men.

Gherardini, Via Belsiana 48
Tel: (06) 6795501
Open: Mon 4pm–8pm, Tues–Sat 10:30am–1:30pm 4pm–8pm
Credit cards: AE, DC, MC, V

This baggage and hand-luggage specialist has long been famous in Florence and now looks like being equally popular in Rome. Elegant, beautiful leatherware at high prices, though there are some cheaper items such as purses and key cases that would make great gifts.

Ginocchi, Via Sistina 35
Tel: (06) 463925
Open: Mon 4pm–8pm, Tues–Sat 9:30am–1:30pm 4pm–8pm
Credit cards: AE, DC, MC, V

A beautiful range of elegant, hand-made leather goods. You won't find clothes or shoes but the choice of other items is vast – handbags, shoulder bags, leather-bound boxes and caskets, wallets and purses in a wide range of colors. All hides are of the finest quality. Prices are fairly high.

Gucci, Via Condotti 8
Tel: (06) 6789340
Open: Mon 4pm–7:30pm, Tues–Sat 10am–7:30pm
Credit cards: AE, DC, MC, V

Plenty of bags, briefcases, belts, shoes, towels, sandals, even ashtrays – most marked with the unmistakable Gucci logo. Prices are high but you can assess the potential damage to your wallet by looking in the window at the price tags. Always crowded but the sales staff are very attentive and speak English. There's another branch at Via Borgognona 25.

Hermès, Via Condotti 60
Tel: (06) 6797687
Open: Mon 4pm–7:30pm, Tues–Sat 10am–7:30pm
Credit cards: AE, DC, MC, V

Hermès needs little introduction – a world-famous store selling beautiful, top quality clothes and accessories. All the old favorites can be found here from scarves to handbags and belts. A super elegant shop.

Herzel, Via di Propaganda 14
Tel: (06) 6795114
Open: Mon 3:30pm–7:30pm, Tues–Sat 10am–1:30pm
  3:30pm–7:30pm
Credit cards: AE, DC, MC, V

A wonderful range of exciting fashion footwear for women. Fake fur trimmings, saucy laces, glitzy sandals, these are fun shoes for extroverts. The staff speak English and though the shop is small the choice is wild and wonderful.

Il Cervone, Via del Corso 38
Tel: (06) 6793850
Open: Mon 4pm–8pm, Tues–Sat 9:30am–1:30pm 4pm–8pm
Credit cards: AE, DC, MC, V

A shoe shop stacked with all kinds of wonderful footwear from loafers through slingbacks to classy evening high-heelers. Prices are low and styles fashionable. A great choice of good quality shoes and boots for both men and women.

Mara, Via Borgognona 49
Tel: (06) 6795448
Open: Mon 4pm–8pm, Tues–Sat 9:30am–1:30pm 4pm–8pm
No credit cards

Marvelous designer-milliner patronized by the haughtiest heads in town. Mara will discuss the material, fit and style of the hat you want and have it ready (after hours of painstaking work) in a couple of weeks. Off-the-peg hats are also sold here.

Maurizio Righini, Via Vittoria 63
Tel: (06) 6784655
Open: Mon 3:30pm–7:30pm, Tues–Sat 10am–1:30pm
  3:30pm–7:30pm
Credit cards: AE, DC, MC, V

This luxurious store is a long-time favorite with Roman shoppers. Originally famous for its superb luggage, the store also offers all sorts of wares including shoes, bags, belts, bathrobes and more. The staff is extremely courteous and helpful.

Mondo Antico, Via dei Pianellari 17
Tel: (06) 6561261
Open: Mon 3pm–6pm, Tues–Sat 10am–12:30pm 3pm–6pm
No credit cards

The charming proprietor sells glass-fronted boxes containing hand-tinted prints which he has cut up and arranged in three-dimensional perspective. The work is painstaking, so stocks are irregular but pop in and you may be lucky enough to find an original, collector's item.

Myricae, Via Frattina 36
Tel: (06) 6781448
Open: Mon 4pm–8pm, Tues–Sat 10am–1pm 4pm–8pm
Credit cards: AE, DC, MC, V

Plenty of handicrafts, colorful, attractive and appealing. Painted trays, glassware, ceramics, Italian regional pottery and all kinds of popular folk art at reasonable prices. A lovely place for gifts or souvenirs.

Naj Oleari, Via di San Giacomo 25
Tel: (06) 6780045
Open: Mon 4pm–8pm, Tues–Sat 10am–1:30pm 4pm–8pm
Credit cards: AE, DC, MC, V

Super modern household items, all to their own exclusive designs. Lots of pretty soaps, bath salts and pot pourris, as well as chic umbrellas in designer fabrics. Not expensive for great Italian style. Very popular with Romans and a good place to find an unusual gift.

Nazareno Gabrielli, Via Sant'Andrea delle Fratte 3
Tel: (06) 6791461
Open: Mon 3pm–7pm, Tues–Sat 10am–2pm 3pm–7pm
Credit cards: AE, DC, MC, V

Famous leatherware store for women. This little shop stocks goods with the exclusive Gabrielli label. Prices are high but so is the quality. Lovely bags in leather and tweed for traveling, plus leather handbags.

Odette, Via Nazionale 224
Tel: (06) 454767
Open: Mon 4pm–7:30pm, Tues–Sat 10am–7:30pm
Credit cards: AE, DC, MC, V

This store offers a wide range of leather clothes for men and women at reasonable prices. Some of the styles won't be to everyone's taste but all the garments are well made. Lovely soft leather dresses and silk-lined trousers for women, plus long jackets for men.

Pineider, Via Due Macelli 68
Tel: (06) 6789013
Open: Mon–Sat 9:30am–1:30pm 4pm–8pm
Credit cards: AE, DC, MC, V

The most elegant and exclusive stationery shop in Rome. Inside, the walls are panelled in marble and walnut. You'll find sets of gorgeous writing paper and envelopes made from traditional rag paper, plus diaries and note books available in a fantastic range of colors to match your mood, your wallpaper, your eyes . . .

Pitti, Via di San Giacomo 19
Tel: (06) 6795930
Open: Mon 4pm–7:30pm, Tues–Sat 10am–1:30pm 4pm–7:30pm
Credit cards: AE

This is basically a store selling household goods but some of the designs are pretty and original enough to make lovely gifts. There's a crazy tea service by Fornesetti, famous for his original porcelain. Each piece (cups, sugar bowls, teapot) is a miniature copy of the Colosseum. Expensive but fun.

Rampone, Via del Babuino 98
Tel: (06) 6784231
Open: Mon 4pm–8pm, Tues–Sat 10am–1:30pm 4pm–8pm
Credit cards: AE, DC, MC, V

Stylish Italian shoe store displaying some leading designer names. Other accessories also for sale include bags, belts and purses. English-speaking assistants offer helpful advice on fitting.

Regal, Via Nazionale 234
Tel: (06) 2330929
Open: Mon 3:30pm–7:30pm, Tues–Sat 9:30am–1pm
   3:30pm–7:30pm
Credit cards: AE, DC, MC, V

A busy store packed with bargain-price accessories. Belts, bags and purses in a range of styles and prices to suit all tastes and pockets. A good place to shop for lower-priced Valentino goods.

Roeckl, Via Sistina 83
Tel: (06) 6790376
Open: Mon 4pm–7:30pm, Tues–Sat 9:30am–7:30pm
Credit cards: AE, DC, MC, V

Beautiful accessories in leather of every type and color. Belts, bags, grips, pocket books and luggage, all handmade, all of the highest quality and all reasonably priced.

Salvatore Ferragamo, Via Condotti 73
Tel: (06) 6798402
Open: Mon 4pm–7pm, Tues–Sat 10am–7pm
Credit cards: AE, DC, MC, V

This recently-opened branch of the famous Ferragamo store offers an extensive range of modestly-priced, quality footwear in a terrific assortment of sizes, shapes and colors. A good selection of hand and shoulder bags are on sale, too.

Sermoneta, Piazza di Spagna 61
Tel: (06) 6791960
Open: Mon 4pm–7:30pm, Tues–Sat 9:30am–7:30pm
Credit cards: AE, DC, MC, V

This store has been supplying the Romans with high-quality leather gloves for years. Designs in suede, pigskin, kidskin and all kinds of other skin are available, some lined with comfy cashmere. All the leather is of the most superb quality.

Soleiado, Via dell'Oca 38
Tel: (06) 3610402
Open: Mon 3pm–7:30pm, Tues–Sat 10am–1:30pm 3pm–7:30pm
Credit cards: AE

This is the shop for bolts of beautiful, traditionally patterned French Provençal cottons and silk. You'll also find shirts and dresses in the same pretty fabrics, plus all kinds of bags and wallets, serviettes and table cloths.

Spazio Sette, Via dei Barbieri 7
Tel: (06) 6547139
Open: Mon 4pm–8pm, Tues–Sat 10am–1:30pm 4pm–8pm
Credit cards: AE, DC, MC, V

Probably the only Renaissance *palazzo* in the world where you'll find a kitchenware store. Terrific selection of kitchen knives as well as traditional Italian cooking utensils like pasta saucepans and sieves. Lots of lamps and glass ashtrays too, at reasonable prices.

Stilvetro, Via Frattina 55
Tel: (06) 6790258
Open: Mon 4pm–8pm, Tues–Sat 10am–1pm 4pm–8pm
No credit cards

Inexpensive glass and china, all Italian, much of it from Tuscany.

Search carefully and you should be able to find some attractive pieces at bargain prices. Plenty of great ideas for gifts here.

Tanino Crisci, Via Borgognona 4M
Tel: (06) 6795461
Open: Mon 4pm–8pm, Tues–Sat 9:30am–1:30pm 4pm–8pm
Credit cards: AE, DC, MC, V

This long-established store has made footwear for men and women for years. The leather used is of the finest quality. Items range from walking shoes and boots through loafers, sandals and oxfords to superb evening styles.

Tommasini, Via Sistina 119
Tel: (06) 461009
Open: Mon 4pm–8pm, Tues–Sat 9:30am–1:30pm 4pm–8pm
Credit cards: AE, DC, MC, V

A small shop selling exquisite lingerie fit for a queen. Marvelous lacy, beribboned nightdresses, camisoles and underclothes at deliciously affordable prices. Friendly service from English-speaking assistants.

Trussardi, Via Bocca di Leone 27
Tel: (06) 6780280
Open: Mon 4pm–7pm, Tues–Sat 10am–7pm
Credit cards: AE, DC, MC, V

One of Rome's most exclusive stores, here you'll find some of the best leather accessories available. Oozing with designer-chic, items are marked with a greyhound-head motif. The canvas tote bags are fun and almost affordable. Also check out the stationery collection which runs to address books and diaries.

Valentino Più, Via Condotti 13
Tel: (06) 6795207
Open: Mon 4pm–8pm, Tues–Sat 10am–1:30pm 4pm–8pm
Credit cards: AE, DC, MC, V

A whole range of gift items by Valentino. Beautiful porcelain, pens, lighters, keyfobs, linens and china. Glass and ceramics are hand-painted; colors and designs bright and witty. Helpful English-speaking staff will gift-wrap your choice, then pack it carefully to prevent damage.

Vertecchi, Via della Croce 70
Tel: (06) 6783110
Open: Mon 4pm–8pm, Tues–Sat 9:30am–1:30pm 4pm–8pm
Credit cards: AE, DC, MC, V

This is the place for artists' supplies, from watercolors to fine papers. They also have a great selection of notebooks, pencils and pens. Lots of expensive fountainpens plus ballpoint pens of original design as well. Great for cheap and cheerful gifts.

JEWELRY

Baci e Gioie, Via Cola di Rienzo 278
Tel: (06) 6530555
Open: Mon 4pm–8pm, Tues–Sat 9:30am–1:30pm 4pm–8pm
Credit cards: AE, DC, MC, V

A fun mixture of costume jewelry and cheaper pieces made of silver and semi-precious stones. Plenty of plastic with chunky necklaces, bracelets and earrings. Some very attractive hand-made silverwork set with turquoises, lots of pearls and gold. Reasonable prices.

Buccellati, Via Condotti 31
Tel: (06) 6790329
Open: Mon 4pm–8pm, Tues–Sat 10am–1:30pm 4pm–8pm
Credit cards: AE, DC, MC, V

A traditional, classic shop selling Florentine jewelry. Lots of silver pieces – the quality and style are unbeatable. A great place for window shopping as well. Prices are high but well worth it if you fall in love with something. English-speaking assistants on hand to help you choose.

Bulgari, Via Condotti 10
Tel: (06) 6793876
Open: Mon 4pm–8pm, Tues–Sat 10am–1:30pm 4pm–8pm
Credit cards: AE, DC, MC, V

Perhaps the greatest jewelers in the world, certainly Rome's most famous. The magnificent marble facade conceals jewelry of staggering beauty and quality; most of us can only dream of possessing pieces like these. Great for window shopping; this is the Tiffany's of Rome.

D'Arosso, Via Borgognona 6A
Tel: (06) 6785158
Open: Mon 4pm–8pm, Tues–Sat 10am–1pm 4pm–8pm
Credit cards: AE, DC, V

Exclusive, hand-crafted individual pieces here. Beautiful wide silver rings set with tiny stones, heavy gold link bracelets and necklaces, and earrings of pearls. Expensive but the craftsmanship is superb.

Feriozzi, Via delle Vergini 17
Tel: (06) 6798431
Open: Mon 4pm–8pm, Tues–Sat 10am–1pm 4pm–8pm
Credit cards: AE, DC, V

Orlando Feriozzi is a craftsman who has been making fine jewelry for almost 50 years. The designs are traditional and the craftsmanship superb. He makes magnificent rings set with beautiful stones. English-speaking assistants. Expensive.

Fornari, Via Condotti 80
Tel: (06) 6794285
Open: Mon 4pm–8pm, Tues–Sat 10am–1pm 4pm–8pm
Credit cards: AE, DC, MC, V

Fornari specializes in gold jewelry but also has some fine silver pieces. The service is very helpful and attentive. Prices reasonable for such high quality. Helpful, English-speaking staff. A traditional Roman store for jewelry.

Fumis, Piazza San Silvestro 14
Tel: (06) 6792510
Open: Mon 4pm–8pm, Tues–Sat 10am–1pm 4pm–8pm
Credit cards: AE, DC

Not the most expensive shop in town with a great selection of silver jewelry. All the pieces are exclusive and made to Fumis's own design, so you are buying something special. Friendly staff speak English.

Fürst, Via Veneto 42
Tel: (06) 483992
Open: Mon 4pm–8pm, Tues–Sat 10am–1pm 4pm–8pm
Credit cards: AE, DC

Right on the Via Veneto near the big hotels, this first class jewelry shop sells all kinds of high quality pieces but they specialize in rubies and emeralds. The staff speak English. Expensive.

Galleria Antiquaria Dell'Arco, Via Giulia 178
Tel: (06) 6541520
Open: Mon 4pm–7pm, Tues–Sat 10am–1pm 4pm–7pm
No credit cards

This store specializes in delightful pieces of 18th- and 19th-century jewelry, with lots of semi-precious stones in all kinds of settings.

Well chosen pieces and fine craftsmanship but the prices are high.
A friendly welcome from English-speaking assistants.

Helietta Caracciolo, Via di Villa Albani 8
Tel: (06) 6867105
Open: Mon 4pm–8pm, Tues–Sat 10am–1pm 4pm–8pm
Credit cards: AE, DC

For stunning, ultra-fashionable jewelry designed by the Countess
Caracciolo. This shop is a favorite with Roman ladies. Expensive
but the best of modern Italian style. You'll find her jewelry on
sale also in the boutiques near the Piazza di Spagna.

I. Leuzzi, Via di Ripetta 1
Tel: (06) 67857051
Open: Mon 3:30pm–7:30pm, Tues–Sat 10am–1pm
   3:30pm–7:30pm
Credit cards: AE

Right by the Piazza del Popolo, this is the store for diamanté
costume jewelry. There are brooches and pins, huge pearly earrings surrounded with diamanté, watches with pearl straps and
Carmen Miranda necklaces. Not expensive and a lot of fun.

L'Oriuolo, Via di Santa Maria dell'Anima 40
Tel: (06) 6877105
Open: Mon 4pm–8pm, Tues–Sat 10:30am–1pm 4pm–8pm
Credit cards: AE, DC

There is a huge selection of costume jewelry in this tiny store,
with everything from tiaras and rings for women, to cufflinks and
tie-pins for men. Plenty of 20s jewelry – beads and bakelite galore
– and a great selection of way-out earrings. Not expensive.

Massoni, Largo Goldoni 48
Tel: (06) 6790182
Open: Mon 4pm–8pm, Tues–Sat 10am–1pm 4pm–8pm
Credit cards: AE, DC, MC, V

This is a long-established family firm. Rather grand but with
attentive service. Massoni delights in creating jewelry made to the
client's own specifications. A favorite with film stars from all over
the world. Expensive.

Pon Pon, Via Nazionale 22
Tel: (06) 461466
Open: Mon 3:30pm–7:30pm, Tues–Sat 9:30am–1:30pm
   3:30pm–7:30pm
Credit cards: AE, V

A tiny two-story shop selling all kinds of crazy costume jewelry. Some of the imitation pieces are very convincing and extravagant. You can find accessories such as belts, shoes, combs and hair ornaments too. Great fun and the prices are low.

Roberto Bolla, Via Borgognona 26
Tel: (06) 6786418
Open: Mon 4pm–8pm, Tues–Sat 10am–1pm 4pm–8pm
Credit cards: AE, V

Tucked away in a beautiful little courtyard off the Via Borgognona, this shop specializes in antique watches. All the great names are here – Patek Philippe, Jaeger, Le Coultre and Vacheron. Very expensive, these watches are not only exquisite but an investment.

Sutrini, Via Borgognona 2A
Tel: (06) 6784168
Open: Mon 4pm–8pm, Tues–Sat 10am–1pm, 4pm–8pm
Credit cards: AE, V

A lovely little jewelry shop with lots of rings, pendants, beads and pearls. Chunky African-style necklaces of beads and wide marbled bracelets rimmed with gold, plus some beautiful lapis lazuli pieces. Expensive.

KIDS' STUFF

Baby House, Via Cola di Rienzo 117
Tel: (06) 351933
Open: Mon 4pm–8pm, Tues–Sat 9:30am–1:30pm 4pm–8pm
Credit cards: AE, DC, MC, V

A fairly large and delightful store selling charming children's clothes at very reasonable prices. Baby House also stocks the Valentino range – prices are higher but the clothes are stunning. Lots of lovely sweaters and classic print dresses.

0-12 Benetton, Via Condotti 19
Tel: (06) 6790042
Open: Mon 2pm–7:30pm, Tues–Sat 9:30am–7:30pm
Credit cards: AE, DC, MC, V

Benetton elegance for under-12s. Your child will be the classiest kid on the street after a visit to this stunning store. Prices are surprisingly low considering the chic. Good for jeans, Benetton-style, and colorful sweatshirts.

Cir, Via Barberini 88
Tel: (06) 483470
Open: Mon 4pm–8pm, Tues–Sat 9:30am–1:30pm 4pm–8pm
Credit cards: DC

A wonderful shop selling lace from Florence, but prices are high.
Beautiful clothes for small girls ranging from two- to 10-year-olds.
Your daughter won't be able to resist the "Princess for a Day"
look. Exquisite clothes for that very special occasion.

Children's Club, Via Vittoria 27
Tel: (06) 6783115
Open: Mon 4pm–8pm, Tues–Sat 9:30am–1:30pm 4pm–8pm
Credit cards: AE, DC, V

Chic clothes for the up-to-10-year-olds, in marvelous materials
and styles. Another branch for 10-to-14s is situated opposite (No
52). Clothes are a little more expensive but equally smart. Everything from classic frocks to denim jackets and not wildly
expensive.

Emporio Armani, Via del Babuino 140
Tel: (06) 6788454
Open: Mon 3:30pm–7:30pm, Tues–Sat 9:30am–1pm
    3:30pm–7:30pm
Credit cards: AE, DC, MC, V

Fantastic fabrications for infant followers of fashion. Styles to suit
girls and boys up to the early teens. Chic like this is not cheap,
unfortunately. This is where fashion for children is taken very
seriously.

Galleria San Carlo, Via del Corso 114
Tel: (06) 6790571
Open: Mon 3:30pm–7:30pm, Tues–Sat 10am–1pm
    3:30pm–7:30pm
Credit cards: AE, DC, MC, V

A wonderful collection of toys to delight children of all ages.
Cuddly animals, dolls' houses and a whole menagerie of rockers
– elephants, dogs and, yes, even horses! Not too expensive, unless
you buy the elephant.

Iraci Sport, Via Cola di Rienzo 147
Tel: (06) 3595423
Open: Mon 4pm–7:30pm, Tues–Sat 9:30am–1:30pm
    4pm–7:30pm
Credit cards: AE, DC, MC, V

Specializing in sports styles for small people. Designer names (Fila and Ellesse) kit out kids of all sizes and ages for that athletic look. Shorts, tennis shoes, tracksuits, rugby shirts and authentic Italian football gear for boys. Not expensive.

Irene Perini, Via del Babuino 31
Tel: (06) 6789044
Open: Mon 4pm–8pm, Tues–Sat 9:30am–1pm 4pm–8pm
Credit cards: AE, DC, MC, V

The Roman cognoscenti flock here to kit their kids out in designer wear. Burberry, Dior, Hechter and Les Copains are some of the famous names Perini matches up to her adolescent clientele. Prices are correspondingly classy. Exclusive.

La Cicogna, Via Frattina 138
Tel: (06) 6791912
Open: Mon 4pm–8pm, Tues–Sat 9:30am–1:30pm 4pm–8pm
Credit cards: AE, DC, MC, V

There are several La Cicogna branches in Rome, this is the flag-ship, and the most central. Delightful clothes for tots to 12s in a vast array of styles, colors and cuts. Moderately priced. This is the place to buy your boy a tuxedo – or a sailor suit for your daughter.

La Città del Sole, Via della Scrofa 65
Tel: (06) 655404
Open: Mon 3pm–8pm, Tues–Sat 9am–1pm 3pm–8pm
Credit cards: AE, DC, MC, V

An enormous range of toys for children of all ages. Italy has several of these stores but this is the biggest. It stocks kites, puzzles, puppets, dolls, whistles, trains, yo-yos and books. You name it, for kids they've got it.

L'Erbavoglio, Via del Fiume 5
Tel: (06) 3606714
Open: Mon 3:30pm–7:30pm, Tues–Sat 10am–1pm
    3:30pm–7:30pm
No credit cards

Mechanical toys in row after row to delight kids of any age, as well as children. This minuscule store is full of traditional clock-work wind-up toys at reasonable prices. Friendly staff will demonstrate on request. Captivating clockwork animals and hundreds of little cars make wonderful, travel-proof gifts.

Leri, Via Barberini 48
Tel: (06) 4740834
Open: Mon 3:30pm–7:30pm, Tues–Sat 9:30am–1:30pm
  3:30pm–7pm
Credit cards: AE, DC, MC, V

Delightful clothes for newborns and toddlers. Leri has several stores in the city, all tiny, and all selling well-cut outfits in sturdy materials at moderate prices. Lots of nice summer dresses for fashionable young ladies.

Marina Menasci, Via del Lavatore 87
Tel: (06) 6781981
Open: Mon 3:30pm–7:30pm, Tues–Sat 9:30am–1:30pm
  3:30pm–7:30pm
No credit cards

A beautiful little shop which specializes in hand-made toys from Northern Italy, particularly our old friend Pinocchio in all shapes and sizes. Situated close to the Trevi Fountain, the service is delightfully friendly. A real joy for children.

Naj Oleari, Via di San Giacomo 25
Tel: (06) 6780045
Open: Mon 4pm–8pm, Tues–Sat 10am–1:30pm 4pm–8pm
Credit cards: AE, DC, MC, V

Pretty clothes at their cutest for boys and girls in Naj Oleari exclusive fabrics available throughout Italy. The colorful, inventive fabrics and styles are highly popular. Lots of pretty sundresses and overalls in bright colors. Good Italian styling at reasonable prices.

Piccadilly, Via Sistina 92
Tel: (06) 6793697
Open: Mon 4pm–8pm, Tues–Sat 9:30am–1:30pm 4pm–8pm
Credit cards: AE

If you believe girls will be girls and boys will be boys, this is the store to visit. Charming traditional children's clothes at reasonable prices. Friendly English-speaking assistants to help you choose. Expensive but these clothes will last for years.

Upim, Via del Tritone 172
Tel: (06) 6783336
Open: Mon 4pm–8pm, Tues–Sat 9:30am–7:30pm
Credit cards: V

A cheap chain store, on the lines of Woolworths, but useful for basic children's gear such as sunhats, swimming trunks, socks and sandals. Upim also stocks toys. A good place to stock up on cheap beachballs, drawing books and pencils. The basic necessities at chain store prices, right in the middle of Rome.

MENSWEAR

Angelo Litrico, Via Sicilia 51
Tel: (06) 4754313
Open: Mon 4pm–7:30pm, Tues–Sat 9:30am–7:30pm
Credit cards: AE, DC, MC, V

Litrico dresses some of the most famous men in the world, including Russia's Gorbachev. This tiny, old-fashioned little tailor's shop just off the Via Veneto is the place to come if you want to dress with the best. The styles are modern and the finishing superb. Prices are high.

Battistoni, Via Condotti 61A
Tel: (06) 6786241
Open: Mon 4pm–7:30pm, Tues–Sat 9:30am–7:30pm
Credit cards: AE, DC, MC, V

Battistoni began almost 50 years ago as a small shirt-making concern and its reputation hasn't stopped growing since. Stunning tailor-made suits and shirts at high prices but the quality and fit are superb.

Benetton, Via Condotti 19
Tel: (06) 6790042
Open: Mon 4pm–7:30pm, Tues–Sat 9:30am–7:30pm
Credit cards: AE, DC, MC, V

A by-word for Italian quality clothes at reasonable prices the world over. Colorful, relaxed casual wear with plenty of Italian stylishness. Smart English-speaking assistants.

Emporio Armani, Via del Babuino 140
Tel: (06) 6788454
Open: Mon 3:30pm–7:30pm, Tues–Sat 9:30am–1pm
    3:30pm–7:30pm
Credit cards: AE, DC, MC, V

A "must" for the fashion-conscious male this large store offers a good selection of designs. Materials, colors or cut often have touches a little out of the ordinary to make them more fun. Some interesting shoes on display here too.

Gianfranco Ferré, Via Borgognona 6
Tel: (06) 6797445
Open: Mon 4pm–7:30pm, Tues–Sat 9:30am–7:30pm
Credit cards: AE, DC, MC, V

Elegant, rather off-beat men's clothes in a tiny store. A great place to come and find a new "in" look, Italian-style. All the clothes are beautifully finished but prices are sky-high. Very chic English-speaking assistants.

Gianni Versace, Via Borgognona 29
Tel: (06) 6795292
Open: Mon 3:30pm–8pm, Tues–Sat 10am–1:30pm 3:30pm–8pm
Credit cards: AE, DC, MC, V

Classic clothes for men who prefer not to stand out in the crowd. Quality fabrics, elegantly cut, with perfect finishing. Terrific silk pajamas and Sherlock Holmes raincoats in a cotton and silk mixture.

Iraci Sport, Via Cola di Rienzo 145
Tel: (06) 3595423
Open: Mon 4pm–7:30pm, Tues–Sat 9:30am–1:30pm
   4pm–7:30pm
Credit cards: AE, DC, MC, V

There are plenty of sportswear shops in Rome but this is probably the best. Tennis clothes, tracksuits, polo shirts and casuals – all perfect for that outdoor sporty look. Prices (even for bigger-name designers) are reasonable.

Lello Calia, Via Veneto 151
Tel: (06) 493505
Open: Mon 3:30pm–8pm, Tues–Sat 9am–1pm 3:30pm–8pm
Credit cards: AE, DC, MC, V

Designer names such as Cerruti and Valentino are on sale here, plus Calia's own line which is the epitome of the Italian man's casual look. Chic, adaptable and affordable.

Lombardi, Piazza Vittorio Emanuele II 137
Tel: (06) 733359
Open: Mon 4pm–8pm, Tues–Sat 9:30am–1:30pm 4pm–8pm
Credit cards: AE

The place to visit if you always fancied yourself in a Borsalino hat. Traditionally-made from felt, these classic wide-brimmed hats could transform your entire image. For those of a less radical disposition you'll also find stylish panama hats for summer picnics and expeditions.

Polidori Uomo, Via Borgognona 4C and 4A
Tel: (06) 6784843
Open: Mon 4pm–8pm, Tues–Sat 9:30am–1:30pm 4pm–8pm
Credit cards: AE

A store specializing in silks, you'll also find a stylish selection of menswear – traditional, elegant and flattering. As you would expect, the fabrics are superb. The shop at 4A sells beautiful silks by the meter, to have made up into shirts when you get back home. English-speaking assistants.

Schostal, Via del Corso 158
Tel: (06) 6791240
Open: Mon 4pm–8pm, Tues–Sat 9am–1pm 4pm–8pm
No credit cards

A delightfully old-fashioned store which has been catering to the Romans for more than 100 years. Here you can buy terrific value pure cotton and woolen socks, pajamas and sweaters, all at exceptionally reasonable prices.

To You Uomo, Via Cola di Rienzo 242
Tel: (06) 6530605
Open: Mon 3:30pm–8pm, Tues–Sat 10am–1:30pm 3:30pm–8pm
Credit cards: AE, DC, MC, V

A collection of clothes from fashionable, fun and reasonably priced designers for men, such as Byblos, Luciano Soprani and shoes by Cesare Paciotti. Pants, jackets, shirts and a good line in casual wear.

Uomo In, Via Attilio Regolo 15
Tel: (06) 311177
Open: Mon 3:30pm–8pm, Tues–Sat 10am–1pm 3:30pm–8pm
Credit cards: AE, DC, V

An enormous store full of clothes from just about every top-name Italian designer. Prices vary according to the label but on the whole they're pretty reasonable. Pants, jackets, jeans, and knitwear are all available here.

Valentino Uomo, Via Mario dei Fiori 22
Tel: (06) 6783656
Open: Mon 4pm–8pm, Tues–Sat 10am–1:30pm 4pm–8pm
Credit cards: AE, DC, MC, V

Indisputable Italian chic, and prices here are certainly more reasonable than anywhere in the States. Classic suits, plus leather or suede jackets and casual polo shirts are favorites here. Helpful, English-speaking sales assistants.

Visconti, Via del Corso 25
Tel: (06) 3613308
Open: Mon 4pm–7:30pm, Tues–Sat 10am–7:30pm
Credit cards: AE, DC, MC

A large store stocking some big-name designers as well as its own pleasant line of casual wear. Heavy cotton Bermuda shorts and Trussardi jeans are good buys. Prices are not out of reach. English-speaking assistants.

WOMEN'S FASHION

Alicia Rosas, Via Borgognona 9–10
Tel: (06) 6792334
Open: Mon 4pm–8pm, Tues–Sat 10am–1:30pm 4pm–8pm
Credit cards: AE, DC, MC, V

Flamboyant designer clothes for peacock people. Beautiful evening gowns made from yards of gathered silk, chic and sexy beachwear for those not shy of showing some skin. Prices are correspondingly exotic.

A Più A, Via dei Greci 27
Tel: (06) 6794370
Open: Mon 4pm–8pm, Tues–Sat 9:30am–1:30pm 4pm–7:30pm
Credit cards: AE, V

A delightful shop with classy and original clothes for daytime and evening wear. This shop opened quite recently and is doing well. Good materials, beautifully cut. Prices are not too steep.

Benetton, Via Condotti 19
Tel: (06) 6790042
Open: Mon 1:30pm–7:30pm, Tues–Sat 9:30am–7:30pm
Credit cards: AE, DC, MC, V

The whole Benetton range of classic, sporty clothes at the usual reasonable prices. This is the most central of several Benetton stores in Rome – a beautiful interior beneath a high vaulted ceiling. Well-made clothes in a wide choice of colors. Helpful English-speaking assistants.

Bomba de Clercq, Via dell'Oca 39
Tel: (06) 3612881
Open: Mon 4pm–8pm, Tues–Sat 10am–1:30pm 4pm–8pm
Credit cards: AE

This shop specializes in marvelous hand-knitted sweaters for all kinds of weather and occasions. The sweater displays are artworks in themselves – some on dummies, some decoratively framed. Prices are reasonable for such fine workmanship.

Box, Via Nazionale 233
Tel: (06) 4754518
Open: Mon 4pm–7:30pm, Tues–Sat 9:30am–7:30pm
Credit cards: MC, V

A busy store displaying fun clothes for teenagers – mini-skirts and dresses, sweaters, slacks, jeans. Prices are reasonable, clothes dashing, with true Italian style. This store is on the crowded Via Nazionale, a popular street with bargain-hunting Romans.

Cucci, Via Condotti 67
Tel: (06) 6791882
Open: Mon 4pm–8pm, Tues–Sat 9:30am–1pm 4pm–8pm
Credit cards: AE, DC

Dateless clothes from the famous house of Cucci (not to be confused with Gucci). Beautifully cut, tasteful garments with a classic look which will never go out of style. Prices are fairly high but the quality is superb.

Fiorucci, Via Nazionale 236A
Tel: (06) 463175
Open: Mon 4pm–8pm, Tues–Sat 9:30am–8pm
Credit cards: AE, DC, MC, V

Here's where to stock up on all your Fiorucci favorites – casual, elegant clothes and heaps of fun accessories. Young, English-speaking staff are helpful and attentive, and the prices reasonable.

Giorgio Armani, Via del Babuino 102
Tel: (06) 6793777
Open: Mon 4pm–7:30pm, Tues–Sat 10am–7:30pm
Credit cards: AE, DC, MC, V

Giorgio Armani is that very talented designer from Milan and his clothes can't fail to please – marvelous mixtures of fabrics, colors and styles. This, his main store, is a pleasure to visit – full of flowers and plants and staffed by charming assistants. Chic and expensive.

Gucci, Via Condotti 22
Tel: (06) 6798343
Open: Mon 4pm–7:30pm, Tues–Sat 10am–7:30pm
Credit cards: AE, DC, MC, V

This is *the* Gucci shop for Gucci clothes. A bright, light shop with plenty of well displayed casual wear. Lots of beautiful linen skirts and trousers, exquisitely cut. The styles are traditional and prices, of course, very high. But you're buying Gucci.

Krizia, Piazza di Spagna 77
Tel: (06) 6793419
Open: Mon 4pm–7:30pm, Tues–Sat 9:30am–7:30pm
Credit cards: AE, DC, MC, V

Devotees flock to this tiny store, where most of the Krizia lines are on display. Beautiful clothes and fun costume jewelry at staggeringly high prices, in the most elegant shopping area in Rome.

Laura Biagiotti, Via Borgognona 43
Tel: (06) 6791205
Open: Mon 4pm–8pm, Tues–Sat 10am–8pm
Credit cards: AE, DC, MC, V

This recently-opened store boasts an immaculate white interior. Lots of silks and asymmetrical hemlines. Smart, fashionable, flattering clothes displayed with plenty of delectable accessories. English-speaking assistants. Expensive but very chic.

Lionello Ajô, Via Borgognona 35
Tel: (06) 6782660
Open: Mon 4pm–7:30pm, Tues–Sat 10am–1:30pm 4pm–7:30pm
Credit cards: AE, DC, MC, V

A tiny store stocking a staggering number of clothes by well-known designers such as Alma-Spazio, Moschino, Koshino, Vicky Tiel, Sonia Rykiel, Angelo Tarlazzi and more. Cast your eye over the stock and you'll get a pretty good picture of what the big-name designers are doing at the moment. Exclusive and pricey.

Missoni, Via del Babuino 96–97
Tel: (06) 6790050
Open: Mon 3:30pm–7:30pm, Tues–Sat 10am–1:30pm
    3:30pm–7:30pm
Credit cards: AE, DC, MC, V

Missoni is based in Milan but this Roman store has an excellent range of beautiful clothes and accessories. Stylish cut with beautiful finishing and, of course, stunning knitwear in myriad colors and unusual texture combinations.

Touche, Via del Babuino 91
Tel: (06) 6792487
Open: Mon 3:30pm–7:30pm, Tues–Sat 9:30am–1:30pm
    3:30pm–7:30pm
Credit cards: AE

Stylish, simple, casual clothes. This is not the store to visit if you like shocking pink or frills. There are plenty of natural fibers and muted colors for an easy-going look. Expensive and elegant.

Ungaro, Via Bocca di Leone 24
Tel: (06) 6799931
Open: Mon 4pm–8pm, Tues–Sat 10am–1:30pm 4pm–8pm
Credit cards: AE, DC, MC, V

Enormously expensive but still hugely popular, Ungaro's new store displays the usual classic up-market look. Tailored linen and silk suits, plenty of elegant dresses cut to flatter. One of Italy's star designers, this shop is almost a national monument.

Valentino, Via Bocca di Leone 16
Tel: (06) 6795862
Open: Mon 4pm–8pm, Tues–Sat 10am–1:30pm 4pm–8pm
Credit cards: AE, DC, MC, V

Last, but not least, in this round-up of women's fashion, here you'll find those familiar broad-shouldered, slim-waisted outlines. Simple and beautiful clothes (both custom-tailored and off-the-peg) in silk, leather and cashmere. Exclusive evening wear; adaptable accessories. Sophisticated and tactful English-speaking assistants are on hand to assist.

RESTAURANTS

ABC, Via Veneto 66   LLL
Tel: (06) 4740950
Open: Daily until 11:30pm
Credit cards: AE, DC, V

This super-smart restaurant is situated opposite the American Embassy on the busy Via Veneto. Excellent food, attentive service, sophisticated atmosphere and up-market clientele. Deluxe and very fashionable.

Al Moro, Vicolo delle Bollette 13   LLL
Tel: (06) 6783495
Open: Mon–Sat until 11:30pm   Closed: Sun and Aug
No credit cards

A small and popular restaurant situated between the Corso and the Trevi Fountain. The decor is nothing to write home about. What makes it such a favorite is the excellence of the cuisine. Noisy and crowded but some of the best food in Rome.

Alfredo alla Scrofa, Via della Scrofa 104   LLL
Tel: (06) 564519
Open: Mon–Sat until midnight   Closed: Sun
Credit cards: AE, DC, MC, V

There are three Alfredo's in Rome and this is certainly the best of all. An institution for over 50 years, there are hundreds of photographs of famous past and present customers covering the walls. The pasta is highly recommended. Good wine and music.

Al Vicario, Via Uffizi del Vicario 31   LLL
Tel: (06) 6791152
Open: Mon–Sat until 11pm   Closed: Sun and Aug
Credit cards: AE, DC, MC, V

A luxurious and pleasant restaurant where classic Roman dishes are served in traditional surroundings. Sophisticated ambience and courteous, efficient service.

Andrea, Via Sardegna 28   LLL
Tel: (06) 4937073
Open: Mon–Sat until 11:30pm   Closed Sun and 2 wks Aug
Credit cards: AE, DC, MC, V

Delicious, classic Roman cuisine prepared with great care. All is of the best quality and fresh from the market. Delightful atmosphere and close to the Via Veneto.

Angelino ai Fori, Largo Corrado Ricci 40 LLL
Tel: (06) 6786198
Open: Wed–Mon until 11:30pm   Closed: Tues
Credit cards: DC, MC, V

A large and popular restaurant just opposite the Forum, with a pleasant atmosphere, attentive service and good food. The superb fish dishes are a speciality here.

Antico Falcone, Via Trionfale 60 LL
Tel: (06) 353400
Open: Wed–Mon until midnight   Closed: Tues and Aug
No credit cards

Situated near St Peter's, this was originally a post station dating from the 15th century. Delicious, filling, beautifully cooked Roman dishes. The house wine is excellent.

Charley's Saucière, Via San Giovanni in Laterano 268 LLL
Tel: (06) 736666
Open: Mon–Sat until 11:30pm   Closed: Sun and most of Aug
Credit cards: DC, MC, V

This unpretentious restaurant run by a Swiss is not far from the Colosseum. Fine wines and delicious cuisine in a welcoming, relaxed atmosphere.

Ciceruacchio, Via del Porto, Trastevere LL
Tel: (06) 5806046
Open: Tues–Sun until midnight   Closed: Mon and Aug
Credit cards: AE, DC, V

A cellar restaurant situated in dungeons dating from the 15th century. Straightforward Roman fare in romantic surroundings. Also a very pleasant summer garden. Good music and singing with plenty of atmosphere.

Coriolano, Via Ancona 14 LLL
Tel: (06) 6541095
Open: Mon–Sat until 11:30pm   Closed: Sun
No credit cards

Delicious dishes from Central Italy. Pleasant, friendly atmosphere; extremely courteous service. Reservations are advised. This is very popular with Romans.

Da Amato, Via Garibaldi 62, Trastevere   LL
Tel: (06) 5809449
Open: Mon–Sat evenings only until 11pm
Closed: Sun
No credit cards

A pleasant restaurant serving both traditional Italian dishes and Spanish ones. Excellent service and intimate atmosphere. The wine list includes a choice of Spanish wines, as well as many Italian favorites.

Da Mario, Via della Vite 55   LL
Tel: (06) 6783818
Open: Mon–Sat until midnight   Closed: Sun and Aug
Credit cards: AE, DC, V

A busy and popular restaurant serving delicious down-to-earth dishes from Tuscany. This traditional *trattoria* is always crowded. Prices are reasonable and the food always good. A plate of beef stew – *stracotto* – washed down with the house wine makes a hearty lunch.

Dal Bolognese, Piazza del Popolo 1–2   LLL
Tel: (06) 3611426
Open: Tues–Sun until 11:30pm   Closed: Mon and 2 wks Aug
Credit cards: AE, DC

A very popular and fashionable restaurant serving mainly Bolognese specialities. Service is rapid and efficient. You can also dine out on the terrace in winter behind glass panels. The food is, quite simply, excellent.

Da Pancrazio, Piazza del Biscione 92   LL
Tel: (06) 6561246
Open: Thur–Tues until midnight   Closed: Wed and Aug
Credit cards: DC, V

Situated in Old Rome, this marvelous cellar restaurant is in part of the ancient Theater of Pompey, which is 2,000 years old. There's nothing extra-special about the food but the surroundings take some beating.

Galeone, Piazza di San Cosimato 27   LLL
Tel: (06) 5803775
Open: Tues–Sun until 11:30pm
Closed: Mon and last 2 wks Dec
Credit cards: AE, DC, V

Fish is the speciality here and the restaurant is decked out to look like a sailing ship. Beautifully cooked, generous portions; friendly, attentive service and a good atmosphere.

George's, Via Marche 7   LLL
Tel: (06) 484575
Open: Mon–Sat until 11:30pm   Closed: Sun and Aug
Credit cards: AE, DC, V

George, an ex-barman, established this restaurant in the days of *dolce vita*. It remains, if not the most fashionable, certainly one of the most prestigious of Rome's restaurants. There's a beautiful garden terrace and a really exceptional wine list. Terrific steaks and pasta. Book well in advance.

Giggetto, Via Portico d'Ottavia 21   LL
Tel: (06) 6561105
Open: Tues–Sun until 11pm   Closed: Mon
No credit cards

This restaurant is situated in the heart of the fascinating old Jewish ghetto and specializes in Roman-Jewish dishes. Busy, lively atmosphere and efficient service. Don't miss the artichokes!

Giovanni, Via Marche 19   LLL
Tel: (06) 493576
Open: Sun–Fri until 11:30pm   Closed: Sat and Aug
No credit cards

A traditional no-nonsense *trattoria* which has been a Roman favorite for years. Delicious regional dishes served in a family-style atmosphere. Superb fish dishes and pasta made freshly every day.

Hostaria dell'Orso, Via dei Soldati 25   LLL
Tel: (06) 6564250
Open: Mon–Sat until 11:30pm   Closed: Sun
Credit cards: AE, DC, MC, V

This was a palace in the 13th century. You dine in a high-ceilinged room with ancient beams. Dante ate here when it was an inn. It's now very fashionable and expensive. Great on atmosphere, plus there's a nightclub here too.

Il Buco, Via San Ignazio 8   LLL
Tel: (06) 6793298
Open: Tues–Sun until 11:30pm   Closed: Mon and Aug
Credit cards: AE, DC

This Tuscan restaurant has been run by the same family since its humble beginning in 1891. It's since expanded into a prestigious restaurant regularly visited by Italian senators and Embassy staff, while presidents and famous faces are not uncommon. The pictures around the restaurant are by a well-known Italian artist, Conte Premoli. The local specialities are hearty Tuscan dishes; also *vinsanto*, a wine liqueur into which you dip delicious homemade almond biscuit pieces.

Il Cerchio e la Botte, Via Lucca della Robbia 15   **LL**
Tel: (06) 572500
Open: Thur–Tues until midnight   Closed: Wed
No credit cards

The *Hoop and Barrel* offers a highly original and inventive menu which changes daily. It's a very small restaurant just off Piazza Testaccio, well worth hunting down. This can be difficult as it doesn't have a sign outside. Good wines from Sardinia and Sicily.

I Preistorici, Vicolo Orbitelli 13   **LLL**
Tel: (06) 655971
Open: Mon–Sat until 11:30pm   Closed: Sun and Aug
No credit cards

A fun restaurant with an original, if not extravagant menu. The name means "the cavemen", but this is an elegant and stylish place to dine. Fashionable with Romans.

Il Tentativo, Via della Luce 5   **LLL**
Tel: (06) 5895234
Open: Mon–Sat until 11:30pm   Closed: Sun
No credit cards

This intimate restaurant situated in Trastevere has gained enormously in popularity over the past few years. Sophisticated cuisine, attentive service and a fine wine list. Reservations advised. This is the place where Roman gourmets come to dine.

La Campana, Vicolo della Campana 18   **LL**
Tel: (06) 655273
Open: Tues–Sun until 11pm   Closed: Mon and Aug
No credit cards

This is one of the oldest *trattorie* in Rome, first mentioned in the Census of 1518. Delicious, straightforward, traditional Roman dishes. The wine list is limited – not unusual in Rome – but perfectly chosen for such hearty fare.

La Rosetta, Via della Rosetta 9   LLL
Tel: (06) 6561002
Open: Mon evening, Tues–Sat until 11:30pm
Closed: Sun, Mon lunch and Aug
Credit cards: DC, V

Situated near the Pantheon, this famous little sea-food restaurant serves delicious fish imported every day from Sicily. Grilled scampi is a speciality. Prices are high but the cuisine is superb. Reservations are necessary as this is a popular place with Romans, too. Good Sicilian white wines to choose from.

L'Eau Vive, Via Monterone 85   LL
Tel: (06) 6541095
Open: Mon–Sat until 10:30pm   Closed: Sun
Credit cards: AE, DC, V

An extraordinary restaurant run by the long-winded Christian Virgins of Catholic Missionary Action Through Work. Young lady missionaries, dressed in their national costumes, serve classic French and colonial fare. Best at lunchtime, this is popular with politicians from the Senate across the road. The Pope used to eat here, too.

Le Rallye, Grand Hotel, Via V. Emanuele Orlando 3   LLL
Tel: (06) 4709
Open: Mon–Fri until 11:30pm   Closed: Sat–Sun and Aug
Credit cards: AE, DC, V

Although attached to the Grand Hotel, Le Rallye deserves a mention as a restaurant in its own right. Superb cuisine and excellent service in elegant and tasteful surroundings. Classic, formal cuisine – try the bar-buffet for a more informal meal.

Mandarin, Via Emilia 83   LLL
Tel: (06) 4755577
Open: Tues–Sun until 11:30pm   Closed: Mon
Credit cards: AE, DC, V

The best Chinese food in Rome. Peking dishes are the speciality and this is where fashionable Romans come to eat duck Peking-style. Expensive and good. The service is swift and attentive.

Nihonbashi, Via Torino 34   LLL
Tel: (06) 4756970
Open: Mon–Sat until 11pm   Closed: Sun
Credit cards: AE, DC, V

The place to eat, Japanese-style, in Rome. The Japanese reckon it's so good they could be back in Tokyo. They show their appreciation by crowding in in vast numbers. Very popular with Romans too. The *tempura* and *suki-yaki* are terrific.

Otello alla Concordia, Via della Croce 81   L
Tel: (06) 6791178
Open: Mon–Sat until 11pm   Closed: Sun
                                  No credit cards

A charming little family-run *trattoria* in the heart of this fashionable shopping district. Simple, straightforward Italian food, efficiently served. There's a delightful vine-shaded courtyard. Excellent value in charming surroundings with good set menus.

Polese, Piazza Sforza Cesarini 40   L
Tel: (06) 6561709
Open: Wed–Mon until 11:30pm
Closed: Tues and last 2 wks Aug
No credit cards

A large, pleasant *trattoria* serving traditional Italian cuisine with Genoese specialities. Unpretentious decor and friendly service amidst a lively atmosphere. Dine under the trees on the piazza in summer. Good value and ambience.

Ranieri, Via Mario dei Fiori 26   LLL
Tel: (06) 6791592
Open: Mon–Sat until 11pm   Closed: Sun and 2 wks Aug
Credit cards: AE, DC, V

This restaurant was established in 1865 by Giuseppe Ranieri, a Neapolitan who was one-time chef to Queen Victoria. The atmosphere remains charmingly traditional and little appears to have changed over the years. International style cuisine.

Re degli Amici, Via della Croce 33B   L
Tel: (06) 6795380
Open: Tues evening, Wed–Sun until midnight
Closed: Mon, Tues lunch and 3 wks Jun
Credit cards: AE, DC, MC, V

This delightful *trattoria* has been serving traditional Roman/Italian cuisine for more than 60 years. Situated in the "bohemian" quarter near the Spanish Steps, there's plenty of atmosphere and great pizzas.

Regno di Re Ferdinando, Via dei Banchi Nuovi 8   LLL
Tel: (06) 6541167
Open: Mon–Sat until 11:30pm   Closed: Sun
Credit cards: AE, DC

A traditional tavern in the old city of Rome, this restaurant is the place for fine seafood and Neapolitan specialities. Popular with the locals, book your table in advance.

Sabatini, Piazza Santa Maria in Trastevere 13   LLL
Tel: (06) 582026
Open: Thur–Tues until midnight   Closed: Wed and 2 wks Aug
Credit cards: AE, DC, V

A delightful restaurant full of genuine Trastevere ambience. Eat in the spacious, frescoed salon or outside at night with a charming view of the flood-lit church. Roman and fish dishes are the specialities. It's popular, so you'll have to book.

Santopadre, Via Collina 18   LL
Tel: (06) 489405
Open: Mon–Sat until 11pm   Closed: Sun and Aug
No credit cards

This little restaurant is situated near the Piazza Fiume and the British Embassy. The menu comprises classic Italian dishes, beautifully prepared, filling and delicious. Don't miss the authentic *risotto*.

Spaghetteria, Via Arno 80   L
Tel: (06) 855535
Open: Tues–Sun until 1am   Closed: Mon and Aug
Credit cards: DC

Paradise for pasta-lovers with over 30 variations on spaghetti. Situated in the Salario district and open until late. Delicious garlic bread and reasonable prices.

Taverna Giulia, Vicolo dell'Oro 23   LLL
Tel: (06) 6569768
Open: Mon–Sat until 11:30pm   Closed: Sun and Aug
Credit cards: AE, DC

A popular and distinguished restaurant situated near the Vatican in Old Rome, specializing in Genoese dishes. The decor is pretty unsophisticated but the food is consistently good. Lots of pesto sauce on the pasta.

El Toulà, Via della Lupa 29B   LLL
Tel: (06) 6781196
Open: Mon–Sat until midnight   Closed Sun and Aug
Credit cards: AE, DC, MC, V

A great favorite with the famous, from film stars to millionaires.

Superb Venetian and international cuisine in luxurious and sophisticated surroundings. Impeccable service. Book well in advance.

Vecchia Roma, Piazza Campitelli 18   **LLL**
Tel: (06) 6564604
Open: Thur–Tues until 11:30pm   Closed: Wed and 2 wks Aug
No credit cards

A particularly lovely restaurant in Old Rome. On a summer evening you can dine out on the beautiful piazza. Traditional, beautifully prepared Roman cuisine.

FAST FOOD AND PIZZAS

If you don't have time to sit down for a meal, do as the Romans do and have a quick bite at a *pizzeria* or a snack bar. There's one on just about every street in Rome. The variations of pizzas and snacks on offer are countless. Pizzas come with everything from sea-food to artichokes. In snack bars you'll find hot croissants stuffed with cheese, ham and many other different fillings. Great with a cold beer or a cappuccino. Here are a few suggestions:

FAST FOOD

California Via Leonida Bissolati 54

Franchi Via Cola di Rienzo 204

Frontoni Viale Trastevere 52

Il Delfino, Corso Vittorio Emanuele 67

Italy Italy, Via Barberini 2/12

McDonald's Piazza di Spagna 46

Nipponya Via della Vite 102

San Carlo Via del Corso 119

Willy's Corso Vittorio Emanuele II 215

PIZZERIAS

Ai Fori Largo Corrado Ricci 2

Il Boscaiolo Via degli Artisti 37

Ivo Via San Francesco a Ripa 158

La Fiorentina Via Andrea Doria 22

Montecarlo Piazza Mastai, Trastevere

San Marco Via Tacito 29

CAFÉS

Alemagna, Via del Corso 181
Tel: (06) 6792887
Open: Mon–Sat 7.30am–10pm   Closed: Sun

Right in the center of Rome, near the Piazza Colonna, this is a favorite spot for a quick snack between shops, a pre-lunch aperitif, or a milk-shake in the afternoon. Grandiose decor with candelabra and mirrored walls. Always busy but well worth a visit – the grandest café in Rome.

Babington's Tea Rooms, Piazza di Spagna 23
Tel: (06) 6786027
Open: Fri–Wed 9am–8:30pm   Closed: Thur

This is Rome's only tea room and was opened by Anna Maria Babington in 1896. Miss Babington's original recipes are still used in the preparation of home-made scones, muffins and pastries but the price for such exclusive "English" fare is very high. Breakfasts, light lunches and teas are served. Babington's still has a faithful following among the famous and wealthy.

Bar San Filippo, Via di Villa San Filippo 8
Tel: (06) 879314
Open: Tues–Sun 6am–midnight   Closed: Mon

A choice of 60 ice creams are on offer here, including blueberry, chestnut, watermelon, pistachio, tangerine, pear, fig, mango, melon, grape and prune. Delicious ice cream cakes for parties. Try a water-ice or the amazing *zabaglione*. The best ice cream in Rome – a must.

Café de Paris, Via Vittorio Veneto 90
Tel: (06) 465284
Open: Fri–Wed 8am–2am   Closed: Thur

The *dolce vita* days of this famous café have passed but it's still a tourist favorite. Watch the world go by from an outside table or enjoy the delicious *tavola fredda* – cold dishes and salads – from a wide choice in the air-conditioned bar. Prices are high but the service is excellent.

Caffè Greco, Via Condotti 86
Tel: (06) 6782554
Open: Mon–Sat 8am–9pm   Closed: Sun

This was Rome's most famous bar during the latter part of the 19th century. A gathering place for such talented writers and drinkers as Mark Twain and Oscar Wilde, and heroic figures such as Buffalo Bill. The decor has been beautifully preserved together with a collection of paintings, busts and photographs of famous former customers. Still popular with writers and artists. The atmosphere is sedate and prices high.

Canova, Piazza del Popolo 16
Tel: (06) 6797749
Open: Tues–Sun 7:30am–11:30pm
Closed: Mon

Rosati's arch-rival, on the opposite side of the piazza. This smart modern café caters to the up-market Roman lunchtime set and prices are fairly high. There is a huge choice of delicious snacks to eat at the bar inside. Or sit outside in the sun over a cold beer and watch the action on the beautiful square.

Doney, Via Vittorio Veneto 145
Tel: (06) 493407
Open: Tues–Sun 8am–1am   Closed: Mon

Doney's reputation among the cognoscenti is rising. This is the Roman café to be seen in. Smart, up-market and fashionable. There's a restaurant behind the terrace. Prices are high but service is efficient. A good place to sit out over a last drink at night and watch the passing crowds.

Giolitti, Via Uffici del Vicario 40
Tel: (06) 6794206
Open: Tues–Sun 7am–2am   Closed: Mon

The most popular place in Rome for *gelati* (ice cream) for over 20 years. Giolitti offers an extraordinary range of home-made ice creams. Very reasonable *tavola calda* (hot snacks) are served as well.

Rosati, Piazza del Popolo 4/5
Tel: (06) 3611418
Open: Tues–Sun 7:30am–midnight
Closed: Mon

Traditional, elegant café with great service and a view of the most beautiful square in Rome. A good place to rest your feet at an outdoor table. The cocktails are terrific. Fellini and Mastroianni practically lived here in their *dolce vita* days and the café is still popular with successful writers and actors. The bar also offers splendid pastries and chocolates.

Tre Scalini, Piazza Navona 28
Tel: (06) 659148
Open: Thur–Tues 7am–2:30am   Closed: Wed

With its lovely terrace on the stunning Piazza Navona, this is a favorite place to linger over an ice cream. The number one treat is *tartufo*, a very rich chocolate-based ice with equally rich whipped cream and whole cherries. If the terrace tables are overflowing, there are quieter tables inside.

HOTELS

All hotels in this section are open throughout the year.

Alexandra, Via Vittorio Veneto 18   LLL
Tel: (06) 4619343
Amenities: ☎ Credit cards: AE, DC, MC, V

This hotel is in a very popular position near the Spanish Steps.
The Via Veneto is constantly busy, so try to get a room at the
back to cut down on noise. All 45 largish rooms have baths or
showers. The atmosphere inside the hotel is rather quiet and
peaceful. Pleasant service.

Ambasciatori Palace, Via Vittorio Veneto 70   LLL
Tel: (06) 480251
Amenities: ☎ ▥ ✕ ♀   Credit cards: AE, DC, MC, V

This deluxe hotel has a prime position on the ever-busy Via
Veneto, right opposite the American Embassy. Recently refurbished, the 147 rooms all have baths (some twin rooms have twin
baths too). Luxurious furnishings and superb courteous service.
The terrace restaurant is open to non-residents.

Atlante Star, Via Giovanni Vitelleschi 34   LLL
Tel: (06) 6564196
Amenities: ☎ ▥ ✕ ♀ Credit cards: AE, DC, MC, V

Centrally-situated near the Tiber, close to St Peter's and many
other major sights. Fully air-conditioned with ultra-comfortable
rooms, each with a color TV. Bright, up-to-the-minute decor and
attentive service. There's a roof garden too, with great views.

Aventino, Via San Domenico 10   L
Tel: (06) 5755231
Amenities: ☎ No credit cards

This little hotel is situated in a pleasant, quiet spot on the Aventine
Hill. The Roman Forum is a few minutes walk away and the
subway and major bus routes conveniently nearby. Relaxed,
family atmosphere.

Bologna, Via Santa Chiara 4A   LL
Tel: (06) 6568951
Amenities: ☎ ♀ No credit cards

Located in the center of Old Rome, near the Pantheon and Piazza
Navona. A large, quiet hotel with 118 rooms. Most with baths.
Pleasantly and comfortably furnished with no unnecessary frills.
Efficient service and peaceful atmosphere.

Boston, Via Lombardia 47   LLL
Tel: (06) 473951
Amenities: ☎ 📺 ✕ 𝚼   Credit cards: AE, DC, MC

Pleasant hotel with comfortable furnishings and cheerful decor, very close to the Via Veneto and the best shops in Rome. Via Lombardia itself is a quiet street, so city noise is no problem. Good restaurant, too.

Cavalieri Hilton, Via Cadlolo 101, Monte Mario   LLL
Tel: (06) 3151
Amenities: ☎ 📺 🅿 ✕ 𝚼 ⇥ ℺   Credit cards: AE, DC, MC, V

There's a spectacular view of Rome from this hilltop hotel situated well away from the noise and bustle of the city. There's a regular courtesy bus providing a link-up with the city center. All 386 rooms are large, comfortable and quiet, with baths. The overall atmosphere may lack character but the service is impeccable. Marvelous roof-top disco/restaurant.

Cicerone, Via Cicerone 55   LLL
Tel: (06) 3576
Amenities: ☎ 📺 🅿 ✕ 𝚼   Credit cards: AE, DC, MC

This hotel is situated in the Prati district, conveniently near the main shopping area and major sights such as St Peter's. Large and extremely modern, with good service and comfortable furnishings.

Colonna Palace, Piazza Montecitorio 12   LLL
Tel: (06) 6781341
Amenities: ☎ 📺 𝚼   Credit cards: DC, V

A beautiful old Roman palace in a quiet square facing Bernini's Palazzo Montecitorio. Very quiet despite its central location, it offers a charming old setting with modern comforts. All 100 rooms have baths. Service is good.

Columbus, Via delle Conciliazione 33   LL
Tel: (06) 6564874
Amenities: ☎ ✕ 𝚼   Credit cards: AE, DC, MC, V

The 15th-century *palazzo* housing this hotel was built for Cardinal Domenico della Rovere and many of the original features remain. Of the 107 rooms, 80 have baths or showers. All are comfortably furnished with handsome decor. The public lounge is superb.

De La Ville, Via Sistina 69   LLL
Tel: (06) 6733
Amenities: ☎ 📺 🅿 ✕ 𝚼   Credit cards: AE, DC, MC, V

This hotel is part of the British Grand Metropolitan Group so good service is taken for granted. It has a pleasant location near the top of the Spanish Steps, with a lovely garden attached. A hotel which has never fallen out of favor.

Delta, Via Labicana 44 **LLL**
Tel: (06) 770021
Amenities: ☎ 📺 🅿 ✗ ⚲ ↝   Credit cards: AE, DC, MC, V

A super-modern hotel with all the style of present-day Rome. Right by the Colosseum in the heart of the ancient city – but here the comforts are right up-to-date. There's a swimming pool, too, and great service.

D'Inghilterra, Via Bocca di Leone 14 **LLL**
Tel: (06) 672161
Amenities: ☎ 📺 ⚲   Credit cards: AE, DC, MC, V

Excellent location for shopping enthusiasts, very near the Spanish Steps. Quiet discreet atmosphere, pleasant decor, excellent service. Good bar but no restaurant.

Diplomatic, Via Vittorio Colonna 28 **LL**
Tel: (06) 6542084
Amenities: ☎ 📺 ✗ ⚲   Credit cards: DC, V

Situated in the bustling Prati shopping district conveniently near bus routes and subway. This is a medium-sized hotel with fully air-conditioned rooms. Efficient, attentive service and pleasant, comfortable furnishings.

Eden, Via Ludovisi 49 **LLL**
Tel: (06) 480551
Amenities: ☎ 📺 ✗ ⚲   No credit cards

Long-established deluxe hotel in an exclusive quarter near the Via Veneto. All 110 quiet, comfortable and well-equipped rooms have bath. The Penthouse Bar (closed weekends and during August) provides a breathtaking view of the city. This is an all-time favorite with American visitors.

Esperia, Via Nazionale 22 **LL**
Tel: (06) 487245
Amenities: ☎ ⚲   Credit cards: AE, V

This large 19th-century hotel is well situated for shopping and sightseeing but rooms tend to be noisy – get one at the back if you can. All 98 rooms have baths. The public rooms still retain a flavor of the 19th century. Pleasant atmosphere, traditional-style service.

Excelsior, Via Vittorio Veneto 125   **LLL**
Tel: (06) 4708
Amenities: ☎ 📺 🅿 ✕ 𝖸   Credit cards: AE, DC, MC, V

Luxurious, palatial white-fronted hotel, right on the Via Veneto. An amazing 394 bedrooms, all with baths, and some suites too. Rich decor and plush furnishings include many beautiful antiques. Relaxed atmosphere; attentive service. There are two fine restaurants and a delightful piano bar provides entertainment far into the night.

Farnese, Via Alessandro Farnese 30   **L**
Tel: (06) 386343
Amenities: ☎ 📺 𝖸   No credit cards

This is a beautiful villa near the Tiber in the Prati district. Bus routes and the subway are conveniently close at hand. All 23 rooms with baths; breakfast only. Pleasant atmosphere, clean, quiet and comfortable.

Flora, Via Vittorio Veneto 191   **LLL**
Tel: (06) 497821
Amenities: ☎ 📺 ✕ 𝖸   Credit cards: AE, V

Many of its 177 rooms overlook the Villa Borghese. The decor is rather old-fashioned but no less charming for that. Service is traditional and attentive. Elegant furnishings with many fine antiques. A thoroughly pleasant and comfortable hotel.

Fiorella, Via del Babuino 196   **L**
Tel: (06) 3610597
No special amenities.   No credit cards

This tiny *pensione* is in an excellent central location but book well in advance – it's very popular. Clean and comfortable with unpretentious decor and furnishings. Reliable and good value. No restaurant.

Forum, Via Tor dei Conti 25   **LLL**
Tel: (06) 6792446
Amenities: ☎ 📺 🅿 ✕ 𝖸   Credit cards: AE, DC, MC, V

This hotel was originally a Renaissance palace constructed from materials taken from the ancient ruins nearby. Fairly small rooms, but all 75 have bathroom and pleasant, elegant decor. Delightful roof-top restaurant overlooks the Roman Forum. There's also a pleasant summer terrace running alongside the restaurant.

Genio, Via Zanardelli   LL
Tel: (06) 6542238
Amenities: ☎ No credit cards

Conveniently near Piazza Navona, Via Zanardelli carries a lot of heavy traffic. Ask for a room at the back of the hotel. It's an efficient and unpretentious hotel, making for a comfortable stay. Good value for money.

Giulio Cesare, Via degli Scipioni 287   LLL
Tel: (06) 310244
Amenities: ☎ Ⓜ ⚏ Credit cards: DC, V

This hotel, situated in the Prati district, was once the home of Roman aristocrats. It still retains the atmosphere of a private villa. Decor is elegant and tasteful, furnishings comfortable and service extremely attentive. Beautifully quiet with a lovely garden terrace. No restaurant but a delicious breakfast buffet.

Grand Hotel et de Rome, Via Vittorio E. Orlando 3   LLL
Tel: (06) 4709
Amenities: ☎ Ⓜ ℗ ✕ ⚏ Credit cards: AE, DC, MC, V

A first-class, traditional deluxe hotel, founded in 1894, now the proud possession of the CIGA chain. Palatial rooms with sumptuous furnishings and impeccable service. The hotel is much frequented by international VIPs and royalty. It combines sheer luxury with the best of taste. The restaurant Le Rallye is excellent (see Restaurant section).

Gregoriana, Via Gregoriana 18   LL
Tel: (06) 6794269
Amenities: ☎ ✕ Credit cards: AE, V

This hotel has become increasingly popular in recent years. There are only 19 rooms, so you'll need to book well ahead. Situated near the Spanish Steps, handy for shopping, you'll enjoy good service in comfortable furnishings. Breakfast only.

Hassler-Villa Medici, Piazza Trinità dei Monti 6   LLL
Tel: (06) 6792651
Amenities: ☎ ℗ ✕ ⚏ No credit cards

Part of the exclusive Hassler chain, housed in the former Villa Medici, the hotel boasts one of the most splendid situations in Rome overlooking the Spanish Steps. All 101 rooms have sumptuous bathrooms. The luxurious decor is exquisite; the service impeccable. A famous roof-top restaurant commands a superb view over the city; it's also open to non-residents.

Holiday Inn, Via Aurelia Antica 415   **LLL**
Tel: (06) 5872
Amenities: ☎ 📺 ✕ ⛾ ⚡ ⚲   Credit cards: AE, DC, MC, V

An all-American hotel, with every kind of home comfort, right down to the ice machines, and air-conditioning. Modern, set in large grounds, it's just outside the city but a frequent free bus service takes you into the center. Decor is pure Hollywood and there's a swimming pool. Great if you have children.

Hotel Carriage, Via delle Carrozze 36   **LL**
Tel: (06) 6795166
Amenities: ☎ 📺 ✕ ⛾   Credit cards: AE, DC, MC, V

This excellent two-star hotel is in a quiet location at the center of downtown Rome. It is tastefully decorated, with an American bar and grill. As it is situated off Piazza di Spagna, it's very handy for the shops. Pleasant furnishings include some period pieces. Unmodernized but perfectly adequate bathrooms.

Hotel Fontana, Piazza di Trevi 96   **LLL**
Tel: (06) 6786113
Amenities: ☎ ✕ ⛾   Credit cards: AE, DC, MC, V (guests must advise beforehand if they mean to pay by credit card)

The hotel, housed in a 13th-century monastery building, is clean and efficient, with an extremely helpful and courteous staff. The rather dark decor may not be to everyone's taste. As the hotel is situated opposite the Trevi Fountain, it tends to be rather noisy but you may enjoy being right in the center of the action. There are 28 rooms, all with a shower or a bath.

Internazionale, Via Sistina 79   **LL**
Tel: (06) 6793047
Amenities: ☎ ✕ ⛾   No credit cards

Situated near Trinità dei Monti, this is a fairly small hotel with comfortable rooms. It's fast gaining a name for itself, so book in advance. Quiet, friendly atmosphere and pleasant service. Breakfast only.

Jolly, Corso d'Italia 1   **LLL**
Tel: (06) 8495
Amenities: ☎ 📺 🅿 ✕ ⛾   Credit cards: AE, DC, MC, V

Beautifully situated by the Villa Borghese, many of the hotel rooms overlook the park. Although you're not far from the Via Veneto, noise is not a problem as all 200 rooms are sound-proofed. Ultra-modern inside and out; extremely comfortable; efficient, courteous service. All the amenities are up to the usual Jolly standard.

La Residenza, Via Emilia 22   LL
Tel: (06) 6799592
Amenities: ☎ P ⏦   No credit cards

A no-fuss-no-frills hotel situated in a former town house. Very pleasant decor, comfortable furnishings and friendly, attentive service. Conveniently near Via Veneto for shopping enthusiasts. A great buffet breakfast is available, but no restaurant.

Londra e Cargill, Piazza Sallustio 18   LLL
Tel: (06) 473871
Amenities: ☎ Ⓜ P ✕ ⏦   Credit cards: AE, V

A short walk from Rome's major shopping district, the hotel is set on a lovely piazza. It's a pleasant converted 19th-century *palazzo* offering 105 rooms, all with bath. Shining modernistic decor; large, elegant public rooms. Pleasant grill room.

Lord Byron, Via G. de Notaris 5   LLL
Tel: (06) 3609541
Amenities: Ⓜ ✕ ⏦   Credit cards: AE, DC, MC, V

A small, exclusive hotel in a tranquil district near the Villa Giulia. Quiet luxury among tasteful furnishings. The overall atmosphere resembles that of an elegant private house. Fifty rooms, all with baths, and a good restaurant (Le Jardin) serving wonderful classic cuisine. Make reservations well in advance.

Orsini Residence, Via Orsini 4   L
Tel: (06) 312829
No special amenities.   No credit cards

This pleasant *pensione* occupies a 19th-century villa in a quiet part of the Prati district, across the Tiber from Piazza del Popolo. Only 12 rooms, eight with baths, so don't leave it too late. The upstairs rooms tend to be more attractive, though all are clean and comfortable. There's a pretty garden too.

Pace Elvezia, Via Quattro Novembre 104   LL
Tel: (06) 6795105
Amenities: ☎ ⏦   Credit cards: DC, MC, V

Pleasantly situated hotel overlooking the Roman Forum and the Piazza Venezia. Comfortable rooms, pleasant decor and efficient service. Elegant and central, it offers good value for money.

Portoghesi, Via dei Portoghesi 1   L
Tel: (06) 6564231
Amenities: ☎   No credit cards

In a good central position, the hotel fronts onto a pretty little

Renaissance piazza in the heart of Old Rome. Recently refurbished with 27 rooms, 20 with bath. Pleasant atmosphere, clean and comfortably furnished. It's best to book in advance as this has long been a popular spot.

Quirinale, Via Nazionale 7   LLL
Tel: (06) 479901
Amenities: ☎ Ⓜ ℗ ✕ ⍭   Credit cards: AE, DC, MC, V

Very central location, handy for most of the major stores. Good-sized comfortable rooms, attentive English-speaking staff and luxurious decor. There's a beautiful garden courtyard; also a private entrance to the Rome Opera House next door. Verdi stayed here in 1893 awaiting the première of *Falstaff*. Many singers and musicians still frequent the Quirinale's bar.

Raphael, Largo Febo 2   LLL
Tel: (06) 6569051
Amenities: ☎ Ⓜ ✕ ⍭   Credit cards: AE

A small but stylish hotel situated in the center of Old Rome. The ivy-covered facade conceals a haven of taste, comfort and luxury. The Senate is nearby so the hotel is a favorite with politicians. Comfortable rooms, all 85 with bath, charmingly decorated. Pleasant atmosphere, efficient service.

Sant'Anna, Via Borgo Pio 134   LL
Tel: (06) 6541602
Amenities: ☎ No credit cards

A small hotel with a friendly atmosphere close to the Vatican. Comfortable rooms, all with bath and pleasant decor; courteous, unpretentious service. A family-style hotel and not expensive. No restaurant.

Scalinata di Spagna, Piazza Trinità dei Monti 17   LL
Tel: (06) 6793006
No special amenities.   No credit cards

An ideal location at the top of the Spanish Steps makes this delightful *pensione* extremely popular. It's fairly expensive and reservations should be made well ahead as there are only 14 rooms (all with bath). Pleasant atmosphere plus a roof-top terrace for summer breakfasts accompanied by a stunning view.

Sheraton Roma, Viale del Pattinaggio, EUR   LLL
Tel: (06) 5453
Amenities: ☎ Ⓜ ℗ ✕ ⍭ ⇲ ℺   Credit cards: AE, DC, MC, V

A popular conference center much favored by businessmen, the hotel favors the suburbs of Rome, with easy access to the city center and airport. Modern design (opened in 1983), absolutely enormous and extremely comfortable. The atmosphere is business-like and the service is excellent.

Sicilia Daria, Via Sicilia 24   L
Tel: (06) 493841
Amenities: ☎ ✕ ♀   No credit cards

Housed in a large building near to Via Veneto, this reliable *pensione* is well-placed for the city center. Spacious rooms, clean and comfortably furnished. Unpretentious, friendly, family-style atmosphere.

Siena, Via Sant'Andrea delle Fratte 33   LL
Tel: (06) 6796121
Amenities: ☎ ✕ ♀   No credit cards

Excellent central location near the Spanish Steps, handy for all the shops and sights. Tiny but comfortable rooms, cordial atmosphere. The hotel is small so book in advance. Breakfast only.

Sole al Pantheon, Via del Pantheon 63   LL
Tel: (06) 6793329
Amenities: ☎ ♀   No credit cards

This is one of Rome's oldest inns, dating from the 15th century. Ariosto, author of the epic *Orlando Furioso*, stayed here in the early 1500s. Although the hotel was recently renovated, it has lost none of its historic atmosphere. There are 28 small rooms, most with bath; some have a view of the Pantheon.

Suisse, Via Gregoriana 56   L
Tel: (06) 6783649
No special amenities.   No credit cards

Convenient location near the Spanish Steps, handy for both shops and sight-seeing. Twenty-eight large, immaculately clean rooms, nine with bath. Unfussy decor, comfortable furnishings, pleasant lounge. This old-established *pensione* is reliable and efficiently run in a friendly, relaxed manner.

Tiziano, Corso Vittorio Emañuele 110   LL
Tel: (06) 655087
Amenities: ☎ ▥ ✕ ♀   Credit cards: AE, DC, MC, V

This was once a large *palazzo*, now converted into a fine hotel with 50 large, comfortable rooms, 45 with bath or shower. Huge public rooms with both antique and modern furniture. Corso Vittorio Emanuele has some of the heaviest traffic in Rome, so do ask for a room at the back. Central situation, near St Peter's.

Victoria, Via Campania 41   **LLL**
Tel: (06) 480052
Amenities: ☎ 🅿 ✕ ⛋   Credit cards: AE, MC

Quietly situated, although it's near the Via Veneto, the hotel faces the Aurelian Wall. All 110 rooms (with bath) are delightfully furnished; some of the upper windows look over the Villa Borghese. A regular and devoted clientele, plus excellent service, makes for a quiet, pleasant stay.

Villa Borghese, Via Pinciana 31   **LL**
Tel: (06) 859648
Amenities: ☎ ⛋   Credit cards: DC, V

Centrally-situated near the Via Veneto, the hotel is handy for major sights and shopping. Relaxed, friendly atmosphere. Bedrooms are large and comfortably furnished; several have a lovely view over the park.

Villa San Pio, Via Sant'Anselmo 19   **L**
Tel: (06) 5755231
Amenities: ☎ ⛋   No credit cards

Handsome old villa with a pleasant garden, set in a quiet area outside the city center. Sixty rooms with bath. Good value for money and friendly atmosphere.

NIGHTSPOTS

Bella Blu, Via Luciani 21
Tel: (06) 3608840
Open: Daily 9pm–3:30am

This is perhaps the hottest nightspot in the city, in the unlikely setting of the Roman suburbs. The clientele is ultra-smart – top sportspeople, Italian aristocrats, movie stars and VIPs all mingle in sophisticated surroundings. Obviously it's difficult to get in. It's very exclusive but well worth the effort. Tiny dance floor, up-market disco music and a minuscule restaurant serving excellent food.

Easy Going, Via della Purificazione 9
Tel: (06) 4745578
Open: Daily 11pm–3:30am

As the name implies this is a lively, uninhibited club. Although the clientele is predominantly gay, you won't be turned away if you're not. The club is equally happy to welcome gays and straights. Marvelously over-the-top pink-and-red decor in the foyer; a downstairs disco that's always jumping.

Folkstudio, Via Gaetano Sacchi 3, Trastevere
Tel: (06) 5892374
Open: Tues–Sat 9pm–2am   Closed: Sun–Mon

This jazz club has been going for years. It's almost an institution these days. An international program of folk, country music and jazz with lots of new talent on offer. Very popular with the locals and the music is authentic too.

Il Dito al Naso, Via del Fiume 4
Tel: (06) 3612389
Open: Mon–Sat 7pm–3am   Closed: Sun

Literally translated, *dito al naso* means "a finger in your nose". This intimate and romantic bar is the place for a quiet and relaxing drink, early evening or very late at night. No dancing but great ambience.

Jackie-O, Via Boncompagni 11
Tel: (06) 461401
Open: Daily 11pm–3:30am

Still one of the smartest Roman nightspots with a clientele to match. You may find it difficult to get in as the club tends to cater to the movie mogul and starlet set. Plush, mock-Liberty decor with a piano bar and restaurant hidden away downstairs. Just the place to watch the "beautiful people".

La Cabala, Hostaria dell'Orso, Via dei Soldati 25
Tel: (06) 6564250
Open: Mon–Sat 10:30pm–3am   Closed: Sun

American disco music in a fabulous palace dating from the 13th century (Rabelais and Dante used to stay here). The club is situated over the restaurant Hostaria dell'Orso, a pleasant place to wine and dine. Drinks are expensive.

Much More, Via Luciani 52
Tel: (06) 870504
Open: Tues–Fri 11pm–3am, Sat–Sun 4pm–8pm 11pm–3am
Closed: Mon

This ex-cinema was converted in 1978 into a top-class nightclub. Youngish clientele dance to excellent disco or live music, from rock to jazz. Fantastic lighting effects make this one of the most exciting spots in town. On Saturdays famous Italian faces flock to Much More and the dancing goes on until dawn.

Piper 80, Via Tagliamento 9
Tel: (06) 854459
Open: Tues–Fri 10pm–3am, Sat–Sun 4pm–7:30pm 10pm–3am
Closed: Mon

The first of Rome's discos, and it's still taking the pace. The crowd is young, the music loud and the excitement high. Plenty of bizarre lighting effects and videos, one room packed with Space Invader machines and a funky atmosphere. If you want to know the latest Roman disco craze, this is the place to be. Lots of fun.

Tartarughino, Via della Scrofa 2
Tel: (06) 6786037
Open: Mon–Sat 9pm–3am   Closed: Sun, Jul–Aug

This tiny exclusive establishment is Rome's top piano bar (piano bars are generally used by single people – a great way to make new friends in a strange city). Formal dress is essential. Even dressed in your best you may not be able to get in. Small and excellent restaurant upstairs; piano player and drinks below.

DAY TRIPS AROUND ROME

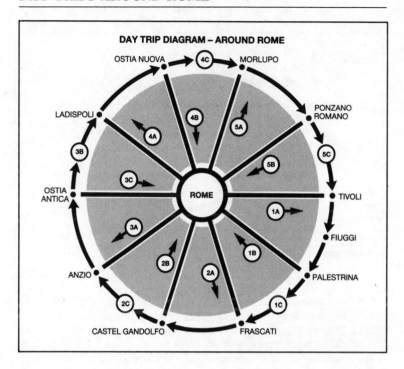

DAY TRIP DIAGRAM – AROUND ROME

These short tours from Rome are delightful in themselves, but they're designed so you can adapt and alter them as you like. With Rome as the hub, they're like spokes of a wheel, connected by the rim. Follow the day tours as outlined for easy enjoyment, or build your own variations as time and inclination dictate. Route A of each tour gives the main story; Route B is the quick return route to Rome; Route C is a variation you might like to try, linking the tours and extending the route.

TOUR 1: VISIONARY VILLAS (A1 90kms; A2 adds 156kms)

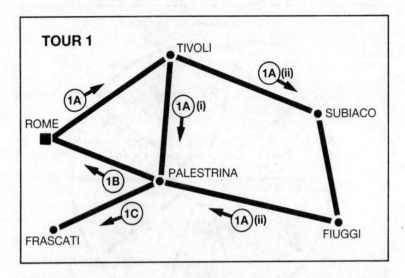

Venturing out to the east of Rome, there's so much to see it would be impossible to take it all in in a single day. Following the Build-A-Tour concept, you'll find a one-day tour (**Route A1**) visiting world-famous **Tivoli**, site of Emperor Hadrian's villa-city, and **Palestrina**, an ancient sanctuary where the Romans built a magnificent temple to the goddess of fortune. Its remains spread over a large part of town and contain a cathedral and a palace. If you have more time to spare, extend your route from Tivoli further east to **Subiaco** for the fabulous medieval frescoes of St Benedict's monastery, then stay overnight in **Fiuggi**, and take a dip in Pope Boniface VIII's favorite spa waters before rejoining the main route at Palestrina (**Route A2**).

ROUTE A: Rome – Tivoli

*Starting from central Rome, take **Viale del Muro Torto** from **Piazzale Flaminio** driving east along the city walls opposite **Villa Borghese**. Keep left on this fast inner-city road as it runs through a series of tunnels for 2½kms, then bear right following a sign for **Policlinico**. Keep left at the next fork (also signed Policlinico), re-emerging by the city walls on **Via Giovanni Battista Morgagni**. Just over ½km later, at a traffic light, turn right following a small blue sign for **Tiburtina ss5**. This road becomes **Viale Regina Elena**, passes the university and ends by a major intersection 1km later. You have to bear right here, before inching left around a clutch of bus stops.*

Exit on to the tree-lined **Via Tiburtina** *where there is a high cemetery wall running along on the right-hand side of the road.*

Via Tiburtina runs straight out of Rome under the GRA outer-city ring road 10kms later. You reach **Bagni di Tivoli** *10kms further on, accompanied by a powerful whiff of sulphur from the thermal baths praised by Pliny the Younger over one thousand years ago. The springs pump a total of 260 million liters of water into the busy public bathing pools each day, maintaining a constant 70°F. Nearly 3kms on, the road forms a narrow bridge between two enormous quarries with huge blocks of Travertine marble stacked along the roadside. A by-product of the thermal springs, this marble has been used by Roman builders since the days of the Colosseum.*

Just under 3kms ahead, there's a right turn for **Villa Adriana.** *You might choose to turn off here and visit the villa before driving into Tivoli. (For full details, see below.) The road climbs for a further 4kms to a plateau, with a garden on the left where you'll find the* **Tourist Office,** *Largo Garibaldi. (Tel: (0774) 21249. Open: Mon–Sat 8am–2pm year round; also 2:30pm–6:30pm in summer.)*

TIVOLI

The vaunted *Tibur* of ancient Roman civilization, Tivoli is caught in a loop of the River Aniene overlooking the *Campagna* in the lee of the Sabine Hills. By the first century it had grown into a summer resort for illustrious Roman citizens who built numerous villas along the shaded slopes. The greatest of these is Villa Adriana, below modern Tivoli, where the reclusive Emperor Hadrian built himself a miniature city. The town center is dominated by the massive walls of the 15th-century Rocca Pia, built by Pius II over a former amphitheater. To the west, Cardinal d'Este's fabulous gardens tumble down the hillside; and further north, Villa Gregoriana surrounds an historic cult site of the legendary prophetess Sibyl.

WHAT TO SEE IN TIVOLI

Villa Adriana
Open: Daily 9am–1½hrs before sunset
Admission: L4,000
Directions: Follow signs from turn-off indicated in route into town (1½kms).

Before you start your walking tour, stop off at the scale model of the Villa in a small hut by the bar. With this filed in your memory the ruins will come alive in the course of your wanderings.

Built by Hadrian between 125–134AD, Villa Adriana is one of the greatest monuments of the ancient world. A dedicated connoisseur of art and architecture, the Emperor sought to build a retreat reflecting the finest forms of artistic expression he'd witnessed on his travels through Egypt and Greece. Within a perimeter measuring almost three miles he constructed a dream city, and its magic is no less strong today after four centuries of excavations.

Highlights of your tour should include the moated **Teatro Marittimo**, accessible only by movable pontoons, where the Emperor could escape from his court. To the south is the **Canopus**, lined with statuary and designed after an Egyptian canal with a temple dedicated to Seraphis and Hadrian's young companion Antinous who drowned in the Nile. At one time the **Palazzo Imperiale** incorporated guest rooms, barracks, baths and a library courtyard. Now planted with olives, it's a perfect spot to stroll among the classical forms. To the south of the palace is the rectangular **Piazza d'Oro** named by archeologists for the spectacular discoveries and treasures uncovered here. At the far end there's an intriguingly designed series of chambers in a complex plan based on the Greek cross – an early example of architectural conceit.

Before departing, you may wish to visit the gift shop. It stocks a good range of postcards and souvenirs.

Villa d'Este, off Largo Garibaldi, Tivoli
Open: Daily 9am–1½hrs before sunset
Admission: L5,000

Founded on the site of a former Benedictine monastery, the Villa d'Este's lush gardens provide a vivid counterpoint to the older palace. The porch, decorated with a ceiling fresco by Pirro Ligorio, leads you into a lovely colonnaded courtyard with the ticket office tucked around on your right. To reach the gardens, you walk through a series of apartments built for Cardinal Ippolito d'Este in 1550. They're sparsely decorated with dusty divans and antique wooden furniture, so you'll concentrate on the ornately painted ceilings alive with a riot of figures, intricate designs and princely motifs. Do catch the views over the valley, too.

At the bottom of the stairs, a bar-cum-gift shop ensures you have enough film in the camera. Then it's out onto the terrace where the air quivers with the sound of water sparkling from a cat's cradle of terraces leading down the hillside. Along the paths, neat box hedges briefly reveal grottoes, steps, balconies and seats edged with floral mosaics. The **Viale delle Cento Fontane** runs almost the breadth of the gardens in a rogue's gallery of moss edged, bat-eared and pig-nosed gargoyles burbling into troughs, providing backing music to the flashy song of the water jets. No wonder composer and one-time guest Franz Liszt was inspired to dedicate a musical tribute to *Les Jeux d'Eau à la Villa d'Este*. Other treats include the rose garden in summer, and strikingly twisted and gnarled cypresses. Once the gardens were open and floodlit during summer evenings but sadly this is no longer the case. There's a chance the practice may be revived – so it's well worth checking with the Tourist Office for developments.

Villa Gregoriana, Largo Sant'Angelo, Tivoli
Open: Daily 9am–1½hrs before sunset
Admission: L1,500

The park of Villa Gregoriana provides a beautiful natural setting for the magnificent **Grande Cascata** (Great Cascade) where the River Aniene plunges over 500ft through a series of waterfalls. It's named for Pope Gregory XVI who cured the river of its propensity to flood by digging a channel through the mountain in the 19th century. This both eased water pressure and created the main falls. Electrified by summer sunshine, the crashing waters and rainbow-colored clouds of spray are a fantastic sight.

SHOPPING IN TIVOLI

Not a shopping mecca by any stretch of the imagination; this is true of most towns within easy reach of Rome. However, you might like to explore the Old Town center off Largo Garibaldi, so take Via Pacifici past the ubiquitous **Benetton** to **Piazza San Croce**. There are a couple of good delis here for picnic makings – cheese, cold meats, bread and snack foods – and another opposite a second Benetton at **Via Trevio** (No 25). **Effe**, Via Trevio 15 (Credit cards: AE, DC, V) stocks gorgeous leather handbags by Furla, designer umbrellas, silk scarves, chic costume jewelry and accessories. Along the street are **Longines** and **Stefanel** on the good quality chain store front.

WHERE TO EAT IN TIVOLI

Ristorante Alfredo di Gino e Toni, Via Mazzini I   L
Tel: (0774) 20304
Open: Daily 9am–4pm 7pm–midnight
No credit cards

Directly across the street from Villa Gregoriana, this is a welcoming restaurant with outdoor seating in a garden patio among pot plants or inside beneath high ceilings and chandeliers. The walls are decorated with pen and ink sketches of Tivoli and historic scenes, plus a large mural depicting the Grande Cascata. Good regional food with delicious homemade pasta.

Ristorante-Pizzeria Il Cioceo, Via Ponte Gregoriana 33 LL
Tel: (0774) 292482
Open: Tues–Sun 1pm–4pm 7pm–midnight
Closed: Mon, and first week in Aug
No credit cards

Within walking distance of Villa Gregoriana, a highlight here is the spectacular view over Grande Cascata and the amphitheater. There are two levels of patio seating at the rear of the restaurant with steps leading down to the falls. Built into the hillside, the interior dining room has an open grill carved out of the bare stone and window sills laden with wine bottles. There's a great atmosphere and one of the brother-owners is a former New York chef so menu translations are no problem. The pasta and fish dishes are recommended, plus a mouthwatering *filetto al pepe verde* (green pepper steak).

WHERE TO STAY NEAR TIVOLI

Millepini, San Polo dei Cavalieri   **LL**
Tel: (0774) 560088/560064   Open: Year round
Amenities: ☎ 🅿 ✕ ⚲ ⚘ ⚲   No credit cards
*Directions: Take the Subiaco road for 3kms (see **Route A2**) to the left turn for **San Polo dei Cavalieri**. Follow signs for San Polo climbing steadily for 7½kms into the village. Look for the big green and white nameboard, then follow signs to the right.*

If you're looking for an overnight stop in the Tivoli area, Millepini makes up for its rather dreary modern decor with a friendly welcome and good facilities. The 50 rooms, all with shower and private balcony, are comfortable and simply furnished. The pizzeria sports checked tablecloths, a relaxed holiday atmosphere and an uncomplicated menu. There's a nightclub (open during the summer) and mini-golf which keeps children endlessly amused and out of your hair.

*   *   *

If you wish to take **Route A2** to Subiaco and Fiuggi, turn to page 139 for details.

ROUTE A1: Tivoli – Palestrina

*From the center of Tivoli make your way back downhill on **Via Tiburtina** past the turn-off for **Villa Adriana** (3½kms) to the left turn for **Palestrina/Zagarolo** 1km further on. Pass the turreted tower of an Augustan tomb on your right, and continue for a dreary 4½kms through scattered factories to a junction beyond the highway. Turn left, then bear right for **Zagarolo** along a tree-lined road into a pretty stretch of countryside. Take a left for **Palestrina** 8kms later, and a narrow tree-lined avenue leads to a junction in Palestrina after 9kms.*

*This is **Viale Pio XII** where you turn left; at the top turn right following signs for **Duomo** along a lower terrace of the ancient **Tempio della Fortuna**. At the end of the terrace you can continue straight up to the temple or bear left and park at the end of the street in **Piazzale Santa Maria d'Angeli**. Walk down narrow **Via***

*Anicia to **Piazza Regina Margherita** where you'll find the Duomo and occasional **Tourist Office** on the right. (Open: Mon–Sat 9am–1pm 4pm–6pm in summer.)*

*   *   *

*For details of **Palestrina**, see page 142.*

ROUTE A2: One-Day Extension: **Tivoli – Subiaco – Fiuggi – Palestrina**   (156kms)

*Leaving Tivoli, follow the walls of the **Rocca** and signs for **Villa Gregoriana** round to the left. This leads around the town center until you cross a bridge. Bear right, away from Villa Gregoriana, uphill for 200m where you keep left for **Subiaco** running out of town above the railroad. Follow signs for **Carsoli** through dry, stony hills peaking to either side of the road, then pick up signs for **Avezzano** as you near **Vicovaro** 12kms from Tivoli. You effectively bypass the town by a convenient lower road, moving swiftly through wooded slopes to a junction 2kms beyond **Roviano**, where you turn right for Subiaco.*

*This road, known as **Via Sublacensis**, follows the course of the River Aniene below sweeping wooded slopes strung with vertiginous villages perched on outcrops of rock or simply built into the hillside. Driving into **Subiaco** 15kms later you pass the 14th-century **Ponte di San Francesco** on the right, then continue under an arch and up the main street following signs for **monasteri**. The road runs uphill for 2kms, when you veer across to the left past the ruins of Nero's Villa once fronted by a man-made lake. While the villa was under construction, the workmen were housed below the extent of the lake "sublaqueum" (under the lakes) – hence Subiaco. Twist and turn your way up to the first monastery, **Santa Scholastica** (which can also be visited), and continue for ¾km to a sharp left turn for **San Benedetto**. Another ¾km of hairpin bends brings you to the parking area below the monastery.*

Convento di San Benedetto, Subiaco
Open: Daily 9am–noon 3pm–6:30pm   (winter until 5:30pm)
Admission free

The monastery is built around a mountain grotto where St Benedict spent three years living the life of a hermit in around 500AD. During this solitary period the only person who knew of his whereabouts was St Romanus who lived in a nearby religious house. He kept Benedict alive by lowering food on a rope with a bell attached to rouse the hermit saint from his contemplations. This spartan regime was disrupted when Benedict was discovered by a group of shepherds who spread the word and encouraged a gathering of disciples. This eventually led to the foundation of 13 monasteries in the surrounding area. One of these was Santa

Scholastica, dedicated to St Benedict's twin sister who came to join him.

From the parking lot there's a steep climb through a beautiful ilex grove, with wonderful views across the hills, to a small gateway and watchtower. Another flight of steps leads to a belvedere and small vestibule decorated with 15th-century Umbrian frescoes. Pause to sign the visitors book, then walk through a cloister to the chapel on the left. The single ribbed nave is richly painted with scenes from *The Crucifixion, The Life of St Benedict* and other biblical stories, most dating from the 14th-century Sienese school.

You descend through a series of galleries, the first being the Lower Church also called the **Sacro Speco**. These fabulous frescoes are the work of 13th-century Roman master, Conxolus. They are remarkable for their clarity, the deep azure blue and green tones warmed with terracotta and touched with gold. **St Benedict's Grotto**, on the right, houses a 17th-century statue of the saint by Antonio Raggi, a pupil of Bernini. There's a silver cover on the foot to preserve the marble which takes a heavy toll from kissing pilgrims. In the top right-hand corner you can also see a fresco showing St Romanus lowering food.

Down a second flight of steps, the **Santa Scala**, there are further Sienese frescoes which represent *Triumph over Death* and *Scenes from the Virgin's Life* in the **Cappella della Madonna**. At the very bottom you'll come to the **Grotta dei Pastori**, where St Benedict preached to the shepherds. On the right-hand wall, there's a primitive eighth-century Byzantine fresco of the Madonna with St Luke painted before the present monastery was built in the 12th century.

If you're lucky enough to have a monk on duty who speaks English, he'll be happy to answer questions and explain the stories behind the frescoes. There's also a shop selling postcards and a soft drink machine, plus the cleanest public toilets in Italy.

Retrace your route back to the junction by Nero's Villa. Take the sharp left turn carefully, following signs for **Altipiani di Arcinazzo/ Fiuggi** *through a short tunnel. This is a beautiful drive through the country, where old habits die hard: stone crofts nestle in small plots of brilliant green vines, donkeys crawl along beneath piles of golden straw and rich streams teem with trout. Follow this road, the* **ss411**, *for 16kms until it bears off for Guarcino and you continue on for* **Fiuggi**. *As you approach Fiuggi you have a choice of destinations:* **Fiuggi Citta**, *the medieval town center; or* **Fiuggi Fonte**, *where the spas and main hotels are found. There is a* **Tourist Office** *at Piazza Frascara 4, Fiuggi Fonte. (Tel: (0775) 55019.) It's in the main square opposite the spa, but its opening hours are unreliable and the tourist hotels are better equipped to answer questions and provide information.*

FIUGGI

If the ancient Romans had owned cars *Tibur* (Tivoli) would probably have been founded here on the fresh green slopes of Monti
Ernici. A copybook spa town in a wooded valley, Fiuggi banishes
the muggy climate of the plains with a light, dry breeze and offers
quiet, relaxed surroundings to those in search of a cure or just
looking for a bed for the night. Like most spas, it's strictly a
summer resort and it's popular so try to book ahead. Fiuggi's
celebrated waters have been recommended by no lesser personage
than Michelangelo, and during the 13th century, Pope Boniface
VIII despatched relays of servants to collect water from the spring
which now bears his name. If you'd like to give it a try, the
entrance fee is L10,000 with an additional charge for extras such
as massage (L22,000 for the complete works, or you can go half
way at L15,000).

SHOPPING IN FIUGGI

Fiuggi Fonte plays host to all the smart shops (and shoppers). For
the best choice head for **Corso Nuova Italia**, where you'll find
Diego Cataldi (Credit cards: AE, DC, MC, V), bulging with good
things from designer watches, accessories and leather goods to
silver, lovely stained glass ornaments by Torrigiani, and glass by
Verrini. The prices are not to be sniffed at. If you've got a sweet
tooth, visit the **Pasticceria** at No 23: a wonderful pastry and candy
store with all kinds of delicious treats including divine coconut
cookies which can be packaged to travel. You can also pick up a
bottle or two of the local water.

WHERE TO EAT IN FIUGGI

Pizzeria La Grotta, Via G. Garibaldi 2, Fiuggi Citta   L
Tel: (0775) 54072
Open: Daily noon–3pm 7pm–midnight (or when the customers
   leave)
Credit cards: AE, MC, V

A good excuse to make the trip to Fiuggi Citta, this restaurant is
down a flight of steps off the main square in the medieval heart of
town. There's a pretty vine-draped patio with cheerful checkered
tablecloths for outdoor dining, while the inner sanctum is a maze
of five small rooms linked by arched doorways, the stone walls
hung with antique farm tools. On cool evenings the central fireplace and hearty cuisine provide warmth and atmosphere. Everything on the menu is freshly prepared, so take the time to enjoy
your meal Italian-style. Starters include melon with fresh cheese;
the *penne al Gorgonzola* is a delicious cheesy pasta dish or there's
steak, lamb and homemade sausages. No English spoken, but the
friendly staff are anxious to help.

WHERE TO STAY IN FIUGGI

Hotel Boschetto, Corso Nuova Italia 6, Fiuggi Fonte   **LL**
Tel: (0775) 55771   Closed: Jan–Feb
Amenities: ☎ 🅿 ✗ ⚲ Credit cards; AE, DC, MC, V

Centrally located opposite the entrance to L'Aqua de Bonifacia VIII, the Boschetto is a relaxing haven after a day on the road. Passing from the elegant wood and marble reception area to the cool beige and peach decor in the bedrooms, you'll feel fully revived in no time. Each spacious room has bath/shower and a small balcony or patio. There's a garden and flowery terrace downstairs and the attractive dining area is up a spiral staircase. Meals can be included with the price of a room, and reception staff are happy to arrange spa appointments for guests.

*Leaving Fiuggi Fonte, follow signs for **Anagni** out of **Piazza Giuseppe Frascara**. Turn right ½km later, then keep left when the road divides 1km after that. This brings you out on the easy-to-follow **Via Casilina (ss155)** bordered by wooded hills. You drive through **Parca Selva Nature Reserve** after 8kms; beyond that the road veers left for **Roma**.* It's a straight run to *Cave (28kms) and a further 5kms to the edge of **Palestrina**. After ¾km, bear off to the right signposted **Palestrina**, up a narrow and unpromising street (**Via della Stazione**) for a further ¾km to a junction facing a stone wall. Turn right; as the road curves left you can either continue straight ahead for **Palazzo Barberini**, or around to the left for the **Duomo**. The route to the Duomo leads to a parking area in **Piazzale Santa Maria d'Angeli**. Continue on foot down **Via Anicia** to the cathedral and **Tourist Office** in Piazza Regina Margherita. (Open: Mon–Sat 9am–1pm 4pm–6pm in summer.)*

PALESTRINA

Legend has it that the original settlement of *Praeneste* was founded by Telegonus, son of Ulysses and Circe. It was the site of a famous sanctuary that Sulla destroyed in 82BC. He then rebuilt on a monumental scale, and the medieval city now occupies much of the site. Dedicated to the goddess of fortune, the temple's terraces climb the hill in four levels to a sanctuary area in Piazza della Cortina, across the road from Palazzo Colonna-Barberini. Bomb damage in 1944 exposed a wealth of interesting information including the fact that concrete had been used in the construction: a world first. Current excavations mean large parts of the lower temple are closed to the public. Down in Piazza Regina Margherita, there's a monument to composer Pierluigi Palestrina, born here in the 16th century. His hometown celebrates with an annual music festival held in May–June. The Romanesque **Duomo San Agapito** (cathedral – open daily 9am–1pm 4:30pm–7pm) dates from the fifth century, when it was built over a Roman temple. It was later reconstructed in the 12th century.

WHAT TO SEE IN PALESTRINA

Museo Nazionale Archeologico Prenestino and **Tempio della Fortuna**, Palazzo Colonna-Barberini, Piazza della Cortina
Open: Tues–Sun 9am–1½hrs before sunset   Closed: Mon
Admission: L1,000

The museum is housed in a restored 17th-century summer palace of the Barberini family, although the Colonnas founded the original structure at least 500 years earlier on top of the sanctuary. Glass windows set in the marble floors reveal column bases covered by the new building. On the next level there's a scale replica of the first *Tempio della Fortuna Primigenia*, thereafter the displays take over. These provide a visual journey through the sanctuary's history from its earliest origins in the eighth century BC to its gradual disappearance in the fourth century AD. There's pottery, miniature works of art in bronze, carved capitals and the fabulous *Nile Flood* mosaic which once adorned one of the sanctuary walls. From the museum walk to the temple's upper sanctuary lined with truncated columns for a view down to the terraces below; you can also visit the remains of the theater.

SHOPPING IN PALESTRINA

If you're in Piazza Regina Margherita, look in the windows of No 11, **Orafo**, an excellent modern jeweler with terrific designs in gold and silver, some set with precious stones. Palestrina is famous for beaten copper and there's a great little workshop, **De Paolis Benito**, Piazza della Cortina 3, tucked into the wall of the Palazzo Colonna-Barberini (open Mon–Sat, also Sun am in summer). Most of the stock is modern and made in the workshop next door: pots and pans (L35,000), urns, bowls and mini-colanders (L8,000). There are also a few antique pieces including 18in-wide platters (L45,000) which could easily fit into a suitcase. On the way out of town there's usually a roadside market where you'll find other bits and pieces of copper and embroidery stitched in old-fashioned "Palestrina Point".

WHERE TO EAT IN PALESTRINA

Ristorante Stella, Piazzale della Liberazione 3   L
Tel: (06) 9558172
Open: Daily 1pm–4pm 7pm–10pm
Credit cards: AE, DC, V

This is a modern bare brick restaurant with tiled floors and small tables sprouting breadsticks. You can select *antipasto* from the

center table, choosing from various cold dishes or salads. For
starters try *scamorza alla griglia* (melted cheese with prosciutto
ham). There are omelettes, seafood risotto, numerous pastas and
meat dishes. For dessert they offer Antica Gelateria del Corso ice
creams, which are delicious and definitely a name to look out for
on your travels.

ROUTE B: Palestrina – Rome

*Make your way down to **Via degli Arcioni** which runs one rung
below Piazza Regina Margherita and follow it to the end. Turn left
onto busy **Viale Pio XII**; then right for **Roma** at the bottom of the
hill. This is **Via Casilina (ss155)**. At **San Cesareo**, 8kms later, you
turn right for **Roma**. Also known as the ss6, this road runs straight
into Rome, after the GRA (city ring road) almost 20kms later.
Routes to the town center are marked **Roma-Centro**.*

ROUTE C: Palestrina – Frascati (25 kms)

*Make your way back down to **Viale Pio XII**, and turn right at the
bottom of the hill for **Roma**. The **Via Casilina** carries you to a
junction 8kms later; you turn right for **Roma** into **San Cesareo**. Just
over 1km later, turn left for **Montecompatri**, swiftly abandoning the
vineyards for the woodlands below town. Drive through the outskirts of Montecompatri following signs for **Frascati** and zigzagging
down into **Monte Porzio** 3kms later. It's a mere 3kms to a set of
traffic lights on the edge of Frascati; turn left here for the town
center, climbing up past a small park on the right. Take a right at
the top and follow the road down into **Piazzale G. Marconi** where
you can park and visit the **Tourist Office**, Piazza Marconi 1. (Tel:
(06) 9420331. Open: Mon–Sat am summer 9am–1pm 4pm–7pm;
winter 9am–1pm 3:30pm–6:30pm.)*

*   *   *

See **Tour 2 – Route A** (page 146) for full details of **Frascati** and
the **Castelli Romani** drive.

TOUR 2: THE CASTELLI ROMANI (80kms)

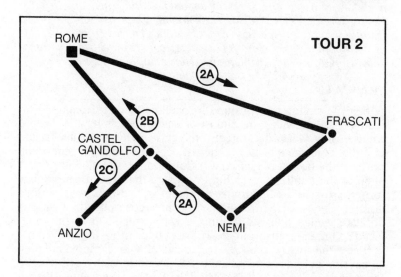

A tour of the Castelli Romani region south of the Eternal City is considered a must for all visitors to Rome. Along the way you can stop off in the famous wine town of **Frascati**, and sample fresh air amid the lakeside scenery of **Lago Albano** or **Lago di Nemi** while enjoying a leisurely lunch. You'll see medieval castles and villas, including the Pope's summer residence at **Castel Gandolfo** where you might choose to spend the night before returning to Rome or linking up with **Tour 3** for a day at the beach near **Anzio**.

ROUTE A: Rome – Frascati – Marino – Nemi – Albano – Castel Gandolfo

*The starting point in Rome is **Piazza Barberini**, where you take **Via delle Quattro Fontane** and drive straight ahead for 1km to **Santa Maria Maggiore**. Keep right of the church and exit onto **Via Merulana** which runs south to **Piazza di San Giovanni in Laterano**. Bear round, following the traffic flow to the right. Ahead you'll see a row of arches: take the first on the right driving down **Via Appia Nuova** to the traffic circle at **Piazza dei Re di Roma**. Take the exit after the continuation of Via Appia Nuova into Largo Vercelli, then turn immediately right. **Via Vercelli** is a residential street leading down to **Via Tuscolana** where you turn right.*

*From now on it's easy, if slow, as you follow Via Tuscolana (ss215) out through an old city gate 3kms later, and past **Cinecitta**, the Italian Hollywood tucked behind a long orange wall on the left*

*3½kms further on. Just after the GRA 1½kms later, bear off to the left for **Frascati** where you arrive after 8kms. Drive up through a clutch of hotels for 2kms to an intersection, then turn left for **Centro** to emerge in **Piazzale G. Marconi**. Opposite, by the streets leading into the town center, you'll find the **Tourist Office**, Piazzale G. Marconi 1. (Tel: (06) 9420331. Open: Mon–Sat am summer 9am–1pm 4pm–7pm; winter 9am–1pm 3:30pm–6:30pm.)*

FRASCATI

A favorite summer playground for well-connected Romans, Frascati's beautiful villas are almost as celebrated as its crisp, white wines. Above Piazzale Marconi, the classical 17th-century facade of **Villa Aldobrandini** heads the list, designed by Giacomo della Porta at the behest of Cardinal Aldobrandini. The villa itself isn't open to the public, but it's fun to explore the overgrown gardens turned over to small groups of roaming livestock and curious visitors. The great central alleyway is now covered with a curious box-like wedge of trees forming a leafy tunnel up to the main facade. (Free permits from the Tourist Office Mon–Fri 9am–1pm.)

Below the square, the former gardens of Villa Torlonia are now a beautiful public park containing the dramatic **Teatro delle Acque** fountains by Carlo Maderna. Moving into the town center, **Piazza San Pietro** is edged on one side by a wonderfully ornate 18th-century cathedral by Girolamo Fontana who also designed the decorative fountain. To the left of the main entrance, there's a memorial to the Young Pretender, Bonnie Prince Charlie. His brother Henry rose in the Church to become Bishop of Frascati.

If you feel it would be a crime to leave town without a drop of Frascati wine passing your lips, head for the **Gran Caffe Roma**, Piazza Roma. You'll see the outdoor terrace near the entrance to the town center. This is a great place to watch the world go by with a glass of wine and a tasty club sandwich if you're in the mood for a snack.

SHOPPING IN FRASCATI

If you can't buy a villa, then the next most obvious local speciality is wine, so call in at **Dante Tosti**, Piazza San Pietro 8 (Credit cards: DC). There's a good choice of wines at varying prices available by the bottle or crate. The typical round bottomed bottles in straw containers make great souvenirs if you can keep them that long. Off the square, **Ellisse**, Via Bezzecca 12, specializes in hand-crafted items including glass, pretty wooden boxes and some handsome painted bowls and lamps. Tucked around the back you'll find a small antique-cum-oriental bric-à-brac shop, **Antichita Paola Correani**, Via Piave 40. It's an eclectic mixture of 19th-century furniture, ornamental headboards, ceramics and wooden crafts including toys imported from India. On the way back to the main square, **Blasi**, Via C. Battisti 11 (AE, DC, V), carries a small selection of colorful Gubbio crockery.

WHERE TO STAY IN FRASCATI

The main hotels are all situated out of town on Via Tuscolana, but if you'd like somewhere right in town try:

Bellavista, Piazza Roma 2   LL
Tel: (06) 9421068   Open: Year round
Amenities: ☎ Ⓜ ◻   Credit cards: AE, DC, MC, V

The friendly owners have recently revamped this pleasant old *pensione* located on the third floor of the Lloyd Adriatico building near the Tourist Office. There's a rather temperamental elevator, so best you climb the marble staircase to reception. All 23 rooms have bath/shower and the views across the Roman plain are terrific.

*Make your way back to the intersection below Piazzale G. Marconi, and turn left for **Marino** following a well-signposted route through **Grottaferrata** to a traffic circle 4kms later. Take the first exit. You'll reach Marino 2kms later (the signboard's well hidden by an oleander bush). There's an arrow to a small parking area on the right ½km ahead if you'd like to stop for a look around or bite to eat. (At the bottom of the street you can see the Fontana dei Mori in **Piazza Matteoti**.)*

MARINO

There are several good reasons to stop off in Marino: one is good food; another is the famous wine. If it happens to be the first Sunday in October, that fountain you see before you is running with wine for the annual grape festival. Quite a thought isn't it? Sadly, these happy coincidences occur all too rarely and it's probably not October, let alone the first Sunday in that bounteous month. Walk down to the fountain in any case and spare a thought for the chained moors which make up its base. If there are shoppers among you, check out **La Rua**, Via Cavour (Credit cards: AE, DC) on the right of the square. Here you'll find gorgeous hand-painted, multi-colored Milanese glass, plus silverware and a small selection of figurative china. Walk down **Corso Trieste**, the main street to the town center, and you'll reach pretty **Piazza San Barnaba** with a fountain, viewing platform and restored 17th-century church. A little further down on the right, you'll also find one of the two restaurants suggested here.

WHERE TO EAT IN MARINO

Ristorante Quattro Mori, Piazza Lepanto 2   **LL**
Tel: (06) 9386178
Open: Thur–Tues noon–4pm 7pm–midnight   Closed: Wed
Credit cards: v

This cozy restaurant is "un antica tradizione nel cuore di Marino" which translates to "an old tradition in the heart of Marino". In short, the locals have given it the thumbs up. There are two small outdoor seating areas decorated with flowers and a simple whitewash and pine-panelled dining room. The food is great with delicious pasta, and fishy specialities such as *scampi Mazzancalle* or *risotto alla pescatora*. Helpful service in a relaxed atmosphere.

Trattoria Il Corazziere da Mario, Via A. Fratti 21   **L**
Tel: (06) 9388978 – no reservations
Open: Wed–Mon noon–2pm 6:30pm–10pm   Closed: Tues
No credit cards

You'll have no trouble finding the orange facade of this popular spot just off Piazza Matteoti. Through the dining room there's outdoor seating on an attractive wicker-shaded terrace. It overlooks the vineyards and woodlands of the valley below; get here early for the best tables. You'll rub shoulders with all sorts from builders to local businessmen and the equally diverse menu ranges from pizzas to veal or steak dishes. They also serve very good salads. Service is efficient, and there's a special emphasis on the excellent dry local wines.

*In **Piazza Matteoti**, take the narrow lane on the far right, bearing round to the left; then keep right for **Via dei Laghi** downhill to an intersection (1¼kms). Turn left for **Nemi/Velletri**. The road climbs along above **Lago d'Albano** plentifully supplied with parking areas where you can pull over and admire the view. Exactly 5kms later you'll spot the left turn for **Rocca di Papa**; 1¼kms along this road is the turn-off for the toll road up to **Monte Cavo** (L800).*

MONTE CAVO

As you climb the toll road up the mountain (4½kms) you'll see the flagstones of the Roman *Via Sacra* which led to the Temple of Jupiter at the summit. In the fifth century BC this was a meeting place of the Latin League. Delegates from the 40-odd member cities came here to perform religious rites and to discuss trade, defense and political matters on neutral territory. In the fourth century BC, Rome assumed leadership of the other members, creating the independent region of Latium. Later the temple was replaced by a monastery. Now it's a scenic restaurant with spectacular views stretching off to the horizon. Return to the main road, turning right into Rocca di Papa where you'll see the shrine of **Madonna del Tufo**. A traveler is said to have halted a landslide at this spot by invoking the spirit of Our Lady. At a fork in the road, keep right following signs for **Centro**, parking where you can and continue on foot.

ROCCA DI PAPA

The highest and, arguably, the prettiest of the Castelli Romani, Rocca di Papa is a maze of centuries-old cobbled streets and overhanging houses balanced precariously on the hillside. Piles of fresh fruit and vegetables decorate shop fronts, while some of the tiny restaurants display whole roast pigs outside the door. When the town shuts up for siesta nothing stirs except the odd slinking cat and you really have found a secret corner of Italy only an hour from Rome.

*Return to the main **Via dei Laghi** and turn left. Less than 3kms later take a right for **Nemi**. At the junction ¹/₄km ahead, fork left driving steeply downhill for 4kms. You'll pick up signs for **Nemi-Centro** which lead through the town center and out by a portal belonging to the ninth-century Ruspoli Castle. A cobbled road, the **Via Tempio di Diana**, rattles you down the narrowest lanes past orchards, terraces of vines and flower nurseries to the lakeshore (3kms).*

LAGO DI NEMI

The lake was once a volcanic crater, later filled by rain and local springs. Long ago, when the pagan temple and woods on the lakeshore were clearly reflected in the striking blue waters, it was known as the Mirror of Diana. In 1929, the lake was partially drained, revealing two boats dating from Caligula's reign in the first century AD. It's thought they were used to ferry visitors across to the temple for important ceremonies. The boats were destroyed in 1944. In June, the valley swarms with fruit pickers gathering the famed sweet wild strawberries the size of a button (a small one at that). Very few get taken home; they're just too good once tasted.

*From the junction near the lakeshore you can turn left to circle the lake and inspect the ruined site of **Tempio di Diana**, rejoining the route in Genzano; or keep right, climbing to an intersection in **Genzano** 2kms ahead. Turn left at the intersection down a broad cobbled road which leads to the main **Via Appia**. If you feel in need of food with a view:*

WHERE TO EAT IN GENZANO

Ristorante da Titto, Via Fratelli Cervi 1   **L**
Tel: (06) 9398450
Open: Thurs–Tues noon–2.30pm 7pm–10pm   Closed: Wed
Credit cards: AE, DC, MC, V
*Directions: Turn left onto Via Appia in Genzano. Take another left turn ¾km ahead by a large sign for **Da Palozzo***; *the restaurant is 300m ahead on the right.*

Tucked away off the general tourist track down a quiet street, Da Titto overlooks the lake with beautiful views from both the dining room and a large covered patio. Typical, regional cuisine starting with a wonderful *caprese* (tomatoes, mozzarella cheese, fresh basil and olive oil), or there's a savory *pizza crostino*; homemade pastas, a good *filetto florentina* and generous servings of locally-grown mushrooms or strawberries.

*If you're not stopping for a meal in Genzano, turn right onto **Via Appia** and follow signs for **Roma** into **Ariccia**.*

ARICCIA

Via Appia runs straight through Ariccia, once a full member of the Latin League. Unable to resist Roman domination, it became an important camp guarding the approach to Rome. As you drive through, you might like to stop in **Piazza della Repubblica** and visit Bernini's beautiful **Chiesa Santa Maria dell'Assunzione** on the south side of the square (open daily 9am–7pm). Its magnificent double-porticoed facade rises into a splendid dome and the entire church is built in the round. Inside, there's a 17th-century fresco of *The Assumption* by Ambrogio Borgognone. Twin fountains are the centerpiece of the square, while the north side is occupied by **Palazzo Chigi**, built for the Chigi banking family.

*Pope Pius IX's thousand-foot long viaduct carries you from Ariccia into the outskirts of **Albano**. Drive straight down the main street for 1½kms to **Piazza G. Mazzini**, an open square with a bus station on the left. Turn left at the end of the square, and keep over to the right. There's parking here, and the **Tourist Office**, Via Olivella 2. (Tel: (06) 9321323/9320298. Open: Summer only Mon–Sat am 9am–1pm 4pm–6:30pm.)*

ALBANO

Albano's name is a corruption of ancient *Alba Longa*, the name of Emperor Domitian's extensive villa and estate. When built in the first century AD, it stretched from Castel Gandolfo across to present day Albano. Septimius Severus founded a great camp (*Castra Albana*) here in the second century. He also constructed a massive gateway, **Porta Pretoria**, the remains of which you'll see at the end of Via Saffi. It wasn't discovered until the bombing raids of World War II. Off Via Saffi, you should also visit the **Chiesa di Santa Maria della Rotonda** (open daily 9am–7pm), a medieval church created in the ruins of a *nymphaeum* which was once part of Domitian's estate. Since then it's also acquired a fine 13th-century Romanesque belltower. Back at Piazza G. Mazzini, take a moment to look over the belvedere down to the **Villa Comunale** gardens. It's a pleasant walk across the tree-lined lawns where you'll see evidence of a first-century BC villa owned by Caesar's arch-enemy, Pompey.

Just outside Albano, below the viaduct on the road back to Ariccia, is a legendary memorial and the supposed **Tomb of the Horatii and Curiatii**. As the Latin League disintegrated in the face of Roman domination, the inhabitants of Alba Longa tried to cut their losses by pitting three of their champion warriors against three Roman counterparts: Curiatii for Alba; Horatii for Rome. In the first bout, two Horatii fell. In the second, Horatio (Latin for 'one Horatii') cunningly separated the Curiatii then slew them one by one, giving victory to Rome.

*To reach **Castel Gandolfo**, turn left out of Piazza G. Mazzini, then right down a pretty tree-lined road signposted **Frascati**. There's a right turn for **Castel Gandolfo-Centro** 1½kms later. Following directions for **Palazzo Papale**, drive through an archway (past signs for Hotel Castel Vecchio) up to **Piazza della Libertà** and the yellow facade of the Pope's summer cottage. On the right, you'll see a **Tourist Office**, Piazza della Libertà 6. (Tel: (06) 9360340. Open: Summer only Mon–Sat am 9am–1pm 3:30pm–6:30pm.)*

CASTEL GANDOLFO

This attractive village sits on the lip of a volcanic crater pitching steeply into the waters of Lago Albano. It's the ancient site of *Alba Longa*, capital of Aeneas's son Ascanius, and the oldest settlement in Latium. Castel Gandolfo's modern day claim to fame is, of course, hosting the Papal summer retreat – traditionally mid-July to mid-September. There are no visits to the palace which, together with the rest of the estate, maintains the same extraterritorial status as Vatican City. However, the Pope holds an open audience in the courtyard every Sunday at noon during his stay. This gives you a chance to see past the armed police and admire Urban VIII's 17th-century villa designed by Maderna.

You'll find several souvenir shops in the square which have added reproduction-Etruscan ceramics, leather handbags and silk scarves to their repertoire of postcards and frankly garish religious memorabilia. There's also a clutch of handy cafés to stave off dehydration.

WHERE TO EAT IN CASTEL GANDOLFO

Antico Ristorante Pagnanelli, Via A. Gramsci 4   **L**
Tel: (06) 9360004
Open: Wed–Mon noon–2pm 7pm–10pm   Closed: Tues
Credit cards: AE, DC, V

On the street below Piazza della Libertà, this restaurant has French windows opening onto a balcony with superb views of the lake. The cuisine is Roman, and the house speciality is superbly cooked trout. Local wines are just the thing to accompany fish, with a cool bottle of slightly sparkling Frascati top of the list. Friendly, efficient service plus a reasonable command of English makes this a best bet for a pleasantly relaxing break.

WHERE TO STAY IN CASTEL GANDOLFO

Hotel Castel Vecchio, Via Pio 23   **LL**
Tel: (06) 9360308   Open: Year round
Amenities: 🅿 ☎ ✕ ⚲ 🗗 Credit cards: AE, DC, MC, V

This attractive modern villa is situated in a quiet street less than ½km from Piazza della Libertà. Great care has been taken with decor and facilities, from the pretty bedrooms to the gym. Most rooms overlook the lake, and there are several small apartments (bungalows) for four people (two in bunks) with a kitchenette and balcony. There are inner and outer terraces with good views; room rates include a generous breakfast with plenty of fresh fruit and yogurt as well as the traditional staples; the restaurant is open for very reasonably-priced dinners Mon–Thur.

ROUTE B: Castel Gandolfo – Rome

*It's a one-way system out of **Piazza della Libertà** down **Via Massimo d'Azeglio** to a junction. Turn right here, then left after 200m for **Roma/Appia (ss7)**. Twin ranks of Roman pines line the route to **Via Appia** where you turn right for **Roma**. In just 7½kms you drive under the GRA, then follow signs for **Roma-Centro** into the heart of the city.*

ROUTE C: Castel Gandolfo – Aprilia (Anzio)   (45kms)

*Leave the square in Castel Gandolfo and drive down **Via Massimo d'Azeglio**. At the bottom prepare to turn sharp left, retracing your route to **Albano**. Cross Via Appia into **Piazza G. Mazzini** following the traffic around to the left, then exit to the right for **Cecchina/ Anzio**. Follow the signposted route through the lower town, keeping watch for a left turn after a rail bridge ¾km later. This takes you into a residential suburb and across a badly marked junction ¼km ahead, driving uphill to a T-junction opposite a smartly painted gateway 150m later. Turn right, through a small shopping area,* *and leave Albano on ss207. The route to **Anzio** is well-marked through **Cecchina** (4kms ahead) to **Campoleone Scalo**. It's a further 8kms, bypassing **Aprilia**, to the junction with ss148 where this route links with **Tour 3**.*

*   *   *

See **Tour 3 – Route A** (page 156) for details of the route to **Anzio** and north along the coast to **Ostia Antica**.

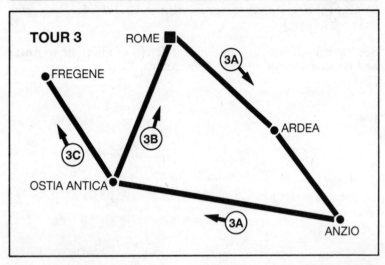

This itinerary has a treat in store for all tastes. Leaving Rome due south for **Anzio**, there's an optional detour to the delightfully picturesque village of **Pratica di Mare** near the ancient sixth-century BC site of *Lavinium* and the sculpture museum in artist Giacomo Manzù's hometown of **Ardea**. Sunseekers can sample the beaches from Anzio north to **Lido di Ostia**, with Roman history on the doorstep at the monumental site of **Ostia Antica** which probably deserves a day trip of its own. With this in mind, you might choose to stay in Anzio overnight after a day on the beach. **Fregene**, on **Route C** (see page 161), is one of the smartest Roman weekend resorts. It's a short drive from Ostia and the first leg of **Tour 4**, the **Via Aurelia**.

ROUTE A: Rome – Pratica di Mare – Ardea – Anzio – Ostia Antica

*Leave Rome from **Piazza Bocca di Verita** (Tempio di Vesta) and take **Via di Greca** onto **Via del Circo Massimo**. At the end of the street turn left onto **Viale Aventino**, preparing to turn right 50m later (signposted **Napoli A2**). Keep tightly to the right and drive down a separate lane from the main traffic flow. This lane leads you straight down **Viale delle Terme di Caracalla**, through parkland for 1½kms, to the four arches of **Porta Ardeatina** which marks the beginning of **Via Cristoforo Colombo**. This broad three-lane road runs through the modern EUR district, past the tall Marconi monument after 5½kms and around the domed **Palazzo dello Sport** stadium where you pick up signs for **Via Pontina (ss148)**. A kilometer* *later, keep in lane for **Pomezia/Aprilia**, driving under the GRA 2kms further on.*

*The dual-lane highway, if not picturesque, is admirably fast and you reach the exit for **Pratica di Mare** 10kms later. If you're in a rush for the beach head straight on towards Aprilia (21kms).*

SIDE TRIP TO PRATICA DI MARE AND ARDEA

*Head off the highway for **Pratica di Mare** and follow a country lane for 10kms. Where the road bears sharp right, you turn left through an archway into the tiny walled village of terracotta houses, each door and window frame edged in yellow.*

PRATICA DI MARE AND LAVINIUM

A five-minute walk around the village which basks in the sun like a sleepy Roman cat is irresistible. Flowers and window grilles decorate house fronts gathered around the central church. Palms and plane trees shade wooden benches and **Caffe Enea** is a good stop for coffee or a cold drink. At the back of the church you'll find a small shop selling fresh mozzarella cheese and salami, eggs (you could probably cook one on the hood of the car when you reach the beach) and other picnic snacks.

To reach **Lavinium**, walk out of the archway, turn right and 50m downhill (on the right), you'll find a gateway and well-marked path leading across a field to the excavations. The sixth-century BC town was founded by Aeneas after his escape from Troy, and named after his wife Lavinia. This was a cult area, the touchstone of Roman religious practice, with a total of 13 altars and the tufa tomb of Aeneas. An inscription dedicated to the Dioscuri (worshippers of Dionysus), who were later outlawed for their orgiastic rituals, suggests that sacrifices may have been performed here at meetings of the Latin League. Aeneas's tomb has yielded an important collection of funerary vases, ornaments and terracotta objects representing various parts of the anatomy: a head, hands and feet among others. This is housed in a private collection currently closed to the public (Borghese Castle, Pratica di Mare. Tel: (06) 9120558). Excavations are still underway, and recent finds include a chamber tomb and the remains of a large bath house.

*From the archway at Pratica di Mare drive straight ahead for ½km to a junction: turn right. There's a small copse of pine trees on the right 2¾kms later where you turn left for **Camposelva**, picking up signs for **Ardea** a little further on. The country road bumps along to the misleadingly named **Nuova Florida** (no palms, no beach) 3kms ahead. After a left-hand corner just under 1km later, you turn left for **Ardea**. This road is even worse, a real test for your hire car's suspension. After 4kms you'll come to an intersection:*

turn right. In 1km there's a row of white railings on your right: turn here and park outside the Manzù museum.

Raccolta Manzù, off Via Laurentina, Ardea
Open: Tues–Fri 9am–7pm, Sat–Sun 9am–1:30pm   Closed: Mon
Admission free
Take your passport with you so they can inscribe your name in the visitors book.

Born in Bergamo in 1908, Giacomo Manzù is one of Italy's most celebrated 20th-century artists. The Friends of Manzù donated this collection to the State in 1979 and it forms part of the Galleria Nazionale d'Arte Moderna in Rome. A sculptor of sublime technical ability, his bronzes cover a range of subjects and styles from the enchanting children in *Giulia e Mileto in carrozza* (1966) to a somber *Porta della Morte* (Door of Death – 1963) for St Peter's in Rome and the abstract theme of *Idea per un monumento*. There's a rugged bust of *John Huston* and the touchingly leggy *Big Striptease* with tumbling stockings and child's hair-bow. You'll find a collection of commemorative medals and coins struck for such diverse events as the 1960 Rome Olympics and the Vatican Council, Picasso-esque gold reliefs and sculpted still lifes in matt gold. Manzù's bust of his personal friend Pope John XXIII (Papa Giovanni), who's revered as one of the most humanitarian and genuinely saintly holders of that office, reveals all the sorrow and resilience in his sturdy face.

Small scale reliefs of the St Peter's door are displayed alongside miniatures of the dying bird and turtle battling with the serpent. There are also examples of the two other great church doors he's completed: Salzburg Cathedral (1958), and St Laurenz in Rotterdam (1964). A new interest in the 1960s was theater design: first the costumes for Stravinsky's *Oedipus Rex*; later *Tristan and Isolde* and *Electra* among others. A series of gouache sketches and collages bear witness to his success in this field.

Turn right out of the museum into Ardea where you take a left for **Aprilia,** *rejoining* **Via Pontina** *(the main route) 4kms later. Via Pontina bypasses Aprilia to the right, and you take the exit for* **Anzio/Nettuno** *onto* **Via Nettuense (ss207),** *passing* **Beach Head War Cemetery** *12½kms later. Surrounded by the oak woods of Bosco de Padriglione, this cemetery is dedicated to the British Forces who lost their lives here during the battles of 1944. There's a church and campanile on your left as you enter* **Anzio** *3kms on, then turn left after ½km for Information and the* **American War Cemetery**. *At a traffic light 300m later (with the rail station on your left), turn right down a palm tree lined street following the yellow* **Information** *signs until you emerge facing the sea. Park the car and walk back to the harbor where you'll find the summer season* **Tourist Office,** *Riviera Zanardelli 105. (Tel: (06) 9846119.)*

ANZIO

An ancient seaport of Volscian origin when it was named *Antium*, Anzio has been a popular resort since Roman times. Coriolanus spent two enforced holidays here, once when he was banished from Rome and again to escape the toga-and-dagger political struggles of the Republican Senate. Arsonist fiddler Nero was born here, and you can visit the remains of his harbor villa, where he hoarded such treasures as the *Maiden of Anzio* (Museo Nazionale Romano) and the *Apollo Belvedere* (Vatican), on the road out of town.

From the busy cafés and restaurants along the harbor, you can look south along the beach to the modern skyline of Nettuno and watch the ferries (three-hour journey) or hydrofoil (one hour) leaving for the island of **Ponza**. This is a favorite weekend spot with good swimming and boat trips around the jagged cliffs. The Anzio Tourist Office has further information and you buy *aliscafi* (hydrofoil) tickets from a yellow caravan on the dock. There are four sailings daily at the weekend; twice daily during the week. Ferries sail daily from June to September.

Anzio's name is synonymous with the Anglo-American landings of 1944 when a beachhead was established under heavy resistance from the Germans. More than 8,000 American troops lost their lives in the offensive. They are buried in the American Military Cemetery near Nettuno where a small museum traces the course of the Italian campaign from 1943 to 1945 (see page 316).

SHOPPING IN ANZIO

Piazza Pia around the church sports a number of useful perfumeries including **Profumeria Bartoli**, Piazza Pia 5 (Credit cards: AE, MC, V), where you can pick up a great Italian beachbag or two in colorful, flowery prints. Opposite is **Pasticceria la Mimosa**, Via XX Settembre 32, full of delicious pastries and some packaged items which make good gifts. The **Positano Shop**, Via Asnanir (AE, MC, V) offers chic swimsuits and resort wear, plus designer suits from Sabbia and Parah. They also run a souvenir shop (directly opposite) stocked with hats, rafts and Anzio T-shirts. **Via Gramsci** should grab your attention, and probably your pocketbook. **Eberhard & Co** at No 7 (AE, DC, V) do a terrific line in rococo-baroque costume jewelry laden with cherubs, bunches of beads, tassles, hearts, bows and ritzy cameos. **No 9** (AE, DC) displays a good gift selection from colored Milanese glass to Italian crystal, silver, reproduction copper utensils and decorative china. Chic Italian and European designs for men and women are the draw at **Il Nostro Bazaar**, No 22 (AE, DC, V). Check out the silk scarves and ties, designer luggage, clothes and accessories.

WHERE TO EAT IN ANZIO

Trattoria da Pierino, Piazza C. Battisti 3   **L**
Tel: (06) 9845680
Open: Tues–Sun noon–3pm 8pm–11pm (10pm in winter)
Closed: Mon
Credit cards: DC

Sit outside if you can and appreciate the fresh breeze off the harbor; if you can't, the wood-panelled interior is lit by large windows and there will be flowers on the table. No surprise that fresh fish is the speciality around here, but the *antipasto di mare* is something else – try it. Be prepared to select your fish from a tray before it's cooked for you: you can pick the ugliest mother on offer and it'll come back tasting superb. Excellent service and generous portions ensure you won't be disappointed or go hungry.

Il Turcotto Ristorante, Riviera Mallozzi 44   **LL**
Tel: (06) 9846340
Open: Fri–Wed noon–3pm 7:30pm–10:30pm
Closed: Thur and Jan
No credit cards

A little way out of the center, Il Turcotto perches on the rocks overlooking Nero's Grottoes. It's named after its Spanish founder, and present day patron Enrico Garcia is the sixth generation to run it. The exterior is shabby, but inside three windows open onto the view, there are shell-decorated pillars, abundant climbing plants and a patio where King Farouk used to dine surrounded by his entourage. Signor Garcia's two fishing smacks supply the kitchens, so there's a huge choice of imaginative fish dishes. You can start with *cannelloni alla Turcotto* (fish-filled pasta topped with octopus, mussels and prawns). The *antipasto di mare* is so enormous it could easily serve two with generous portions of clams, prawns, cuttle fish, squid stuffed with fish and a superb batter-fried delicacy containing anchovies, cheese and mortadella. The chef recommends fish charcoal grilled (*alla griglia*).

WHERE TO STAY IN ANZIO

Grand Hotel Dei Cesari, Via Mantova 3   **LL**
Tel: (06) 9844353   Open: Year round
Amenities: ☎ 🖵 ✕ ♀ ⇄ 🗖   Credit cards: AE, DC, MC, V

A large and pleasant, if not exactly "grand", hotel situated 2kms from the town center on the road to Lido di Ostia. You'll find over 100 recently decorated modern rooms all with bath/shower and small balconies which overlook the beach; a spacious peach and gray-tiled reception area scattered with carpets, palms and seating areas; and outside, there's a terrace with tables and chairs.

The dining room is large but screens of vine leaves afford a measure of privacy, and the Italian-international menu is attractive and well presented. Good facilities include a tunnel under the road to a private beach annex and Olympic-size pool; sauna and massage are available; plus a discotheque in summer.

From the center of Anzio follow signs for **Roma** *back to the railroad station where you turn left and soon pick up signs for* **Ostia** *(straight on). There's a sign for* **Villa e Grottes di Nerone** *(Nero's Villa and Grottoes) ³⁄₄km ahead; turn left here if you wish to visit the site.* **Via Ardeatina** *(or* **Via Severiana***) runs right along the coast to Lido di Ostia. If you're looking for a good stretch of beach, just under 5kms from the turn-off to Nero's Villa there's an ERG gas station on the right before you reach* **Lavinio***: turn off down a narrow road on the left. You'll find a section of public (free) beach right next to a pay beach. The pay beaches are cheap (approx. L2,000 per person) and often preferable to the free beaches as you can hire sun loungers and use family-style restaurants in the facility.*

The road cuts inland at **Lavinio***, then returns to the coast 24kms later. For the next 11kms a long section of dunes line a public beach which runs all the way into* **Lido di Ostia***. Cross straight over a traffic circle on the outskirts of Ostia, and continue along the beachfront for 4kms to a mini traffic circle. Turn right, following the small sign to* **Via del Mare/Roma***. The pines provide a welcome canopy as you drive out of town, keeping in lane for Rome for 4kms. At a traffic light you'll see signs for* **Ostia Antica***. To reach the site bear off slightly to the right, looping left to a second light and across Via del Mare to a junction where you turn left. The entrance to the site is 300m along on the right opposite* **Castello di Giulio II***.*

Scavi di Ostia Antica
Open: Tues–Sun Summer 9am–7pm; Winter 9am–4pm
Closed: Mon
Museum: Tues–Sun Summer 9am–1pm 2pm–4pm Winter 9am–1pm   Closed: Mon
Admission: L2,000 inc. museum

The name Ostia comes from the Latin *ostium* (mouth). Rome's ancient trading port was built close to the mouth of the Tiber, and linked to the city by Via Ostiensis which runs parallel to the modern, more prosaically named, Via del Mare. It's said that if you only have time to visit Pompeii or Ostia Antica, then visit the latter: its relatively recent excavation (early this century) means it's still in excellent condition and the process of discovery isn't over yet. The site is enormous; thus far around 35 hectares have been uncovered, probably half the city at the height of its power when it housed 100,000 souls busily engaged in building, trading, worship and entertainment. Ostia's value to the study of Roman urban life is incalculable.

It's estimated that the city was founded around the fourth or possibly early third century BC. Initially, Ostia was a small port and unimportant trading post which scratched a living from the salt marshes. It grew steadily through the first century AD with help from Emperors Augustus, Claudius and Nero. Trajan added a "Trajan ditch", or basin, which regulated the flow of water from the Tiber to ensure safe anchorage on the Tyrrhenian Sea. This increased trade and spread wealth: Antonius Pius added baths, while Agrippa and Septimius Severus contributed a theater.

Off the main street, **Decumanus Maximus**, you'll find beautiful mosaics decorating the Terme di Nettuno (Neptune's Baths) in front of the barracks. Via della Fortuna contains a Roman tavern with a mosaic welcome mat exhorting customers to drink their fill. **Piazzale delle Corporazione**, the business center, was surrounded by 70 offices which housed shippers, foreign representatives, grain dealers and craftsmen. Each trade corporation was identified by its own mosaic symbol. Next you'll come to the **Theater** where three marble masks adorn a wall. The main street continues to the **Forum**, the heart of the city, with temples to north and south; baths to the east; and the **Curia** (senate) to the west. Follow the arrows round the site and you'll find the massive warehouses (*horrea*) for grain storage. The second-century **Horrea Epagathiana et Epaphroditana** once belonged to two freed slaves – as you'll see, they came a long way.

The museum is a must – visit it before the ruins. It's packed with finds including terracotta pottery, sculpture, votive ornaments, sarcophagi and carvings depicting scenes from everyday life.

ROUTE B: Ostia Antica – Rome

*Return to **Via del Mare** (ss8) in the direction of Rome and drive through **Ancilia**. The River Tiber runs alongside the road for several kilometers before you reach the GRA. Follow Via del Mare running west of the EUR towards **Roma-Centro**.*

ROUTE C: Ostia Antica – Fregene – Via Aurelia   (40kms)

*Leaving the site at Ostia Antica, turn away from Rome and continue to a junction ½km later. Here you turn right for **Fiumicino** (A12), around the edge of the ruins. Cross the Tiber after 2kms, and keep straight ahead for the airport (A12) for 4kms to a traffic circle. Exit right for **Roma**, driving around the airport to a second traffic circle and right turn for Roma onto the highway signposted **Civitavecchia** (A12). After 5kms you join the A12, racing swiftly cross-country for 12kms to the exit for **Fregene**. (The toll gate will relieve you of L1,000). Drive straight onto **Maccarese** (2kms) where you turn left. Take a right after a bridge 300m ahead; and again 2kms later. You* *enter Fregene with the beach straight ahead. Halfway down the tree-lined alley you can take a left (following a sign for Hotel Villa Fiorita) onto the main shopping street. Look on the right for the summer **Tourist Office**, Via Castellamare 58. (Tel: (06) 6460596.)*

FREGENE

Colonized back in 245BC, Fregene occupies the site of Etruscan *Fregenal*. Nowadays, it's colonized every summer by smart, contemporary Romans intent on avoiding the less exclusive crowds south of the Tiber estuary. Enclosed by scented sea-pine forest, Fregene is a fashionable resort with a number of lovely villas scattered under the trees and a fine white sandy beach. You'll find good shopping on the main street, Via Castellamare; and the cheery local bar/ice cream parlour **Bon Caffe Bondolfi**, which serves special coffees and ices until late in summer. The nightlife is good too, with keen clubbers driving all the way from Rome to catch the action (Roman clubs often shut July–August). This is a great stop-over before you pick up **Tour 4** on Via Aurelia in the morning, or stay for a few days to brush up your tan.

WHERE TO STAY/WHERE TO EAT IN FREGENE

La Conchiglia, Lungomare Ponente 4 LL
Tel: (06) 6460229   Open: Year round
Amenities: ☎ 📺 🅿 ✕ ⍩ Credit cards: AE, DC, V

This hotel requires a minimum stay of three days, so it's not an overnighter. However, if you're planning a few days at the beach you're only a stone's throw from the shore at the end of the main street into town. Soothing modern brown and white decor; 36 comfortable rooms with bath/shower and a pleasant restaurant (full board is included in the room rate). You've also got free entry into the Lido pay beach across the road.

Villa Fiorita, Via Castellamare 86 LL
Tel: (06) 6460435   Open: Year round
Amenities: ☎ 🅿 ✕ ⍩ Credit cards: AE, DC, MC, V

Right on the main street, Villa Fiorita's garden is a lush mixture of flowers, manicured lawns with shady trees and a generous sprinkling of outdoor tables. Both the reception area and bedrooms favor cool blue/green decor, comfortable modern furniture plus the odd antique. There's an open fireplace crackling in winter. Good pasta and fish dishes are served in the dining room with outdoor seating in summer. Backed by pine forest, the hotel is quiet, central and welcoming.

*Leave Fregene and retrace your route to **Maccarese**. Bypass the old village with the railroad tracks to your left, and drive on through* *a built-up area to a modern bridge 2½kms later. Exit left off the traffic circle in the middle of the bridge, crossing the railroad. Continue out of town, under the A12 1km further on, until you see the* **Via Aurelia** *roadbridge 4½kms later. Immediately after the bridge turn left: this country road joins the Aurelia at* **Aranova** *(2kms).*

*   *   *

See **Tour 4 – Route A** (page 163) for details of the route onward to **Bracciano** via Ladispoli and Cerveteri.

TOUR 4: TAKING TO THE WATER (125kms)

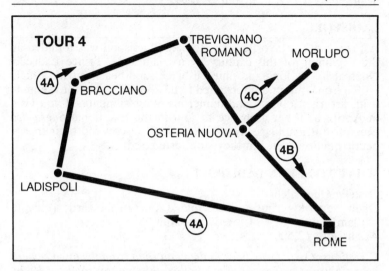

This tour takes you west of Rome to the seaside resort of **Ladispoli**, north to the ancient Etruscan necropolis at **Cerveteri** and encircles beautiful **Lake Bracciano** in an easy day's drive. There are a couple of hotels listed along the route in case you feel inclined to stay over for sun or watersports before returning to Rome or linking up with **Tour 5** at Osteria Nuova.

ROUTE A: Rome – Ladispoli – Cerveteri – Bracciano – Trevignano Romano – Osteria Nuova

*Our tour commences on **Via della Conciliazione**, driving west towards the Vatican. Bear left around **Piazza San Pietro**, and keep left into **Piazza Sant'Uffizio**. At the traffic light, turn right for **Porta Cavalleggeri** onto **Via Gregorio VII** and drive under a pair of bridges. The splendors of the Vatican are replaced by residential suburbs as you continue to **Piazza Pio XI** 2kms further on. Keep straight ahead following a small blue sign for **ss1 Aurelia**, driving uphill for ³/₄km. Keep right at the top of the hill; then move to the left lane, turning left ¹/₄km later onto **Via Aurelia**.*

*The broad boulevard transforms into a fast divided highway. Bound for **Civitavecchia**, it leads out of the sprawling suburbs into the eccentrically sculpted countryside for 24kms to **Palidoro**. An uneasy truce of smallholdings and billboards lines the next 8kms to the left turn for Ladispoli. Leave the ss1 here, entering Ladispoli 1km later. It's ¹/₂km to the main square; park under the trees. For information in the summer season, cross the road and turn down by the **Gran Bar**. Take the first right, passing Hotel Villa Margherita* *on your left, and ask at the **Tourist Office** (Pro Loco), Via Duca degli Abruzzi 149. (Tel: (06) 9913049.)*

LADISPOLI

A town that's a favorite with Romans, Ladispoli was founded at the beginning of this century by its namesake, Prince Ladislao Odescalchi. Its long and unusual black sand beaches with a high (70%) iron content are reckoned to be a surefire cure for rheumatism, arthritis, obesity and numerous other ailments. If you visit in April you'll get a chance to join in the traditional *Sagra del Carciofo* (artichoke festival). We haven't discovered their therapeutic qualities yet, but they sure taste good.

WHAT TO SEE IN LADISPOLI

Castello Odescalchi
Open: Sep–May Thur & Sun. Guided tours of the garden only at
   10am and 2pm   Closed: Jun–Aug
Admission: L2,500

Directions: On the way back to the main road from the town center, bear right just before a bridge. Follow this bumpy road for ¼km to the castle gates on the right.
Originally built by the Orsini family, this castle was used as a refuge by 16th-century Pope Leone X to foil a kidnapping attempt by Turkish pirates. Later it passed to the princely Odescalchi family, perhaps the most noble Roman dynasty, who converted the castle and its gardens in spectacular style. Centuries on, the gardens are still a delight. They featured in scenes from John Huston's screen epic *La Bibbia* (The Bible), and have crept into several movies from Italy's Roberto Rossellini (he spent part of his childhood here). Guided tours are few and far between (see above – closed in high summer), but keen garden-lovers shouldn't miss the magnificent displays of exotic plants, California cypresses, palm trees, Australian eucalypts, Japanese specialities and much more.

SHOPPING IN LADISPOLI

Rather limited after the delights and excesses of Rome. Souvenir hunters and those in need of lightweight gifts to take home might profit from a visit to the **Coral Shop**, Via Duca degli Abruzzi 131 (Credit cards: AE). You'll find a good stock of attractive multicolored coral jewelry from necklaces (L90,000–370,000) to earrings (L24,000) and rings (L13,000). Other useful extras such as postcards, beachwear, sun oil and toys can be found at **Leonardo di Monte & Figli**, Via V. Cantoni 4, and Piazza della Vittoria 17.

WHERE TO EAT IN LADISPOLI

Ristorante Cielo e Mare, (Hotel Villa Margherita,   **LL**
4th floor) Via Duca degli Abruzzi 147
Tel: (06) 9929089
Open: Apr–Nov daily 12:30pm–3pm 8pm–10pm
Closed: Dec–Mar
Credit cards: AE, DC, MC, V

Take the elevator from the first floor for an excellent view of the Tyrrhenian Sea en route to the "Sky-and-Sea" of the restaurant's title. Artful decor complements the location with large aquaria, pictures of seagulls and tile mosaics of fish. The 30 tables sport blue and green tablecloths, flowers and bowls of seasonal fruit. Fresh fish serves as the house speciality accompanied by an excellent pesto sauce if you're lucky. There's a full menu of *antipasto*, pasta, fish and desserts. Tourist prices, but good food to complement the great view.

Ristorante Sora Olga, Via Odescalchi 99   **LL**
Tel: (06) 9929088
Open: Thur-Tues noon–3pm 8pm–11pm   Closed: Wed
Credit cards: AE, DC, MC, V

No sea view, but this restaurant, with a large printed marine mural on one wall, does have a seaside appeal. There are 16 tables in two rooms, with wood panelling and watercolors of sea scenes along three walls. The menu kicks off with *antipasto di mare* or fish soup, then spaghetti with mussels, followed by a fish dish with rice. Tasty, filling and good value all round.

Gran Bar Nazionale, Piazza della Vittoria 19   **L**
Open: Daily until late
No credit cards

This coffee bar/snack shop has a shoal of small tables set up in a corner of the main square to accommodate summer crowds. It's a good location for a spot of people-watching. You can take in all the local characters and resort activities over a cool drink or an ice cream.

WHERE TO STAY IN LADISPOLI

Hotel Villa Margherita, Via Duca degli Abruzzi 147   **LL**
Tel: (06) 9929089   Closed: Dec–Mar
Amenities: ☎ 🅿 ✕ ⦿ Credit cards: AE, DC, MC, V

This modern hotel is located in a quiet but central part of town off the main square next to the Tourist Office. You enter by a narrow brick driveway flanked by potted plants, white tables and swinging chairs beneath the trees. Eighty spotless and compact rooms offer private bath/shower, terraces overlooking the ocean and central heating; plus there's a sunny breakfast area directly behind the entrance overlooking a garden.

*Drive back up **Via L. Odescalchi**, out to the main road and turn left for **Civitavecchia (A12)**. It's 2½kms to the right-turn for **Cerveteri-Necropoli Etrusco**. Here you bear off and reach town 1½kms later. Keep right ½km ahead; then bear left, following signs for **Museo Etrusca**. Drive uphill, past a sign for Bracciano, to the parking lot in the central square beneath medieval city walls. Facing back downhill, there's a fine old building on the right-hand corner which houses the **Tourist Office** (Pro Loco), Via delle Mura Castellane. (Variable opening hours.)*

CERVETERI

Founded in the eighth century BC, ancient Cerveteri (or *Caere*) was a bastion of the Etruscan empire. A major trading city, operating behind the busy ports of *Alisium* (Palo Laziale), *Pyrgi* (Santa Severa) and *Punicum* (Santa Marinella), *Caere* expanded rapidly. The city's galleys helped defeat the Phoenicians and it offered sanctuary to the Vestal Virgins after the Gaulish invasion of Rome in 390BC, then gradually declined in importance. The medieval fortifications around the town center are still shored up by Etruscan remains. Cerveteri's winding streets are crammed with revelers for the annual Flower Festival (last Sunday of May) and Wine Festival (last Sunday in August). The latter includes a parade of decorated trucks, as well as free grapes and wine for all.

WHAT TO SEE IN CERVETERI

Museo Nazionale Cerite (Archeological Museum), Piazza Santa Maria
Open: Tues–Sun Summer 9am–2pm 4pm–7pm; Winter 9am–4pm
Closed: Mon
Admission: L4,000

Follow the well-signposted route up by the Tourist Office to the gates of the former Ruspoli Castle, donated to the State in 1967. The majority of finds from the burial grounds (*necropolis*) of *Caere* are spread throughout the great museums of Europe – notably London and Paris. Nearer home (for the relics), the largest collection is housed in the Villa Giulia in Rome. This, however, is a good introduction to Etruscan culture, commencing in chronological order (oldest first) and running the gamut of treasures from pottery fragments to statuettes and jewelry, plus furniture. Much on display underlines this ancient civilization's firm belief in an afterlife.

Necropoli Etrusca, 2kms north of Cerveteri (follow yellow and black signs)
Open: Tues–Sun 9am–1 hr before dusk   Closed: Mon
Admission: L4,000

Buy an English guide book to the site in the parking area before you embark on this complex voyage of discovery. The clearly indicated route marked by arrows takes several hours to complete, but armed with a booklet you're free to tailor your own tour. Such was the Etruscans's faith in an afterlife, they not only equipped their tombs with all the necessary home and social comforts (as did the Egyptians), they even built burial chambers to replicate their own houses.

The original colorful decor has often faded beyond imagination, but marvel at the elegant doorways, designer roof beams and graceful divans all carved from smooth tufa stone. **Via Sepolcrale Principale** is the main thoroughfare, lined with tombs from the eighth to first centuries BC. Here you'll see the intriguing **Tomba dei Rilievi** (Tomb of Reliefs), built by the influential Matuna family around the mid-sixth century BC. Richly carved with scenes from everyday life, it provides an invaluable historic insight. Other highly individual designs include the Tomb of the Shields and Saddles and the Tomb of the Painted Animals.

Before returning to Cerveteri, cool drinks and snacks are available at the bar opposite the entrance.

SHOPPING IN CERVETERI

If you're in an Etruscan mood after the previous two visits but can't see yourself outbidding the Getty Museum for original antique artworks you might settle for the modern replicas on sale at the **Etruscan Shop Center**, off Piazza Risorgimento. Traditional designs have been incorporated on hanging plates and other pottery pieces (L10–120,000); copies of funeral masks cost around L9,500; or you can select an oxidized bronze (green) statuette (L12–16,000).

WHERE TO EAT IN CERVETERI

Trattoria da Pino a L'Oasi, Via R. Morelli 2   L
Tel: (06) 9953482
Open: Tues–Sun 1pm–4pm 7pm–11pm   Closed: Mon
No credit cards

On the southern edge of town as you approach from Ladispoli, this restaurant occupies a large modern house with front and side yards enclosed by trees and hedges. There are about 30 tables indoors; 15 outdoors on the side lawn. Windows all around give the place a light, open feeling and there's a large open oven where you can see the chef preparing food. Specialities of the house include fresh fish, homemade pasta and great desserts temptingly displayed by the entrance. Do try the delicious *tiramisu*: a cream pudding with cocoa-espresso coffee. The staff speak English.

*From the parking lot, head downhill past the Tourist Office for 200m, then execute a swift left-right-left onto the **Bracciano** road (ss2). Leaving Cerveteri the road runs along a valley edged with slabs of bare-faced rock interspersed with luxuriant foliage. This gives way to rounded hills and patches of vines. At a junction 16kms further on, cross over for Bracciano and drive under a bridge. There's a terrific view of the 15th-century castle off to your right 200m later. Continue uphill, bearing right for **Cassia/Viterbo** ½km ahead. Turn right at the top of the street. You'll soon reach **Piazza Giuseppe Mazzini** at the foot of the castle walls.*

BRACCIANO

The popular small resort town of Bracciano sits proudly at the head of Lago di Bracciano, the eighth largest lake in Italy. Above the lakeshore, Bracciano's Old Town is dominated by the imposing **Castello degli Orsini-Odescalchi**, which lays claim to being Italy's finest baronial stronghold. For outdoor types, there's plenty of action on the lake with sailing, windsurfing and fishing: a brief list of possibilities is included below. (Further information available from the Tourist Office which is moving as we go to press.)

WHAT TO SEE AND DO IN BRACCIANO

Castello degli Orsini-Odescalchi, Piazza Giuseppe Mazzini
Open: Tues–Sun for hour-long guided tours (English spoken) four
    times a day.
    Jul–Aug 9am, noon, 4pm, 7pm
    May–Jun, Sep 9am, noon, 3pm, 6pm
    Oct–Apr 10am, noon, 3pm, 5pm
Admission: L5,000

Founded by Napoleone Orsini in 1470 and completed by his son 15 years later, this magnificent Renaissance fortress passed to the Odescalchi family in 1848 – as did many other Orsini-inspired properties. Built in the shape of a pentagon, the battlements link five rounded towers and afford spectacular views across the lake. It's a steep hike up to the 16th-century portal, past a collection of 15th-century frescoes by Antoniazzo Romano, then into the triangular courtyard.

    The tour whisks you through two floors of gorgeous apartments with hand-painted wooden casement ceilings. The ceilings and frescoes took 60 painters nine solid years to complete. Don't miss the portraits of imperious Orsini and Medici profiles; Paolo Giuseppe Orsini married Isabella de'Medici here in 1560. She was later strangled: some say by her jealous husband. The ancient brick floors are laid over the remains of a ruined 11th-century fortress. You'll also find a handsome museum section with a superb collection of armor and antique weaponry.

Sports Opportunities On and Around Lago di Bracciano

The lake covers an area of 58 sq. kms enclosed by the volcanic crater of Monte Sabatino. Its waters are well-stocked with game fish including trout and pike – plus a vast eel population. If you're keen to get out on the lake you can hire various wind-propelled craft, or take a leisurely trip on the sightseeing boat *Sabazia*. Beach bums can hire umbrellas and budding tennis pros can keep their elbow in at several clubs near Bracciano.

Tennis Clubs (call to make reservations; hours and prices vary by season):

Simiorato, Via Settevene Palo
Tel: (06) 9022707

Centro Sportivo Athena, Via Ansuini
Tel: (06) 9023674

Sailing (summer weekends only):

Da Alvaro's near Bracciano's lakeside restaurants
Boats cost around L150,000 for three hours

Windsurfing (Board Sailing), Hobiecats, and Paddleboats:
Rentals on the beach at Bracciano and Trevignano Romano
Costs per hour: Windsurfer L10,000; Hobiecats L30,000; paddleboats L10,000

Beach Equipment:
Again along the beach at Bracciano and Trevignano Romano.
Costs: Beach chairs L5,000 half day; L8,000 entire day; Umbrella L8,000 a day

Sightseeing Boat *(Sabazia):*
Leaves from **Sporting Club Trevignano**, Via Della Reno, Trevignano. It takes about 1½ hours to motor around the lake, stopping at Bracciano and Vicarello.
Cost: L5,000 per person. Five trips a day: three in the morning (before 1pm), two in the afternoon (after 3pm) – times vary. Coffee, drinks and snacks sold on board.

WHERE TO EAT IN BRACCIANO

Both these restaurants are on the lakeshore at the bottom of the hill leading back to Cerveteri.

Ristorante Luccio d'Oro, Lungolago G. Angenti   L
Tel: (06) 9024135
Open: Thur–Tues 1pm–3pm 7pm–midnight   Closed: Wed
No credit cards

This restaurant has an excellent view of the lake, its sunbathers and windsurfers, and you can park along the lake road. There are 12 tables on a deck separated from the beach by an iron railing, plus a small dining room decorated with an Etruscan painting, bright pink and white napery and flowers on every table. The main restaurant is large and open with a patio area for extra seating in the summer season when it offers coffee and snacks to hungry sunbathers. The menu is simple, inexpensive and good; particularly the fresh fish such as trout caught in the lake. A bottle of local wine is good value too.

Casina del Lago, Lago di Bracciano   L
Tel: (06) 9024025
Open: Wed–Mon noon–3pm 7pm–9pm   Closed: Tues
No credit cards

The open-air decking is a popular spot with young windsurfers and sunseekers taking a break from the beach. There's a large indoor restaurant to the right of the bar with long tables suitable for family groups and a casual holiday atmosphere. The menu covers plenty of ground from pasta and seafood to veal, served in plentiful quantities. (The Casina also has rooms, but they're rather expensive considering they don't view the lake.)

Drive downhill on **Via Umberto I** *from the castle and take the first right after 50m. Keep right as the road forks, winding gently down* **Via del Lago** *to the lakeshore and a junction. Turn left for Trevignano, encircling the lake bordered by villas and vines, olive orchards and gargantuan fringes of reeds. Just over 9kms later you'll see a sign on the left for* **Bagni di Vicarello**. *Closed to the public for some time, these ancient springs were favored by the Romans for treating gout and arthritis. It's another 2kms into Trevignano Romano; the parking lot is on the right 1½kms ahead.*

TREVIGNANO ROMANO

This picturesque lakeside village clambers steeply uphill from an enchanting tree-lined esplanade overlooking the glassy-still waters of Lago di Bracciano. Walk up to the **Chiesa dell'assunta**, entering the Old Town through the archway. Follow the ramshackle cobbled Via Umberto I until you pick up signs for the church leading up to the left. From the square outside the church, there's a lovely view over the rooftops; above you can see the crumbling ruins of yet another Orsini castle. The interior of the church is also worth a visit. (Open: Daily 10am–1pm, 5pm–7pm. Admission free.) Its Gothic-Roman origins received a battering during the Baroque period, but a beautiful early 16th-century fresco of *The Virgin's Coronation* from the school of Raphael decorates the apse.

WHERE TO STAY/WHERE TO EAT IN TREVIGNANO ROMANO

Villa Valentina, Via della Rena 96, (Lungolago)   **LL-L**
Tel: (06) 9019038
Open: Year round   Restaurant closed Wed
Amenities: ☎ 🅿 ✕ ♀   Credit cards: AE

This pleasant hotel/restaurant occupies a peaceful setting on the left of the road as you drive into town from Bracciano. The entrance is through a fenced-in garden (also used for outdoor dining beneath straw umbrellas); tiled floors, bright decor, copious greenery and open windows create a fresh, welcoming atmosphere. The rooms are simple but comfortable with twin beds in the doubles; all have showers.

   The menu is equally straightforward, well prepared and excellent value. Freshwater fish must leap from the lake into the frying pan and the pasta's "like Mama used to make it".

*Continue clockwise around the lake, past pretty houses overlooking the esplanade and out of town beneath a steep wooded escarpment. After 6kms bear right for **Anguillara**. You'll enjoy the magical view of this pretty lakeside village rising from its own reflection in a jumble of haphazard terracotta roofs and soft yellow buildings a further 6kms on. Opinion differs on the origins of the name "Anguillara". Some say it was named for a Roman villa built where the shoreline forms a sharp angle (angularia). Others, more prosaically insist it refers to the quantities of eels in the lake (anguillae).*

   The next 9kms of badly-rutted road to a T-junction in Osteria Nuova are best not mentioned. From here our routes divide.

ROUTE B: Osteria Nuova – Rome

*Turn left for **Roma** at the T-junction, rejoining **Via Braccianese** from Bracciano. This leads out into the countryside although the Italian billboard blight still plagues the roadside. There's another junction in the built-up area around **La Storta** 7kms later: turn right. This is the **Via Cassia (ss2)**. After a brief pine-shaded respite from the sun you reach the outskirts of Rome, driving over the GRA 6kms from La Storta, then past the **Tomba di Nerone** on the left 4½kms further on before a patch of open ground. Now on the **Via Cassia Nuova**, you join **Corso di Francia** after ½km which leads straight down to **Ponte Flaminio**. You can bear off for **Ponte Milvio** just before the bridge, or cross the river keeping right at the end until you reach a junction with **Viale Tiziano/Via Flaminia**.*

ROUTE C: Osteria Nuova – Campagnano – Morlupo (30kms)

*Turn left at the T-junction in Osteria Nuova, signposted **Roma**. At the next crossroads turn left for **Cesano**, heading out into open countryside obscured on your right by a high gray stone wall. After 3kms, a narrow bridge jack-knifes you into Cesano: follow the road through town. At the top of the hill, turn left onto **Via di Monte Sant'Andrea**; then sharp right ¾km later to a T-junction with the **Via Cassia (ss2)**. Drive north toward **Viterbo** for 2½kms, before making a right turn to **Campagnano**. Follow the signs, keeping right 1km later, until you reach the ancient heart of the town.*

CAMPAGNANO

A small town with its origins buried deep in Etruscan history, Campagnano still retains a glimmer of its medieval appearance with a show of Renaissance towers, portals and fountains. It's also the regional center for simple, but delicious produce specialties including artichokes, cucumbers, cheese made from sheep's milk and red Baccanale wine. Towards the end of April to early May the **Sagra del Baccanale** (wine festival) is in full swing; at other times of the year, the best place to sample all these delights is **Da Righetto** (see below), on the main street 100m from the archway.

Da Righetto, Campagnano   **L**
Tel: (06) 9091036   No credit cards
Open: Wed–Mon 1pm–4pm 8pm–11pm   Closed: Tues

Situated right on the narrow main street, sporting enormous window shutters, Da Righetto is a deliciously cool, dim retreat from the heat. Its walls are decorated with landscapes and you'll find samples of the robust local wines perched on every ledge. Game dishes are a speciality: hare and pheasant are highly recommended. Artichokes (in season) are cooked on a large open fire, or you can opt for generous servings of pasta – all washed down with quantities of good local red wine.

*At the traffic circle by the gateway, bear right for **Sacrofano** on Via Sebastiano which bundles you out of town along a badly-finished road. When the road divides take the left-hand fork signposted **Magliano**. This is a real country road. It twists and turns along a narrow ridge with fine views over valleys to right and left. After 10kms you'll reach a junction with Via Flaminia; turn right, and then left for **Morlupo** 1½kms later. Follow this road to a right fork, signposted **Comune/PT**. Bear left at the bottom of the slope, and park in **Piazzale Armando Diaz**.*

*　　*　　*

See **Tour 5 – Route A** (page 174) for full details of Morlupo and a tour of picturesque hill towns.

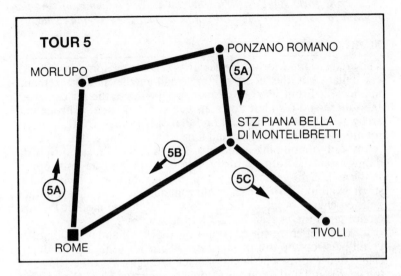

TOUR 5

MORLUPO

PONZANO ROMANO

5A

STZ PIANA BELLA
DI MONTELIBRETTI

5B

5A

5C

ROME

TIVOLI

Our final tour involves a gentle excursion to a selection of small hill towns north of Rome. There are no major historic or architectural sights, but photographers should definitely stock up on film for this one. You'll be rewarded with stupendous views from these eagle's eyries, picturesque cobbled streets, ancient castles and hidden alleyways opening into further breathtaking vistas.

ROUTE A: Rome – Morlupo – Fiano Romano – Ponzano Romano – Stz Piana Bella di Montelibretti

*To reach the northbound **Via Flaminia**, follow **Lungotevere Flaminio** alongside the River Tiber, crossing the river on **Ponte Duca d'Aosta**. Turn right after the bridge to **Piazzale Ponte Milvio**, followed by a left and right onto **Via Flaminia** (you'll see **Ristorante La Vigna** on the corner). Houses and shops line the narrow street. Drive under a road bridge ¹/₂km ahead; then cross straight over a traffic light. At a junction 2kms later (with a burnt-orange turreted building off to the right), turn left, driving out through the industrial suburbs along a divided highway and under the GRA in the direction of **Prima Porta/Terni**.*

*As you climb out into the countryside, you'll see a run of wonderful flower stalls strung along the roadside bursting with anemones, lilies, carnations, cyclamen, irises, roses and many other colorful blooms. On Sunday the crowds swarm in en route to the cemetery at the top of the hill. Via Flaminia heads directly north, through fields and scattered houses, bypassing the center of **Riano** after*

*16kms before **Castelnuovo di Porto**. Less than 2kms later, on the outskirts of **Morlupo**, turn right and follow this road for 1½kms to a right fork signposted to the town center (**comune**). At the bottom of the hill bear left and park in **Piazzale Armando Diaz**.*

MORLUPO

The area around Morlupo is heavily strewn with Roman weekenders' villas, but the heart of this small medieval town remains unaffected. From Piazzale Armando Diaz, take the far exit from the square and turn left down a steep cobbled street. Through an archway at the bottom you'll find **Piazza Giovanni XXIII**, a pretty square ringed by historic buildings. Facing you is the recently renovated salmon pink exterior of **Chiesa di San Giovanni Battista** dating from the 16th century (open daily 10am–1pm 4pm–6pm). It forms a right-angle with a 15th-century oratory which houses small exhibitions of local art throughout the year. Yet another belfried chapel occupies the far corner, while the modest **Palazzo Orsini** faces the church behind barred windows.

If you happen to hit Morlupo on the last Sunday in October you'll be swept up in the *Sagra della Salsiccia* (Sausage Festival), celebrated with much slicing of spicy sausages. At other times of the year you'll find a warm welcome at the *trattoria* by the parking lot.

WHERE TO EAT IN MORLUPO

Agostino al Campanaccio, Piazza Armando Diaz 13   L
Tel: (06) 9030008
Open: Wed–Mon 1pm–3pm 7pm–midnight   Closed: Tues
No credit cards

This jolly *trattoria* extends into two small rooms, through the pretty enclosed patio. Simple rustic decor in the dining room with whitewashed walls, low ceilings supported on bare beams and copper pots filled with flowers. Pen-and-ink sketches slot in between the wine racks and the lamplit atmosphere is as friendly as the open hearth. Good country cooking features, naturally, plates of local sausage (*antipasto*) or you can sample it chopped up in pasta with tomatoes. Other good bets are delicious *galleto* (a chicken speciality), and local wines from Capena.

*Take the far exit from **Piazzale Armando Diaz**, across the road leading down to the church, and follow signs for **Capena** along **Via Cesario Battisti**. Follow this narrow backstreet, winding out of Morlupo through a jumble of villas and olive groves to Capena 5kms later. Named after the ancient Etruscan territory of Capenati, Capena has yielded numerous archeological finds including tombs which date from the sixth century . These are now displayed at Villa Giulia in Rome. Continue through the town for 3kms; just* *before the left turn to **Fiano Romano**, you'll see the Hotel Feronia on your right.*

WHERE TO STAY/EAT NEAR CAPENA

Hotel Feronia, Via Provinciale (Loc. S. Marco) LL
Tel: (06) 9032682/4 Open: Year round
Amenities: ☎ 🅿 ✗ ⏲ ⹁ ⚲ Credit cards: AE

Set in a small park and surrounded by fragrant pine trees, this unpretentious modern hotel offers 35 pleasant, simply-furnished rooms with bath. Cool color schemes and potted plants abound; there's a relaxed holiday atmosphere in summer, although it's very quiet in winter.

The restaurant, in a separate building, overlooks the Olympic-size pool. It offers a mixed menu of Italian and international dishes.

*Turn left for **Fiano Romano** after the hotel, then right (by an electricity generating station) 3/4km later. Climb uphill and down through the town for 4³/4kms before making a left turn. Then turn right ¹/2km later and park in the street leading down to Fiano's Old Town. It's entered by a portal with the 15th-century castle on the left.*

FIANO ROMANO

It's a Kodak-eating view across little Piazza Cairoli to the ancient city gate. On the inside you'll find Piazza Giacomo Matteotti where **Chiesa di San Stefano** faces the **Castello Ducale**: another Orsini country retreat. This is now in the sticky hands of an infant school run by nuns. The holy sisters have their hands full most days, but on Sundays between 3pm and 4pm they're happy to accompany you around the frescoed apartments pointing out carved doors, sculpted fireplaces and antique tapestries. If you get a chance, climb the belltower for a 360° view across the Tiber valley to the mountains.

The church is easier to visit (open daily 9am–1pm 4pm–6pm). Simple gray pillars support stucco arches in its small square interior and modern stained glass casts colored shadows. The walls are decorated with ornate reliefs and fine paintings. At the top of the right-hand aisle, the frescoes of two angels flanking a *Madonna* are attributed to Pinturicchio; other 15th-century works include fragments of a *Crucifixion* and a gentle *Nativity* from the Umbrian school.

*Drive back uphill from the Old Town, turn right at the top and follow the road round to the left for **Nazzano**. Climb steeply through the villas and vines and a scattered hilltop village – evidence of the great Roman exodus. Over the last 10 years, thousands of Romans* *have opted for the life of country commuter and a recent amnesty on building restrictions has led to a rash of modern eyesores mushrooming along every roadside. Turn right for Nazzano 5kms later; there's an uninterrupted view off to your left to the village of* **Sant'Oreste** *clinging to its sheer-sided peak beneath the immense bulk of* **Monte Soratte**. *Turn left 1km later; and left again after 5kms with Nazzano down to your right clustered round its 15th-century castle now inhabited by monks (no admission). You've got a good, if brief, view of this copybook example of "spiral" town planning: the main street wraps itself in serpentine fashion around a hill topped by the castle.*

Take a left for **Ponzano** *1km on; then another left (2kms) opposite a fine avenue of trees. Just ¼km into Ponzano, fork right for* **Chiesa Parrochiale**. *There's parking as you drive up the hill, and a small parking lot marked off to the left below the main square.*

PONZANO ROMANO

Walk up from the parking lot to the twin squares, Piazza Vittorio Emanuele and Piazza della Nativita di Mario Santissima: big names for two tiny rectangles perched on a hilltop. (The **Tourist Office** (Pro Loco) is rumoured to operate sometimes out of the crumbling 18th-century Palazzo Vescovile, but it was probably despatched by dry rot.) There's another great view clear over the river plain from the balcony; in the foreground you'll see the ancient abbey of **Sant'Andrea in Fulmine**. This is now being restored to save its frescoes. A keen medico during a 16th-century outbreak of the plague slathered them all in disinfectant, which may have saved a few lives, but did nothing for their color scheme.

The narrow streets are worth exploring. To do so take Via XX Settembre off Piazza Vittorio Emanuele and wend your way to Piazza San Nicolo. In the top corner you'll find the newly decorated **Chiesa di San Nicolo**, its Baroque interior a riot of buttercup yellow and tangerine paint. (If the door isn't open try at the town hall opposite or the convent next door.) Lit by chandeliers and lovingly filled with fresh flowers, the church also boasts a beautiful 16th-century gilt-framed *Madonna*, attributed to the Zuccari brothers. It hangs in the first chapel on the left, an harmonious group with attendant saints in gentle blues and ochers: quite a contrast to the pastel pastiche surrounds.

WHERE TO EAT IN PONZANO ROMANO

Porto Vecchio Fani, at Sant' Oreste-Ponzano   L
Open: May–Sep daily 1pm–4pm 7pm–11pm; Oct–Apr weekends
   only
No credit cards
Directions: Take the road down past San Andrea in Fulmine to the river. The entrance is 300m ahead up a dirt road.

A real home-on-the-ranch style restaurant on the banks of the Tiber. There are tables and chairs outside with a great view of the countryside and river; inside, the converted farm buildings are hung with antique tools above bench seats. This family-owned business starts 'em young: all five children aged 8–14 serve at table. Mom's in the kitchen preparing hearty home-cooking full of regional character: try the skewers (*spiedino*) of various meats (lamb, beef, pork) with spicy pasta for an unusual and delicious combination.

Drive back out of Ponzano to the junction by the avenue of trees: turn right signposted Roma. At a T-junction 2½kms later, make a left for **Torrita Tiberina** *and you'll see the entrance to the Old Town on your right after 3kms.*

TORRITA TIBERINA

A medieval fortified village, which the Orsini and Savelli families lorded over in turn, Torrita still has two of its solid 12th-century towers, but the drawbridge has been replaced with a solid version. There are plenty of photocalls here for those keen to explore the tiny streets linked by covered passages, abrupt twists and turns, and sudden views of Nazzano's castle above the snake-like sweep of the River Tiber. Italian politician Aldo Moro, murdered by the Red Brigade in 1978, was born here, and buried in the local cemetery, hence the main street carries his name.

The road from Torrita runs down to the valley, crossing the river at **Rieti**, *toward* **Passo Corese**. *After 17kms bear right, cross the railroad tracks and drive through Passo to a junction 2½kms later. Turn right here onto the tree-lined* **Via Salaria** *signposted for* **Roma**. *Just under 5kms later, near Stz Piana Bella di Montelibretti, there's a left turn for* **Palombara** *which marks the start of* **Route C** *to Tivoli.*

ROUTE B: Stz Piana Bella di Montelibretti – Rome

The Via Salaria runs directly back into Rome, through **Torre Mancina** *and* **Monterotondo Scala**. *You drive under the A1 after 14kms, 4kms short of the GRA in an ugly sprawl of billboards and factories. Keep following signs for* **Roma-Centro**: *you'll pass Urbe airport and cross the Tiber before the road skirts* **Parco Pubblico Villa Ada**, *finally running out of steam at* **Piazza Fiume**, *a short distance east of* **Villa Borghese**.

ROUTE C: Stz Piana Bella di Montelibretti – Tivoli   (30kms)

Heading east toward **Palombara**, *the landscape is a lush carpet of vines and fruit trees which stretches all the way to the horizon and the great swell of* **Monte Gennaro**. *You cross a main road 9kms further on and reach Palombara 5kms later; keep left for* **Tivoli** *and skirt the base of the town. There's a left turn for Tivoli in the unmarked village of **Marcellina** 5kms further on. This leads down a valley and along a superb, twisting hillside route into Tivoli after 10kms. Follow yellow signs for **Information/Villa d'Este** over a stone bridge across the River Aniene and through town until you see the imposing stone turret of the Rocca on your right. The road curves right, then left opposite a garden. There's a small parking lot on the right next to the **Tourist Office**, Largo Garibaldi. (Tel: (0774) 21249. Open: Mon–Sat 8am–2pm year round; also 2:30pm–6:30pm in summer.)*

*   *   *

See **Tour 1 – Route A** (page 135) for full details of **Tivoli** and a choice of tours east of Rome.

A LONGER TOUR NORTH TO LOWER TUSCANY AND UMBRIA

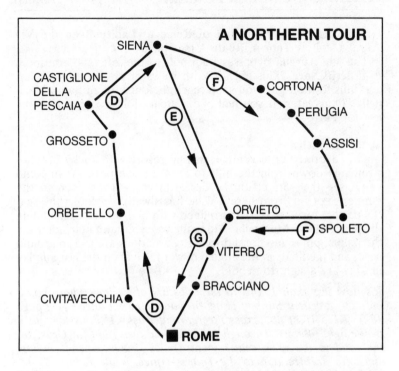

This is an opportunity to explore further afield. Starting from Rome, this tour follows the coastline north via the important Etruscan site at **Tarquinia** to the sunny beach resorts of **Orbetello** and **Castiglione della Pescaia**. Next, you cut across country to **Siena**, one of Tuscany's most beautiful and historic towns. It's built on three of those famed Tuscan hills (**Route D**).

Here, there's a choice of onward routes depending on the time you have available. If your vacation is drawing to a close, there's a fast route south to the celebrated cathedral and wine town of **Orvieto (Route E)**. Those with more time to spare can continue east from Siena to the Umbrian art center of **Perugia**; **Assisi**, St Francis's home town; and ancient **Spoleto**. Then head west again to join up with the fast route from Siena in **Orvieto (Route F)**.

From Orvieto, there's a fast highway back to Rome. However, the scenic route isn't much longer. It winds through the vineyards to **Bolsena**, scene of a 13th-century miracle; superb medieval **Viterbo**; and lakeside **Bracciano** with its magnificent 15th-century feudal castle (**Route G**).

ROUTE D: LADISPOLI – (CIVITAVECCHIA) – TARQUINIA – ORBETELLO – (GROSSETO) – CASTIGLIONE DELLA PESCAIA   (Approx. 170kms)

For details of the route out of **Rome** to **Ladispoli** on the Via Aurelia, follow **Tour 4, Route A** (see page 163).

The **Via Aurelia** bypasses Ladispoli to the left, and continues to **Osteria Nova** 2kms ahead. With views of the sea to your left and hills to the right, you soon reach the outskirts of **Santa Marinella** 20kms later. If you feel like a break, follow signs off to the left for **Porto**.

Santa Marinella

This is a pretty little summer sailing resort with rocky beaches stretching down from the hills to an attractive port. At one end you'll see the 15th-century Odescalchi castle (not open to the public). Not far from here a wide boardwalk overlooks the sea. It's perfect for a stroll; it's also lined with bars and cafés including the pleasant **Bar Marinella**. Along the way you can't help admiring the palms, pines and floral displays. Carnations are a crop around here, and the floats at the annual flower festival on the last Sunday in May are a sight to behold.

*It's now less than 10kms to the outskirts of **Civitavecchia**. You'll pass the excellent Sunbay Hotel on your left 1km ahead (see page 182). Keep right and cross the railroad tracks 1¼kms later to a traffic light (400m). Through traffic should turn right for **Grosseto**; the road to the town center (centro) lies straight ahead. Follow signs for Information to the **Tourist Office**, Viale Garibaldi 42. (Tel: (0766) 25348. Open: Mon–Sat 9am–12:30pm 3:30pm–6:30pm.)*

A SIDETRIP TO CIVITAVECCHIA

Bombed out of recognition during World War II, the town of Civitavecchia is no great beauty. The real reason for a stop here is the chance to relax at the Sunbay Park Hotel (see page 182). After a hectic few days in Rome, a short spell by its pool is a welcome respite. There are several sights to visit in the main town, a port founded by Emperor Trajan in the second century AD. The harbor is guarded by Forte Michelangelo, begun by Bernini under instructions from Julius II in 1508, and finally completed by Michelangelo himself. You can only view the painter's unusual leap into military architecture from the outside these days. Next to the fort you'll find ferries to Sardinia, an 8½-hour trip away. There are two daily sailings: 9:30am and 9:30pm. (Return ferries from Sardinia leave at the same times.)

WHAT TO SEE IN CIVITAVECCHIA

Museo Civico, Largo Plebiscito, Civitavecchia
Open: Tues–Sun 9am–2pm only   Closed: Mon
Admission free

This small, two-story museum is filled with relics of previous civilizations from the Stone Age, through the Etruscans to the Romans. On one wall upstairs, a chart explains the 10 different layers of earth that have been excavated and shows which items have been discovered at what point. The thermal spa north of the town attracted many visitors, and the findings in these areas are particularly rich including gold jewelry, stone vases, and delicate miniature masks. You'll also see tools, pottery and numerous funerary objects.

Terme Taurine (Trajan's Baths), 3kms N. on road to Allumiere
Open: Summer Tues–Sun 9am–1pm   Closed: Mon
         Winter: check with Tourist Office
Admission free

The site is fenced in but there's a gate near the caretaker's office (on the left in a patch of bushes). Past this you'll find the crumbled brick walls which once formed a villa surrounding the well-preserved baths. These were built by Trajan's successor, Emperor Hadrian, in the second century. They provided a convenient spot to enjoy the natural springs. Walk through the baths (take care not to step on the remaining mosaics) and note the intricate brick and stonework. The largest section, called the *calidarium*, must have accommodated hundreds of bathers among its pillars.

SHOPPING IN CIVITAVECCHIA

There are plenty of shopping opportunities in the streets leading off **Largo Plebiscito**, and several on this busy thoroughfare itself. If you're on the look out for Italian fashion, **Boutique La Perla**, Largo Plebiscito specializes in Versace designs, hand-painted T-shirts (L40,000) and some great but pricey swimwear. **Intrigo**, at No 22, offers a more affordable range of lingerie and bathing suits as well as beach/daywear outfits. For cute kids' and babies' clothes you can't beat **Prenatal**, Largo Cavour 10, round the corner from the museum. Not only clothes and swimsuits, but neat toys too.

WHERE TO EAT IN CIVITAVECCHIA

Trattoria alla Lupa, Via San Fermina 5, Civitavecchia   L
Tel: (0766) 25703
Open: Wed–Mon 10am–4pm 8pm–midnight   Closed: Tues
No credit cards

Right by the Tourist Office, on a corner to the left, this restaurant's attractions definitely derive from its food rather than its view. The half-panelled dining room is rather dark and they don't muck around with outdoor seating (or speak English for that matter), but all is forgiven when you've tucked into the seafood specials. Try the sea salad as an *antipasto*, then mussels or shrimp on a skewer as a main course.

Trattoria O'Pescatore, Largo San Francesco d'Assisi 15   L
Tel: (0766) 25662
Open: Tues–Sun noon–3pm 7pm–11pm   Closed: Mon
No credit cards

This family-run restaurant, located next to the church of St Francis, also specializes in great value seafood which is displayed on a large table by the entrance. Tables in the dining room enjoy a spectacular view of the sea, and there's outdoor dining in a vine-shaded patio. It's small, it's friendly and the owner speaks English; red and white tablecloths, pictures of fish and sea scenes plus Chianti bottles strung about like Christmas lights make this a dictionary definition of *trattoria*. Wonderful food too: fish or lobster soup (from a local recipe), smoked swordfish, pasta with clams (*vongole*) and skewered shrimp.

WHERE TO STAY IN CIVITAVECCHIA

Sunbay Park Hotel, Via Aurelia-Sud (1km inside southern city limits)   LLL
Tel: (0766) 22801   Open: Year round
Amenities: ☎ 📺 🅿 ✕ ♀ ⸚ 🖥   Credit cards: AE, DC, MC, V

Turn off Via Aurelia and into the left-hand entrance to this elegant four-star hotel. Flowering plants line the lobby that leads to a comfortable seating area and attractive restaurant with picture windows overlooking the sea. There are 90 spacious and attractive rooms with bath/shower (plus 25 suites), all with private balcony and seaview. The sea itself is not recommended for bathing, but there's an Olympic-size pool surrounded by loungers for sunseekers. Down at the private boat pier, you can hire a craft for the day; or should you fancy a spot of tennis, the reception staff can arrange it. The dining room (L–LL) features a large aquarium accommodating future chef's specials. Save room for the desserts: delicious *gelati* (ice-cream) or banana flambé Italian-style.

*   *   *

*There's a well-signposted route out of Civitavecchia for **Grosseto** which leads to the last leg of the **A12 autostrada**. You turn off to the left for **Roma**, then keep left for **Aurelia ss1** through an abandoned tollgate. After 8kms, the A12 peters out, but the Aurelia picks up for a swift 10km run to **Tarquinia**. If you're feeling historically-minded, Tarquinia is a major Etruscan site.*

A SIDETRIP TO TARQUINIA

Bear off Via Aurelia to the right and follow signs for **centro** *uphill to a junction facing the medieval town walls. Turn left following the wall to a parking lot on the right at the entrance to the Old Town (¹/₂km) in* **Piazza Cavour**.

One of the not-to-be-missed Italian archeological sites, Tarquinia dates back to the 12th century BC. In the sixth century BC the city was far more important than Rome, ruling the entire coast of Etruria and Latium. In the seventh century, the inhabitants moved northeast of the original site to the present magnificent position on top of a rocky plateau facing the sea.

A stroll through Tarquinia's narrow medieval streets brings you to secluded squares, palaces and churches. The church of San Francesco in Via di Porta Tarquinia has a beautiful Romanesque rose window and a monumental 16th-century campanile. There's also a Roman aqueduct in working order, and good beaches 5kms away. The Etruscan site, however, is the main attraction here.

WHAT TO SEE IN TARQUINIA

Museo Nazionale Tarquiniese, Palazzo Vitelleschi, Piazza Cavour
Open: Tues–Sun 9am–noon, summer only 4pm–7pm
Closed: Mon
Admission: L4,000 (tickets valid also for the Necropolis)

This museum, housed in a delightful Renaissance palace built in 1439 for Cardinal Giovanni Vitelleschi, still retains certain Gothic features such as the window shapes. You enter through a court-yard which displays some of the best Etruscan sarcophagi in Italy. These date from the sixth to fifth century BC. Unfortunately, the rooms off the courtyard are closed (though you can peep through the grilles to admire their ancient splendor). Heading upstairs to the second floor, the first room on the left holds the museum's most prized possession: two winged horses that once stood guard on a temple constructed at the end of the fourth century BC. Their position high up on the wall seems a bit silly but they were intended to be viewed from below. In other rooms you'll also see vases, urns, votive offerings, bowls, amphorae and some lovely terracotta figures.

Etruscan Necropolis, Tarquinia
Open: as for Museum; Tours summer hourly 9am–7pm, winter
  hourly 9am–1pm
Admission: L4,000 (tickets valid also for the Museum)
Directions: From the parking lot, turn left down away from the center; take the first left-hand turn and follow this road for 4kms until you see the fenced-in Necropolis on your left.

The Necropolis extends for about 5kms and comprises thousands of tombs dating from the sixth to the first century BC. From the outside these tombs look like grassy hillocks with gray concrete doorways built at one end. These are the new entrances to the tombs that have been opened. You'll probably find only a few open on any given day because they're extremely sensitive to moisture and air, but those that you can see are remarkable works of art. The restored wall paintings in some of the tombs depict details of Etruscan life, with banquets, festivals and dances, elaborate lovemaking, horse racing and fishing, funeral rites and religious symbols.

WHERE TO EAT IN TARQUINIA

Il Bersagliere, Via Benedetto Croce 2, Tarquinia   L
Tel: (0766) 856647
Open: Tues–Sun 12:30pm–2:30pm 7:30pm–10:30pm
Closed: Mon
No credit cards

This simple restaurant (square wooden tables with candles) serves tasty food with the emphasis on what's available in the market each day. Their *risotto alla pescatore* (rice with seafood) is a good bet. So are the local white wines. Staff speak enough English to help you cope; service is on the casual side.

WHERE TO STAY IN TARQUINIA

Tarconte, Via della Tuscia 19, Tarquinia   LL
Tel: (0766) 856141   Open: Year round
Amenities: ☎ ▯ ✗ ♀ Credit cards: AE, DC, V
Directions: Follow signs for Necropoli Etrusca to Piazzale Europa. Turn right on Viale L. Dasti; Via della Tuscia leads off down to the right (25m).

Located in a quiet residential street a short distance from the town center, this is a pleasant provincial hotel with 53 rooms, all equipped with bath/shower, balcony and air-conditioning. Although the staff speak little English, they are generally anxious to please. There's a large, modern restaurant and a cheerful taverna strewn with antique rusticana, dried corn cobs, garlic and flowers. Behind the hotel outdoor terraces overlook the plain.

*To rejoin the main route, drive downhill from the parking lot for just under 2kms, then turn left for **Grosseto**, curving around onto Via Aurelia.*

*   *   *

*The landscape west of Tarquinia would delight bicyclists with its even camber; the road unreels like tape across the flat fields and into **Tuscany** just over 30kms further on. Off to the right there's an* *outcrop of small lumpy hills, polka-dotted with olives. As you approach the **Orbetello** exit (20kms ahead) the imposing bulk of **Monte Argentario** looms out of the bay with Orbetello clinging to the shoreline in its shadow. If you're looking for lunch and a swim, you won't find a better opportunity or a prettier rendezvous than here.*

A SIDETRIP TO ORBETELLO

*Exit Via Aurelia, following signs for **Orbetello** across the narrow 2½km causeway linking Monte Argentario to the mainland. As you enter the city gate, there's a shady square on the left. Turn right at the end of the square for **Monte Argentario** following the road up to a parking lot on the left in **Piazza della Repubblica**. Take the left-hand alleyway, **Via Solferino**, into the town, emerging in **Piazza G. Garibaldi**.*

ORBETELLO

Orbetello is a delightful summer resort built on a sandy strip of land surrounded by a lagoon. The famous Lombard painter Caravaggio (1569–1609) drowned in the lagoon while on the run from a murder charge. Other momentous events in the town's history include its annexation in the 16th century by the Spanish. They were responsible for much of the architecture you see around you. The first Italian transatlantic airplane crossing departed from the local airstrip in 1931, eventually coming down in Rio de Janeiro.

The faded elegance of Piazza G. Garibaldi makes a lovely break from driving. You can admire the ornate stucco decorations on the peach-colored arcade from beneath an umbrella outside one of the busy cafés spilling over the cobbles. You'll pass the Orsini-built cathedral by the parking lot. The gracious 14th-century facade is animated by carved figures and the portal wreathed in clambering vines. Feel like a swim? Your best bet is **Porto Santo Stefano**, 8kms west of the main town. It's well marked (left out of the parking lot, to a junction where you turn right at the signs).

SHOPPING IN ORBETELLO

Corso Italia, where you'll find most of the restaurants and bars, also offers a good few shops but side streets such as **Via Mazzini** offer the best choice. Just off Corso Italia and Piazza G. Garibaldi, you'll find **Antichita Venezia**, Via Mazzini 14–22, displaying a wide-ranging selection of antiques: sturdy Victorian country furniture including dressers and blanket boxes; bird and flower prints; glass and embroidery plus a few dressy pieces such as an ornate mirror surrounded by gilt curlicues. Next door at No 12 there's another **Antichita**, with a mixture of antique and modern silver from toastracks to chocolate pots; also painted glass, monster wooden candleholders, cigarette cases and some jewelry. At the other end of the scale, opposite these antiques shops you'll see **Schema**, Via Gioberti 88–90, which proclaims its slick style with black and white checkerboard tiles. Here they deal in the most up-to-date designer home furnishings: sleek chrome and leather chairs, hi-tech lighting, a fine selection of tongue-in-cheek crockery and wall furniture from clocks to colorful hangings.

WHERE TO EAT IN ORBETELLO

Osteria del Lupcante, Corso Italia 103, Orbetello   **LL**
Tel: (0564) 86718
Open: Thur–Tues 12:30pm–3pm 7:30pm–11:30pm
Closed: Wed
Credit cards: AE, DC, V

Bright red paint, a striped awning and boxed shrubs provide a crisp welcome here. The whitewashed interior is decorated with bunches of dried flowers, and subdued lighting creates a pleasantly relaxed atmosphere. There's also a popular outdoor patio area in summer. Special care is taken to offer a few unusual dishes on the menu, such as spaghetti with sea urchin sauce; plus you'll be offered a good value *menu turistico* in high season, but this is not served on the patio.

WHERE TO STAY IN ORBETELLO

I Presidi, Via Mura di Levante 34, Orbetello   **LL–LLL**
Tel: (0564) 86701   Open: Year round
Amenities: ☎ 🅿 ⚲   No credit cards

A short walk from Piazza G. Garibaldi, the ivy-covered Presidi overlooks the lagoon (1km from the parking lot on the way out of town). It's a friendly, helpful place with 63 modern rooms (all have bath/shower) and outdoor terraces which catch sea breezes off the palm tree-lined promenade. It's a great place to watch the sun set over the bay.

Leaving Orbetello, turn left out of the parking lot following the road around the seawall back to the gateway and across to the mainland.

*   *   *

Ten kilometers past Orbetello, **Via Aurelia** *is separated from the shore by a thick wedge of pine trees packed with tents and caravans. After 4kms it ends in a promontory tipped by a ruined castle. The road now cuts inland along a valley bordered to the west by the* **Parco Naturale di Maremma**, *an unspoilt area of forested hills with teeming wildlife and a sprinkling of old stone watchtowers. All along the Maremma coastline, north to Punta Ala, the mixture of thick scrub-covered hills and coastal marshlands makes this a favorite haunt of birds and game including wild boar.*

*After the **Alberese** exits (8kms), the valley opens out and you reach **Grosseto** 16kms later. Capital of the Maremma district, Grosseto is a modern town with little of interest. For an overnight stop, this route continues to **Castiglione della Pescaia**.*

GROSSETO

*If you need to break your journey in Grosseto, drive on into town for ½km, then take a right for **Centro**. At the end of the street turn left; then left again, and follow signs round a complicated but well-marked route for **Centro** to the city walls. Turn left as you face the high brick walls, then take the first entrance into the town center (on your right). You will be facing the **Bastiani Grand Hotel**.*

WHERE TO EAT IN GROSSETO

Enoteca Ombrone, Viale G. Matteotti 69/71, Grosseto   L
Tel: (0564) 22585
Open: Mon–Sat 12:30pm–2:30pm 7:30pm–10:30pm
Closed: Sat eve–Sun, first 2 wks Jan, Jul
No credit cards

Giancarlo Bini and his family have made this small, stylish restaurant a local favorite. The menu is extensive and changes with the season's produce. The *antipasto* of pear cooked in cheese is delicious, as is the spicy *pasta e fagioli* (pasta with white beans). The wine list is as long as your arm: let Giancarlo recommend some of his unknown treasures. Great for a romantic evening out.

WHERE TO STAY IN GROSSETO

Bastiani Grand Hotel, Piazza Gioberti 64, Grosseto   **LLL**
Tel: (0564) 20047   Open: Year round.
Amenities: ☎ 🗺 🅿 ✕ ⍾ ▱   Credit cards: AE, DC, MC, V

Located in the heart of the old town, this modern hotel has been cleverly tucked inside an historic building. Room decor is reminiscent of an elegant US airport motel but the public areas abound with marble and thick carpets. All 48 air-conditioned rooms have bath/shower. The pleasant, English-speaking staff are helpful and friendly. Breakfast, included in the price, consists of a spoilt-for-choice buffet.

*   *   *

*To bypass Grosseto en route to **Castiglione della Pescaia**, turn left for **Livorno** 150m into the town, driving under a railroad bridge. Keep left for **Marina/Livorno** and you'll pick up signs for Castiglione at a traffic circle ½km later; turn right. The tree-lined **ss322** cuts through the edge of **Principina** and crosses the River Bruna after 8kms. Turn right for Livorno at a junction 1½kms later, and drive through a scented pine forest to Castiglione (10kms), crowned by its medieval Old Town. Cross a bridge, then turn left for Infor-*

*mation. Take another left turn and you'll see the port ahead; a parking lot on the right houses the excellent **Tourist Office**, Piazza Garibaldi 6. (Tel: (0564) 933678. Open: Mon–Sat, Sun am 8:30am–12:45pm 3pm–6pm; Jul–Aug mornings and 4pm–7pm.)*

CASTIGLIONE DELLA PESCAIA

This is a great spot to break for the night, or even for a couple of days. It's smack in the middle of the Maremma coast. Once a desolate marshland region sparsely populated by herdsmen and wildlife, the Maremma is now an attractive tourist haven of beautiful beaches and pine forests. Further up the coast, Punta Ala is a fabulous resort well worth a visit. Castiglione is really two towns: the unspoilt medieval village built on a precipice dominated by the castle; and a modern fishing village down by the port.

There are three gateways to the citadel, one of which still preserves its original 14th-century doors. Once inside, it's a delight to explore the picturesque, narrow flagstoned streets where climbing plants and pots of brilliant geraniums festoon doorways and window grilles. The castle is privately owned, but you get a terrific view down the coast from a belvedere where a snack bar does a roaring trade in *gelati*.

There are 25 miles of beach (mainly public) around Castiglione, and a huge choice of watersports are on offer. The Tourist Office has a wealth of information in English, including handy booklets describing short driving tours and nature trails where you might end up snout to snout with a wild boar (mother boars don't appreciate efforts to entrap their enchanting offspring). Bird fanciers should dust off their binoculars and focus on the enormous variety of waterbirds or the antics of the brightly-colored bee-eaters. There's something for everyone in this town that bustles with happy holidaymakers and yachtsmen.

SHOPPING IN CASTIGLIONE DELLA PESCAIA

The main shopping street is **Corso della Liberta** running in from the harbor. There's a good handful of boutiques laden with beachwear and casuals, small supermarkets, souvenir and postcard shops, plus the **Enoteca Porrini Bar**, Corso della Liberta 9 (Credit cards: AE, DC, V), which is not only a bar but also a good wine shop. Try a glass or two of vino at the bar before purchasing bottles to take out. From mid-August to September, the town hosts a mini-wine festival. A real find is **Creazione**, Via Palestro 9 (AE, MC, V), the local pottery outlet (you can see the tiny workshop off to one side). If you're looking for unusual, portable gifts at very reasonable prices there's some great jewelry made from terracotta pegs, plain, enameled or gilded and strung with beads. Their necklaces (L40,000) and earrings (L20,000) are excellent buys. They also sell fun hand-painted bowls decorated with bright fish, parrot and animal motifs, decorative masks and house number plates.

WHERE TO EAT IN CASTIGLIONE DELLA PESCAIA

Da Romolo, Corso della Liberta 10, Castiglione L
Tel: (0564) 933533
Open: Daily 12:30pm–3pm 7:30pm–midnight
No credit cards

This modest restaurant boasts a wall full of certificates attesting to its culinary expertise but don't expect any frills. In summer try to get here early enough to secure one of the sidewalk tables, thus avoiding the brightly-lit interior. Food here is serious. Fabulous wafer-thin and tender prosciutto; the delicious local speciality is inky-gray *spaghetti in padella con frutti di mare e crostacei* which tastes and even smells of the sea. Don't be put off by the color: that's the tiny baby squid no bigger than your little fingernail mixed with shrimp and clams. To finish, the chilled chocolate desserts come highly recommended.

WHERE TO STAY IN CASTIGLIONE DELLA PESCAIA

L'Approdo, Via Ponte Giorgini 29, Castiglione LL
Tel: (0564) 933466 Closed: Jan
Amenities: ☎ ✕ 🍷 Credit cards: AE, DC, MC, V

A friendly, modern hotel on the port with parking on the street or by the Tourist Office. All 48 comfortable rooms have shower. There's a piano bar in summer. Children are most welcome. You'll need to book in advance during the season.

Roma, Via Cristoforo Colombo, Castiglione LL
Tel: (0564) 933542 Open: Year round
Amenities: ☎ ✕ 🍷 ▯ Credit cards: AE, DC, MC, V

Just up the street from L'Approdo and a little nearer to the beach, this is another family-style hotel with a long, sunny sitting room and a rather gloomy reception area. The 34 bedrooms in fresh blue-and-white (with bath/shower) are much more attractive than the public areas. Some benefit from a port side view.

ROUTE D1 : CASTIGLIONE DELLA PESCAIA TO SIENA (Approx. 95kms)

There are two routes north to **Siena** from Castiglione/Grosseto. The faster and shorter (70kms from Grosseto) is the main **ss223**; the more arduous, scenic route takes the **ss73** (95kms) off Via Aurelia 10kms north of Grosseto. If you're in a hurry, or don't feel enthusiastic about twists and turns (there are many on the second route), the **ss223** is well signposted to Siena, where you briefly join the A2 Rome–Florence route heading north before exiting for Porta San Marco. Both routes meet up at **Porta San Marco**, the southwestern gateway into Siena. Follow the instructions out of Castiglione, then if you wish to take the **ss223** turn to page 191 to rejoin the **ss73** route outside Siena.

*Leaving Castiglione, take **Via Fratelli Cervi** away from the harbor, then turn right on **Via San Bernedetto** for Siena/Grosseto. Keep straight ahead for Grosseto, leaving Castiglione on sp3 and heading for the hills. Some impressive avenues of alternating cypress and pine trees lead off the road to sunbaked farmhouses before the routes to Siena diverge after 9½kms. If you're taking the ss223 follow the road around to the right across a bridge.*

*If you've opted for the scenic route, turn left in front of a café-bar for **Buriano**. Drive across the plain for 7kms (ignoring turns for Buriano), then take a right for **Braccagni** on sp72. Another 6kms (1km after Montepescali railroad station) brings you to a junction with Via Aurelia. Turn left for 1km, before a right turn signposted **Roccastrada/Siena** (ss73). This country road snakes gently through a valley edged with olive trees and small modern villages adrift from their ancient beginnings which still cling to the slopes.*

*The road starts, imperceptibly at first, to climb into the cooling embrace of gnarled cork oaks. Many are still marked by a thick collar just below the branches that shows their trunks have been 'harvested'. So as not to damage the trees forever, on average the bark is only stripped away once every seven years. Clear views lead you up to **Roccastrada** 10kms further on, at 475m above the plain. A tremendous flourish of brilliant green vines clambers across the terraces at **Piloni** (10kms). Corkscrewing through the woodlands to **Monticiano** is thirsty work, so you might appreciate an ice-cream or a cold drink at **Rick's Bar** in the square. As you descend to a valley an interesting pepper-pot roof rises from a wooded outcrop to the left. This is the little **Cappella di Montesiepi**, a Romanesque chapel above the ruined abbey of **San Galgano**.*

A SIDETRIP TO ABBAZIA DI SAN GALGANO

Open: Daily 9am–dusk
Admission free
*Directions: Four kms beyond Monticiano, turn left for **Massa Marittima** (ss441). Just over 2kms later turn left again, then right into the parking lot by the abbey.*

One of the earliest examples of Cistercian architecture in Tuscany, the beautiful ruins of this enormous Gothic abbey stand in the middle of the countryside with tremendous views across a patchwork of fields and woodland.

The abbey was once the centerpiece of a powerful 13th-century

Cistercian community, but now its roof is open to the sky. Lofty
arches and windows in its soaring walls silhouette patches of blue,
simple capitals decorate the pillars and there's grass underfoot.
Outside you can see a right-angled remnant of a delicate cloister.
With its elegant tracery, this stands in a small garden; while the
adjacent Chapter House boasts a fine rib-vaulted roof. The romantic stillness is broken only by the chime of goatbells and birds, or
the occasional scuffle of lazy cats sunning themselves on a low
wall. The circular chapel, further up the hill, is in the process of
being restored, so it can't be visited. But you get a wonderful
view back down to the abbey, and the chapel's striped exterior
has plenty of charm.

Make your way back to the main road.

*   *   *

Back on the ss73, you reach **Frosine** *(5kms): an enchanting tiny
village gathered around an old manor house. There's a bar up on
the right where you can pull over, then walk back for the views.
This is followed by a very windy stretch of road which ends in a
narrow wooded gorge before* **Rosia** *(10kms). Then it's another
10kms to* **Costalpino** *and your first glimpse of Siena. You arrive at
the edge of town having crossed the* **Rome–Florence ss2** *just 3½kms
later. At the traffic light, ignore signs for Centro and drive straight
ahead, signposted* **Porta S. Marco.** *A winding road leads up to
Porta San Marco 2kms further on. Here you bear right, driving up
to a junction ½km later; follow signs for* **Duomo** *and you'll reach*
Via Tito Sarrocchi. *At its end, take a left and stick to this road,
crossing* **Via di Citta,** *to* **Via del Capitano** *and the Duomo. Park the
car, walk back to Via di Citta and turn downhill for the* **Tourist
Offices,** *Via di Citta 43. (Tel: (0577) 42209. Open: Mon–Sat
8:30am–1pm 4pm–7pm.) Also Piazza del Campo 56. (Tel: (0577)
280551. Open: Mon–Sat 8:30am–12:30pm 3:30pm–7pm.)*

SIENA

The most archetypal of Tuscan towns and considered by some
more beautiful than Florence, Siena "the beloved" welcomes you
with the motto "Wider than her gates does Siena open her heart."
Other towns may boast grander palaces, taller towers and bigger
cathedrals but none have the warmth, harmony and gentleness of
this beautifully preserved medieval city. Enclosed by massive
stone walls, the steep winding streets spread elegantly over three
converging red clay hills, after which the paintbox color "burnt
Siena" is named. You'll need a few days to take in all the sights
which are spread out over the city's three sections. You often
have to cross steep valleys to get from one part of town to the
other. Most of the historic center is closed to cars which has
helped protect the glowing red buildings from discoloration and

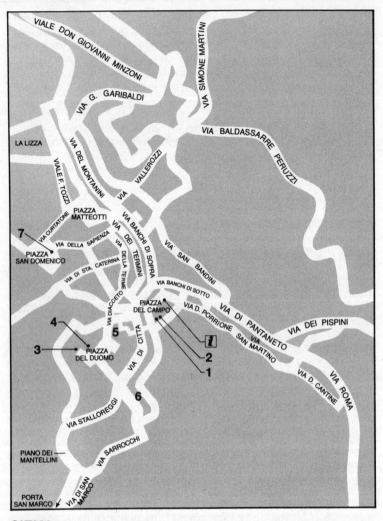

SIENA

 Tourist Office
1 Piazza del Campo
2 Palazzo Comunale
3 Duomo
4 Libreria Piccolomini
5 Pieve di San Giovanni
6 Pinacoteca
7 Chiesa di San Domenico

adds to the general feeling of tranquility.

The city was originally Etruscan and then became a Roman colony, believed to have been founded by Remus's sons. You'll notice the coat-of-arms showing a she-wolf with the twins, Romulus and Remus, which she is said to have nursed. After the Roman period, Siena's history is muddled but it later emerged as a self-governing commune continually at war with neighboring Florence. In one battle the Florentines tried to start a plague by catapulting dead donkeys and excrement over Siena's walls. Economic rivalry and territorial conflict came to a head in 1260 when the Sienese defeated the Florentines at Montaperti, a hill just outside the town.

Siena became an important banking center and remained prosperous despite wars, famines and the devastating Black Death (1348). There was a long period of French and Spanish invasions in the late 14th century, ending in Siena's surrender to the Spaniards in 1555. Two years later, King Philip II of Spain handed over the city to Florence; and in 1861, Siena became part of the Italian Kingdom.

The rivalry with Florence still continues. You'll find taxi drivers cursing cars with Florentine license plates, firm declarations that Florentine painters merely copied the Sienese, and when it comes to the question of speech, the Florentines apparently grunt like pigs and the Sienese of course have exquisitely pure accents. It's best not to get involved.

At the heart of Siena lies the magnificent Piazza del Campo. The Sienese mystic St Bernadine liked to preach here, Henry James admired its elegant proportions, and the *contrade* (districts) of Siena use it for games and contests. The most popular is the *Palio delle Contrade*, a terrifyingly dangerous horserace held twice yearly which attracts thousands of tourists. The horses tear round the mattress-padded Campo chased by frenzied Sienese in medieval costume. The event seems to be at odds with Siena's normally serene disposition.

The buildings round the Campo are exceptionally beautiful. At the bottom of the fan you'll see the most graceful Gothic palace in Tuscany – the brick and marble Palazzo Comunale where the medieval commune conducted its affairs. To the left rises the ironically slender Torre del Mangia (Tower of the Glutton), nicknamed after a medieval gourmand bellringer whose job was to strike the hours. It was from a wooden pulpit not far from the tower's base that St Bernadine used to condemn the lustful habits of the Sienese women.

The Via dei Pellegrini on the Campo's east side leads you up to the magnificent cathedral – a masterpiece of Gothic Renaissance design. It's been said that the cathedral "has the look of a bishop" who "has been obliged to assume oriental costume." Nothing could be more Christian than the cathedral's profile, but its black and white horizontal marble stripes have a definite Moslem feel. The interior is overwhelming – all that is best in Church art competes for your attention. In the north aisle, you'll find the entrance to Cardinal Piccolomini's famous library built in memory of his uncle, Pius II.

At the top of a stairway leading down from Piazza del Duomo, you pass through a gigantic freestanding wall of striped marble arches. In 1339, inspired by the news rival Florence was about to build a bigger cathedral, the Sienese drew up plans to extend their cathedral. The present edifice would have represented a mere transept of the new model. This plan was abandoned 10 years later when it became clear the town's affluence couldn't match its artistic aspirations. Moreover, religious convictions were at a low ebb after the devastating 1348 plague. These arches are all that remain.

The area around the cathedral is the *Selva* (forest) neighborhood and its symbol is the rhinoceros. If you go down the stairs west of the cathedral to Piazza della Selva, you'll see a bronze rhino which commemorates a past victory.

The Via Banchi di Sotto, one of Siena's main streets, runs northeast of Piazza del Campo through the *contrade* of the Unicorn and the Elephant to the eastern 'third' of the city. A short distance along, you'll come to the 1460 Palazzo Piccolomini where Siena's archives have been kept for centuries. It contains fascinating documents, letters and account books. Some of the tax ledgers have beautiful *tavolette* (wooden covers) painted by leading artists.

Siena's largest and most lively 'third' runs north along the Via Banchi di Sopra, the main shopping street. You'll pass the medieval palaces of the great banking families – Palazzo Tolomei (1200) and to the north, Palazzo Salimbeni, restored by a modern Sienese bank and now used for special art exhibitions.

Head west of Banchi di Sopra and you'll find yourself in the *contrada* of the Goose, a maze of steep narrow streets that rise above the red roofs to give one of the best views of the cathedral. Here you'll find the Church of St Dominic (San Domenico) and the house of St Catherine who was one of medieval Italy's great mystics and reformers. Later in life she was proclaimed a Doctor of the Church and was somehow able to continually knock the Pope over his crooked affairs without coming to harm. Determined to conquer sleep and hunger, she eventually survived on nothing more than the Communion Sacrament and half an hour's sleep a night. Her austerities eventually overcame her and she died exhausted at the age of 39.

Continue uphill from San Domenico to La Lizza, on the western edge of town. You can enjoy a picnic in the shady grounds of the Fortezza Medicea. This fortress was built in 1560 by the triumphant Duke Cosimo I of Florence to keep watch over conquered Siena. It's more like a grand country villa than a military fortification. Nevertheless, the Sienese, not wishing to be reminded of their defeat, turned the grounds into a municipal park called Piazza della Libertà. You can quench your thirst at Enoteca Italica Permanente in the munitions cellars. Here you'll find an exhibition of some of Italy's finest wines. (See **Shopping in Siena**.)

WHAT TO SEE IN SIENA

Piazza del Campo, Siena
Siena's main square, the piazza is paved with marble and orange-pink brick in the shape of a scallop shell (romanticists have called it heart-shaped). Nine individual ribs radiate from the hub – each segment a marvel of herringbone brickwork. The segments represent the city's medieval "Government of Nine", and slope gently down to the facade of the **Palazzo Communale** (see below). The delightful central fountain, **Fonte Gaia** (Fountain of Joy), is a copy of the original by famous Sienese architect and sculptor, Jacopo della Quercia (1374–1438).

Next to the Palazzo Comunale, the magnificent brick **Torre del Mangia** is topped with white stone. At 287 foot high, it commands a wonderful view over Siena – for those who can face the flight of 503 steps. By the base of the tower, you'll see the carved canopy of **Cappella di Piazza**. This beautifully decorated open loggia was built in 1378 to commemorate Siena's deliverance from the Black Death plague in 1342. In a courtyard to the right, you'll spot the bellringing glutton's statue – he of the Torre del Mangia.

Palazzo Comunale (Town Hall), Piazza del Campo, Siena
Open: Apr–Oct Mon–Sat 9:30am–6:30pm, Sun 9:30am–1pm;
      Nov–Feb daily 9:30am–1pm
Admission: L5,000

The Palazzo Comunale is an austere yet graceful Gothic structure built in 1297–1310 from stone and pinkish brick. Government offices occupy the first floor, but the upper floors are open to the public and here you'll see some marvelous examples of Sienese art. In the Sala del Mappamondo (named after a map by Ambrogio Lorenzetti), you'll find a *Maesta* by Simone Martini (1315), showing the Madonna surrounded by saints and apostles. Sadly, it's badly in need of restoration. Martini's enormous fresco of the victorious Sienese general, Guidoricco da Fogliani (1328), also adorns the room. To the right, in Sala della Pace o dei Nove, a famous cycle of frescoes by Lorenzetti graphically illustrate the *Effects of Good and Bad Government* (1337–39). You'll notice how scenes of diligent smiling workers thriving away under the influence of Temperance, Prudence and Strength contrast with scenes of urban blight and corruption. It would seem Lorenzetti's abject lesson was largely ignored, however. After visiting Siena in 1495, Philip de Commines thought it "governed the worst of any in Italy" and always "divided by factions". You should also take time to admire Taddeo di Bartolo's frescoes in the Cappella del Consiglio (Council Chapel). Painted between 1407–14, they depict scenes from the *Life of Christ and of the Virgin*.

Duomo (Cathedral), Piazza del Duomo, Siena
Open: Daily 9am–12:30pm 2:30pm–5:30pm
Admission free

Dedicated to the Assumption, the cathedral was founded in the 13th century and completed late in the 14th century. Its restored Romanesque Gothic facade is spectacularly beautiful, and complemented by a slim Romanesque campanile in alternating black and white marble stripes pierced by windows which increase in size at each succeeding level.

As if the outside weren't striking enough, the splendid interior has black and white banded walls with pillars and 14th-century vaulting painted in blue with gold stars. There's a cornice with 172 busts of popes and lords, dating from the 15th and 16th centuries. One of the major highlights is the highly decorative paving. Created by more than 40 medieval and Renaissance artists, it's always partially covered for protection and only revealed in its entirety for a few days in mid-August.

Libreria Piccolomini (Piccolomini Library), Piazza del Duomo
Open: Daily Mar 12–Oct 9am–7:30pm; Nov–Mar 11 10am–1pm
   2:30pm–5pm
Admission: L1,500

Leading off the north aisle of the cathedral, Cardinal Piccolomini (later Pope Pius III) built this library in 1495 to house his family's collection of manuscripts and books. The bulk of these came from his uncle, Pope Pius II, a poet, diplomat, religious reformer and great geographer much admired by Christopher Columbus. Many antique illuminated manuscripts are on display and they are incomparably beautiful.

The walls are decorated with colorful frescoes by Umbrian master Pinturicchio (1505), depicting scenes from Pius II's life. They're a fascinating document of *la dolce vita* at the height of the Renaissance: you'll notice intriguing details of clothes and hairstyles. In pride of place at the center of the library stands a Roman copy of the *Three Graces* of Praxiteles, three marble lovelies draped in classic Greek daywear.

Pieve di San Giovanni (Baptistry of St John), Piazza San Giovanni
Open: Daily 9am–1pm 3pm–7pm
Admission free

The cathedral's 14th-century baptistry, with twisted barley-sugar columns edging a triple portico, stands in a small piazza separate from the main building. Its gloomy interior is decorated with 15th-century frescoes (undergoing restoration) by Vecchietta and Michele di Matteo. However, the real highlight is the polygonal font (1417–30) by Jacopo della Quercia, surrounded by five exquisite bronze reliefs including one by Ghiberti, and another by Donatello. Of the six figures, two (*Faith* and *Hope*) are also by Donatello, while the statue of St John and some of the figures on the tabernacle are by della Quercia himself.

Pinacoteca (Gallery), Palazzo Buonsignori, Via San Pietro 29
Open: Tues–Sat 8:30am–7pm, Sun 8:30am–1pm
Closed: Mon
Admission: L3,000

The Palazzo Buonsignori is a lovely Gothic building in faded rose-colored brick, with two rows of arched windows and slender columns of white marble. This houses probably the world's most complete collection of Sienese art, displayed in chronological order from the 13th to the 16th century. There are fabulous examples of works by Duccio di Buoninsegna, Simone Martini and Taddeo di Bartolo, and equally beautiful pieces by Matteo di Giovanni, the Lorenzettis and Sano di Pietro. Works by other important painters such as Il Sodoma and Dürer can also be admired in this extensive collection.

Chiesa di San Domenico (Church of St Dominic), Viale Curtatone
Open: Daily 9am–1pm 3pm–7pm
Admission free

Although this church is dedicated to St Dominic, there's more emphasis here on local-born St Catherine of Siena. The building itself is something of a hybrid with parts dating from the 13th to 15th centuries.

The 21st child of a Sienese dyer, Catherine (1347–80) entered the Dominican order in this church at the age of 13. She had mystical experiences from an early age and several of these miracles and visions occurred in the chapel at the west end. The Cappella di Santa Caterina halfway along the nave contains a series of frescoes by Il Sodoma (1526). These illustrate scenes from St Catherine's life, which wasn't without political incident.

For over 200 years a long-term religious/political power dispute raged between the Empire and the Papacy. As a gesture of independence (and a desire to escape the sordid intrigues of Roman politics), Clement V moved the papal seat to the French city of Avignon in 1309. Through her writings and a visit to Pope Gregory XI in Avignon, St Catherine was one of the major forces responsible for the Pope's eventual return to Rome in 1377. She was frequently consulted by his successor, Urban VI, maintained a lively correspondence with church and lay leaders throughout Europe, and fired off a series of fiery tracts urging unity within the Catholic community.

You can also visit Catherine's house, **Casa di Santa Caterina**, in Via Benincasa. (Open: Daily 9am–12:30pm 3pm–6pm. Admission free.) This is a pretty medieval building, with a cloistered courtyard containing a well. The rooms were converted into a series of small chapels in the 15th century, and contain numerous artefacts and paintings of the saint's life.

SHOPPING IN SIENA

You name it, and you'll probably need to look no further than the shopper's paradise gathered in the general arc of **Via Banchi di Sopra** and **Via di Citta**. A stone's throw from both is the mind-boggling **Fratelli Falchini**, Via Banchi di Sotto 26–32 (Credit cards: AE, DC, MC, V), with its fabulous stock of Italian leatherwear. Elegant evening bags from Emilio Pucci; sturdy leather-to-last-a-lifetime handbags (L160,000) and attaché cases (L388,000) made by Il Ponte (The Bridge) in Florence. There are pigskin filofax holders, crocodile clutch bags and monogrammed pocket books. Designs from France include a collection by Guy Laroche and Ungaro; plus there's Mandarin Duck and Samsonite luggage if you're running out of storage space. Still hunting for leather goods? You can also try **Furla**, Via Banchi di Sopra 21 (AE, DC, MC, V), for terrific belts and accessories as well as gold and tortoise shell costume jewelry.

Ceramics are a justly favorite buy in Italy, and Siena is no exception. At the top of the scale (and top of the price range too) is **Falconi Oggetti di Artigianato**, Via di Citta 116 (AE, DC, MC, V). They offer superb reproductions of classic patterns. **Terra di Siena**, Via dei Pellegrini 15 (AE, DC, MC, V), stocks beautiful modern Sienese pottery, but it's also expensive: fruit and salad bowls are marked up to L180,000. It's better to go for the lovely fruit-patterned jugs (L27,000), boxes (L26,000), small plates (L28,000) or cute unglazed cherub faces (L16,000) which will look great out by the barbecue area back home. **No 102**, Via di Citta (AE, DC, V), is more down to earth with plenty of mugs decorated with *contrada* emblems and Marciotti china. It's on sale all over Italy but made here. The plump ducks are bestsellers. There are some attractive platters (L66,000) with good copies of old-fashioned designs; cook's containers for herbs, flour and condiments (L15,000); ceramic masks; bon-bon dishes; and several unglazed terracotta pieces from flower pots to table decorations.

All over town you'll see delis, cake shops and even tobacconists selling **Sapori** products. These local cookie manufacturers have a virtual monopoly on the production of *ricciarelli* (almond pastries) and *panforte*, the chewy Sienese cake made with almonds and candied peel. Buy a slice from a coffee bar or cake shop. If you like it, make tracks for **Il Salotto di Siena**, Via di Citta 7, where you'll find it beautifully gift packaged. On the gift front, don't miss the temptations of **Il Papiro**, Via di Citta 37 (AE, DC, MC, V), where gorgeous Venetian paper has been put to good use covering address books, diaries, blotters and even pencils. Small photograph frames cost around L18,000, there are unusual cigarette or trinket boxes (L40,000) and stunning papier-mâché ducks (L180,000) with each feather painstakingly applied in pastel tones.

Antique shops are everywhere. For the best, **Saena Vetus**, Via di Citta (AE, DC, MC, V), has showrooms dotted down the street which gradually haul you in to the main store at No 53. This houses the jewelry division: a wonderful selection of elaborate 19th-century gold and gemstones; enameled lockets; colored-glass Art Deco scent bottles with silver surrounds; plus a few unusual semi-precious pieces. A general display of fine furniture and ceramics makes up the rest. **Antichita Monna Agnese**, Via di Citta 45 (AE, DC, MC, V), also stocks women's jewelry, and men's accessories such as fob watches and tie pins. The silver here is excellent and includes silver-backed dressing table sets and Georgian table decorations. Elaborate 19th-century porcelain ornaments compliment intricate marquetry side tables, both displayed beneath the fine art collection. **Bottega dell'Antiquariato**, Via del Capitano 13 (AE, DC, MC, V), lies just off Piazza del Duomo. This is the place for larger-scale antique furniture, notably 17th- to 19th-century oak. You'll also find fragile Venetian glass, books, prints, tapestry and 18th- to 19th-century fine art. If you're serious about furniture, there are several restorers at work in Via di Stalloreggi.

Finally, a couple of truly practical hints. If you're running short of reading matter, **Libreria Senese**, Via di Citta 62–66, and **Freltrinelli**, Via Banchi di Sopra 64–66 (both take AE, DC, MC, V), stock a good selection of English language books. Picnickers and gourmets should stop in at **Salumi Typici di Siena**, Via di Citta 95, for a cornucopia of tasty local salamis and cold meats, fresh cheeses (including Parmesan), olive oil, monster green olives, dried mushrooms, and numerous other delicacies. On the wine front, head for **Enoteca Italica Permanente** in the Fortezza Medicea off La Lizza. There's a pretty tacky Wednesday market here, but you can pick up some good brass and copperware. The Enoteca is in the old fort itself, and stocks a fabulous range of Italian wines in old brick vaults, plus there's a bar where you can taste the goods first (open 3pm–midnight).

WHERE TO EAT IN SIENA

Guido, Vicolo P. Pettinaio 7, Siena   LL
Tel: (0577) 280042
Open: Tues–Sun noon–3pm 7pm–midnight   Closed: Mon
Credit cards: AE, DC, MC, V

Tucked away off Via Banchi di Sopra, Guido's dining rooms
boast pretty rosy-red vaulted brickwork which dates from the 14th
century. Well-lit by wrought iron chandeliers, the walls are hung
with photographs and pictures, while potted greenery and flowers
add color and a caring touch. Aperitifs materialize as you study
the menu. Before deciding on a starter, maybe ravioli stuffed with
ricotta served with meaty wild mushrooms (*porcino*), check out
the tasty selection of *antipasti* on the center table. Choices include
salty-garlicky prawns, stuffed tomatoes, cold meats and various
salads – or you can have them all. Generous main courses run to
steaks, lamb cutlets cooked with artichokes, roast veal, or a rich
risotto with truffles (*tartufo*). Make sure you try the homemade
bread. Their special brown bread is deliciously moist and flavored
with bits of olive. Some white breads conceal pockets of cheese.

Le Campane, Via delle Campane 4, Siena   L
Tel: (0577) 284035
Open: Tues–Sun 1pm–3pm 7pm–midnight   Closed: Mon
Credit cards: AE, V

Just off Via di Citta, Le Campane's small terrace is covered by
an awning and surrounded by plants. This makes it a good shady
spot in high summer. The owner is Sicilian, and his fish cannelloni
are quite something, as is the escalope with truffles. The traditional menu is wide ranging but the chef's special touches make
it stand head and shoulders above local competition. The atmosphere is friendly in the main dining room with its ancient arches.

Nello-La Taverna, Via del Porrione 28, Siena   LL
Tel: (0577) 289043
Open: Tues–Sun lunch 1pm–3:30pm 7pm–midnight
Closed: Sun pm–Mon
Credit cards: AE, DC, V

Behind Il Campo, this cheery small restaurant opens onto a quiet
street. Barebrick walls, rushbottomed chairs, thick pottery water
jugs decorated with *contrada* emblems and action photographs of
the Palio on the walls all contribute to the relaxed atmosphere.
Individual table lamps add an intimate note. Delicious homemade
pasta is displayed in trays: try their *ravioli alla fonduta* (deliciously
cheesy), or simple noodles lightly-flavored with herbs (*erbe*). If
you've built up an appetite, *arristino misto*, a rich seasonal game
stew, is a surefire answer.

WHERE TO STAY IN SIENA

Palazzo Ravizza, Piano dei Mantellini 34, Siena   LLL
Tel: (0577) 280462
Open: Year round   Restaurant closed Jan–Feb
Amenities: ☎ ✕ ♀   Credit cards: AE, DC, MC, V

Only just in the LLL category, this lovely *pensione* occupies a wonderful old town house near Porta San Marco, with a private garden overlooking the Tuscan hills. If you're lucky, your bedroom's tall, shuttered windows will overlook them as well. Spacious bedrooms are furnished in spartan style with unmatching antiques. This all adds up to a faded charm. There are excellent modern bathrooms in 21 of the 25 double rooms. The dining room has painted ceilings: one section is decorated with boughs of chestnut, olive and pine; the other with ornate patterns and figures. Admirable home cooking provides a choice of risottos, roasts and omelettes at dinner (three courses); breakfast is buffet-style and they're happy to provide a decent packed lunch.

Jolly Hotel Excelsior, Piazza La Lizza, Siena   LLL
Tel: (0577) 288448   Open: Year round
Amenities: ☎ 🖾 ✕ ♀ 🖰   Credit cards: AE, DC, MC, V

North of the town center near Fortezza Medicea, the Jolly is a seven-minute walk from Il Campo. This good international-style hotel belongs to Italy's largest chain. The reception area is elegant. The 102 comfortable, modern rooms all have bath and full air-conditioning. There's an "American" bar (Italian for well-stocked) and a fine restaurant. Dining here is extremely good value, and the menu is full of temptations from salmon mousse to rich strogonoff or panfried veal with red pepper.

Hotel Chiusarelli, Viale Curtatone 9, Siena   LL
Tel: (0577) 280562
Open: Year round   Restaurant closed Jan–Feb
Amenities: ☎ 🅿 ✕ ♀   Credit cards: AE, DC, MC, V

Behind an elegant facade close to San Domenico, the Chiusarelli has been completely modernized in rather bland style, but it's convenient and pleasant, with a pretty terrace shaded by vines. All 57 quiet rooms have bath and modern furnishings. The restaurant offers a simple menu if you're too tired to hit the town after a hard day's sightseeing.

Hotel Continental, Via Banchi di Sopra 85, Siena   LL
Tel: (0577) 41451   Open: Year round
Amenities: ☎ ♀   Credit cards: AE, DC, MC, V

Short on amenities but long on style, the Continental has a place of its own in Siena. Right in the town center so you can't drive to it, it's worth a mention for the gorgeous old surroundings. Built in the 16th century, its painted ceilings, marble doorways, beautiful parquet floors, lived-in antique furnishings and courteous staff sketch a gentle salute to a bygone age.

*   *   *

If you're traveling on to **Perugia** and **Spoleto**, turn to **Route F** (see page 203).

ROUTE E: SOUTH FROM SIENA TO ORVIETO
(Approx. 135kms)

If time doesn't allow you to continue to Perugia, Assisi and Spoleto, this quick route south to the famous wine-producing town of **Orvieto** will enable you to connect with **Route G**, the last leg of the tour down to Bolsena, Viterbo and Bracciano before returning to Rome.

*To link up with **Via Cassia** (ss2) southbound you can leave direct from **Porta Romana**. Alternatively, make your way back to the junction of the Castiglione road (ss73) and the Rome–Florence (A2) on the outskirts of Siena. Here you follow signs for **Roma**. (ss2)/**Porta Tufi** (left at the traffic light if you're coming from Porta San Marco), along a small road running below the town. Drive past the exit for Porta Tufi 2¼kms further on. It's after a series of road bridges, and you'll come to a junction with the road from Porta Romana 1km later. Turn right, leaving Siena 1km further on. In no time at all, you're out in the lazily contoured hills crowned with wooded topknots and freckled with houses.*

* **Ponte a Tressa**, after almost 6kms, prefaces a dreary run of villages stretching a further 6kms; then continue past **Buonconvento** 10kms later. Quite suddenly the prospects improve: traffic lessens and the scenery is lovely. Beyond **San Quirico d'Orcia**, the landscape becomes much wilder. This area features rocky hills covered with dense scrub which is home to flocks of hardy sheep and a few stone crofts. Nearly 24kms later, there's a long tunnel, followed by a final flourish of hills. You then descend to the Paglia River valley. From here, Via Cassia climbs into **Acquapendente**; follow signs for **Roma** through the town, on to **San Lorenzo Nuovo** 11kms later. Turn left here for **Orvieto** (ss74). This takes you out onto a pleasant country road. Take another left 15kms later. Just 5kms further on you'll have a striking view across to Orvieto with the cathedral's facade glittering in the sun as the road winds downhill for 4½kms to the lower town. Now the road climbs for 2kms, through the Porta Romana gateway and on to a junction 100m later. Turn right up a narrow winding street for ½km following signs for **Duomo/ Information**. At a junction, with San Francesco's church on your right, take another right and you'll emerge by the Duomo 200m*

later. You can park on the right, near the **Tourist Office**, *Piazza del Duomo 24. (Tel: (0763) 41772. Open: Mon–Sat 9am–1pm 3pm–7pm (May–Aug 2:30pm–8pm), Sun Mar–Oct 10am–1pm 4pm–7pm; Nov–Feb 10am–1pm only.)*

*   *   *

For full details of **Orvieto** and the route back to **Rome**, turn to page 270.

ROUTE F: SIENA – CORTONA – PERUGIA – ASSISI – SPOLETO – ORVIETO (Approx 270kms)

From your hotel in Siena, make your way to the junction of the ss73 and A2 on the outskirts of the city. If you've parked by the Duomo, turn right out of **Via del Capitano** *onto* **Via di Stalloreggi**. *Along* **Piano dei Mantellini** *you turn right, signposted* **Roma**, *which leads you back to* **Porta San Marco** *and down to the junction where the southern roads converge.*

At the traffic light follow signs for **Roma/Perugia**, *then pick up signs for* **Arezzo** *as you cross a road bridge and turn off to the left. After 2¼kms keep right for* **Arezzo/Perugia**, *before the road runs through a series of tunnels and viaducts. Signs for Arezzo are the key to success, and 4kms later you're driving down the Siena-Bettolle ss326 through the rolling Tuscan hills. It's a lovely drive eastwards at any time of year, though the tree colors in fall make a particularly magnificent contribution to the landscape.*

After 51kms, at **Bettolle**, *the old road runs out, and is replaced by an excellent two-lane modern highway which runs direct to Perugia bypassing the beautiful hill town of Cortona. Fortunately, Cortona is only a short distance north, so this route makes a detour, then returns to the highway on the shores of* **Lago Trasimeno**.

The exit for **Cortona** *lies 4½kms from Bettolle, and then climbs steeply uphill. As you crest a rise 5kms later, you'll see the wedge-shaped white triangle of Cortona spilling down the broad hillside ahead. There's a bumpy bridge on the outskirts of* **Camucia** *8kms further on, then keep right for* **Centro** *and follow signs around a one-way system for Cortona to a right turn after 1km. This leads you up through the terraces, past the beautiful Renaissance church of* **Santa Maria del Calcinaio** *for 4kms to a fork in the road. Drive straight on for* **Centro-Piazza Repubblica** *and a parking lot 20m ahead. You enter Porta Sant'Agostino, climbing the perpendicular slope to Piazza della Repubblica where you'll see signs to the right for the* **Tourist Office**, *Via Nazionale 70. (Tel: (0575) 603056.)*

CORTONA

Situated in the province of Arezzo, midway between the Mediterranean and the Adriatic coasts, Cortona clings to a ridge on the slopes of Monte Sant'Egidio. From this elevated position, the dizzy fortress town has one of the finest views in Italy looking out over the fertile plain of the Val di Chiana with glimpses of the Sienese mountains to the far end.

One of Italy's most historic towns, Cortona was a venerable settlement before the arrival of the Etruscans. Conquered by the Romans in 390BC, the town benefitted briefly from its position on the Via Cassia trade route north from Latium. Then it slowly sank into a decline. In the Middle Ages, its star rose again as a center of the arts. Fra Angelico lived in a Dominican monastery here in the early 15th century; and Luca Signorelli, whose work was much admired by Michelangelo, was born in Cortona (1450). You'll find works by both these artists in the superb Museo Diocesano. Pietro da Cortona continued the town's artistic tradition in the 17th century. His Baroque splendors are best illustrated by the facade of Santa Maria della Pace in Rome and frescoes in the Palazzo Pitti in Florence.

The prosperous medieval commune of Cortona survived wars with Perugia and Arezzo. Then, in 1409, it was conquered by King Ladislao of Naples. He sold it to the Florentines. Because the people of Cortona had been sympathetic to Florence, they were well treated and Cortona itself developed into an attractive middle-class Renaissance town. Its narrow centuries-old flagstone streets are still lined with Renaissance houses. This tight little community has a timeless, secretive air somehow bounded both physically and mentally by the ancient ramparts. Being built on a ridge, the town had nowhere to expand; it thus remains delightfully unspoiled.

You approach Cortona via a series of hairpin bends which swing up through olive groves and vines, passing some beautiful villas and churches. The massive medieval ramparts, worn by centuries of wind and weather, were built on the site of the original Etruscan walls. You'll spot rugged Etruscan stonework in the base of the walls and you can visit Etruscan tombs on the hillside below town. The most famous of these are Tanella di Pitagora and the Melone.

In Piazza della Repubblica, the heart of town, you'll see the 13th-century Palazzo del Comune with its clocktower and gigantic staircase. To the right, in Piazza Signorelli, stands Palazzo Pretorio (Prefect's Palace) also called Palazzo Casali after the family who ruled Cortona until the Florentine takeover. It now houses the Museo dell'Accademia Etrusca's magnificent collection of bronzes including a chastity belt and an astonishing fifth-century BC oil lamp which weighs 130 lb. The lamp has a gorgon's head for its base. Cortona's post office is just off Piazza della Repubblica. The iron hooks outside were used in the Middle Ages for hanging up criminals.

Wander downhill from the Palazzo Pretorio to the quiet seclusion of Piazza del Duomo. Here you'll enjoy a bird's eye view from the ramparts over the valley. The original Romanesque cathedral was rebuilt several times during the Renaissance period and, being on the edge of town, it seems isolated. Across the piazza stands the Museo Diocesano which is more interesting. Inside are two exquisite paintings by Fra Angelico as well as important works by Sassetta, Duccio, Lorenzetti and Signorelli.

Take a steep climb up Via Santa Margherita, to the top of town and Santuario Santa Margherita, dedicated to the patron saint of Cortona. Inside the church, you'll find her beautifully decorated 13th-century tomb. Further uphill, on Via di Fortezza, stand the ancient tree-filled ruins of the Fortezza Medicea, built on the remains of an Etruscan fortification. You can enjoy the breeze and another excellent view over the surrounding countryside to Montepulciano and the glittering expanse of Lago Trasimeno.

WHAT TO SEE IN CORTONA

Museo Diocesano, Chiesa Gesù, Piazza del Duomo, Cortona
Open: Tues–Sun 9am–1pm 3pm–6:30pm (5pm Oct–Mar)
Closed: Mon
Admission: L3,000 (Ring the bell for entry)

Housed in a former church, this collection should bring any art lover post-haste to Cortona. The first section is largely devoted to Luca Signorelli (1450–1528) and the *bottega* (studio) he founded in Cortona towards the end of his career. It was a successful, workmanlike operation specializing in altarpieces, none of which touched the intensity of his early works. For a glimpse of this, there's a striking *Descent from the Cross* in rich, glowing colors and dazzling gilt. The impassioned grief of the central characters is masterfully contrasted and focussed by the gentle picturebook townscape in the background.

The immediate focus of the second main room, the old church itself, is Michelangelo Leggi's fantastic blue and gold sculpted ceiling (1536), alive with birds, animals, serpentine reptiles, piles of fruit and fir cones, tools and religious impedimenta. At the far end, above a Florentine marble font, you'll find one of Fra Angelico's finest works, a glorious *Annunciation* echoing the blue and gold of the ceiling. Its extraordinary clarity and minute detail is at once awe-inspiring and enchanting – each tiny feather of the angel's wings, delicate flower picked out of the dark green garden, rosy fruit and fringed palm has a character of its own. The richness of the cloth and the Madonna's gentle expression invests an unusual warmth to this classically stylized form. In the final room, there are a pair of beautiful 14th-century *Madonnas* from the

Sienese school – one by Duccio, the other by Lorenzetti. They flank the tremendously ornate Vagnucci reliquary (c.1458 Florence), colorfully enameled and bejeweled with seed pearls and precious stones.

Museo dell'Accademia Etrusca, Palazzo Pretorio, Piazza Signorelli, Cortona
Open: Tues–Sun Apr–Sep 10am–1pm 4pm–7pm; Oct–Mar
    9am–1pm 3pm–5pm   Closed: Mon
Admission: ʟ3,000

The entrance to the museum lies behind a great gray 17th-century facade on Piazza Signorelli. Walk through the covered archway, lined with former governors' coats-of-arms, and up a flight of steps into the original castle built in the 13th century but heavily remodeled during the Renaissance period. Cortona's ancient past has furnished this museum with a notable collection of Etruscan art as well as Roman and Egyptian antiquities. Down the center of the enormous Great Hall glass cabinets contain a magnificent array of statuettes from goddesses garlanded with laurels to dancing girls waving trumpets and tamborines; statues of Hercules by the dozen; and bronze farm animals including pigs, dogs, goats and ducks. A collection of 15th-century miniature ivory carvings decorated with figures and a pretty acorn design provide light relief. At the far end, a painting by Francesco Signorelli (no relation) shows Cortona's four patron saints arranging the town's protection with a Madonna, while a Pinturicchio hangs in a crazily warped and cracked frame.

This museum is enormous. From the sarcophagi and framed fragments of hieroglyphics on papyrus, you move through to fine arts and furniture. There's a superb 18th-century inlaid dresser sporting intricate townscapes with jumbled houses, churches and towers peeking over city walls behind trees and marshland. In the latter rooms you'll find terrific high ceilings and several frescoes, plus a collection of Etruscan pottery and carved Roman capitals. Check out the monster 18th-century globe too: this shows California as an island.

SHOPPING IN CORTONA

Antiques are big news in Cortona; they even host an annual antiques fair here in September. You can start at **Bottega d'Arte**, Piazza della Repubblica 6 (Credit cards: v), where the antique prints make useful souvenirs. Antique and reproduction silver is available in quantity and there are some attractive 19th-century china figurines. **Giorgio Billi**, Piazza Signorelli 29, is one of several small traders in this square. Apart from impressive country furniture, you'll find a good selection of collectables from antique tools, copper jelly molds and apothecaries' pestle and mortars to pretty cut-glass scent bottles with silver stoppers. A quick trip down Via Nazionale will reveal a cook shop at **Nos 6–8**, which stocks unusual modern glass by IVV and Alessi coffee percolators. More antiques at **Antichita**, Via Nazionale 37 (MC, V), displayed in a spacious showroom ideal for several elegant 18th-century armoires and divans. Also silver, old maps and 18th- to 19th-century ceramics including chemists' jars. Lastly, a brief mention for **Giulio Lucarini**, Via Nazionale 56 (with a studio around the corner), who designs attractive country-style pottery and some fun speckledy salad bowls.

WHERE TO EAT/WHERE TO STAY IN CORTONA

If it's lunchtime, make tracks for **Ristorante La Loggetta (L)**, Piazza di Pescheria 3, just above Piazza della Repubblica. (Tel: (0575) 603009. Open: Tues–Sun 12:30pm–3pm 7pm–11pm. Closed: Jan–Feb.) Below green shutters, this is an old wine store with outdoor tables in summer and a good family atmosphere pervading the common sense cuisine. For overnight stays, **Albergo San Luca (LL)**, Piazza Garibaldi 2, is a pleasant surprise. (Tel: (0575) 603787. Open: Year round. Amenities: ☎ Ⓜ ✕ ♀ Credit cards: AE, DC, MC, V.) In a quiet, shady square, the San Luca is blessed with superb views over the plain, comfortable modern decor and 75 rooms all with bath. The verandah is a must for the sunset, and there's a convenient restaurant. (Closed: Tues in winter.)

*Wend your way back downhill from Cortona into **Camucia** and turn left. Pass the right turn for Foiano (the road you arrived on) and continue straight on down ss71 where you'll pick up signs for Perugia en route to **Riccio** 5kms later. The intersection with the highway is 5kms on: drive under the road bridge, then take the first left for **Perugia**. There are terrific views across Lago Trasimeno 6kms later, and the road bores through a series of tunnels.*

*Approaching Perugia after 28kms, you pass exits for **Perugia-Ferro di Cavallo** and **Madonna-Alta**; take the third exit indicating **Centro** 3kms later. Keep right, entering the city limits ½km on. Drive uphill in the left lane through a series of tunnels and on for 2kms up **Via San Galigano** to a traffic light by a portal. Turn sharp right along **Viale Orazio Antinori** around the city walls for a further 2kms to **Piazza dei Partigiani** by the Hotel Lilli. At a set of traffic lights turn left around the Garibaldi monument in **Largo Cacciatori delle Alpi** onto **Via G. Marconi**. After an archway (¼km), turn left for **Centro**, bearing around in front of a church to a further intersection, where you keep right for **Hotels-Centro Storico**. Park wherever you can now – **Piazza Italia** is at the top of the hill where you'll find signs for the **Tourist Office**, Corso Vannucci 94. (Tel: (075) 23327. Open: Mon–Sat 8:30am–1:30pm 3:30pm–6:30pm; Sun 9am–1pm.)*

PERUGIA

Capital of Umbria, Perugia ("the Gentle") successfully combines its roles as a medieval hill town, an important arts center, a sophisticated university city, and a famed chocolate producer. The city rises on a hilltop above the plain. As you approach you'll see the gray stone buildings silhouetted against the blue Umbrian sky. Don't be put off by the modern development on the town's outskirts – Perugia has had to make sacrifices in the name of progress – you'll find fascinating medieval quarters tucked away within the modern exterior. The oldest part is naturally nearest the top of the hill. As the city grew, a second level developed, known as the Lower City.

Perugia was the site of a flourishing Etruscan cultural center before the Romans took it over in 310BC. The city later became a Lombard duchy (592AD). From then on it was one disaster after another: bloody wars with neighbors interspersed by violent feuding between rival local families. This culminated in a massacre on August 14, 1500 which successfully removed most of the leaders. Pope Paul III seized the town in 1535; it was annexed to the French Empire in 1809, then restored to the church in 1815. Finally it became part of united Italy (1860).

An English pilgrim in the Middle Ages, hearing of the town's bloodbaths, referred to it as "the terrible city of Perugia", and described its citizens as "the most warlike of the people of Italy". To toughen themselves up, the Perugini dressed in padded clothing, divided into teams and stoned each other until the streets were littered with corpses. Legend has it that their families took the deaths calmly and bore no resentment.

Amazingly, in the midst of this perpetual bloodbath, Perugia calmly flourished as the center of the great Umbrian painting school which reached its height in the 15th century. The school produced masters such as Boccati, Bonfigli and Lorenzo, but the local celebrity was Pietro Vannucci (1445–1523), better known as Perugino. He was also Raphael's teacher. You can see the best of his frescoes in the Collegio del Cambio (Stock Exchange).

The city's main street, Corso Vannucci, runs along its highest ridge and is a mixture of old and new. It's closed to motor traffic, but during the evening *passeggiata* (strollers' hour) human traffic is almost as bad. At the northern end, you'll find the Duomo, Fonte Maggiore (Great Fountain) and Palazzo dei Priori (Priors' Palace), all conveniently situated around Piazza IV Novembre (see below) in the heart of the old city.

The austere Gothic cathedral is on the square's north side, its steps a favorite meeting and resting place for students and tourists alike. Begun in 1345 to replace an earlier building, it was completed in 1490 – except for one wall which was to be covered in pink marble (and has remained uncovered ever since). Above the

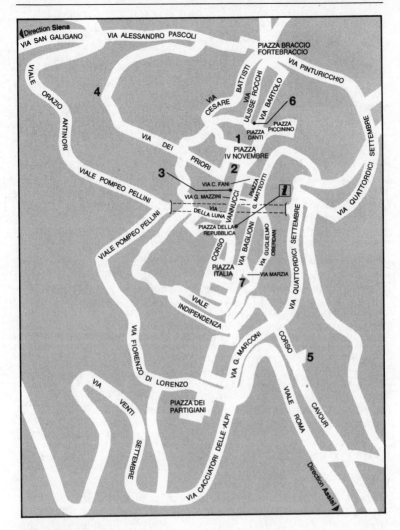

PERUGIA

- **ℹ** Tourist Office
- **1** Piazza IV Novembre
- **2** Galleria Nazionale dell'Umbria
- **3** Collegio del Cambio
- **4** Oratorio di San Bernadino
- **5** Museo Archeologico Nazionale dell'Umbria
- **6** Pozzo Etrusco
- **7** Rocca Paolina

main entrance there's a large crucifix protected by glass. It was placed there 600 years ago by a guilt-ridden soldier who'd mistakenly fired at the cathedral.

A climb up Via del Sole, leading from Piazza Danti next to the cathedral, brings you to the lovely Piazza Michelotti, the city's highest point. Retrace your steps to Piazza Danti and head down Via Ulisse Rocchi to the Arco di Augusto: a magnificent gate built over a period of two thousand years. Etruscans built the lower part; Romans added the upper section; and the pretty loggia on top was completed in the 16th century. Beyond the gate, you'll see the 18th-century Palazzo Gallenga Stuart, home of the Universita Italiana per Stranieri (University for Foreigners). Students come to this center of Italian language and culture from all over the world. The University of Perugia, founded in 1307, lies to the north in a former Olivetan monastery.

At the southern end of Corso Vannucci, you'll find Piazza Italia and the Giardini Carducci. From these unremarkable terraced gardens there's a wonderful view over the San Pietro quarter. An escalator in Piazza Italia leads down to the 16th-century Rocca Paolina fortress built by Sangallo. The fortress contains a confusing and sinister roofed-over city of grim walls, dark archways and deep shadows, which was incorporated into the design by order of the hated Pope Paul III. He wanted a hidden stronghold which could also serve as a prison. In 1848, the Perugini revolted and most of the hidden city was knocked down.

After dark take a stroll through the old city. You'll find the stone buildings, archways and cobbled alleyways give you a true taste of the Middle Ages. Afterwards return to the bright lights and cosmopolitan atmosphere of Corso Vannucci and enjoy a drink in one of the elegant cafés.

WHAT TO SEE IN PERUGIA

Piazza IV Novembre, Perugia

This piazza has always been at the center of important events in Perugia. During the Middle Ages it was the scene of violent and bloody conflict during struggles between the town's leading families, and silver-tongued St Bernardine preached to gathered crowds from the pulpit at the side of Palazzo dei Priori. A famous 15th-century preacher and pacifist, St Bernardine needs all his persuasive powers to bargain for the souls of the advertising industry. He was proclaimed their patron saint in 1959.

The **Fonte Maggiore** at the center of the piazza is considered to be Perugia's most important monument. It was built at the end of the 13th century to celebrate the completion of an aqueduct carrying fresh water to the town from a spring eight kilometers away. Sculpted in white marble, it's an elaborate structure, rather like an enormous three-tiered wedding cake. A frieze around the base begins its tale with the story of Original Sin, works its way through Roman and Perugian history throwing in the signs of the zodiac for good measure, and finishes with tablets devoted to philosophy. Twenty-four saints surround the middle basin, while three water-nymphs balance on top. The sculptors were celebrated father and son, Nicolo and Giovanni Pisano.

On the west side of the piazza, **Palazzo dei Priori** is now the town hall (Palazzo Comunale). (Open: Tues–Sat 9am–1pm 3pm–7pm, Sun 9am–noon 3pm–7pm. Admission free.) Begun in around 1293–97, it was enlarged and completed in 1443. The older facade overlooks the piazza, and from here you'll see a flight of steps up to a doorway flanked by a Perugian griffin and a lion holding chains. The latter was supposedly looted from the gates of Siena after a successful Perugian offensive. To the right of the steps is St Bernardine's pulpit. The entire pink and white Gothic-style structure is outstanding.

Galleria Nazionale dell'Umbria, Palazzo dei Priori, Perugia
Open: Mon–Sat Summer 9am–2pm 3pm–7pm, Sun 9am–1pm;
   mornings only in winter
Admission: L4,000

This gallery occupies the top floor of Palazzo dei Priori. Its early rooms are dedicated to the great Tuscan masters of the 13th to 15th centuries: Fra Angelico, Piero della Francesca, Nicolo and Giovanni Pisano (who designed the Fonte Maggiore) and Duccio. Then it's the turn of the Umbrians headed by Perugino; this collection includes works by Boccati, Bonfigli, Caporali, Fiorenzo di Lorenzo and Pinturicchio. Art lovers shouldn't miss this.

Collegio del Cambio, Corso Vannucci, Perugia
Open: Mar–Oct Tues–Sat 9am–12:30pm 2:30pm–5:30pm, Sun
   9am–12:30pm; Nov–Feb Tues–Sat 8am–2pm, Sun
   9am–12:30pm   Closed: Mon
Admission: L1,000

Just like the *cambio* signs in the bank, this building was constructed for the money changers. They obviously had quite a bit to spare, and lavished it on superb decoration. The highlights are Perugino's fabulous frescoes which billow across the Council Chamber like dream sequences. Raphael was Perugino's pupil, and it's believed that the figures of the *Eternal Father with Prophets and Sibyls* were painted by the young Raphael at the tender age of 17.

Oratorio di San Bernardino, Piazza San Francesco, Perugia
Open: Daily 9am–noon 3:30pm–7pm
Admission free

This superb Renaissance oratory is linked to the Chiesa di San

Francesco by an arch. Its beautiful 15th-century sculpted facade in multi-colored marble is by the great Florentine artist Agostino di Duccio. Inside, the altar is an enormous, ornately carved third-century sarcophagus.

Museo Archeologico Nazionale dell'Umbria, Piazza G. Bruno, Corso Cavour, Perugia
Open: Mon–Sat 9am–2pm 3pm–7pm, Sun 9am–1pm
Admission: L2,000

Entrance to this museum, which houses one of the finest collections of Etruscan relics in existence, is through a large and beautiful cloistered courtyard. Inside, the exhibits include tombs, vases, bronze lamps, statuettes, and objects worked in gold and terracotta.

Pozzo Etrusco (Etruscan Well), Piazza Danti 18, Perugia
Open: Tues–Sun 9am–12:30pm   Closed: Mon
Admission free

The Etruscan city of Perugia was built around this well, which dates from the fourth to third century BC. Originally it was the town's only water supply, holding around 450,000 liters and fed by natural springs. Reached by a flight of narrow, slippery stairs through low tunnels hewn out of the rock, it's awe-inspiring to stare down into the well's bottomless green depths.

Rocca Paolina
Open: Daily 9am–1pm 4pm–7pm
Admission free

Reached from the Etruscan Porta Marzia (in Via Marzia) or by a series of escalators connecting Piazza dei Partigiani with Piazza Italia (there's one opposite the Hotel Brufani), Rocca Paolina is an area of pure medieval Perugia. Astonishing as it seems, this ancient quarter was vaulted over and incorporated in the foundations of the town's enormous 16th-century fortress, preserving for posterity the shells of houses, stores and workshops. Walking through streets which were once open to the sky is an amazing experience. Now the underground city, much of it once owned by the powerful Baglioni family, is lit by dim lights, giving a spooky film-set atmosphere to the place. There's some great modern sculpture too, which makes the setting even more surreal.

SHOPPING IN PERUGIA

If you've been in Italy for two weeks or two days, it's more than likely you've encountered a "Perugina". Wrapped in silver-and-blue paper, these delicious chocolates are on sale at every confectionist, tobacconist, and newsstand throughout the land. They usually lurk in hotel minibars too. If you haven't tried them already, now's the time. **Corso Vannucci** is the heart of Perugia's shopping district, a broad pedestrian throughfare leading from Piazza Italia to the Duomo where the student population sun themselves on the steps. Constantly busy, from noon to late at night, this is the heart of Perugia's fashionable boutiques: they're all chic, rather over-priced (compared with Rome) and of similarly high quality. The fabulous **Trussardi** (Credit cards: AC, DC, MC, V), typifies Italian fashion wizardry with elegant knitwear designs trimmed in leather, beautiful scarves, casually expensive men's and women's clothing, plus all the accessories from monogrammed key rings and luggage to designer fountain-pens decorated in a rich walnut-wood pattern. **Vannucci**, No 14 (AE, DC, MC, V), stocks menswear from Ferre, Bonas and Mazza; **Ritzino**, Piazza Danti 24 (AE, DC, MC, V) equips quality-conscious kids, as well as their adult counterparts, in English-style sweaters and prints, Italian cords and Timberland footwear.

Rufini, Piazza IV Novembre 31 (AE, DC, MC, V), is practically next door. There's lots to attract the antiques buff's magpie eye here. Carefully displayed beneath painted ceilings, an elegant 18th-century dressing table is decorated with Venetian glass scent bottles, silver-and-tortoise shell trinket boxes and china figurines. Heavy mahogany desks; dainty occasional tables on finely tapered legs; beautifully inlaid display cabinets; silver traveling clocks from another era; and glittering early 20th-century paste jewelry for secret showgirls all make an appearance.

On the crafts side, there's a fun market around the Duomo every Tuesday and Saturday morning, where you can pick up pottery bargains. The nearby town of Deruta is one of Italy's major ceramics producers, and you'll find a good selection on sale at **Maioliche Artistiche Umbre**, Via Baglioni 32 (AE, V). Less overpowering than the Sienese designs, Deruta specializes in delicate blue and white swirls and scrolls with colors added in the central design – the clockfaces make very pretty and unusual gifts or souvenirs. There are also some attractive antique-style patterns decorated with fish and animals in soft greens and oranges. **Bottega d'Arte Cellucci**, Corso Vannucci 38 (AE, DC, MC, V), stocks a little bit of everything: pretty enameled mugs and coffee services; antique and reproduction copper pots and trays; eyecatching fabrics and tapestries which make great wall hangings; Umbrian hand-embroidered bedspreads; yet more ceramics; plus an unusual collection of walking canes sporting decorative silver tops. **Laboratoria Artigianale**, Via Marzia 3, is a terrific glass "workshop" selling highly original hand-painted and colored glassware. Rainbow-colored brandy snifters and stoppered decanters are decorated in deep pinks, greens, blues and purples outlined in gold. Local crafts don't come a lot more traditional than wine-making, and for the best selection visit **Enoteca Provinciale di Perugia**, Via

Ulisse Rocchi (DC, V). Outside you'll see an impressive 15th-century wine press atop a stone trough.

WHERE TO EAT IN PERUGIA

Ristorante del Sole, Via della Rupe, Perugia   **L**
Tel: (075) 65031
Open: Sun–Fri 1pm–3:30pm 7pm–11pm   Closed: Sat
Credit cards: AE, DC, MC, V

Furnished in bright modern blues and yellows, this sunny restaurant is tucked down a covered passage off the top of Via Oberdan surrounded by a clutch of smart little stores. The garden is set inside the original medieval stone walls with beautiful views over the Umbrian valley to Assisi, and the food is first class. Local specialities include rice with chopped vegetables and pasta with mushrooms; service is attentive.

Falchetto, Via Bartolo 20, Perugia   **L**
Tel: (075) 61875
Open: Tues–Sun 1pm–3pm 7pm–11pm   Closed: Mon
Credit cards: AE, DC, V

This is a tiny restaurant with a barrel-vaulted ceiling behind the Duomo. Don't be put off by the rather grotty wood-panelling visible from the street, but barely noticeable once you're inside. At the back, there's an open kitchen with a barbecue grill reached by a flight of steps flanked by bowls of fruit; pretty tables in the body of the room are decorated with posies of dried flowers. Charming service. Chef's specials include *risotto alla fregoli* (rice with a rich sauce flavored with ham and shavings of truffles), good grills and desserts such as *tirami su*, a rich coffee gateau. Also, a special mention for the wondrously succulent prosciutto.

La Taverna, Via delle Streghe 8, Perugia   **LL**
Tel: (075) 61028
Open: Tues–Sun 1pm–3pm 7pm–midnight
Closed: Mon, mid–end Jul
Credit cards: AE, DC, MC, V

You can understand why this is called "the street of the witches" (*streghe*) as you plunge down the steps of this covered alley off Corso Vannucci. La Taverna, decorated with potted greenery, is a comforting sight tucked in a small square at the bottom. Vaulted ceilings and archways link a series of connecting dining rooms. Pasta with truffles is always a good bet as are various rich risottos for the hungry diner. Milk-fed lamb is deliciously tender and served in generous quantities, and tempting seasonal desserts are on display.

WHERE TO STAY IN PERUGIA

Brufani, Piazza Italia 12, Perugia   **LLL**
Tel: (075) 62541   Open: Year round
Amenities: ☎ Ⓜ Ⓟ ✗ ⚲ ▯   Credit cards: AE, DC, MC, V

This gem of a small hotel has a mere 24 rooms (including three suites). The Brufani occupies a prime position in the corner of Piazza Italia at the top of the town. You have to share the shady belvedere with the rest of the world, but the views from your bedroom window are all yours. The attractive rooms are furnished with a sprinkling of antiques. Downstairs, there's an elegant seating area, polished art deco bar and chic little restaurant serving Umbrian cuisine.

La Rosetta, Piazza Italia 19, Perugia   **LL**
Tel: (075) 20841   Open: Year round
Amenities: ☎ Ⓜ Ⓟ ✗ ⚲   Credit cards: AE, DC, MC, V

Conveniently located at the top of Corso Vannucci, the hotel encircles a pretty medieval courtyard, though La Rosetta's interior has been thoroughly modernized. Efficient reception and car parking service make for a pleasant welcome; all 103 comfortable rooms have bath/shower and some antique furniture. There's a bar area downstairs, a very good value restaurant (L) boasting a handful of culinary awards and tables in the courtyard during summer. Try the vol-au-vent filled with tortellini in a meat sauce, ravioli with nut sauce and a delicious light vegetable mousse topped with tomato.

Hotel Signa, Via del Grillo 9–16, Perugia   **LL**
Tel: (075) 61080/22393   Open: Year round except 1 wk Xmas
Amenities: ☎ Ⓟ ⚲   Credit cards: AE, DC

The Signa is well-signposted from Largo Cacciatori delle Alpi, where you take Viale Roma. Follow signs off to the left and through St Peter's Gate then park on the pavement. The hotel is up a narrow alley (they'll arrange garaging for the car). A 10-to-15 minute walk below the town center, the Signa is small and friendly, but has few frills. There are 25 comfortable, modern rooms all with bath, also a separate building housing mini-apartments (excellent value, but minimum one-week stay). There's a quiet patio garden, small breakfast room and TV room so compact it's like an airplane.

PERUGIA TO ASSISI

*The route to **Assisi** is marked right out of **Piazza Italia**, driving back down **Viale Indipendenza** to **Largo Cacciatori delle Alpi**. Here you turn left, taking **Viale Roma** along the city walls for 1¼kms; then* *turn right (with Porta San Constanzo on your left). Another 3kms brings you to the highway, turning right for Assisi/Foligno just after a small yellow church. After 6½kms the Cesano road bears off to the left; 2kms later you turn left for Assisi (ss147) into Ospedalicchio. There are superb views of Assisi, crowned by its medieval fortress, as you drive across the valley. To the left, St Francis's Basilica juts out above the sheer stone facings of the monastery. Climbing into town 10kms later, there's a further magnificent vista back to the great dome of Santa Maria degli Angeli on the plain. Just after the Assisi sign, you can drive straight ahead and park near San Francesco or continue uphill for another 1½kms to a parking lot by the summer season Tourist Office. From the lower parking lot, walk up Via Fontebella to the main Tourist Office, Piazza del Comune. (Tel: (075) 812534. Open: Mon–Sat 9am–1pm 3:30pm–6:30pm; holidays 9am–3pm.)*

ASSISI

The tiny Umbrian city of Assisi clings to the slopes of Mount Subasio. Rising on a series of ledges and terraces, the city overlooks the valleys of the Topino and Chiascio rivers. A town of great charm and tranquility, Assisi developed from the Roman town of *Asisium*. Assisi's past wasn't always so tranquil: in the early Middle Ages it was fought over by the dukes of Spoleto. It then became an independent commune in the 12th century, engaged in local feuds and wars with Perugia and was annexed to the Papal States. Assisi finally joined the Kingdom of Italy in 1860.

Set against the soft beauty of the Umbrian countryside, this is a fitting birthplace for St Francis (1182–1228). As a young man, he had a taste for good living and high society. But later, after imprisonment during a Perugian war, he became devout and devoted his life to prayer and penitence. With a deep love of nature and animals St Francis was known as "God's songwriter".

Despite the never-ending stream of pilgrims and tourists, Assisi retains a serenity and peace which have earned it the title of "City of birds and silence". To experience the tranquility, take an evening stroll through the delightful cobbled lanes of pink and white stone buildings and flower-decked balconies. Still enclosed by ramparts, Assisi has hardly changed since the Middle Ages.

You'll find that almost any building worth looking at is in some way associated with St Francis. The most striking is the Basilica di San Francesco: an elaborate, majestic 13th-century monument enriched with frescoes and paradoxically dedicated to a saint who preached poverty.

Assisi, all steps, steep alleyways and more steps, is a fitness freak's dream city. That said, it's worth the climb from the basilica up Via San Francesco with its fine medieval houses, to Piazza del Comune. You'll pass the Casa dei Maestri Comacini (Como Masons' Guild) – most of the workmen who built the basilica came from Como in northern Italy; the charming frescoed Oratorio dei Pellegrini, a 15th-century pilgrims' hospice; and Monte Frumentario, a 13th-century hospital converted into a granary. The adjacent fountain still has a notice warning that anyone caught washing their clothes here will be fined and have their laundry confiscated.

Though hardly in the center of town, Piazza del Comune is the town center, built on the first piece of level ground you've seen. Remains of Roman *Asisium* jostle with medieval buildings here. What at first looks like a dilapidated bank, is in fact the Roman Temple of Minerva, now Santa Maria's church. The monstrous blackened Corinthian columns supporting the facade date from the first century BC, and present a striking contrast to the well-preserved medieval buildings all around. Among the sights of this later period, you'll see a 13th-century tower and the Palazzo Comunale which houses the **Civic Gallery**. (Open: Daily Mar–Oct 10am–7pm; Nov–Feb 11am–1pm 2:30pm–6:30pm. Admission: L3,000.) Also known as *La Pinoteca Comunale*, the gallery displays a fine collection of works by Umbrian masters and Giotto's followers. The truth is, after the overwhelming treasures in the basilica these by comparison tend to be rather disappointing, despite their quality.

East of the piazza, along Corso Mazzini, you'll find the Chiesa Nuova built over the house where St Francis's parents lived; and the gorgeous candy-striped facade of Chiesa di Santa Chiara. A hike up the steep Via San Rufino brings you to Piazza San Rufino. Straight ahead you'll see the Duomo with its massive belltower and impressive Romanesque facade. From the cathedral, you can easily reach Rocca Maggiore, a well-preserved 12th-century fortress.

A short drive due south out of town takes you to the Convento di San Damiano. One of Italy's most sacred shrines, it stands in peaceful silence, surrounded by cypress and olive trees. This is where St Francis heard Christ telling him "Francis, repair my falling house." At which, the young man rushed home, sold a bale of cloth from his father's warehouse to raise money (getting himself disinherited in the process) and began a new life of poverty and simplicity. Later, he brought St Clare and her nuns here, solving the problem of housing his female converts; and composed his lovely *Canticle of All Things Created* on a visit to this convent.

If you have time, take the scenic drive east up Monte Subasio to **Eremo delle Carceri**. (Open: Daily 8am–dusk. Admission free.) This simple hermitage in the hills is far more in keeping with the spirit of St Francis than all the ostentatious basilicas in the world. Established by St Bernardine in the 15th century, the original cave cells are part of a larger complex of buildings. The warren of tiny rooms is connected by steep, twisting stairs and there are two tiny chapels where the hermits prayed. In the pretty terraced courtyard there's a tree where St Francis supposedly preached to the birds.

Below Assisi, rising from the plain like a mirage, is the elaborate frescoed church of Santa Maria degli Angeli, built over the Chapel of the Porziuncola (which literally means "a small portion of earth"). This chapel was given to St Francis by the Benedictines in return for a yearly basket of carp from the River Tescio – still faithfully paid today by the Franciscans. You'll see the cell where St Francis lay on the bare earth to die. Nearby is the rose garden into which he threw himself when wrestling with temptation. Since then, the roses have bloomed without thorns.

Assisi is a city of many religious celebrations which are joyous occasions for feasting, processions and amusements. Easter week brings thousands of visitors to see the processions and mystery plays; *Calendimaggio* (May Day) celebrates the return of spring. Townspeople wear magnificent medieval costumes and parade along the streets in two groups which compete in a playful singing competition.

WHAT TO SEE IN ASSISI

Basilica di San Francesco, Via San Francesco, Assisi
Open: Daily 9am–noon 2pm–1 hr before sunset
Admission free

Assisi's famous basilica was built on a site once known as "Infernal Hill" because criminals were executed here. With characteristic humility, St Francis asked to be buried in this spot; the Pope granted his wish and the name was changed to "Hill of Paradise". The 13th-century basilica comprises two superimposed churches, a crypt and adjoining monastery all designed by Brother Elias, St Francis's successor. The upper church is a beautiful and imposing white stone building with a magnificent arched door and intricate rosette window. Its lofty interior is painted throughout and the choir stalls at the far end are works of art in their own right. Take time to enjoy the beautifully crafted marquetry portraits of saints, a caged bird, organ pipes and unusual still-life vistas through windows and doors or the contents of a broom cupboard in immaculate perspective.

In the lower church, you're treated to one of the most important collections of frescoes in Italy. As a tribute to this well-loved saint, the very finest masters journeyed to Assisi to decorate these chapels: Giotto, Cimabue, Simone Martini and Pietro Lorenzetti all joined forces with the unknown "Maestro di San Francesco" to create a treasure of unsurpassed beauty and immeasurable artistic importance. Below the lower church is the secret vault where Brother Elias placed the saint's remains. Determined to thwart relic-robbers, he hid the coffin so well that it wasn't discovered until 1818. Now it's on view in a small chapel.

Chiesa di Santa Chiara, Piazza Santa Chiara, Via Borgo Aretino
Open: Daily 9am–noon 2pm–1 hr before sunset
Admission free

This is a Gothic gem, with its superb dusty-pink and white striped facade and enormous, intricate rose window. Built between 1257 and 1265, the church dominates a large sunny square overlooking the lower town. The soaring, light-filled interior boasts a graceful high altar supported by 12 pillars. St Clare is buried in the crypt below. Like St Francis, St Clare came from a wealthy family. She deserted them at the age of 18 to follow the teachings of St Francis. Later she founded the Franciscan Order for women, the Poor Clares, and was joined by her sister and widowed mother. In 1215, Pope Innocent III granted the Poor Clares the "privilege of poverty": permission to live off alms alone. St Clare guided her community right up to her death in 1255, suffering constant ill-health bought on by the harshness of her personal regime, though this was never forced on others.

In 1958, Pope Pius XII decreed St Clare the patron saint of television because she once had a simultaneous vision of a Christmas service taking place in the basilica when she was over two kilometers away at San Damiano. You used to be able to buy reception-guaranteed statuettes of St Clare which plugged into your television.

Chiesa Nuova and Casa Paterna di San Francesco, Corso Mazzini
Open: Daily 9am–noon 2pm–1 hr before sunset
Admission free

This small, richly decorated Baroque church, marbled within an inch of its life, was erected in 1615 over the remains of St Francis's parents' medieval home. Inside, you'll see the cell-like niche where the saint was locked up by his father after he sold the bale of cloth to repair San Damiano and announced his intention to become a monk. Finally, he was freed by his mother. She's portrayed with the keys in her hand in a modern sculpture outside the church. The altar is built over what was once St Francis's bedroom. Below the church, through a door marked *Santuario*, is a small courtyard leading down to the room where his father worked as a textile merchant. The house's original *porto della morte* still exists, filled with modern stained glass. It's the door by which the dead were taken out. All medieval houses, rich and poor alike, had one of these doors which was never used by the living.

SHOPPING IN ASSISI

Essentially a tourist trap, you'll find the best bargains in Assisi at the souvenir shops which line **Via San Francesco** and the streets off **Piazza del Comune**. For the best choice of embroidery there are several good shops leading up to the basilica on **Via Frate Elia**, also at **Maioliche di Deruta**, Piazza del Comune 25 (Credit cards: AE, DC, V). Coasters start at around L6,000, place mats at L10,000 and prices climb from here for embroidered or beautiful lacy tablecloths. There are plenty of ceramics on offer such as tiles (L7,000), nativity figures and pretty painted pottery beads (L5,500 each). Antiques stores spring up everywhere. For the most pretentious, it's worth window-shopping in **Antichita Gioelli**, Via Portico 16A (AE, MC, V), where a pair of early 19th-century gold and enamel drop earrings were on offer at a staggering L1,500,000. Lots more jewelry, silver and gorgeous 18th-century marquetry furniture to gaze at. The prettiest shop must be the tiny **Galleria Fontebella**, Via Fontebella 13 (V), with pigeons a meter deep on the low roof and the facade decorated with splendid metal dragons hanging from brackets. Inside this tiny musty store, you'll find lovely religious art and sculpture, pewter tankards and pots, plus some unusual 18th-century porcelain and cruder pottery. Assisi produces its own *digestif* called *L'Amaro Francescano*, which is on sale all over the place. A little wine store, **Tartufi**, Via Portica 14, sells wine (and *grappa*) in handy little bottles, but try it first. Via Portica is also good for tempting cake shops.

WHERE TO EAT IN ASSISI

Frantoio, (Hotel Fontebella), Vicolo Illuminata   **LL-LLL**
Tel: (075) 812977
Open: Daily 12:30pm–3:30pm 7pm–11pm Closed: Wed in winter
Credit cards: AE, DC, MC, V

Built into the hillside below Hotel Fontebella (there's an elevator in the foyer), the Frantoio has been converted from an old olive oil mill. Beyond the vaulted stone ceilings of the dining room, there's a lovely covered terrace edged with greenery for the summer months with views over the lower town. Service is thoughtful and polite; the cuisine Umbrian; the prices quite steep. But there's no doubt about the quality. Delicious crunchy *bruschetta* with olive oil and garlic goes well with a salad (although the Italians sometimes find this odd). A great range of generous meat dishes from grills to country casseroles such as *strangozzi*. The dessert trolly, laden with rich gateaux, is spectacular: macaroon specialities are a must.

Buca di San Francesco, Via Brizi 1, Assisi   L
Tel: (075) 812204
Open: Tues–Sun 1pm–3:30pm 7pm–11pm
Closed: Mon, Sun pm in winter, mid-Jan to Mar
Credit cards: AE, DC, MC, V

Behind an elaborate metal grille at the top of Via Fontebella, this restaurant, with its genuinely rustic atmosphere, serves a selection of traditional Tuscan and Umbrian dishes. Stone walls and rush-bottomed chairs create a homey feel to the dining room, and both the chefs are women. Their excellent cooking explodes the Italian myth that only men can be creative in the kitchen. The local specialities are pigeon, game and crêpes with meat.

La Fontana da Carletto, Via San Francesco 8, Assisi   L
Tel: (075) 812933
Open: Wed–Mon 12:30pm–3pm 7pm–midnight
Closed: Tues and Feb
Credit cards: AE, DC, V

Right on the main street in a pretty vine-covered building, the Fontana is divided into a pizzeria and a restaurant proper, with local specialities of game pâté and pasta with vegetables. The atmosphere is friendly; the pizzas are particularly recommended.

WHERE TO STAY IN ASSISI

Hotel Umbra, Via degli Archi 6, Assisi   LL
Tel: (075) 812240
Closed: Mid-Nov to mid-Dec, mid-Jan to mid-Mar
Amenities: ✗ ♀ Credit cards: AE, DC, MC, V

This 27-room family-run hotel is situated at the end of a pictur-esque arched passageway which leads off the main Piazza del Comune in the center of town. Parts of the building date from the 13th century, but its decor is elegant and modern. The bed-rooms, some of which retain original stonework features, are decorated in an apricot color scheme, with solid wooden furniture. All have either bath/shower. There's a lovely terraced garden with views over the Umbrian countryside, and a restaurant in the leafy courtyard serves regional specialities, superbly cooked and reasonably priced. We recommend you take demi-pension here – bed, breakfast and one other meal.

Hotel Fontebella, Via Fontebella 25, Assisi   LLL
Tel: (075) 812883   Open: Year round
Amenities: ☎ Ⓜ Ⓟ ✗ ♀ Credit cards: AE, DC, MC, V

This hotel is housed in a delightful centuries-old *palazzo* midway between central Piazza del Comune and the basilica, with views over the countryside. It's pleasantly and efficiently run by Signor Giovanni Angeletti, and the staff speak good English. The three-story building has 37 attractive, good-sized rooms, all with bath/shower. There's a garden and highly prized parking lot. Their restaurant, **Il Frantoio** (see page 220), is justly renowned for its Umbrian cuisine.

ASSISI TO SPOLETO

*The ss147 continues from Assisi to rejoin the main **Perugia–Foligno** road (ss75)). Turn left out of the parking area near San Francesco, climbing up past the summer Tourist Office parking lot and then turn right. After 6kms, you're back on the ss75. There's a picturesque view of **Spello**, an ancient fortified town, on the left 6kms later; then the **Foligno** exit 3kms later, where you can make a short detour.*

A SIDETRIP TO FOLIGNO

*You enter the Foligno city limits ½km from the ss75, crossing a bridge and turning left signposted **Centro** ½km later. There's a traffic light after 1km where you cross another bridge, then make a right along the riverbank. At an intersection almost 1km later, turn right and immediately left, driving alongside the old city walls for 1km. At the end of the street lies **Porto Romana** with the Tourist Office on the left. You have to bear right, then left through a block of parked cars. Park as close to here as possible, walking back to the **Tourist Office**, Porta Romana. (Tel: (0742) 60459. Open: Mon–Sat 8am–8pm; Sun in summer only 9am–1pm.)*

FOLIGNO

Unlike most Umbrian cities, Foligno is situated on a plain and stands on the site of Roman *Fulginia*. The street layout still reflects the typically regular Roman arrangement. Via Flaminio, an important trade route built by the Romans in the third century BC, passes through Foligno and accounts for its rapid economic development in the 14th and 15th centuries. The nearby River Topino spurred agricultural development and provided another means of transporting goods, while the area's rich clay soil saw to the production of building materials and ceramics alongside agriculture. During this prosperous heyday, the Trinci family ruled town until it fell to the Papal States in 1439.

Foligno, famous for its important 15th-century painting school, was one of the country's earliest printing centers. Three hundred copies of Dante's *Divine Comedy*, Italy's first book to be published in Italian, are said to have been printed in the town's Palazzo Orfini in 1472, and an old wooden printing press stands in the entrance to Palazzo Trinci in Piazza della Repubblica.

Because of Foligno's favorable geographic position between other Umbrian cities, the town became a hive of industrial and commercial activity in the 19th century. It was considered "a meeting point for consolidating ties of kinship, business relations and matters of public administration". Unfortunately, Foligno suffered heavy bombing in World War II. It has been largely rebuilt, although some of the old quarter around central Piazza della Repubblica has survived. Today the town continues to thrive as an important industrial and commercial center.

The buildings you'll want to see are the Duomo, the church of Santa Maria Infraportas and Palazzo Trinci: all conveniently located around Piazza della Repubblica. The cathedral has an impressive Romanesque facade on Piazza del Duomo, while that on Piazza della Repubblica dates from 1201. Its fine wooden door is ornately carved with saints and angels. The richly decorated interior was rebuilt by Giuseppe Piermarini in the 18th century, but the 12th-century crypt and 16th-century Cappella del Sacramento have survived.

The 15th-century brick-built Palazzo Trinci, joined to the cathedral by an arch, has a neo-classical facade added in the 19th century. It houses a picture gallery and in the chapel you'll see frescoes by Ottaviano Nelli. Santa Maria Infraportas, the oldest building in Foligno, contains 12th-century frescoes which are worth seeing.

*From Porta Romana, take the **Spoleto** road, passing the triumphal arch on your right. Then, keeping the Bar Porta Romana and gas station also to your right, drive directly out of town, over a traffic circle 1km ahead, and through an ugly industrial sector to the **ss3** after 2½kms.*

* * *

*The **ss75** bypasses Foligno and then ends. Here you keep right for **ss3** which eventually runs all the way south to **Rome**. First, however, it passes **Trevi**, pouring down a hillside to your left above the industrialized valley. The landscape clears up around **Campello** 5kms ahead, then you bear off for **Spoleto** 13kms later. Turn left into Spoleto, and left again, driving through the downtown shopping area for ¾km to a triumphal arch. Pass under the arch into **Piazza Garibaldi**, then turn left for **Centro**, climbing alongside the city walls on **Via Anfiteatro** for 1¼kms. When you see a small sign for **Centro/Alberghi**, turn right down a narrow street for ½km to a T-junction signed left for the hotels **Duchi/Gattapone**. Turn left up **Viale G. Matteotti** and you emerge by the **Tourist Office**, Piazza della Libertà 7. (Tel: (0743) 28111. Open: Mon–Sat 9am–12:30pm 3:30pm–6:30pm.)*

SPOLETO

Set among thickly forested hills at the foot of Monteluco, Spoleto is one of Umbria's most beautiful towns. Originally the site of ancient *Spoletium*, the town became an important Roman colony in 241BC. From its strategic position on Via Flaminia, Spoleto successfully repulsed an attack by the Carthaginian general Hannibal, who was forced to take his elephants elsewhere. In the early Middle Ages, Spoleto became the headquarters of a Lombard duchy which ruled most of Umbria, and was the scene of intense feuding between various powerful families.

The town was annexed to the Papal States in 1354. While under papal rule, Spoleto had the dubious distinction of being governed by Lucrezia Borgia – Pope Alexander VI's illegitimate 19-year-old daughter. Then married to the second of her three husbands, she successfully ruled Spoleto for two years. Her power-seeking father subsequently arranged her marriage to the 17-year-old Alfonso d'Este of Ferrara, later murdered by his wife's brother and lover, Cesare. Spoleto became part of the Italian Kingdom in 1860.

Between mid-June and mid-July the town hosts one of Italy's most important cultural events, the *Festival dei Due Mondi* (Festival of the Two Worlds). However, if you visit Spoleto outside the festival season, you'll get a better sense of the town's character – it was a favorite of Assisi's St Francis – and you'll find plenty of entertainment in the piazzas.

The town's most important monument is the majestic Romanesque cathedral. On the steps leading down to Piazza del Duomo, you'll see the charming 12th-century church of Sant'Eufemia. Recently, the Vatican dismissed her sainthood, but in her day she was something of a feminist: her church was the only one in Umbria to provide a *matroneum* (women's gallery). In Via dei Duchi there are medieval artisans' workshops-cum-stores with narrow wooden doors and stone shop counters. At the end of the lane, you reach Piazza del Mercato adorned by Costantino Fiaschetti's 18th-century fountain. The market is held here every Friday morning. Wander through the twisting lanes leading from the piazza and you'll come across vaulted passageways, beautifully carved arches and stairways. Via del Municipo leads to the 13th-century Palazzo Comunale, where two clocks ring out the hours to keep the townsfolk on their toes.

Interesting relics of Spoleto's Roman past include the ruins of a small Roman theater dating from the first century AD. A medieval church was built over the old stage, but the semicircular tiers of seats have been recently restored for use at festival time. A Roman arch marks the entrance to the town at the top of Via Bronzino, and there's a luxurious villa on Via de Visale. Complete with atrium, bedchambers and a mosaic bath, the villa reputedly belonged to Emperor Vespasian's mother. On the northern edge of town, you'll see the remains of an amphitheater. Today it's part of a military barracks.

Further round to the east, you can stroll through gardens surrounding the Rocca, a massive six-towered fortress looming high above Spoleto. Constructed with recycled stone from the Roman amphitheater, it was built by Gattapone for Cardinal Albornoz in the 14th century. Until 1983, the fortress was used as a prison; now it's open to visitors. A short walk along Via del Ponte is a must for a view of the amazing Ponte delle Torri (Bridge of Towers).

Michelangelo found "true peace" among the oak trees of Monteluco, and when you've feasted long enough on the riches of Spoleto, the woods make a great picnic spot.

WHAT TO SEE IN SPOLETO

Duomo, Piazza del Duomo, Spoleto
Open: Daily 9am–noon 2pm–7pm
Admission free

The jewel in Spoleto's crown, this cathedral makes an arresting sight from the steps of Via dell'Arringo. Its broad white facade stretches the full width of the pink-paved piazza, and the central mosaic glitters with gold in the sunshine. There's a magnificent Renaissance porch, eight rose windows of varying sizes and a soaring belltower to one side. Consecrated in 1198, then restored during the 17th century, the cathedral's interior is largely unadorned at first sight. Make your way across the busily-patterned mosaic floor to the apse (behind the altar). Here you'll find a series of fabulous 15th-century frescoes by fun-loving monk, Fra Filipo Lippi. An incorrigible womanizer, he was allegedly poisoned to death by a jilted lover. His ornate tomb in the transept was commissioned by Lorenzo "The Magnificent" de Medici. In the first chapel on the right there are frescoes by Pinturicchio depicting scenes from the Virgin's life.

Ponte delle Torri (Bridge of Towers), Via del Ponte, Spoleto
Open: Daily
Admission free

This 14th-century masterpiece is a magnificent sight from the eagle's eye position of Via del Ponte. It spans a 250-foot ravine over the River Tessino in 10 awesome arches and links Spoleto with the slopes of Monteluco. It's possible that this too was the work of Gattapone, who built the Rocca, and it's founded on the remains of an earlier Roman construction. Originally, the bridge's main purpose was to transport water to the town, but you'll also see forts at either end designed to defend the town's approaches.

You can walk the length of the bridge and climb up to a belvedere beyond the fortifications for a wonderful view of Monteluco and the lush wooded hillsides of the Tessino valley.

SHOPPING IN SPOLETO

Bored with hotel soap? Feeling tired and footsore? There's welcome relief at **Cosmesi in Natura**, Via Fontesecca 12 (Credit cards: AE). You'll find a great stock of natural preparations from essential oils, cleansers and soap to henna and bathsalts all scented with flowers or herbs and prettily packaged in northern Italy. The gift baskets are cute (L27,000); there's a mixed box of pot pourri with separate compartments so you can blend the scent of your choice (L21,500); and lavender bags (good for slipping in suitcases) from L5,500. **Ceramiche Umbre**, Via Fontesecca 21 (AE, MC, V), mixes lovely reproductions of olde-world pottery designs with a collection of antique copper kitchen utensils. There are small pans at L150,000 or good value copies of frilly-edged jelly molds with fruit designs at L9,000. Next door, at **Antichita Eugenio Milanese**, there's a small antique furniture showroom with some attractive 18th-century landscapes painted on wood in ornate surrounds. Further up the hill, there's a huge showroom at **Palatium**, Via A. Saffi 11 (AE, DC, V), built around a centuries-old well. Enormous 19th-century bookshelves and dressers are displayed to advantage, decorated with candlesticks, china and pewter bowls of fruit or vegetables. Also worth checking out are the antiques stores lining the route to the Duomo down **Via dell'Arringo**.

Foodies will go nuts around Piazza del Mercato. Start with **Antica Umbria**, Via dei Duchi 3, specializing in things Umbrian from little pots of olive paste to gift boxes of gourmet goods carefully packed in miniature wooden crates. **Lo Sfizioso**, Piazza del Mercato 26, is a great deli for picnic makers. There's a large choice of cold cuts, cheese, ready-made salads, olives, wine and bread. **Salumeria**, Via dell'Arco di Druso 22, definitely picks up the charm award for its engagingly old-fashioned atmosphere. Bags of nuts and dried fruit; tiny pots and tins of truffles; piles of *porcini* (dried mushrooms); enormous jars of artichoke hearts; and a deli counter.

WHERE TO EAT IN SPOLETO

Il Tartufo, Piazza Garibaldi 24, Spoleto　　　　　　　　　LL
Tel: (0743) 40236
Open: Thur–Tues 12:30pm–2:30pm 7pm–11pm
Closed: Wed, mid-Jul to mid-Aug
Credit cards: AE, DC, V

Right at the lower end of town, it's well worth descending from the heights of the Duomo to sample Il Tartufo's gastronomic delights. As you might guess from the name, truffles are a speciality here, and the elegant cuisine is a tribute to the chef's imagination as he adds delicate touches to traditional dishes. The results are outstanding: a simple pasta with cream and truffles is as delicious as any of the more complicated dishes.

Pentagramma, Via Martani 4, Spoleto   L
Tel: (0743) 47838
Open: Tues–Sun 1pm–3:30pm 7:30pm–11:30pm
Closed: Mon, first 2 wks Jan
Credit cards: AE, V

Just off Piazza della Libertà, the Pentagramma is relatively cheap and cheerful with a bistro atmosphere, modern paintings on the walls, flowers on the tables and a young staff. Plentiful regional cooking: the *bruschetta* (crisp bread) with chopped tomato is a simple but tasty starter, and *strangozzi* (rolled pork) lightly fried with herbs makes a change from the usual steaks. The standard of service varies enormously – be prepared for rough edges.

WHERE TO STAY IN SPOLETO

Dei Duchi, Viale G. Matteotti 4, Spoleto   LLL
Tel: (0743) 44541   Open: Year round
Amenities: ☎ 🅿 ✗ ⚲ ⊟ Credit cards: AE, DC, MC, V

A very pleasant modern hotel, just below Piazza della Libertà. There are 50 attractive rooms all with bath/shower, pretty furnishings, contemporary and antique prints plus views over the surrounding countryside. There's breakfast on the terrace in summer, a comfortable seating area in the bar and a sunny restaurant decorated with clambering greenery.

Gattapone, Via del Ponte 6, Spoleto   LLL
Tel: (0743) 36147   Open: Year round
Amenities: ☎ ⚲ ⊟   Credit cards: AE, DC, MC, V

Follow signs for Ponte delle Tori right up at the top of the town and you can park along the belvedere with a superb view of the bridge soaring out of the valley. There are only 13 rooms (with bath/shower) in this delightful small hotel right on the brink of a wooded gorge. A gem of 1960s Italian decor, it's like being on board a luxury cruiser with sweeping wooden staircases, polished floors, friendly staff and a sunny American bar furnished with squashy burgundy leather armchairs.

SPOLETO TO ORVIETO VIA TODI

*Leaving Piazza della Libertà, head back downhill on **Viale G. Matteotti**, past Hotel dei Duchi, to the junction with **Viale Martiri***

*della Resistenza 1/2km ahead. Turn right, following the city walls
and signs for **Acquasparta**. Take a left 1 1/2kms later and you'll soon
pick up signs for **Todi**. The **ss418** runs through the outskirts of
Spoleto and valley villages for 8kms, before starting to snake gently
through the vineyards up into the hills around Firenzuola reaching
a junction outside Acquasparta 15 1/2kms later. This is a convenient
spot to detour off the main route for a trip to the spa of **San Gémini**.
Otherwise, keep straight ahead for Perugia and join the **ss3 bis** for
the drive north to Todi.*

A SIDETRIP TO SAN GÉMINI

*Bear off to the right before the main road (ss3), following signs
for **Acquasparta**. At a T-junction 1/2km ahead, turn left for **San
Gémini**, following a country road, which runs almost parallel to
the highway, for 6 1/2kms to the outskirts of the spa village with a
massive bottling plant on your right. You'll see the left turn into
the spa parking areas 1km ahead, marked **Fonte**.*

The Park and Spring of San Gémini, near San Gémini
Open: Daily May–Sep
Admission: L3,500

The mineral water spring of San Gémini rises 380 meters above
sea level, and the waters are taken to cure gastro, kidney, liver
and urinary disorders. In its natural state, the water is slightly
fizzy, but when bottled the fizziness dissipates. There's a fountain
in the park from which you can drink as much as you like. This
beautiful seven-acre park stands amid a forest of tall trees, including great oaks, pines and mountain ash. Among the trees, numerous paths make for perfect leisurely strolls and the famous spring
of the San Gémini mineral water is also located here, where you
can drink free of charge.

Hotel and Restaurant All'Antica Carsulae, San Gémini   L
Tel: (0744) 630163   Open: Year round
Amenities: ▣ ✗ ⌻   Credit cards: AE, DC, MC, V

There are seven simply-furnished bedrooms in the main building
of this friendly modern hotel-restaurant, and another 12 actually
in the park (all have bath/shower). The bright, airy restaurant is
open to non-residents, its high raftered ceiling and tiled floors
making a refreshing break from the midday sun. It won an important culinary prize recently, and the standard of the traditional
Umbrian cooking is very high. The local specialities are truffles
(of course) and pasta with sausages and cream.

*Make your way back towards Acquasparta, and join the **ss3 bis** in
the direction of **Perugia**.*

* * *

*The dual-lane **ss3 bis** cuts a broad swathe through a patchwork of small farms, woodlands and hills to the **Todi** exit almost 20kms further on. Exit here, entering the town 1km later, and climbing to a junction after ½km. Turn left, then take the next right for **Todi-Centro** 50m further on, passing Hotel Villa Luisa on the right. Another 1km uphill and you turn left in front of a stone gateway, following the city walls to the white marble, multi-domed Renaissance extravagance of Santa Maria della Consolazione. Take a right, keeping straight ahead for **Centro-Citta**. There are views down over the valley until you reach **Piazza Umberto I** 1km later. Follow around to the left, through Piazza della Repubblica, and into **Piazza del Popolo**. You can park here, or around to the right in **Piazza Garibaldi**. Walk back to the arches on the corner of the main square, where you'll find the **Tourist Office** (Protodi), Piazza del Popolo 38. (Tel: (075) 882406. Open: Mon–Sat 9am–1pm 3:30pm–6:30pm, Sun 9:30am–12:30pm.)*

TODI

Three ancient towns in one, beautiful Todi parades its illustrious past with style. The first settlers were Etruscans, who contributed the Porta Marzia gateway at the bottom of Corso Cavour. Next, the Romans rebuilt the battlements; and finally prosperous merchants created the superb medieval town center. Piazza del Popolo is the elegant heart of Todi, edged by the Duomo and no less than three 13th-century palaces. First on the right, nearest the cathedral, is Palazzo del Capitano, reached by an outside staircase. It's joined to the Lombard-style Palazzo del Popolo, a Gothic marvel built over an arcade and festooned with battlements. This is one of Italy's earliest "people's palaces", built in 1213. At the bottom of the piazza, you'll see Palazzo dei Priori, where the ecclesiastics kept house with a good view of the office from remodeled Renaissance windows. It was later occupied by a series of regional governors.

The fourth side of the square is given over to stores and the Gran Caffe Duomo. This is an ideal spot to drink in Todi's historic atmosphere with a drop of 20th-century liquid refreshment or an ice-cream. Corso Cavour is the main shopping street running down from Piazza Garibaldi. Via del Duomo, to the right of the cathedral, houses a couple of antiques shops. Todi also hosts a popular spring antiques fair.

Back in Piazza della Repubblica, you'll find **Chiesa di San Fortunato**. (Open: Daily 8am–12:30pm 2pm–7pm. Admission free.) A remarkably harmonious mixture of Gothic and Renaissance architectural styles, this church is the burial place of Jacopone da Todi (1230–1306). A poet and friar, born Jacopo dei Benedetti, da Todi is one of Italy's most important medieval literary figures.

WHAT TO SEE IN TODI

Duomo, Piazza del Popolo, Todi
Open: Daily 8am–7pm
Admission free

Occupying the top end of the piazza, the cathedral's imposing 13th-century facade and Gothic belltower rise gracefully behind a broad flight of steps. These lead up to a fine portal which surrounds a pair of lovely 17th-century carved doors. Their wooden panels depict various saints and Renaissance motifs. The stunningly simple Romanesque interior is supported on twin rows of columns decorated with elegant carved capitals. It culminates in a great dome above the altar. Here you'll find a semicircle of beautifully-worked choir stalls similar to those in the basilica at Assisi. These, however, are more intricate – musical instruments, astrological apparatus, *palazzos* – and they're all the more impressive for their stark surroundings. Take time to admire the rose window and its twin medalions to left and right; also the narrow pencils of colored glass which line the left-hand wall.

WHERE TO EAT IN TODI

Umbria, Via San Bonaventura 13, Todi   L
Tel: (075) 82390
Open: Wed–Mon 12:30pm–2:30pm 7:30pm–10:30pm
Closed: Tues, and mid-Dec to mid-Jan
Credit cards: AE, MC, V

Tucked behind Palazzo del Popolo, this diminutive restaurant is well worth seeking out. The cozy green dining room, hung with photographs and prints, is squeezed around a central table overflowing with a tempting array of *antipasti* and unbelievably calorific desserts. It leads out onto a small terrace where you might be lucky enough to secure a table in summer. Do try, as much for the views over the valley as the joy of dining outdoors. Friendly service and a jolly atmosphere combine with delicious regional cuisine (liberally flavored with truffles) to make this a meal you'll remember.

WHERE TO STAY IN TODI

Villa Luisa, Via Cortesi 147, Todi   L
Tel: (075) 8848571   Open: Year round
Amenities: ☎ 🅿 ✕ ♀ Credit cards: AE, DC, MC, V

Todi's finest is a spick-and-span modern brick affair on the outskirts of town(you pass it on the way in from Spoleto). There are 43 simple, comfortably-furnished rooms with bath; a rather stark seating area in the foyer; and a spacious restaurant which closes on Wednesday from October to March. The garden is a bonus, as is the quiet location.

Leave the center of Todi, driving downhill on **Corso Cavour***, past Piazza Garibaldi, and turn right at the bottom for* **Orvieto***. This brings you back to Santa Maria's church, where you drive straight on and down into the Tiber valley. You've a bird's eye view from the hill with the broad sweep of the river curving through checkered fields and disappearing into a cardboard cut-out of steep ridges. Crossing the river at* **Ponte Cuti***, you reach a junction and turn left for* **Orvieto-Baschi** *(ss448). It's a beautiful drive downstream, following the Tiber's course to the shores of* **Lago di Corbara***, then through a series of galleries carved into the cliffside to a junction 22kms later, where you turn right and cross the A1 autostrada. This is the ss205 which runs into* **Orvieto-Scala** *7kms on.*

Drive on through this ugly industrial quarter, under a railroad bridge after 1½kms, then keep left when the road divides 200m later. Climb uphill for 2¼kms to a right turn on a bend, signposted **Hotels Aquila Bianca/Maitani***, and take this road, following the city walls that are partly formed by natural rock. Turn left at a T-junction, entering the Old Town through Porta Romana. It's a narrow winding street which leads you up to a junction with a church on your right 1km later. Turn right for* **Duomo/Information** *onto cobbled* **Via Lorenzo Maitani** *which emerges in* **Piazza del Duomo** *½km ahead. Keep right and park outside the* **Tourist Office***, Piazza del Duomo 24. (Tel: (0763) 41772. Open: Mon–Sat 9am–1pm 2:30pm–8pm (3pm–7pm Sep–Apr), Sun Mar–Oct 4pm–7pm, Nov–Feb 10am–1pm.)*

ORVIETO

Rising above the plain on an island of volcanic rock, not unlike the mesas of southwest America, Orvieto's setting is the most awe-inspiring of all Umbrian hill towns. Attracted by this impregnable position, the Etruscans settled here until they were ousted by the Romans in 280bc. When the Etruscans departed, their former city was referred to as *Urbs Vetus* (Old City), hence the modern name of Orvieto. The town became an independent commune in the 12th century and, after the usual pitched battles with its neighbors, it was swallowed up by the Papal States in 1448. A perfect natural fortress, Orvieto became a popular refuge for out-of-favor popes in the Middle Ages.

The plateau's constricted space has prevented any expansion of the medieval town. Sadly, noise pollution from angry small cars and motorbikes is another matter and a constant problem. There's also a spot of trouble with subsidence and landslides. On the way into town, you may have noticed scaffolding propping up the brown cliffs. Fortunately, a major civil engineering program is underway to secure the city's foundations.

Like its fine white wine, Orvieto's 13th-century cathedral is one of Italy's greatest. It was built to commemorate the Miracle of Bolsena (see page 237), when a priest witnessed drops of blood appearing on the linen altar cloth as he celebrated Communion. The cloth was later brought to Orvieto. Piazza del Duomo is an ideal setting to appreciate Orvieto's two great treasures: the cathedral on the one hand, and a glass of refreshing wine in the other. Some of the small shops around the piazza have tunnel-like cellars which run underground to the cathedral: always the last bastion in a siege.

Opposite the cathedral, you'll see Palazzo Faina which houses the **Museo Civico**'s collection of Etruscan vases, jewelry and terracotta. (Open: Tues–Sun summer 9am–1pm 3pm–6:30pm; winter 2:30pm–4:30pm winter. Admission: L3,000.) Palazzo Soliano (formerly Palazzo dei Papi) with its external staircase stands to the right of the cathedral. Built between 1297 and 1304, it was here that the popes took refuge. Nowadays, you'll find the cathedral museum in residence.

In contrast to the grandiose cathedral, you'll find the rest of Orvieto an unpretentious, bourgeois medieval town bisected by Corso Cavour, a busy, pedestrianized shopping street. In Piazza del Popolo, where there's a colorful vegetable market, you'll see the 12th-century Palazzo del Popolo: one of the oldest buildings in town. Just north of here, Via della Pace brings you to Chiesa di San Domenico. The first Dominican church ever built, it dates from 1233. Here you can admire Cardinal de Braye's beautiful tomb, carved by the great sculptor Arnolfo di Cambio.

Piazzale Cahen, on the eastern side of town, runs along the Rocca, a fortress built in 1364 by order of another nervous prelate, Cardinal Albornoz. There's a pretty garden among the ruins and great views from the ramparts over the Umbrian plain. A dirt trail to the left of the fortress winds down from Orvieto's clifftop perch, through shady thickets, to Pozzo di San Patrizio (St Patrick's Well) and the fields below.

When you've had your fill of culture and leg-stretching, join the evening strollers on Corso Cavour or return to Piazza del Duomo for a leisurely look at the great cathedral in the soft evening light.

WHAT TO SEE IN ORVIETO

Duomo, Piazza del Duomo, Orvieto
Open: Daily 7am–1pm 2:30pm–dusk
Admission free

Work on this Romanesque-Gothic extravaganza began in 1290. By 1310, the Sienese Lorenzo Maitani had taken over, and his remains the greatest influence although a further 31 architects were involved before work finally ceased in the 17th century. A team of 152 sculptors and 68 painters breathed life into the stone-work, while 90 mosaic artists working from Maitani's designs created the magnificent facade which earned the cathedral its nickname: the "Golden Lily of Cathedrals". The bas-reliefs by Maitani himself, on the lower sections of the pillars, are particu-larly spectacular and depict scenes from the Bible. Considerable controversy surrounded the addition of Emilio Greco's sculpted bronze doors in 1965.

The main body of the cathedral, in bold black-and-white striped marble, is reminiscent of its counterpart in Siena. The same effect is found inside: something of a relief after the glittering brilliance of the facade. There are sumptuous frescoes in the Cappella Nuova, started by Fra Angelico and completed by Luca Signorelli. Perhaps inspired by the French invasions of the late 15th century, Signorelli's powerful renderings of the *Apocalypse* and fierce, pitiless *Coming of the Anti-Christ* reach a dramatic intensity never achieved in his later works.

A large silver shrine in the Cappella del Caporale contains the blood-spotted altar cloth from Bolsena. It's unlocked only for major religious festivals and paraded around town during the Corpus Christi celebrations. You'll see Gothic stained glass and some marvelous statuary, but many of the cathedral's treasures are now housed in the **Museo dell'Opera del Duomo** in Palazzo Soliano. (Open: Tues–Sun 9am–1pm 2:30pm–6pm, 5pm in winter. Admission: L3,000.) This collection includes sculpture by Salvi di Andrea, the Pisanos, and Arnolfo di Cambio, parts of a fine polyptych from Simone Martini and a self-portrait by Signorelli.

Pozzo di San Patrizio, below Piazzale Cahen, Orvieto
Open: Daily summer 8am–8pm; winter until 6pm winter
Admission: L3,000

Trekking downhill from Piazzale Cahen, you pass an Etruscan tomb on the way to the well. Designed and built by Sangallo the Younger between 1528 and 1537, this ingenious engineering feat was commissioned by Pope Clement VII, who took refuge in Orvieto after the sacking of Rome. The 200-foot deep well, intended to supply the town with water in the event of a siege, was never actually used. Two spiral staircases of 248 steps lead down to the well head: one for water carriers going down, the other for those returning to the surface. They never intersect. If you feel inclined to descend to the chilly depths, remember you have to climb back up again. This is not a recommended excursion for devotees of fashion footwear, or those less than sure-footed.

SHOPPING IN ORVIETO

On a par with Chianti and Valpolicella, Orvieto is one of Italy's top three wine-producing regions. The Etruscans planted vineyards long before the Romans arrived and Orvieto's trade in quality wines goes back thousands of years. Cathedral artist, Luca Signorelli, even inserted a clause in his contract with church officials which stated "he be given as much as he wanted of that wine of Orvieto". You'll find Orvieto's wines on sale all over town, but you can taste as well at **Casa Barberani**, Via Lorenzo Maitani 1, near the Tourist Office. (Open: Daily 10am–7pm. Credit cards: AE, DC.) All Barberani's wines, which are grown on the slopes near Lago di Corbara, carry the appellation *Classico*. This means they're grown in the original vineyard region. *Secco* is a dry wine; *abboccato* is medium-dry; and *amabile* (lovable) is sweet. Diagonally across the square, antiques lovers should cast an eye over the treasures in **La Botteguccia**, Piazza del Duomo 4. Beneath the original domed brick ceiling, you'll find an enchanting selection of small furniture, silver, *objets d'art* and antique china dolls.

Surprise, surprise. Pottery is big in Orvieto, too. **Via del Duomo** is one long pottery retail store and it's impossible to prefer one outlet to another except as a matter of personal taste. Suffice to say, **Adami**, Via del Duomo 47 (AE, DC, V), has the best range of Tuscan and Umbrian designs. Many of the smaller stores also sell lacework mats and coasters in a traditional heavily knotted pattern. **Doi Fratelli**, Via del Duomo 11 (AE), makes a brave stand against the ceramic cowboys. This is a great deli selling all sorts of Orvietan specialities from cold cuts, hard cheeses and olives to delicious fresh bread baked with ham and cheese.

At the bottom of Via del Duomo, turn left onto **Corso Cavour**. This is boutique-country and there's fashion for all in various price ranges. Further down on the left, you'll find **Bottega Michelangeli**, Via Albani (AE, DC, MC, V). Do not under any circumstances enter this shop with children – it could cost you a fortune. Michelangeli is a superb woodcarver descended from generations of carpenters. His enchanting shop is a magic garden of wooden trees and animals. Fat little planes and bulging-cheeked cherubs dangle cheekily from the ceiling. Outside, there are wooden horses for the kids to play on and decorative wooden cut-outs around the door frames. You're welcome to browse, but you don't need to be a top-flight mathematician to realize nothing comes cheap here. Single alphabet letters start at L18,000; a simple branch holding four little chicks makes around L54,000; the smallest doll costs L220,000, and the largest well over a million lire. If it all proves too much for you, struggle on down Corso Cavour to the Michelangeli designed interior of **Bar Montanucci** and reward yourself with a *cappuccino*.

WHERE TO EAT IN ORVIETO

Giglio d'Oro, Piazza Duomo 8, Orvieto   LL
Tel: (0763) 41903
Open: Daily 1pm–3:30pm 7:30pm–midnight
Closed: Wed from Nov–Mar
Credit cards: AE, DC, MC, V

You walk up to the second floor for this bright, ultra-chic modern dining room with arty blue glass wall lights and strange blue ceramic pelmets above pretty beige curtains. Strips of gray-and-white marble climb the walls, echoing the Duomo across the square; there are elegant place settings with Villeroy and Bosch china, fresh roses and a casually smart clientele relaxing in comfortable armchairs. The food is delicious, but (unusual for Italy) pays token homage to *nouvelle cuisine* by way of small portions. The *crostino di cacciagione tartufati* (gamey liver pâté with truffles) is divine, but it arrives on a quarter of a piece of bread – you'll need at least two. Spaghetti – very good with salmon – is certainly more filling and there's a rich steak tartare. House wine from the local Barberani winery is light and refreshing. Service is slick but unhurried.

Morino, Via Garibaldi 41, Orvieto   LL
Tel: (0763) 35152
Open: Thur–Tues 12:30pm–2:30pm 7:30pm–10:30pm
Closed: Wed and Jan
Credit cards: AE, DC, MC, V

This casual, chic spot features exquisitely prepared Umbrian dishes. These nearly always include truffles; they don't go for a trifle but they're worth every lire. Made-on-the-premises pasta comes in a cornucopia of shapes and sizes – all are great first courses. Their saddle of veal with *porcini* mushrooms is both tasty and reasonable. House wines are first rate. Staff speak adequate English.

WHERE TO STAY IN ORVIETO

Aquila Bianca, Via Garibaldi 13, Orvieto   LLL
Tel: (0763) 42271   Open: Year round
Amenities: P ♀   Credit cards: AE, DC, MC, V

It would take several pages to describe each twist and turn of the route from the Duomo to the hotel parking lot. However, it's well-marked, but take it slow as the roads are often painfully narrow. Housed in a converted 18th-century town house, the Aquila Bianca is centrally placed, near Piazza della Repubblica. Traffic noise is unavoidable, but the welcome is friendly and helpful. There are 37 comfortable small rooms with bath/shower;

a terribly grandiose lounge area complete with chandelier and musician's gallery; plus a pub-tavern (open Apr–Sep) which serves a simple menu while you sit at trestle tables in the cellar.

Maitani, Via Lorenzo Maitani 5, Orvieto   LLL
Tel: (0763) 42011   Open: Year round
Amenities: **P** ♀   Credit cards: AE, DC, MC, V

A short step from Piazza del Duomo, the Maitani is right at the heart of town and has a tiny terrace – quite an accomplishment here. The foyer is an eclectic mix of modern art and overstuffed chairs, marbled linoleum and fresh flowers. The decor quietens down a little in the 43 rooms (all with bath). Those at the back are relatively peaceful; those on the side overlook the cathedral's facade.

Virgilio, Piazza del Duomo 5/6, Orvieto   LL
Tel: (0763) 41882   Open: Year round
Amenities: ♀   No credit cards

Behind a beautiful antique facade in the cathedral's shadow, you'd never suspect the ultra-modern small foyer awaiting you. Glass-like marble floors, chrome and leather seats, molded plastic coffee tables and a chic bar with highstools – it sounds like a nightmare contrast. In reality, it's thoughtfully and attractively arranged; there's a warm welcome; and 15 pleasant rooms with bath/shower. You can park outside only in the evening, but you'll find public parking on the other side of the cathedral.

ROUTE G: ORVIETO – BOLSENA – VITERBO – BRACCIANO – ROME   (Approx 140kms)

*Retrace your steps from Orvieto's **Piazza del Duomo** along **Via Lorenzo Maitani**. Turn right at the end following blue signs for **Roma**; then left 100m later. You cross **Via Garibaldi** after ¼km and leave town from **Porta Romana**, driving downhill to a traffic circle. Take the exit left for **Roma-Firenze (A1)**. Towards the bottom of the hill you'll pick up signs straight ahead for **Bolsena/Viterbo**. Almost immediately the road starts to climb again; there are terrific views back to Orvieto huddled around its gold-faced cathedral. Just 3½kms from Orvieto, after a short stretch of straight road, the road divides with little warning: keep left for **Bolsena**. After a further 10kms, turn right down a narrow road for Bolsena; as the main route leads off to Montefiascone. Keep right at a junction after 2kms; around the next corner there's a delicious view of **Lago di Bolsena** and Bisentina Island.*

*Almost 4kms later, you pass Bolsena's ancient **Rocca** (castle) and wind downhill to the main parking lot in **Piazza Matteotti**. If you can't park here, continue straight across the traffic lights to the* *lakeshore. There's some confusion at the moment as to where Bolsena will set up its summer season Tourist Office – possibly by the church in Piazza Matteotti. Meanwhile, we're assured that at least it will be well signposted.*

BOLSENA

The ancient settlement of *Volsinii* was founded by Etruscan refugees from Orvieto and perched above the Rocca. As the town grew, it slid downhill and today the most modern buildings are right on the lakeshore. The largest volcanic lake in Italy, Lago di Bolsena is still prey to the odd earth tremor, but it doesn't seem to bother the local fish population, let alone the eels. Bolsena's delicious eels tempted 13th-century Pope Martin IV to abandon all self-control. He features in Dante's *Inferno* sunk in the depths of gluttony – and eels. Not an eel-fan? Well, you can still feast on carp, pike and other freshwater delicacies.

Bolsena's other main claim to fame is the Miracle of Bolsena. A doubting Bohemian priest was celebrating Mass here in 1263. As he blessed the wafers representing the Host (or body of Christ), drops of blood appeared on the altar cloth and the marble steps. The cloth was taken to Pope Urban IV, who was staying in Orvieto. Impressed by this proof of the Transubstantiation, Pope Urban decreed a cathedral should be built in Orvieto to house the cloth, and instituted the Feast of Corpus Christi by Papal Bull the following year. Now one of the most important Catholic festivals, it's celebrated on the first Thursday after Trinity all over the world. While Bolsena was forced to relinquish the precious altar cloth to Orvieto, the steps are on view in the Cappella del Miracolo at Chiesa di Santa Cristina.

For a great view of the lake, it's well worth clambering around the **Rocca**'s 13th-century battlements. (Open: Mar–Dec Tues–Sun 10am–12:30pm 5pm–8pm. Admission: L500.) There's also a small museum here, displaying Etruscan finds from *Scavi di Volsinii* just up the hill. If you'd like to linger a while, head down to the lakeshore promenade which is lined with small restaurants and cafés. You'll also find **Hotel Columbus**, Viale N. Colesanti 27. (Tel: (0761) 98009. Open: Mar–Oct. Credit cards: MC, V.) This quiet, modern hotel offers 39 comfortable rooms with bath/shower. There's a restaurant, and a shady terrace with views of the lake through the trees.

WHAT TO SEE IN BOLSENA

Chiesa di Santa Cristina, Bolsena
Open: Daily 8am–noon 2:30pm–7pm
Admission free. Tour of catacombs L2,000

Walk back to the bottom of the hill in Piazza Matteotti, and turn right through an archway onto Corso della Repubblica. At the end of the main street, across a small piazza, you'll see Santa Cristina's delicately carved Renaissance facade decorated with fish and fruit, shields and quivers of feather-flighted arrows. The interior is dark; low arches rise from stout pillars; and there's a very beautiful 15th-century gilded triptych by Sano di Pietro. The entrance to the *Cappella del Miracolo* is in the left-hand aisle: if it's closed apply to the *Sacristia* (right of the main door). Nothing could be more surprising after the gloom of the main church than this brilliant-white chapel built in honor of the miracle. An enormously ornate reliquary flanked by silver candlesticks contains a portion of the marble steps stained with blood. Through the next door you enter a dingy, sub-zero cavern. Two hundred lire in the slot will reveal a fine terracotta altarpiece in classic blue and white enamel with a flowery border by Giovanni della Robbia, as well as the raised antique altar, surrounded by interlinking arches, where the miracle took place. At the far end of the cavern, Grotta di Santa Cristina houses a lovely unglazed terracotta effigy of St Christina on a platform above the entrance to the ancient Christian catacombs.

At the traffic lights in Bolsena, turn left for **Viterbo** *driving along the lakeshore for most of the 14kms to* **Montefiascone**, *home of "Est! Est! Est!". Montefiascone's white wines have long had their admirers. Back in the Middle Ages, one such enthusiast was a Bishop Fugger of Augsburg. Short of a good guide book, he sent his servant ahead to mark out inns serving good wine with the word "est" (from "Vinum est bonum" or "wine is good"). So comprehensive was this early wine guide, and so fine the local wines, Bishop Fugger died from over-indulgence and is buried in a local church.*

Drive on into Montefiascone for 1¼kms. Bear right around the old town's base; then keep left for **Roma/Viterbo**. *In summer, there are plenty of roadside stalls selling "Est! Est! Est!", or you can drop into* **Cantina di Montefiascone** *1½kms further on at the bottom of the hill. After 15kms, Via Cassia bears off for Rome; keep straight on for* **Viterbo**. *Two kilometers later you drive through Porta Fiorentina into* **Piazza della Rocca** *and turn right for* **Centro/Information**. *At the far end of the piazza, a narrow cobbled street leads to a small square where you turn left down* **Via Cairoli**. *Facing* **Piazza dei Caduti**, *at the bottom of the hill, turn right for the central parking lot. Walk back to the* **Tourist Office**, *Piazza dei Caduti 16. (Tel: (0761) 234795. Open: Mon–Sat 9am–12:30pm 4pm–6:30pm.)*

VITERBO

The city of Viterbo grew at the foot of Monti Cimini on the site of a former Etruscan settlement. It was taken over by the Romans

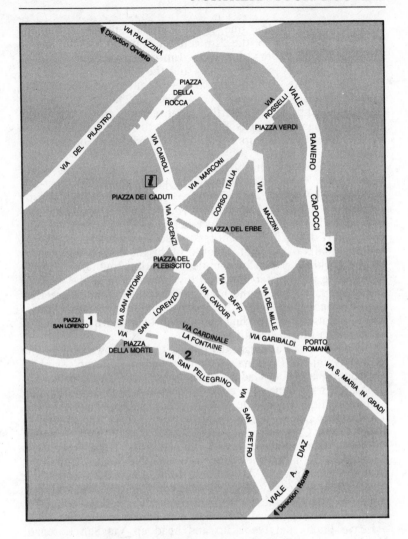

VITERBO

Tourist Office
1 Piazza San Lorenzo
2 San Pellegrino
3 Museo Civico

in 310BC; then became one of the Lombard towns of Tuscany (774AD). By the end of the 12th century, Viterbo had become an important independent commune. Embroiled in three centuries of wrangling between the papacy and the Holy Roman Empire, the city competed with Rome as papal center for a brief time. Over a dozen popes lived, died or were elected here. The city declined in importance after the papal seat moved to Avignon in France. When the popes eventually returned, they settled in Rome: Viterbo ended up as a mere provincial town of the Papal States.

The outskirts of Viterbo were razed to the ground in World War II, then replaced by a sprawling jungle of soulless post-war buildings. However, once you enter Porta Fiorentina, by Cardinal Albornoz's imposing 14th-century *rocca* (castle), you're quickly reassured that the medieval city's heart is still in the right place. On a sunny day, Viterbo's dark, cobbled streets are splashed with brilliant shafts of sunlight, colored by bright flowers and cooled by the trickling waters of countless beautiful fountains. Stormy days define the sinister medieval towers looming above volcanic stone ramparts. Inside the atmospheric Old Town, where they used to honor Our Lady of the Plague, somber gray stone houses exude a sense of foreboding heightened by street names such as Piazza della Morte (Death Square).

Begin your tour at Piazza del Plebiscito in the town center. The sprawling Palazzo Comunale with its stone lion (Viterbo's symbol) overlooks Piazza dei Caduti on the west side. The courtyard is decorated with numerous coats-of-arms, palm trees, a fountain and more lions under the clocktower. Garibaldi stayed in this 15th-century palace in 1876. On the piazza's east side stands the Romanesque Chiesa di Sant'Angelo. A stone coffin said to contain the body of a medieval damsel, known as La Bella Galiana, is embedded in its facade. Her incomparable beauty reputedly caused a war between Viterbo and Rome. Legend has it that the lovely Galiana's purity was such that you could see wine pouring down her throat as she drank. Unfortunately, she refused an offer of marriage from a local nobleman who then murdered her.

Leave Piazza del Plebiscito and head up Via San Lorenzo. You'll pass little Piazza del Gesù – the old market square – halfway to Piazza della Morte. Ironically, the latter, with its 13th-century fountain, is one of Viterbo's loveliest squares despite its sinister name. A little further on, you reach the quiet of Piazza San Lorenzo which replaced the Etruscan acropolis. Straight ahead is the Duomo's swooping Renaissance facade, although the main body of this cathedral is actually Romanesque. On the north side, you'll see the Gothic Palazzo Papale built as a papal residence.

If you retrace your steps to Piazza della Morte and keep straight on for *quartiere medioevale*, you'll come to the San Pellegrino district. This is the wonderfully preserved heart of medieval

Viterbo. To the south, the fountain in Piazza Fontana di Piano was at the center of a 14th-century uprising when the townspeople objected to a member of the papal court trying to wash a puppy in the source of their drinking water. Head north for Piazza della Fontana Grande and you'll see Viterbo's biggest and strangest 13th-century fountain gurgling away. Built in the shape of a huge Greek cross, it's fed by a Roman aqueduct.

Just beyond Porta della Verità stands the former 13th-century convent of Santa Maria della Verità. There are some exquisite frescoes (1469) by Lorenzo da Viterbo, a pupil of the great Quattrocento master Piero della Francesca. The **Museo Civico** is housed next door. (Open: Tues–Sun Apr–Sep 8:30am–1:30pm 3:30pm–6pm; Oct–Mar 9am–1:30pm. Admission: L3,000.) Here you'll find Salvator Rosa's beautiful 17th-century canvas *Incredulita di San Tommaso*, in which doubting Thomas probes Christ's wound with his finger.

Further north, inside the town walls east of Piazza Verdi, is the hideous Santuario di Santa Rosa, built in 1850. In it you'll find the grinning mummified remains of the saint, who died in 1261 and is believed to be too holy to decompose. Her feast day is celebrated on September 3 with terrific processions. Until 1967, the men of Viterbo would carry a massive ceremonial float through the streets to the church. This enormous construction, known as the *macchina di Santa Rosa*, topped 100 feet in height and weighed in at around four tons. During this annual feat of endurance so many people were killed when the *macchina* fell onto the bearers or into the crowd, that it had to be abandoned. You can see sketches of the old designs in the Museo Civico.

If you have time, take a drive 20kms due east of town to Parco dei Mostri (Park of the Monsters) at Bomarzo. You'll be spooked by the wild and fantastic sculptures created for Prince Vicino Orsini in the 16th century. He intended it should be a surprise for his wife. It was. The unfortunate woman took one look and died of heart failure. History doesn't relate whether the prince had an ulterior motive.

WHAT TO SEE IN VITERBO

Piazza San Lorenzo, Viterbo

As you walk down Via San Lorenzo, you'll cross a short bridge just before you reach the piazza. This enhances the illusion that this peaceful cathedral square is out on a limb, slightly distanced from the town center's everyday bustle.

The cathedral dates from 1192, although the facade is a 16th-century addition. To the left, it's supported by a particularly elegant 14th-century belltower, the top half decorated by bands of black-and-white stone with twin arches on each face. The Palazzo Papale (1266) forms a right-angle to the north, extended by the interlocking arches of a beautiful Gothic loggia to a hospital on the east side. Decorated with a veritable pride of Viterbo's lion symbols, the loggia's arches are etched in spectacular clarity against the sky.

A flight of steps leads up to the palace's turreted facade. Conclaves were held here, including the one which finally elected Pope Gregory X in 1271. This lasted for 33 months, causing the Viterbans to become so exasperated they decided to speed things up by locking the cardinals in the palace and tearing off the roof. The cardinals got around this by setting up tents in the Great Hall: its wooden floor still bears the scars. Next, their food supply was cut off. This obviously had the desired effect and Pope Gregory was elected shortly thereafter. The tradition of locking up the conclave until a decision is reached has survived to the present day. However, the fall-out from Pope Gregory's election still wasn't over. The Great Hall roof was replaced, but six years later it caved in on the head of his successor, John XXI, who died of his injuries and is buried in the cathedral next door.

San Pellegrino, Viterbo

The ancient *contrada* (district) of San Pellegrino remains the most important and evocative glimpse of medieval Italy in the country. For 800 years this working-class quarter of sturdy closed-face houses has emerged unscathed from battle and escaped the planner's ax. You won't experience anything like it elsewhere. Its closely-packed buildings reflect the close-knit community; and there's a palpable sense of secrecy in its covered passageways and narrow blind alleys. Crossing yet again from the deeply shaded gloom of an archway into brilliant sunshine, your eyes start to play tricks on you. This is even more true at night when lamps cast grotesque shadows, transforming an evening stroll into a romantic adventure.

You'll notice stone staircases leading to second-story front doors; gracefully arched loggias edged by greenery and decorated with hanging flower baskets; simple, carved friezes; and mullioned windows. Craftsmen still work in the first-floor *botteghe* (workshops) – carpenters, potters and the inevitable horde of antiques dealers. Watchful cats maintain a deceptively languid surveillance on passers-by, appearing and disappearing like fluid shadows. This is a magical corner of Italy you won't forget.

SHOPPING IN VITERBO

Corso Italia, running south from Piazza Verdi through pretty Piazza dell'Erbe, is Viterbo's main shopping street. Here you'll find all the usual up-market pharmacies, gift stores and fashionable boutiques. In typical Italian fashion, the shoe stores tend to outnumber everything else by ten-to-one. If you've already shod yourself well into the 21st century but still crave more of that beautiful Italian leather you'll find a good selection of leather clothing at **Ramirez**, Corso Italia 81–85 (Credit cards: AE, DC, V). Men's and women's leather jackets start at around L300,000 in a wide variety of styles, while neat ladies' cut-off blouson designs cost around L200,000; skirts and trousers in both suede and leather also feature, plus shoes. On the designer clothing front, **Max Mara** at Corso Italia 78 (AE, DC, MC, V), will keep the fashion-conscious female busy. As will **Carillon**, Corso Italia 53 (AE, DC, MC, V), with fatally attractive outfits from a selection of Italian designers including Versace and Genny. Antiques enthusiasts should take a torch to **Via Cardinale La Fontaine** and **Via San Pellegrino**. Firstly, because it's like digging for buried treasure in these cavernous gloomy showrooms buried in the vaults of the Old Town. Secondly, because you'll probably be here all night. It's impossible to single out individual shops for attention: there are so many and they're all worth a browse. Apart from the fantastic surroundings, you'll find the most incredible range of stock from ancient blocks of carved Roman masonry to dusty 17th-century oil paintings; rough Etruscan pottery to elegant 18th-century ceramics. Unless you're an expert, be very wary of exceptionally antique pieces. There are rarely genuine bargains in this field. However – enjoy, enjoy. You're bound to find something which catches your fancy and will always remind you of your trip.

WHERE TO EAT IN VITERBO

Scaletta, Via Marconi 41, Viterbo L
Tel: (0761) 30003
Open: Tues–Sun 12:30pm–2:30pm 7:30pm–10:30pm Closed: Mon
Credit cards: AE, DC, V

A short distance north of Piazza dei Caduti, these sleek black-and-white dining rooms overlook the street behind a jungle of flourishing greenery. Painted lilac borders and colorful modern art brighten the stark decor; friendly staff and a lively clientele create a pleasant atmosphere. There are plenty of tempting snacky starters on offer like *crostini* and *bruschetta* with various toppings, followed by good value pizzas, grills and salads.

Tre Re, Via Macel Gattesco 3, Viterbo L
Tel: (0761) 234619
Open: Fri–Wed 12:30pm–2:30pm 7pm–10:30pm
Closed: Thur and Aug
Credit cards: AE, DC, V

Just off Piazza dell'Erbe, this is a real old-fashioned restaurant. It's small and homey, rather like an English pub with its heavy oak beams and panelled walls. You'll experience regional cooking and hospitality at its best here, not to mention a fine choice of local wines from Montefiascone's *Est! Est! Est!*, to Orvieto Classico. Hearty bean and pasta soups or *osso buco* make great fillers. There's *bombolotti panna e salsiccia* (a rich pasta dish with cream and sausage), or *vitello tonnato* (thin slices of veal served with a spicy caper and tomato sauce). A good shared starter is a generous plate of *fritto misto all'Italiana* (little pieces of meat, vegetables and cheese dipped in light batter, fried and served scorching hot).

Gran Caffe Schenardi, Corso Italia 11, Viterbo   L
No telephone
Open: Thur–Tues 7am–10pm   Closed: Wed
No credit cards

This fabulous café-bar deserves a special mention – in fact, it should be listed with the historic sights of Viterbo. Built as a banking house in 1493, the first floor was transformed into a bar in 1818. Beneath a gracious vaulted ceiling supported by columns, the black-and-white marble-tiled floors lead through the bar and patisserie to double doors opening into a dining room. The brilliant white walls are pierced by alcoves containing classical statues, and smaller niches housing imperious busts. There's a riot of stucco decoration and gilt mirrors behind the bar. On either side of the serving area, chilled cabinets display a mouthwatering choice of gooey gateaux and pastries (to the left); savory pizzas, toasted sandwiches and vol-au-vents (to the right). Collect a drink or a *cappuccino* from the bar, make your selection from the cold cabinets and settle down at one of the small marble-topped tables to survey the scene. Apart from the architectural splendors, there's a richly varied clientele from smart business types holding conferences over tiny cups of *espresso* to dust-covered workmen tossing down a rather stronger brew. If a sandwich or a cake seems small beer after all that sightseeing, there's a self-service salad bar in the dining room with a limited selection of hot dishes. You can sit at a clutch of pretty tables surrounded by attractive modern paintings. They have a piano-player here on Saturday evenings.

WHERE TO STAY IN VITERBO

Tuscia, Via Cairoli 41, Viterbo   LL
Tel: (0761) 223377   Open: Year round
Amenities: ☎ ♀   Credit cards: DC, MC, V

Five minutes' walk from the town center, you'll find the Tuscia's 60 modern rooms spotless and soulless. They all have bath/shower and central heating; there's some parking available too. In contrast to the antiseptic surrounds, the staff are genuinely welcoming and helpful though their English is limited.

From the parking lot, drive up **Via Ascenzi**, through **Piazza del Plebiscito**, onto **Via San Lorenzo**. Just before Piazza della Morte, turn left on **Via Cardinale La Fontaine**, signposted **Roma**. Follow signs for **Roma** across the bumpy cobbles for ³/₄km and out of Viterbo by **Porta San Pietro**. You emerge facing a church, and turn right for **Cassia/Roma**; then left onto the main road 100m later. Keep right for Rome and you'll rejoin **Via Cassia**. There's an overblown intersection 7kms later; follow signs for **Roma**. Via Cassia bypasses the center of **Vetralla** 6kms further on and runs out of **Cura** 5kms later. If you're in a dash for Rome, Via Cassia will take you all the way there. However, if Lago di Bolsena whetted your appetite for lakeside scenery, take a right for **Bracciano (ss493)** after 4kms.

It's a really scenic drive to Bracciano, but the road surface is pretty bumpy and beware the first railway crossing you reach. (Hitting this too fast will register new heights on your personal Richter scale.) In **Vejano**, 9kms later, just beyond the impressive rounded towers of Castello Altieri, there's a lovely view across to a chapel in the valley. Then the road improves, running through **Oriolo Romano** and past **Manziana** to the outskirts of **Bracciano** 20kms on. You pass a military academy: 200m ahead there's a left turn into the town center, dominated by the outline of **Castello Odescalchi**. For details of **Bracciano** and the road around the lake, turn to **Tour 4, Route A** of the Day Trips Around Rome (see page 168).

Via Braccianese bypasses Bracciano and runs into **Ostia Nuova** 15kms later. Keep straight on through town, past the junction with the Trevignano/Anguillara road on your left. You'll find details of the route back to Rome in **Tour 4, Route B** of the Day Trips Around Rome (see page 171).

*　　*　　*

A LONGER TOUR SOUTH TO NAPLES AND THE AMALFI COAST

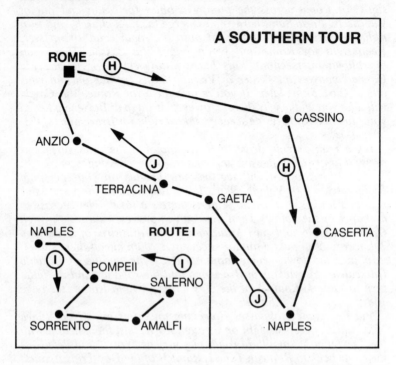

A SOUTHERN TOUR

Driving south from Rome on Via Casilina, you'll pass through lovely medieval **Anagni**, once the "City of Popes", en route to the famous abbey and World War II battleground of **Montecassino**. At **Santa Maria Capua Vetere**, the splendid Roman antiquities include an amphitheater almost as big as the Colosseum. Also on a grand scale, Charles III's magnificent palace at **Caserta** boasts 1,200 rooms. **Naples**, birthplace of Italy's sultry actress Sophia Loren, is a bustling southern Mediterranean port where carnival and crime simmer side by side in the shadow of Mount Vesuvius (**Route H**).

No visitor to the south should miss this opportunity to spend a few days driving around the famous **Bay of Naples** and the **Amalfi Coast**. Just south of Naples, you'll find the petrified cities of Herculaneum at **Ercolano**, and **Pompeii**. The citrus groves of **Sorrento** once echoed with the Sirens' song which drove sailors mad. They were foiled by Ulysses, who plugged his crew's ears with wax while he was tied to the mast so he could listen without jumping ship. Then it's on to the resorts of **Positano** and **Amalfi**, before the cathedral city and port of **Salerno**. From here, you can

continue straight on up the coast for Anzio, or return to Naples
(**Route I**).

Heading back along the west coast for Rome, you could stop off
for a beneficial mud bath at the spa in **Agnano**; check out a semi-
active volcano in **Pozzuoli**; and take a boat trip to the Pontine
Islands from **Gaeta**. It's a beautiful drive around the Gulf of Gaeta
to **Terracina**, then north to the Neanderthal caves and the nature
reserve at **Circeo**, before rejoining the Short Tours Around Rome
at **Anzio** (**Route J**).

ROUTE H: A SOUTHERN TOUR: ROME–ANAGNI– CASSINO–CAPUA–CASERTA–NAPLES
(Approx. 220kms)

ROME TO SEGNI

*From the parking lot in central **Piazza della Repubblica**, turn into*
***Via Nazionale**. Take the fourth street on your left (Via Agostino de*
*Pretis). This leads you into **Piazza Esquilino** with the church of*
Santa Maria Maggiore ahead. Cross the lights and halfway round
*the piazza bear right into **Via Merulana**. Ease into the left lane at the*
*top of the hill before **Piazza San Giovanni in Laterano**. Turn left at*
the lights and follow the road past the church on your right, easing
over to the right. Cross the lights and drive through the central arch
in the city walls. After going through the arch you'll note a concrete
lined central slip lane across the piazza, with a green sign, pointing
to the left, that says "Tangenziale". Get in this lane, then take a left
as the light permits. This takes you down a narrow street for two
blocks into another small square. Get in the right-hand lane here,
not turning right at the Via Tarantino but at the lights beyond it.
Here the sign across the street says "Appio L. Brindisi" but at the
*point at which you turn into it this becomes the **Via la Spezia**. Pass*
four traffic lights along this street; drive halfway round at the traffic
circle, under the arch and across the lights. Turn right after 50m into
***Via Casilina** (signposted ss6) with railroad tracks on your right. You*
cross the tracks 300m later.

After 2kms the built-up area ends and you have a view of the
mountains in the distance. In another 4kms you pass a sign
indicating Rome's city limits. Immediately beyond you'll see a blue
*sign for **Via Casilina** as the road bends around to the right. Take the*
left fork, following the blue sign. Drive under the bridge and at the
*next fork follow signs for **Frosinone**. After several kilometers you*
pass through the village of Torregaia then the road climbs onto an
overpass.

Drive through the villages of Borghesiana and Finocchio, then
there's a view of the plain and the distant hills. Apart from the odd

*factory, you're now clear of the Rome overspill. After a couple of kilometers you drive through the villages of Laghetto, Colonna and Cesario. You're now driving along the **Via Casilina (ss6)** south-east in the direction of Frosinone, the main town of the province of Ciociaria. This is an area of verdant hills and valleys, studded with medieval villages rich with folklore.*

*As the Casilina is only single-lane, you could get stuck behind slow-moving trucks. Forty kilometers from Rome center is the town of Labico. Two kilometers from here you pass through **Valmontone** where the road forks at a white monument: take the left fork. After 8kms you cross the **River Sacco**. Another 2kms and you'll see an enormous factory and a sign indicating Segni to your right. At the fork just ahead, take a right, passing over a small bridge. You now come to the town of **Colleferro** and a small traffic circle. Go straight across, following the sign for **Segni**, which lies 6kms further on. Pass the public gardens on your left and at the lights go straight across. You're now on the **Corso Garibaldi**. You'll then come to a fork: turn right for Segni. As you leave Colleferro the road climbs uphill and you've a fine view of the plain on your left. The road winds through a valley with several hairpin bends and you'll see Segni on the hill ahead.*

*As you enter Segni, turn left at the traffic circle. Drive straight into **Corso Vittorio Emanuele**, at the end of which there's a T-junction. Turn left, then right a few meters ahead at the fork, following the sign for **Duomo**. It's a narrow street, flanked by a high wall on the right. Shortly after this, makes a sharp right U-turn and you can park on this road which leads into the cathedral square.*

SEGNI

Segni's history stretches back as far as the sixth century BC when it was a primitive hill settlement, and the town's walls date from this time. Established by the Barbarians, the town was later occupied by the Romans who used the fortified city as a prison for their captives during the battles with Hannibal. It flourished in the Middle Ages when it was an occasional papal seat. In 1173, Pope Alexander III canonized Thomas à Becket here.

The city walls (*Mura Ciclopiche*) are reached by a footpath. They stretch for more than 1½ kilometers and are about six meters high, made of enormous blocks of stone. You'll find several gates in them, the most notable of which is the Porta Saracena: a massive two-meter long boulder supported by equally huge slabs of rock.

The cathedral, originally Romanesque and rebuilt in the 17th century, is in the medieval town center. The narrow Via Dante, which is full of character, is near the Piazza Duomo. A charming medieval loggia is on your left at the end of the street. The road leading to the top of the hill above the town is called the Pianillo, from which you'll enjoy a magnificent panorama of the Sacco valley. An ancient acropolis and the base of a temple are at the summit.

WHAT TO SEE IN SEGNI

Chiesa di San Pietro Apostolo, Segni
Open: Daily dawn-sunset
Admission free

St Peter's church was built in the 13th century on the site of a Roman Temple of Jupiter. A simple gray stone construction, it commands a wonderful view over the surrounding countryside. This is where Thomas à Becket was canonized by Pope Alexander III. Inside you can see several fine frescoes, some dating from the 13th century.

Cisterna Romana, behind San Pietro, Segni
Open: Daily dawn–sunset
Admission free

This ancient cistern is some 14 meters in diameter. It dates from 530–525BC: the same period, in fact, as the Roman temple which lies beneath the church. The cistern was the site of various pagan rituals as well as the source of the town's main water supply. *La Giostra del Maialetto* (Pig Tournament) dating from Roman times is enacted here to this day in the first half of August. Four blind-folded individuals are armed with brooms. With a small bell tied to one leg, they climb down into the cistern. A small pig, wearing an identical bell, is then let loose into the "arena". The winner – the prize is the pig – is the person who manages to hit the pig with his broom the most often. Usually, to the delight of the crowd, the competitors hit each other.

SEGNI TO ANAGNI

*Leaving Segni's **Piazza Duomo**, retrace your route, turning sharp left down the street with the high wall now on your left. Turn right into Corso Vittorio Emanuele, and halfway down turn right into **Via Traiana**, following the arrow. Drive straight down the hill and turn right at the T-junction for **Colleferro**. After about 5kms you're back in Colleferro. Turn left at the traffic circle, following the sign for Colleferro, and cross the traffic lights. Follow the sign straight ahead for the **Via Casilina**.*

*Go around the public garden and across the traffic circle, still following the sign for Via Casilina. After crossing a bridge you're on the Via Casilina; turn right, following the sign for **Napoli/ Anagni**. You'll come to Anagni after about 9kms. Continue to drive across the plain with the hills in the near distance until you pass* *under a bridge, then there's a sign left for **Anagni**. Leave the main road at the fork and follow a country lane with large gardens on either side. The road now climbs steadily, giving an increasing panorama on your right. Follow the white sign for **Anagni Centro** and shortly after you'll find yourself in a tree-lined main avenue. Pass to the right of the white stone arch (Porta Cerere) and enter the picturesque historic town center. You'll find yourself in a narrow, one-way street. A few hundred meters up on your left is the medieval Casa Barnekov, then a fountain at **Piazza d'Azeglio**. You'll come to **Piazza Cavour** with its white memorial, and on your left is the huge arched entrance to the medieval Palazzo Comunale. The road opens into a small piazza on your left: follow the road around to the right, pass the ancient Palazzo Bonifacio on your right, and you'll enter pretty **Piazza Innocenzo III**. The **Tourist Office** is to the left of the Duomo, on Piazzo Innocenzo III. (Tel: (0775) 727852. Open: Daily noon–6pm or 7pm.)*

ANAGNI

Arriving in the lovely medieval center of Anagni, surrounded by the verdant hills of Ciociaria, is like stepping into the past. Occupied by the Romans in the fourth century BC, Anagni became a church possession in the eighth century. It's called the "City of Popes" as Innocent III, Gregory IX, Alexander IV and Boniface VIII were born here. It was also the Pope's official residence in the Middle Ages.

The main street, Via Vittorio Emanuele, which passes through the town center to the cathedral square at the other end, is lined with medieval buildings including the 12th-century Palazzo Comunale (Town Hall) with its vast arches, and the medieval Casa Barnekov.

WHAT TO SEE IN ANAGNI

Palazzo Comunale, Piazza Cavour, Anagni
Open: Daily 9am–1pm
Admission free

Constructed between 1159 and 1163 by Jacopo del Iseo, this building, also known as the Palazzo Civico, is in Romantic-Lombard style. Its imposing arches are unusual. The side facing the courtyard has bifor and trifor windows and a small fourth-century loggia. The *palazzo* is still the Town Hall today.

Palazzo di Bonifacio VIII, Quartiere Caetani, Anagni
Open: Daily 9am–12.30pm 3pm–1hr before sunset
Admission free

The palace houses a museum which comprises six rooms built in stone and decorated with frescoes. There's a permanent photo-graphic exhibition here of the medieval remains of Anagni and other neighboring towns. The second room, a grand, frescoed chamber, is known as the *Room of the Famous Slap* where Boniface was hit by an emissary of France's Philip the Fair in 1303. The slap was delivered as a result of a long-standing feud caused by Philip's attempts to extract financial dues from the clergy and his subsequent excommunication by Boniface.

Duomo, Piazza Innocenzo III, Anagni
Open: Daily 9am–noon 4pm–6pm
Admission free

Simple and unadorned, the 11th-century Duomo is built on the site of an ancient acropolis. On one side of the cathedral you can see a large statue of Pope Boniface VIII, erected by the townsfolk. The main facade overlooks a square 12th-century belltower and a small piazza to the right of Piazza Innocenzo III. To reach the belltower, walk under an archway to the right of Boniface's statue, climb a flight of steps and you'll see it in front of you.

Don't miss the crypt in the cathedral. (Open by application to the parish priest. Admission by donation.) It's magnificently decorated with 13th-century frescoes covering the walls and vaulted roof. These frescoes depict various aspects of history, geography and religion, and deserve close attention. The beautiful mosaic floor was constructed in 1231 by the Cosmati marble masons. Strictly suitable dress, for men and women, must be worn here.

WHERE TO EAT IN ANAGNI

Ristorante Del Gallo, Via Vittorio Emanuele 164   LL
Tel: (0775) 727309
Open: Daily 12:30pm–3pm 7:30pm–10:30pm
No credit cards

Opposite the imposing Palazzo Comunale is the faded sign for the Del Gallo restaurant. It's easy to miss. You go through the unpretentious entrance into a white-walled, oak-beamed cottage. Two cozy rooms, furnished with rustic pieces, lead into a third room with a pretty, painted-wood ceiling and a magnificent view of the plain. There's a charming, homey atmosphere provided by the owner-chef, Signora Marisa Pampanelli, whose family have lived here for generations. Genuine home-cooking and regional cuisine, including *macaroni*, and *timballo alla Bonifacio* (home-made fettuccini with meatballs and ham). Try *brasata alla Ciociara* (veal steak in white wine) for a main course. For dessert, sample the *zuppa Inglese*: a moist sponge cake with creamy custard laced with liqueur. The house white wine is dry and slightly tangy. Ideal on a hot summer's day.

ANAGNI TO FERENTINO

Leaving Anagni, pass under the arch (Porta Santa Maria) at the far end of the piazza, and follow the road around to the left. At the fork continue straight on for Fiuggi. The road runs downhill, and a short way ahead there's a fork indicating right for Ferentino. There are hairpin bends for a stretch as you follow signs for the Via Casilina, then continue straight across the plain for Ferentino/Frosinone. Shortly after is the T-junction with the Casilina road. Turn left. Along this road you'll find the hills on your left are just a couple of fields away now. After 2kms you'll see a sign left for Ferentino, and you have to cross over the main road onto a smaller one. Follow the white sign for Ferentino centro as the road climbs. After about 500m you enter the built-up area and follow signs for centro. Turn sharp left, then right at the fork, then make a sharp U-turn right, signposted Municipio Carbinari. You'll pass the Casa di Risparmio di Roma on your left and an old gray stone building with a view of the plain on your right. Immediately ahead you're in Piazza Matteotti with its white monument. Next to a café on the right, you'll find the summer season Tourist Office, Piazza Matteotti. (Tel: (0775) 394114. If the office is closed enquire at the café or the newspaper shop in the square for opening times: these vary considerably.)

FERENTINO

This is one of the oldest cities in the Lazio region. The Romans occupied it in the fourth century BC and Hannibal destroyed it in 211BC. The town flourished in the Imperial period when it became popular with the Roman nobility. In the Middle Ages it was the home of several popes.

Ferentino is girdled by polygonal or cyclopean city walls over three meters thick. These consist of immense irregular-shaped boulders that fit neatly together and are one of the most remarkable examples of their kind in Italy. They date from the fifth to second centuries BC with a medieval upper section.

There are a number of gates in the walls; especially interesting are the Porta Sanguinaria (Bloody Gate) which represents the pre-Roman, Roman and medieval eras in Ferantino's history; and the Porta Maggiore (Great Gate), also called Archi di Casamari. Outside the Porta Maggiore is a rare monument: a Roman will carved in the rock. In this will, engraved in the second century BC, Quintilius, illustrious patron of Ferentino, bequeathed his worldly goods to the town. Every five years, on his birthday, May 9, part of the inheritance was to be distributed among the populace. Inside the city walls are the walls of a first-century BC acropolis, built at the same time as the Roman market.

Duomo, Piazza Duomo, Ferentino
Open: Daily 8:30am–12:30pm 4:30pm–7:30pm
Admission free

This Romanesque cathedral is a jewel. Built in the 12th and 13th centuries on top of an acropolis, it stands apart in a little square in the high part of the town overlooking the plain. The facade is small and of the utmost simplicity: gray local stone with faded frescoes in crescent shapes over the three doors. Inside it has lovely Cosmati mosaic work on the floor and a fine pulpit.

WHERE TO EAT/WHERE TO STAY IN FERENTINO

Hotel Bassetto, Via Casilina K.74.6000   LL
Tel: (0775) 394931/244931   Open: Year round
Amenities: **P** ✗   Credit cards: AE, DC, MC, V

This modern, comfortable hotel lies just outside Ferentino, on our route to Cassino. It's named for founder-owner Enrico Concutelli, whose nickname "*Il Bassetto*" means "shorty". All 72 rooms have good-sized bath/shower rooms; children are welcome and there's a play area. The hotel will make arrangements for you to use a local swimming pool and nearby riding school.

The hotel's restaurant is open to non-residents and set in modern surrounds with an air of elegance: a single rose on each table. First course specials include *cavatelli ai frutti di mare* (small pasta with seafood) and *tagliolini alla Mediterrano* (homemade pasta with fresh tomato sauce and basil). For a main course try *pollo alla Sophia* (chicken with tomato and a tasty sauce). The menu also has a special "Mediterranean diet" section for light meals, with the number of calories indicated. At lunchtime the chef prepares the pasta dough in full view of his customers.

FERENTINO TO CASSINO

*From the **Piazza Matteotti** in Ferentino follow the sign for **Frosinone**. As you go downhill turn right after about 50m. The street is extremely narrow. At the T-junction, with the church in front of you, turn left – signposted **A2**. The Hotel Bassetto is 2kms from the piazza, on the right. At the next T-junction turn left, following signs for the **A2**. Keep following signs for **Frosinone/A2**. At the major intersection with traffic lights (7.2kms from the Hotel Bassetto), follow signs for **A2/Napoli**. Drive straight ahead, through the next five sets of traffic lights. You're following signs for **A2/ Napoli/Roma/Latina**. The autostrada sign is green while the more local town signs are blue. After 3½kms from the major intersection, turn right – signposted **A2/Roma/Napoli**. Follow the road to the ticket booth and then bear left for **Napoli**. You're now on the A2 heading south.*

*After about 46kms leave the A2 at the **Cassino** exit. The cost of your trip will be about L3000. After the toll booth turn left for **Cassino** and keep following signs for the town. After 2½kms you'll go over railroad tracks, then turn right for Cassino. Follow signs for **Cassino Centro**. At some major traffic lights follow the white sign for Cassino Centro. The Centro signs look like a bull's eye with a series of circles around it and the town name. Bear left where the road forks right for Napoli. Follow the road around. The Hotel Excelsior is on your left. Immediately thereafter you'll see the Renault showroom, also on the left. Turn left by the dealership into **Via Condotti**, where you should park. Just up on the left, you'll find the **Tourist Office**, Via Condotti 6. (Tel: (0776) 21292. Open: Mon–Sat 9am–1:30pm.)*

CASSINO

Cassino has been completely rebuilt since World War II. Although the Tourist Office is located in the modern town, all the important historic sites are found a steep drive up the mountain behind Cassino, on Montecassino. Here you'll find Roman ruins, the Rocca Janula, the war cemetries and Montecassino Abbey: the most specatcular monastery in Italy.

*Directions: Turn left out of Via Condotti and drive down Via della Repubblica (one-way). After 200m turn left at the traffic lights. At the next set of lights, turn left again into Via Enrico de Nicola. A little further on there's a right turn signposted **Abbazia**. As you climb the twisting mountain road for 9kms to the abbey, you'll pass the sites listed below.*

WHAT TO SEE ON MONTECASSINO

Amphitheater and **Museo Archeologico**, Archeological area
Open: Tues–Sun 9am–1 hr before sunset   Closed: Mon
Admission free

The amphitheater is reached by a grassy path: avoid wearing high heels. Dating from the first century, it was built by the Roman matron, Ummidia Quadratilla, who had a passion for theater and spectacle. You can still see the stone brackets jutting from the walls which secured awnings to shade the spectators. You'll also see the massive gray stone tomb constructed for Ummidia and her family.

The Museo Archeologico is a tiny museum with only two rooms, but the exhibits are very well laid out. There's a collection of excavated items from the ancient site of *Casinum*, including marble statuary, pots, small sculpted heads and marble coats-of-arms.

Rocca Janula, Montecassino
Open: Daily
Admission free

Founded by an abbot in the 10th century, this fortress is now an impressive and commanding ruin. It was apparently built as a fortified defense against the Saracens, and local legend says there's a network of catacombs beneath the *rocca* with tunnels hundreds of kilometers long leading to the catacombs in Rome. An overgrown pathway leads from the roadside to a good vantage point. It's a lovely and relaxing place for a walk or a picnic.

Abbazia di Montecassino, Montecassino
Open: Daily 9am–noon 1:30pm–hr before sunset
Admission: L2,000 (includes museum)

The abbey at Montecassino is the best known and most astonishing monastery in Italy. It stands on a ridge of the mountain overlooking the Garigliano valley and the main southern approach road to Rome. This spot has been sacred since pre-Christian times, when it was the site of a Temple of Apollo. Here St Benedict founded the original Christian monastery in 529 and established the order of monks which took his name: the Benedictines. When the saint died in 543, his remains were buried in the monastery together with those of his sister St Scholastica, though the exact site of his burial remained a mystery until the urn containing his remains was unearthed during rebuilding work following World War II.

In the Dark Ages, traditions of learning and scholarship were preserved in only a few far-flung religious centers. Montecassino became one of the greatest of these. Through the years the monks established a unique collection of Latin and classical literature, as well as religious texts, containing many works which would otherwise have been lost to history.

Unfortunately, the monastery's spectacular and strategic position was to prove its downfall on several occasions. Only 60 years after its foundation, it was laid waste by the Lombards. The Saracens sacked it in the ninth century, as did the Normans two centuries later; then in 1348 it was destroyed by an earthquake. But on each occasion the Benedictine monks patiently rebuilt their monastery. The building remained unscathed until 1944 when the Allies, advancing north through Italy, were halted by the German army at Montecassino. From January until May the German defenses held out against the siege, and by the end of this period the monastery was once again in ruins, victim of the constant barrage of Allied bombing and artillery fire. However, the abbey's priceless collection of illuminated manuscripts and documents had been moved to Rome, where they were housed in the Castel Sant'Angelo. After the war, work began on the reconstruction of the monastery. This was based on documents, photographs and paintings, and a study of the fragments of sculpture and marble in the rubble. Pope Paul VI consecrated the abbey on October 24, 1964. Unfortunately the original paintings and murals were irreplaceable, so contemporary artists have made good the loss: most notably Pietro Annigoni, whose great fresco *The Glory of St Benedict* on the entrance wall was completed in 1979.

The size and splendor of the abbey are overwhelming. It commands a view over the whole of Cassino and surrounding mountains. Stand at the balustrade of the huge central cloister and enjoy a breathtaking panorama at sunset. This cloister has two lateral smaller cloisters and a sweeping stone staircase leads to the Chiostro dei Benefattori (Cloister of the Benefactors) and the facade of the basilica.

Two new bronze side doors designed by Pietro Canonica are set in the facade. The central door, dating from the 11th century, was restored after the war. The basilica, the Church of St Benedict, is richly Baroque with its gold stucco and marble inlay. The crypt is encrusted with gold and brightly colored mosaic, in the manner of Monreale Cathedral in Palermo. Above the altar in the crypt are the tombs of St Benedict and St Scholastica. St Benedict's tomb has now become a symbol of faith and peace for the warring nations of World War II. The tomb supports 13 lamps, as it did before the war. "May the lamp of brotherhood ever shed its bright and holy light at Montecassino", Pope Paul VI said at the consecration.

Abbey Museum, Montecassino (to the left of the basilica)
Open: Daily 9am–12:30pm 3pm–6:30pm
Admission: L2,000

An excellent museum, very well set out and deserving more than a cursory look. The exhibits include many of the most precious items saved from the intensive bombing of 1944. There's statuary and an art gallery: here you can see manuscripts, paintings and a treasury of gold, silver and jewel-encrusted religious objects. The illuminated manuscripts are superb. The collection includes huge music scores for the choir lectern (*corali*). These were written in large print so the chanting monks could read them at a distance. The art gallery includes paintings by Luca Fiordan, two by Andrea di Salerno and two studies by Annigoni for the frescoes in the basilica.

Set in a stairwell after the exhibits are World War II mementoes: bomb shells, metal helmets and machine guns. As you climb the stairs, the walls are lined with photographs documenting the wartime destruction of the abbey: a fittingly ironic touch after the exquisite craftsmanship of the museum's contents.

War Cemeteries, Montecassino
Open: Daily 9am–sunset
Admission free

There are four war cemeteries – Polish, English, German and
Italian – at Cassino, containing more than 30,000 graves. The
Polish cemetery is situated opposite the Abbazia di Montecassino.
In the battle fought here in May 1944 the Allies finally breached
the gates of Cassino, thus enabling them to continue their delayed
march on Rome.

WHERE TO EAT/WHERE TO STAY IN CASSINO

Forum Palace Hotel, Via Casilina Nord   **LL**
Tel: (0776) 481211   Open: Year round
Amenities: ☎ 🅿 ✕ ⚲   Credit cards: AE, DC, V

This is a pleasant, comfortable hotel and the best in Cassino. It's
situated 1km north of town on the road to Frosinone. The large
hall contains two wooden sculptures and the lounge area is circular
and sunny with windows halfway round. The decor is predominantly brown and beige and the 100 rooms are all sound-proofed.
Those overlooking the parking lot have a good view of distant
mountains, but the furniture is a little uninspiring for a four-star
hotel.

The restaurant is open to non-residents. It has an international
cuisine and a varied daily menu (not à la carte). For a real treat try
the homemade fettucine if it's on the day's menu: either *alla
Ciociara* (with meat sauce), or *alla moda dello chef* (with tomato,
peas, bacon pieces and onion). Also homemade are the *gnocchetti
sardi pomodoro e riccotta* (potato dumplings with tomato and
ricotta cheese). There's a selection of meat dishes to follow: the
veal is outstanding.

MONTECASSINO TO CAPUA

*Drive down the road from the monastery. At the bottom turn right
to **Roma** and go back the way you came, retracing your steps to the
A2. Follow signs for **A2**/**Roma**. Don't be concerned that Napoli isn't
shown on these signs. Eventually it will appear. Continue on this
road until you see a left turn with signs A2/Roma, make the left turn
and bear right at the fork, following **A2**/**Roma**/**Napoli** signs. Pick up
a toll ticket and proceed onto the A2 in the direction of **Naples**.*

*After about 44kms you'll see an attractive parking area to your
right where you can picnic. After 50kms on the A2 you leave the
autostrada at the **Capua** exit, paying a toll of approximately L3500.
Follow the road straight ahead. After about 300m turn left at the
crossroads signposted **Capua**. Keep following signs for Capua.
After about 6kms you enter the town of Capua. Follow the main
road round to your left, past the Esso gas station on the right. Bear*

left at the fork signposted Napoli, following the main road. Then bear right at the next fork, continuing to follow the main road. After 300m go over a bridge. Take your third left. Opposite there's a large military building, the turret on its corner is directly opposite your left turn. Drive down the narrow, tree-lined street with a dome ahead. The road ends in a T-junction at the church; turn left, following the sign for the museum. Now you're in Capua's historic center in a narrow, one-way street with two arches ahead. Pass under the first and park where possible. Go back to the first arch and turn right, following a white sign for Municipio. The left side of the street is arcaded. At the end of this street you'll find Piazza dei Giudici. In a building on the far left, with three stone coats-of-arms over the main door, you'll find the Tourist Office, Piazza dei Giudici. (Tel: (0823) 963930. Open: Daily 9am–noon 4:30pm–8pm.)

CAPUA

The town of Capua dates from Etruscan times, and originally stood where Santa Maria Capua Vetere is now situated. When the original Capua was destroyed by the Saracens in the ninth century, the displaced inhabitants built the new town of Capua on its present site, in a bend of the River Volturno. Through the ensuing centuries various nationalities, including Norman, Swedish, French and Austrian, have controlled the town. It suffered damage during a bombardment in September 1943 and, more recently, from the 1980 earthquake.

Before you continue on to Santa Maria Capua Vetere (4kms south), archeology buffs shouldn't miss the **Museo Campano**, in Via Roma. (Open: Tues–Sat 9am–2pm, Sun 9am–1pm. Admission free.) The museum is housed in the Palazzo Antignano, which dates from the 15th-century era of Spanish rule. It has a majestic portal of rare Catalano style and an archway elegantly bordered with carved tufo, surmounted by a crown-like design. You sign the register than a guide shows you around the various collections of historic objects which illustrate the region's rich past. There's an ancient site at Capua from which many Greek vases, Roman mosaics and statues have been excavated. You can also see a fine display of medieval sculpture. (The art gallery and coin collection are at present closed to the public.) Don't miss the museum's amazing collection of about 200 stone mother statues (*madri*). These ancient figurines from the sixth to first centuries BC, each depict a seated woman holding one or more swaddled babies in her arms (one statue holds 12 infants). Among these figures is a taller one, without children, believed to represent the goddess of birth and fertility. These statues were found in the vicinity of Capua and experts believe there must once have been a temple dedicated to maternity on the site.

CAPUA TO SANTA MARIA CAPUA VETERE

Unfortunately, this is a dreary drive through tawdry surroundings.

*Leave Capua's **Piazza dei Giudici** with the Tourist Office on your left and drive under the arch. Continue down **Corso Appio** passing the Chiesa de l'Annunziata on your left and you'll come to the large intersection again. Drive straight across and down tree-lined **Via Napoli**. After about 300m there's a set of lights; turn left for **Caserta** and **SMC Vetere**, following a green sign for **Napoli**. You'll then see a blue sign indicating Caserta straight ahead. Soon you'll see a white sign to indicate you're entering SMC Vetere. Continue straight ahead, following the sign for **centro**. After 1km drive under a bridge and you'll see Arco di Adriano, an ancient brick arch which you drive under. After 100m there's a yellow sign for the amphitheater and a small park on your left. Turn sharp left after the park into a huge piazza, where you'll see the great amphitheater ahead. Follow the road around to the left and park. The **Tourist Office** is at the entrance to the amphitheater. (Open: Tues–Sun 9am–1hr before sunset.)*

SANTA MARIA CAPUA VETERE

Ancient Capua, dating from the eighth century BC, was originally Etruscan. The Romans invaded it in 330BC. The *ozi di Capua* refers to Hannibal's fatal rest in this town. He stopped here to relax before marching against Rome, but meanwhile the Romans mobilized and thoroughly routed his Carthaginian army.

After Hannibal's crushing defeat, Capua remained faithful to the Romans. However, the gladiators' revolt (73–71BC), led by Spartacus, had its origins in the amphitheater and gladiator school of Capua. The great amphitheater was built at the end of the Republican era. During the Roman Imperial period Capua grew in prestige; Cicero called it *"urbus amplissima atque ornatissima"* (a sizeable, well-adorned city). Roman emperors extended the amphitheater and embellished it with columns and statues. The Barbarians attacked the town during the fifth and sixth centuries and in 841 the Saracens destroyed it. The townsfolk fled to the hills and shortly after began to build the modern Capua at *Casilinum*, the river port of old Capua. Santa Maria Capua Vetere grew up from the ruins of ancient Capua. In 1860 Garibaldi based his headquarters here while preparing for the Battle of the Volturno which was decisive in the unification of southern Italy.

WHAT TO SEE IN SANTA MARIA CAPUA VETERE

Amphitheater, Santa Maria Capua Vetere
Open: Tues–Sun 9am–1hr before sunset   Closed: Mon
Admission: L2,000 (includes the Mithraeum)

This is a truly imposing monument, second only in size to the Colosseum in Rome and in a marvelous state of preservation. It measures 170 × 140 meters, and the arena 72 × 46 meters. Here it's possible to conjure up the atmosphere of Roman gladiatorial battles and realize the power and grandeur of their civilization. Underneath the arena is a warren of subterranean galleries where the slaves and wild animals were kept. Unlike the Colosseum, you can wander through these freely, often losing yourself in the confusing maze.

This amphitheater was built before the Colosseum by the Roman Emperor Augustus and subsequently restored by the Emperors Hadrian and Antoninus Pius. Note the arches composed of seven blocks, still in excellent condition after two thousand years. The Romans cut these blocks with mathematical precision and then, with pulleys, lowered all seven simultaneously onto a prepared base. The central or key block is of fundamental importance as it absorbs all the tension and vibration. Only one statue remains in situ: a female torso in one of the alcoves. The rest of the statuary is set out in a small garden next to the amphitheater. A second-century mosaic, laid out in the garden in front of the amphitheater, is visible from the road where you park your car.

Mithraeum, Santa Maria Capua Vetere
Open: Tues–Sun 9am–1hr before sunset   Closed: Mon
Admission: L2,000 (includes the Amphitheater.) Tip the guide

The guide travels with you in your car the short distance from the amphitheater to the Mithraeum. The Mithraeum is a subterranean temple, 25 × 3 meters, dating from the second century and dedicated to the Persian god Mithras. His followers were involved in mysterious and secret rites which excluded women, but were open to all men regardless of social status. Along the walls are partially erased frescoes depicting initiation scenes. The vault is painted with stars and a fresco of the moon goddess riding a chariot. The wall behind the altar is decorated with a magnificent, well-preserved fresco depicting the handsome Mithras in the act of slaying a white bull. This compelling painting warrants close attention. Notice the allegorical figures: a dog representing Goodness; a snake representing Evil; and a crow, scorpion and ant surrounding the bull. There's the sun, with a raised torch; the ocean on the left; the moon with a lowered torch; and the earth on the right. Mithras, looking like a young Apollo, wears an oriental costume and a magnificent cloak lined with stars; unfortunately his face has been erased, possibly by 20th-century vandals. On one wall there's a small marble relief of Cupid and Psyche, believed to be of a later date than the temple.

It's interesting that many buildings in Capua feature pieces removed from the amphitheater over the years before such activities were banned. For example, opposite the Mithraeum entrance is a house with a fragment of stone sculpture of five leaves attached to the wall.

SANTA MARIA CAPUA VETERE TO CASERTA

*Retrace your steps from the amphitheater, turn left at the end of the street to rejoin **Via Moro**. Cross a small square and continue straight ahead down the cobbled street. Cross the intersection and you'll pass a park on your right. The road now becomes paved and there are signs to **Napoli**. Follow the blue signs, for **Caserta**, through the built-up area. After 2kms there's an odd shaped stone tower on your right. Drive under a bridge and after 1km you'll see a sign to indicate you're entering Caserta. You'll see the immense **Palazzo Reale** ahead on the left. Pass the palace and find a place to park nearby. In the summer months you may be approached by an unauthorised individual, possibly on roller skates, requesting L2,000 to keep an eye on your car. You're not obliged to pay but most people do. A few blocks further down on the left, you'll find the **Tourist Office**, Corso Trieste 39. (Tel: (0823) 321137. Open: Daily Jul–Aug 8am–2pm 4pm–7:30pm; Sep–Jun 8:30am–1:30pm 4pm–7:30pm.)*

CASERTA

Caserta's great (and only) distinction is that it has the largest palace in Italy: La Reggia. In World War II this was where the Allied High Command established its headquarters, and the formal surrender of all German and Italian forces in Italy was signed at the palace in 1945.

Construction of this monster began in 1752 for Charles III, the Bourbon King of Naples, and took 20 years to complete. It was designed by the king's favorite architect, who plied his profession under the suitably Italian and artistic name of Luigi Vanvitelli (although he was a Dutchman called Van Wittel). The Reggia was intended to rival Louis XIV's palace at Versailles, and Vanvitelli was given carte blanche and unlimited expenses to do so. The result is a grandiose building covering some fifty thousand square meters and containing over 1,200 rooms. It doesn't rival Versailles and many consider it rather overbearing, but there's lots to see including the Royal Apartments and the famous Cascata Grande. You can spend a very pleasant afternoon here.

WHAT TO SEE IN CASERTA

Appartamenti Storici (Royal Apartments), Palazzo Reggia
Open: Mon–Sat 9am–1:30pm, Sun and holidays 9am–12:30pm
Admission: Adults L3,000, children under 12 free

Walk along the central arcade with an impressive view of the
Cascade beyond. Halfway down on your right is the vast stairway
(117 steps) leading to the apartments. The Royal Apartments are a
succession of sumptuous and richly decorated rooms. The ceilings
are superbly frescoed and hung with huge, glittering chandeliers.
The furniture is largely Empire. Your tour begins with the New
Apartments to your right, so called because they were the last to
be completed. Particularly impressive is the great, gilded throne
room. The king's bathroom is wonderful, with its tub carved from
a block of oriental granite and a fine marble dressing table. On the
pretty painted ceiling, you'll see the goddess Ceres who looks as if
she's clasping a bird dripping with blood. She isn't. The red splash
is ink which an American soldier hurled at the ceiling in a fit of
rage during World War II.

Retrace your steps and turn left into the Old Apartments (the
first to be finished). The splendid glass chandeliers were made by
master craftsmen in Murano. The study has a little sundial perched
on the windowsill outside. Ask the attendant to show you "*la
meridiana*". In the king and queen's bathroom there's a tub of
white sculpted marble with an inner basin of gilded bronze (at
present closed for repairs). The bathrooms are notable not only
for their beauty, but also for their hot and cold water, a luxury
available to monarchs alone in that era. The Grand Court Theater
is also closed at present.

Parco di Palazzo Reale
Open: Daily 9am–6pm (summer), 9am–2:30pm (winter) (It's
advisable to check the opening hours with the Tourist Office if you
come in spring or autumn.)
Admission: L2,000.

Alternative ways to see the park are by car (Mon–Sat), by foot or
by horse and trap. The latter will take you on a romantic trip for
about L20,000 but covers only the lower half of the park. There's
so much to see here, with over 250 acres of beautiful parkland to
visit. Notable highlights are the fabulous Cascata Grande waterfall, decorated with numerous statues telling the legend of Diana
and Actaeon (who was turned into a stag); and the English garden.
Also two huge magnolia trees, the size of great oaks and centuries
old.

WHERE TO EAT IN CASERTA

Antica Locanda Massa 1848, Via Mazzini 55, Caserta   LL
Tel: (0823) 321268
Open: Tues–Sun noon–4pm 7pm–11.30pm
Closed: Mon and 2 wks in Aug
Credit cards: AE, DC, V

Enjoying the reputation of being the best in town, this restaurant, established in 1848, is located in a quaint square a few blocks from Piazza Dante in Via Mazzini. If the road's closed to traffic, tell the traffic warden you want the restaurant and he'll let you through. Park in the piazza or in a parking lot up a narrow street opposite.

Inside there are white walls, oak beams, and an antique open fireplace blazes in winter. The floor is paved with slabs of Vesuvian lava, and the salon is furnished with Bourbon antiques, including confessionals now used as sideboards. There's an outdoor terrace in a pretty whitewashed courtyard under a 100-year-old pergola of vines and giant bougainvillea. The cuisine is typically Campanian. From a wide choice of pasta dishes, we recommend *linguine al cartoccio* (made with seafood and fresh tomato sauce), or *cazzarielli all Borbone* (tiny dumplings in a sauce of four cheeses and black truffles). For dessert there's delicious homemade ice cream: try the *stracciatella* (a type of chocolate chip). In the colder months there's a typical Campanian dessert, *la pastiera*, made with rice flour, ricotta and candied fruit. The wine list is good, and as an aperitif don't miss the orange-based *cocktail al arancia*.

WHERE TO STAY IN CASERTA

Hotel Reggia Palace, Viale Carlo III, Caserta   LL
Tel: (0823) 458500   Open: Year round
Amenities: ☎ ⊡ 🅿 ✕ ⚲ ⌂ ℘ ▮   Credit cards: AE, DC, MC, V

A modern, air-conditioned hotel, just a few kilometers from town, the Reggia offers many facilities including a disco and playground. It has a rather dark, aggressive decor: dark blue carpets and modern paintings in the hall and lounge; red and white walls and grey ceiling in the dining hall. The color schemes on the second and third floors are more restful. Bedrooms look onto the parking lot in front and trees and the distant freeway at the back. Windows are not sound-proofed but the traffic is far enough away not to disturb. The rooms are not large, but the bathrooms are pleasantly spacious. Double and triple rooms or suites are available. The suites are particularly attractive with two double rooms and two bathrooms, one with a tub, the other with a shower.

Hotel Centrale, Via Roma 170, Caserta   **L**
Tel: (0823) 321855   Open: Year round
Amenities: ♀   Credit cards: AE, DC, V

This hotel is situated in the center of Caserta. The exterior, with a round neon sign, is uninspiring, but the interior is rather better with antique-style furniture and some rather tawdry mirrors. The hotel has a generally homey appearance. It's comfortable and good value for money, with friendly staff. There's a small bar on the first floor and a large breakfast room-cum-lounge on the top floor. The 40 simple rooms have pretty tiles on the floors in front rooms and blue carpeting in the larger back rooms. Those facing the street have sound-proofed windows, though the air-conditioning is rather noisy. A few rooms have hip baths where taking a shower requires yoga-like flexibility: do specify a shower-stall or full-size tub when making your reservation. Have breakfast in the bar: for L2,000 you'll get a large cup of excellent *cappuccino* and a huge brioche. The hotel has no restaurant but this poses no problem: Caserta and Caserta Vecchia have many excellent restaurants and cafés.

A SIDETRIP TO CASERTA VECCHIA

*To reach Caserta Vecchia continue down **Corso Trieste** to the white monument at the end. Turn left, following the yellow sign for **Borgo Medievale**. The road bears right and you'll find yourself on a wide road with squat palms down the middle. Turn sharp left at the traffic lights, following the yellow sign for **Caserta Vecchia**. At the T-junction take the right fork (this bears left) and follow the blue signs for **Caserta Vecchia**. Soon afterwards you pass through a village, at the end of which turn right. This narrow, twisting road leads you high up the mountain, giving a superb view to your right. After 5kms the road turns away from the vista to a fork: bear left. Shortly thereafter you come to a parking lot: leave your car here, as the medieval village is closed to traffic. Walk up a short, steep incline flanked by a scruffy pine copse to the stone arched entrance to the village.*

*NOTE: Not all the signs are posted all the time but if you follow the directions you'll come to **Caserta Vecchia**.*

CASERTA VECCHIA

Caserta Vecchia, founded by the Lombards, was the original Caserta, before Charles III built the Reggia. A hilltop community grew in the ninth century when the people of Calazia and Suessola fled here after their towns were destroyed. The Calazians were led by their bishop who established a diocese here. In 1113 it became the Casertan Diocese, and in 1842 this was transferred to the new

Caserta on the plain.

It seems that time stopped centuries ago in this lovely gray-stone village perched 400m above sea level in the shadow of an ancient castle. Although the village has preserved the atmosphere of a bygone age, it's still fully inhabited. Caserta Vecchia is a delightful spot to spend a couple of hours, not only for its charming and picturesque narrow streets, but also its excellent cooking. People flock from all over the area to eat in its many *trattorias* and restaurants. The standard of food and the quality of wines are very high. A must for gourmets.

The Duomo's beautiful 12th- and 13th-century belltower straddles the street to form an arch where you walk through to delightful Piazza del Duomo. The cathedral's Romanesque dome has a complicated geometric shape, and the belltower has five floors and four bells. Originally it was seven meters taller but lightning "shortened" it in 1700. The simple facade is enlivened by no less than 10 stone animals. There are epigraphs on the architraves of the three portals which state that the cathedral was built in the first half of the 12th century. The interior is officially closed for extensive repairs at present, but you can sometimes find someone who'll allow you to peek inside. If you can, it's well worth it. Magnificently spartan, the roof is supported by two arched rows of nine monolithic columns heaved up the hill from the plain. The lovely pulpit, constructed in the early 17th century from 13th-century fragments, is the only piece of elaborate carving in the church.

Cross the square from the Duomo and continue down Via San Michele Arcangelo. On your left you'll pass an ancient house justly famous for its two splendid bifor windows: **Casa delle Bifore**. This is owned by two families, both specializing in pretty hand-painted terracotta-ware. Michele Farraiuolo, his wife and three daughters are all artists and their showroom is in the courtyard. Continue to the end of the street and you're rewarded with a spectacular view of the plain, Caserta and the Reggia.

WHERE TO EAT IN CASERTA VECCHIA

La Castellana, Via Torre 4, Caserta Vecchia   LL
Tel: (0823) 371230
Open: Daily noon–2pm 8pm–11pm
Closed: Thur from Jul 1–Sep 30
Credit cards: AE, DC, MC, V

A stone's throw from the entrance to the medieval village, the restaurant harks back to the olden days, with boars' heads and hams hanging from whitewashed walls (though a color television and jukebox mar the overall effect). Across the road and up a short flight of stone steps is a pleasant, graveled courtyard under a roof of vine leaves: a more casual setting with plastic chairs and, alas, neon lighting. This family-run restaurant specializes in game, including venison and boar, and everything is *alla brace* (charcoal grilled). Try the *antipasto di cinghiale* (boar) and *pappardelle con cinghiale* (pasta with boar meat sauce). A typical Campanian dish is *pettole e fagioli* (wide strips of pasta cut into pieces, served with beans). Then there's the speciality of the house: *stingozzi alla Castellana*, a secret recipe using long, thin pasta with a sauce of tomato, ham and eggplant. There's a wide selection of grilled meat dishes to follow. In summer, try the fresh fruit flan.

Antico Ristorante Mastroangelo, Piazza Duomo   L–LL
Tel: (0823) 371377
Open: Daily noon–2:30pm 7pm–11pm   Closed: Tues in winter
No credit cards

This restaurant-cum-pizzeria is well-known locally for its excellent pizzas and for having had Queen Elizabeth the Queen Mother as a client on June 24, 1988. It's situated opposite the cathedral; you pass under a white arch into a shady courtyard with simple table settings under a pergola of vines, lit by wrought iron lamps. (There's a bar with a jukebox that's open all day.) The restaurant was originally a convent and inside there are white walls, arches and a medieval fireplace. Why not try a pizza made with the delicious local mozzarella cheese. (Pizza isn't served at lunch-time.) Signor Mastroangelo recommends his homemade pasta dishes, particularly his *pasta bestemmia* (swearing pasta) made with a hot, spicy sauce of chillis, mozzarella and ham. On some summer days you can sample the *torta di gelato* (ice-cream cake), made locally for the restaurant. The house wine, made by the owner, has body with a pleasant grapey bouquet.

CASERTA TO NAPLES

*To leave Caserta Vecchia, retrace your steps down the mountain. This time don't drive up Corso Trieste (it's one-way), but go past the white memorial and take the next right into **Via Roma**. Continue past four sets of lights to the large intersection; turn left signposted **A2/Napoli**. After about 1km cross the railroad bridge leading to a T-junction. Turn left here into a wide main road, flanked by oleander bushes. You pass the borough of **San Nicola la Strada** and the Reggia Palace Hotel on your right. You'll drive under two bridges after passing the Reggia Palace. After a few kilometers you reach the right turn for the freeway. You join the toll-paying freeway here for the last 30kms into Naples.*

*It's just over 6kms from the fourth traffic light, where you turned in Caserta, to the right turn for the **A2** to **Napoli**. You'll have to pay on entry to the road, this time – a cost of L1300. You'll also pay L500 as you exit the highway.*

*Drive along the A2 for about 18½kms. Toward the end of the drive follow signs for **Napoli Centro/Tangenziale** (ring road). Follow these and leave the highway at the **Corso Malta** exit. Pay your toll. Drive down the Corso Malta, turning right into the **Plaza Nationale** – drive through the plaza to the **Via Calata Ponte di Cassanova** on its opposite side. Take your second left after the plaza, onto the **Corso Novaro**. Drive down this road, underneath the elevated tracks, as far as you can. Turn right at the "no entry" sign into the **Via Firenze**, then left into the **Via Bologna**. At the end of this street turn left into the parking area in the **Piazza Garibaldi**. You'll find the **Tourist Office** across in the Stazione Centrale. (Tel: (081) 268779. Open: Mon–Sat 8:30am–7:30pm (sometimes closed between 2pm–2:30pm), Sun 8:30am–2pm.) Ask for a copy of the monthly pamphlet* Qui Napoli. *This English-language information booklet lists useful addresses, hours of opening, timetables and so on.*

A word of warning: in summer it's best to avoid driving in Naples except in the early morning or late evening, otherwise you're liable to be stuck in ghastly traffic jams in 33°C of humid heat.

NAPLES

Naples is a city of splendor and squalor. It's set in one of the most beautiful bays in the world, with picturesque islands, an azure sea and the cone of Mount Vesuvius in the background. Yet the sea is so polluted that it's forbidden to eat locally caught fish, and the streets of the city play host to the world's greatest (and noisiest) continuous traffic jam. The city contains over 150 churches, many of them centuries old and some of superb architectural beauty – yet its back streets contain the most notoriously overcrowded slums in Europe. Somehow it seems poetically appropriate that such a city is run by a municipal council which meets in a banqueting hall where 500 years ago the King of Naples invited all his rivals to a grand feast of reconciliation and then murdered them.

Miracles and misery are Naples's stock-in-trade. The main cathedral is dedicated to the city's patron saint, San Gennaro. Twice a year, in May and September, the saint's relics are paraded in joyous procession through the streets, then the crowds gather to witness the Miracle of the Blood. The saint's reliquary contains two phials of his blood. Through the centuries this has become congealed, but on the day of the festival the blood miraculously liquifies. The miracle is expected to take place at each festival; when it doesn't, the superstitious Neapolitans believe it's an evil omen for their city. They recall that in 1527 the city was smitten by plague when the miracle didn't occur, and the next failure in 1569 was marked by famine. More recently, Vesuvius erupted after the miracle failed to take place in 1941.

Naples was first established by Ancient Greek colonists around 1000BC. (The present Italian name for the city derives from the Greek *nea polis*, meaning "new city".) The Greek settlement of *Nea Polis* thrived for at least two centuries before Rome was even founded. Inevitably, as the power of Ancient Rome grew, Naples became part of the Roman Empire. After the Roman Empire's decline Naples had a checkered history of which little record remains, though it is recorded that a Duke of Naples declared the city's independence in 763. In the ensuing centuries Naples remained a kind of quasi-independent kingdom, often ruled by a foreign king who owed his allegiance to some other European power, such as Spain, France or Germany. As a result of these varied influences Naples developed a distinct culture of its own, contributing much in the fields of music, philosophy and painting to European culture. The philosophers Vico and Croce were Neapolitans, and the greatest medieval thinker, St Thomas Aquinas, studied here for several years. Neapolitan classical music produced such figures as Scarlatti and Leoncavallo, its conservatory was the oldest in Europe, and its opera house (San Carlo) predates La Scala in Milan. The popular songs of Naples are part of a unique centuries-old tradition, kept alive by generations of street singers and local performers. So it's no surprise that Naples was the home of the greatest of all Italian singers, Caruso.

Present-day Naples still bears the scars of its recent history. The southern Italian earthquake and the ravages of World War II were devastating for a population already notorious for its poverty. In the 1950s only one-fifth of the city's population had regular jobs, and even today one-third of its inhabitants remain unemployed. Under such conditions it's not surprising that crime flourishes. It's estimated that nearly 40,000 people in Naples live off the proceeds of smuggling: and the smugglers have even formed their own trade union to protect themselves against police harassment. Organized crime also flourishes, with a secret criminal organization called the *Camorra* which is much like the Sicilian Mafia. The *Camorra* are reputed to run the largest organized black market in the world. Yet despite this, Neapolitans are renowned for their open, easygoing friendliness. Visit any restaurant or café, and you'll soon find yourself experiencing this first-hand. The Neapolitans enjoy life – in singing, in the play of emotions, or watching the world go by as they sip their wine on a sunny day. *Dolce far niente* (literally: sweet to do nothing), as the popular Italian expression has it.

Though the Neapolitans have a reputation for doing nothing in style, they have made several significant contributions to industrial development through the centuries. The first steamboat ever to sail in the Mediterranean was launched in Naples in 1818, and just over 20 years later Italy's first railroad steamed out along the shore of the Bay of Naples. Likewise, the first Italian funicular railway opened here in 1880 (and the song they wrote about it remains popular to this day: the celebrated *Funiculi – funicula*).

Many of the finest sights in Europe can be seen on a day trip from Naples. You can take a boat trip to the islands of Ischia or Capri, with its Blue Grotto. Drive a few miles round the Bay of Naples and you come to Pompeii and Herculaneum, the Roman cities destroyed by an eruption of Vesuvius in 79AD. (Nowhere else in the world is it possible to see quite so clearly how people actually lived nearly two millennia ago.) Continue round the Bay of Naples, past Sorrento, and you'll see the superb scenery of the Amalfi Drive. Here the road passes high above the Mediterranean, winding through small unspoilt towns clinging precariously to the steep mountainside. Then of course there's Vesuvius itself, which you can climb to see the spectacular crater at the summit. Or, less energetically, you can visit the steaming lava fields of Solfatara, and the cool, dark waters of Lake Averno, once thought to be the entrance to hell.

WHAT TO SEE IN NAPLES

Palazzo Reale di Capodimonte, Capodimonte Park, Naples
Open: Daily 9am–1 hr before sunset. Picture gallery: (summer) Tues–Sat 9am–7pm, Sun, Mon & holidays 9am–1pm; (winter) Tues–Sat 9am–2pm
Closed: Sun–Mon
Admission free. Picture gallery: L4,000, children under 18 and senior citizens free

Capodimonte Palace is a massive, rather overpowering structure. The building was begun in 1738 and took 10 years to complete. In former days it was a royal estate used by the King of Naples for his hunting expeditions, and is set in a large park with a landscaped garden that has unfortunately fallen into disrepair. (You are strongly advised not to walk in this park as it has become the haunt of local delinquents; the safest way to see it is through a car window.) The Palace itself houses the Royal Apartments and a picture gallery, open to the public.

The Picture Gallery is on the third floor where there are 41 rooms displaying works from various artistic movements. There's a large collection of icons and paintings on wood which include superbly painted crucifixes. The Florentine paintings in Room Five are particularly lovely. Be sure to see the large drawing by Raphael and the magnificent bronze bust of Dante. There are several Titians, a Botticelli and a Lippi.

The Royal Apartments are sumptuous throughout. The rooms are hung with tapestries and contain fine furniture. Outstanding is an enormous round table with a mosaic top supported by three tiers of legs. Don't miss the Porcelain Dining Room, a mirrored salon in which the wall and ceiling are covered with delicately painted, raised porcelain work. Room 77 has a magnificent inlaid marble floor. The porcelain collection and armory are often closed; if so, ask the guardians if they'll open them for you.

Certosa di San Martino, on the summit of the Vomero hill, Naples
Open: (summer) Tues–Sat 9am–7pm, Sun, Mon & holidays 9am–1pm; (winter) Tues–Sat 9am–noon, Sun 9am–1pm
Closed: Mon
Admission: L3,000 (includes admission to museum)

The immense Carthusian monastery of St Martin is magnificently situated on the Vomero hill. It was founded in the 14th century and remodeled in the 16th and 17th centuries. The white-and-gray marble Chiostro Grande (Large Courtyard), with its beautifully-kept gardens, is a haven of grace and harmony. The small doors and adjacent cubby holes under the cloisters were punishment cells for errant monks. Columns on the central wall (1605) are made from a precious African marble and the courtyard served as the monks' burial place.

The area known as the Monks' Walk comprises two terraced gardens with a splendid view over the whole Bay of Naples, the surrounding plains and mountains. Worn pathways lead you under shady arches of thick vines, past flowerbeds and through groves of trees. It's particularly beautiful in springtime.

The church, Sacristy, Treasury and other linked chambers form a stunning display of Gothic grandeur. The church is a lavish profusion of paintings, sculptures, multi-colored marble, and a 17th-century fresco above the altar, *Descent from the Cross*, by Ribera.

The art collection in the monastery's museum includes works by the Neapolitan and Campanian masters. There's also a collection of exquisite glass objects which includes engraved and decorated mirrors as well as oil paintings on glass. The religious statues carved in wood are superb examples of their kind; note especially the pregnant Virgin lying on her bed. The rooms themselves are distinctive, often half-panelled in dark wood or furnished with somber, heavy furniture. (Parts of the art gallery are closed for renovation at present.)

Rooms 32–38 of the museum house nativity models or cribs (*presepii*). These can be found all over Italy at Christmas, in churches and in private houses, but they have always been a speciality of Naples and Sicily. These rooms in the museum house a most remarkable collection of *presepii* and the sculpted figures (*pastori*) that form part of the scenes. The figures are extraordinary in their perfection and detail, and range in size from the enormous tableau by Cuciniello to a tiny nativity scene set in an egg shell. A fascinating and unusual collection. At time of going to press this is closed for renovation, but will be opening again soon. (Enquire at Tourist Office.)

Museo della Cerámica Duca di Martina, Villa Floridiana, Naples
Open: Tues–Sat 9am–2pm, Sun & holidays 9am–1pm
Closed: Mon
Admission: L2,000

This pretty, 18th-century white mansion on the Vomero hill houses the lovely porcelain collection of the Duke of Martina. The collection has grown since his time and now numbers some 6,000 pieces of both European and Asiatic porcelain. Also of interest is the collection of canes with carved ivory handles, the exquisitely painted boxes and the gold and silver objects.

The gardens surrounding the Villa Floridiana (Open: Tues–Sun 9am–dusk) are in a marvelous position high on the Vomero hill overlooking the sea. Paths lead between huge, shady trees and there are plenty of benches for resting and admiring the view. The park is famous for its beautiful camellias and evergreens.

Duomo, Via del Duomo, Naples
Open: Daily 9am–1pm 4:30pm–7pm (subject to variation)
Admission free

This superb Gothic cathedral incorporates over 100 antique columns in its central nave. The paintings of saints over the arches are by the famous artist Giordano (1632–1705). You can also see the tombs of various kings and popes, including that of Andrew of Hungary who was murdered in 1345 by his wife Joan I.

Within the cathedral is the famous chapel of San Gennaro. He is the patron saint of Naples, invoked whenever there is a tragedy. His superb chapel has seven ornate altars and is closed by an immense Baroque gilded bronze grille, the fulfilment of a vow made by the people of Naples during the plague of 1526–29. Behind the main altar the saint's relics are kept including his head and two phials of his congealed blood.

Cappella Sansevero, Via dei Sanctis, Naples
Open: Daily 10am–1:30pm, Sun and holidays 11am–1:30pm
Admission: L2,000

There's a wonderfully melodramatic story attached to this chapel, situated off Via delle Croce in the Old Quarter. Its builder, the Prince de Sansevero, was reputed to be a thoroughly evil man. The two petrified skeletons in the crypt are said to be those of his servants, victims of his diabolical tortures and experiments. He allegedly injected them with a mysterious substance which caused their blood to solidify. We are left to imagine how this was achieved before the invention of hypodermic syringes.

In the center of the chapel, you'll see a statue of the dead Christ laid on a bed. Sculpted by Giuseppe Sammartino, it's a work not only of the most skilful realism, but also of the most exquisite beauty. The sculpted shroud covering the body gives the appearance of being transparent.

NOTE: At the time of going to press the chapel is temporarily closed for repairs, but will be opening again soon. Enquire at the Tourist Office.

Museo Archeologico Nazionale, Piazza Museo Nazionale, Naples
Open: Daily 9am–7:30pm (summer); Mon–Sat 9am–2pm
(winter), Sun & holidays 9am–1pm
Admission: L4,000

This is one of the world's largest and most important museums of antiquity, furnished with priceless treasures from Pompeii and Herculaneum. It's difficult to single out objects from such abundance, but the beautifully preserved frescoes from the two sites are particularly impressive: the colors are superb and extraordinarily vivid. Also note the two white marble sculptures of athletes in the first room after the entrance.

Magnificent large bronzes are housed in the vast Meridian Hall. The hall itself is interesting for its astrological sun-clock. Look up at the far wall on the right and you'll see the tiny hole where a ray of sun would fall on the floor clock. In 1980, this 17th-century palace was damaged by an earthquake and the hole is now out of synch. Housed in the mezzanine is a collection of vibrant and intricate mosaics that's a sheer pleasure to linger over. Note particularly the skill with which animals are depicted. Also in this section is the original little statue of the dancing fawn taken from Pompeii.

NOTE: Due to staff shortages, some rooms are closed in the afternoons.

Appartamenti Storici, Palazzo Reale, Piazza Plebiscito, Naples
Open: Daily 9am–7pm (summer); Mon–Sat 9am–2pm, Sun &
holidays 9am–1:30pm (winter)
Admission: L3,000 adults, children and senior citizens free

These lavish, tapestried apartments bring to life the enormous wealth and power of the former Kings of Naples. Furnished with priceless inlaid tables and ornamental porcelain vases, the rooms are hung with vast, gold-stuccoed mirrors and massive chandeliers. A special mention must be given to the magnificent ballroom with its minstrels' galleries and eight huge frescoed doors. Don't miss the extraordinary wax and glass bust of Maria Caroline d'Asburgo. The altar in the chapel is particularly splendid with its mosaic of inlaid semi-precious stones, and the centerpiece's 3-D design.

The great terrace with its bowered walk is lovely in summertime, affording a magnificent view over the Bay and port. Ask one of the guardians if you can take a peek, but it's usually out of bounds to the public.

Chiesa di Santa Chiara, Strada Santa Chiara, Naples
Open: Daily 8am–12:30pm 4:30pm–7pm
Admission free

This wonderful church was restored to its original Gothic style after being badly bomb damaged in 1943. Simple and unadorned, it has a high, square central nave with Gothic stained-glass windows of singular beauty. It is built in pale stone and has a simple wooden ceiling, giving the impression of space, light and tranquility. In this setting the magnificently carved monumental altar makes the maximum impact. The original church was built in the 14th century for Sancia of Malbrea, wife of Robert of Anyai (France). The tomb of Anyai is behind the altar, and also dates from the 14th century.

The huge 14th-century Chiostro delle Clarisse (Nuns' Cloister) at the back of Santa Chiara's church was transformed, in 1742, with a most unusual garden. The benches and pillars supporting arbor roofs of thick vines have been totally covered with decorated tiles depicting landscapes, flowers, fruit and rustic scenes. Between the covered walks are flowerbeds, fountains and trees of all kinds. The cloister is surrounded by a frescoed arcade and it's a favorite place for students to sit and study – and cats.

The 18th-century *presepe* near the cloister entrance (admission L1,000) was made by local craftsmen. Interestingly, the figures are dressed in 18th-century costumes. Notice the minute details of everyday life.

Castel Nuovo and **Castel dell'Ovo**, near Piazza Plebiscito, Naples
Open: Tues–Sat 9am–2pm, Sun 9am–1pm   Closed: Mon
Admission: L2,000

These two castles on the waterfront are striking landmarks. The **Castel Nuovo** (also known as Maschio Angionino) is situated next to the Palazzo Reale. Built between 1279 and 1282, by Charles of Anjou, it has undergone several restorations over the centuries. The white marble-sculpted triumphal arch commemorates the entry of Alphonsus I into Naples in 1443.

Castel dell'Ovo dominates the seafront and small fishing port at Santa Lucia. It's a massive 11th-century fortress enclosing an entire citadel within its great walls. It served in the past as a prison. There's a legend attached to this castle which says that an egg (*uovo*) was placed beneath the foundations, hence the castle's name. If the egg ever breaks, then the castle and city will fall.

Galleria Umberto, off Piazza Plebiscito, Naples
Open: Daily dawn–sunset
Admission free

Opposite the Teatro San Carlo, this is a beautiful arcade built in the shape of a cross. Dating from 1887, it's a delight of art nouveau glass and its central dome is 56 meters high. Although not as animated as it once was, the arcade is still at the heart of Neapolitan life. People gather here to drink coffee, gossip, or just to argue about issues of the day.

Teatro San Carlo, off Piazza Plebiscito, Naples
Open: Daily 9am–noon
Admission: L3,000, free Sun

This is one of the largest and most famous opera houses in all Italy and, indeed, the world. It pre-dates the celebrated La Scala in Milan by nearly half a century. San Carlo was built for Charles de Bourbon in 1737 and the acoustics are said to be perfect. The interior is sumptuous, with lavish decor and six tiers of boxes. The royal box in the center is particularly magnificent. Its painted ceiling depicts Apollo and the Muses. Stendhal said of the opera house that "There is nothing in Europe . . . which can give you the palest hint of its splendor."

SHOPPING IN NAPLES

Via Toledo and **Via Roma** run in a continuous line from Piazza Plebiscito to the Museo Archeologico Nazionale. They form the main shopping area of Naples and are crowded with every kind of shop imaginable, including Italy's two main department stores, **Standa** and **Rinascente**. Bags and shoes are excellent value; Neapolitan leather workers are famous for their skill in making copies of high fashion styles. **Gay-Odin**, Toledo 427 (no credit cards) is a pretty, old-fashioned shop that makes its own chocolate. It also offers a wide selection of other delicious confectionery.

The network of small streets leading off **Via Benedetto Croce** and **Via San Biagio ai Librai** are also full of interesting shops. Via Croce and Via San Biagio follow the line of an old street that cuts through the heart of ancient Naples. These two streets are known as **Spaccanapoli** (*spacca* means split). Just off the Spaccanapoli in **Via Gregorio Armeno**, from October to December, you can buy the figures (*pastori*) for Christmas creches, made by local craftsmen. In the Italian home, building a nativity (*presepe*) is a tradition and no more so than in Naples.

BOAT TRIPS FROM NAPLES

There are ferry boat (*traghetto*) and hydrofoil (*aliscafo*) services daily to the islands of Capri, Ischia and Procida. Several companies run these trips and between them there are departures every 20 to 30 minutes in summer. Boats leave from **Molo Beverello** and **Mergellina** (the latter only hydrofoils). Prices vary from company to company. Timetables are published daily in the newspaper *Il Mattino* and there's also information including telephone numbers in the *Qui Napoli* pamphlet from the Tourist Office. Bear in mind the timetables are subject to last-minute alterations. For precise details of prices and times enquire at the Tourist Office, or local offices on the quay.

Note that cars with foreign license plates are permitted to travel to Ischia and Procida all year; Italian plates are not permitted in the summer. No cars are allowed on Capri. Some examples of prices are as follows:

Capri and Ischia
Ferry: L10,000 round trip (children under five free), L20,000 car (depends on size). Time needed: 1 hr 10 mins
Hydrofoil: L12,000 one way. Time needed: 35 mins

Capri, a tiny rocky island, is only four miles long and two miles wide. It's a veritable paradise of magical grottoes (including the famous **Blue Grotto**), soaring peaks and lovely coves. Rich in history and legend, it has long been a tourist center for the rich international set and day trippers alike. Although best out of season, Capri shouldn't be missed at any time of year.

Ischia is the largest island in the Bay of Naples and of volcanic origin: it once formed part of the mainland with the Phlegrean fields. Known as the Green Island of Health for its thermal springs and rich vegetation, it also has lovely beaches. A delightful place to visit.

Procida (hotels difficult to find, day trips advised)
Ferry: L8,000 round trip (children under five free). Time needed: 1 hr
Hydrofoil: L8,000 one way. Time needed: 25 mins

Procida is an unspoilt island and the least frequented by hordes of tourists. Considered by many to be the most charming of the Phlegrean islands, it's picturesque and tiny.

WHERE TO EAT IN NAPLES

La Bersagliera, Borgo Maunaro 10, Naples   **LL**
Tel: (081) 415692
Open: Wed–Mon 12:30pm–3pm 7pm–11pm   Closed: Tues
Credit cards: AE, DC, MC, V

This is one of the most popular restaurants, frequented by Neapolitans and tourists alike. It gets its name from the founder, a lady whose father was an officer in the division of *Bersaglieri*. Her photograph has pride of place in the dining room, and the present owner is her son, Signor Agostino Chiosi.

It's situated in the shadow of the ancient Castel dell'Ovo and right on the edge of the quay, with boats bobbing an arm's length away. The tables, set under a plastic awning, are separated from the water by pots of geraniums. Beyond a glass wall is the attractive inner hall with mirrors on three sides and an elaborately moulded ceiling. Delicious and delicately spicy is the *spaghetti ai frutti di mare* (with mussels, clams or spiked with chilli). Also recommended is *spaghetti* or *risotto al pescatore* (with cuttlefish and octopus pieces). Try a dish of *insalata di polipi* (chunks of succulent octopus with parsley on a bed of lettuce). Bookings are appreciated and the musicians should be tipped when the hat comes around. Parking is a problem as the restaurant is at the bottom of a flight of steps leading off a busy road. It's best to walk here along the seafront.

Ristorante d'Angelo, Vomero hill, Naples   LL
Tel: (081) 5789077
Open: Daily noon–3pm 7pm–1am
Credit cards: AE, DC, MC, V

High on the hill, this restaurant provides a glorious vista across the Bay. Sit in the bougainvillea-filled garden, under a pergola of vines, or inside where the two dining rooms have large panoramic windows. The decor inside is simple: white walls, adorned with autographed photos of celebrities and a fireplace at one end. The pasta speciality is *scarpariello* (short pasta with tomato, basil, peppers and Parmesan). There's a good selection of fish and meat dishes to follow. The restaurant is also a pizzeria. For dessert there are crêpes suzette, fresh fruit flans and, in season, delicious wild strawberries, blackberries and mulberries (*frutti di bosco*). The house white wine is light, slightly tangy and very palatable. The bottle label depicts owner Signor Vittorio Attolini's father wearing his famous silver horn which regular clients would touch for good luck.

Ristorante Cavour, Hotel Cavour, Piazza Garibaldi 32   LLL
Tel: (081) 264730/283122
Open: Daily 12:30pm–3:30pm 7:30pm–11pm
Credit cards: AE, DC, MC, V

Residents of the Hotel Cavour and non-residents alike are welcome at this lovely restaurant. It has just opened and the newly decorated salon is tasteful and chic: parquet flooring, pink suede chairs, old prints, and plants in shiny brass pots. Elegant cut glass and silverware on the tables, too. Quiet background music completes the scene. There's an à la carte menu or the fixed price daily hotel menu (L). If you choose the latter, you eat in deluxe surroundings at a low cost. The dishes on the hotel menu are excellent too. Try *farfalle alla fornina* (butterfly-shaped pasta with zucchini, cream and ricotta cheese). The *osso buco di tacchino cremolato* is a turkey leg with the marrow in a tasty sauce of minced carrots and spices. If you prefer a greater choice, the à la carte has an ample selection of the various courses. There's a further menu option: a fixed (higher) price gourmet menu.

Gambrinus, Via Ghiaia 1–2, Naples   L
Tel: (081) 47582
Open: Daily until late
No credit cards

Situated almost directly opposite the Palazzo Reale, this café is one of the most elegant in Naples. Founded in 1850, the decor of the bar and tearoom is pure art nouveau. If you want to escape from the bustle for a while, this is the place to visit. The cakes are typically Neapolitan such as the delicious *sfogliatella* filled with ricotta and candied peel. In the café's heyday the *beau monde* and intellectuals of Naples sat here and listened to an orchestra. Gabriele d'Annunzio wrote verses at one of the marble-topped tables. Gambrinus belongs to the Italian Association of Historic Buildings and its lovely rooms should be seen even if you don't want a drink.

Bar Daniele, Via Scarlatti 104, Naples   L
Tel: (081) 364480/377721
Open: Daily until late
Credit cards: AE, DC, MC, V

Close to the Villa Floridiana on the Vomero hill, this modern café has a good range of savory dishes, including rice salad, roast beef slices, meat patties and various pasta or vegetable dishes. For something sweet, there's an appetizing selection of cakes, ices and ice-cream delicacies. The specialty is *mousse all'arancio*: a scrumptious concoction consisting of an orange, ice-cream, milk and cream which is served inside the orange skin.

WHERE TO STAY IN NAPLES

Hotel Rex, Via Partenope 38, Naples   L
Tel: (081) 416388   Open: Year round
Amenities: ⚲   Credit cards: AE, DC, V

Situated a stone's throw from the seafront, this modern family-run hotel is excellent value for money. On a side street, and with double glazing, you aren't disturbed by traffic. You can even see a bit of the Bay if you crane out of the window. The decor is modern with tasteful antique additions of heavy wood chairs, chests and painted panels. The bathrooms have been recently renovated. Rooms are neat, simple and spruce. A bargain for large families are the special offer rooms without private bath: up to five people for a top price of L85,000. The staff are friendly and helpful.

Hotel Palace, Piazza Garibaldi 9, Naples   **LL**
Tel: (081) 264575   Open: Year round
Amenities: ✕ ⚐   Credit cards: AE, DC, MC, V

A pleasant hotel situated on the opposite side of the square to the station, it has modern decor throughout with attractive colored floor tiles. All 102 rooms have good-sized bathrooms. There's air-conditioning in half the hotel's rooms, which you'd be wise to specify when booking. As there's a lot of traffic in this piazza, you'd also be better with a room on one of the higher floors. Parents of small children note that rooms have French windows opening onto lowish railings. Rooms 101, 102 and 103 have pretty terraces overlooking the square. The elevator doesn't stop level with the floors so not suitable for wheelchairs.

Hotel Cavour, Piazza Garibaldi 32, Naples   **LL**
Tel: (081) 283122/285929   Open: Year round
Amenities: ✕ ⚐   Credit cards: AE, DC, MC, V

A comfortable, centrally situated, three-star hotel run by the same company as the Palace. The hotel has a cozier decor than the Palace: rose-print covers in the hall and an antique print of *Vecchia Napoli* (Old Naples) covering one wall. The bar/breakfast room is furnished in wood and leather and has old-rose covered tables and banquettes. The rooms have flowered wallpaper and antique style furniture. On the first floor there are four steps up for the elevator. The same advice concerning air-conditioning and low railings applies here as for the Palace.

Royal Hotel, Via Partenope 38, Naples   **LLL**
Tel: (081) 400244   Open: Year round
Amenities: ◻ P ✕ ⚐ ≋   Credit cards: AE, DC, MC, V

This hotel is the largest in Naples and offers elegance, comfort and a superb position on the seafront. Two stone lions flank the entrance which leads into an elegant, spacious hall and lounge bar, with parquet flooring and masses of plants. There's a piano bar here in the evenings, and a piano bar in the hotel restaurant. All 300 rooms have balconies, sunshades and good-sized bathrooms. Decor is blond wood and flocked wallpaper. Up on the roof the Royal has the only pool downtown, and it's a beaut: a large, seawater pool with a small waterfall. There's a small sun terrace too, with bar service and snacks. The elevator doesn't reach the roof: you have to climb a flight of steps.

* * *

From Naples, you can make a tour of the **Bay of Naples** and the **Amalfi Coast (Route I)**. Or, return along the coast to **Rome** via **Gaeta** and **Anzio (Route J)**.

ROUTE I: NAPLES – ERCOLANO – POMPEII – SORRENTO – AMALFI – SALERNO – NAPLES

(Approx. 155km)

NAPLES TO ERCOLANO

*Leave **Piazza Garibaldi**, passing the Palace Hotel on your right and head south-west down the main **Corso Umberto I**. At the end of this street you'll come to **Piazza Bovio**. Go around the square and down **Via A. Depretis** (third right turn). After 300m the gardens of the **Piazza Municipio** lie ahead. Follow the road round to the left, then right, passing the Castel Nuovo on your right. You'll have a view of the quay on your left. This road becomes **Via F. Acton** and within 200m there's the Palazzo Reale on your right and gardens on your left. Drive through the 800m tunnel ahead – **Galleria Vittoria** – then cross the intersection into **Via Arcoleo**. At the end of this street **Piazza Vittoria** lies ahead. Once you're in the piazza, turn left and then left again at the traffic lights into **Via Partenope**, retracing your route with the Palazzo Reale and the Castel Nuovo now on your left. The road changes name often. Follow as close to the bay as you can. After about 5kms you'll see a sign, which you follow, for **Autostrade** and **Tangenziale**.*

*You now drive down a divided highway with tram lines in the center. Pass the freeway turn-off and drive under the autostrada. The road now narrows into a single lane and you drive through a dilapidated, shabby zone. Almost 4kms from the underpass you'll see signs for **Ercolano** – **Pompeii** straight ahead. After 2kms there's a yellow sign for **Ercolano** to the right. Turn sharp right into a narrow one-way street. At the intersection after 200m drive straight across and turn left at the sign. You'll have glimpses of the sea on your right then a sign to indicate you're in Ercolano.*

*At the second major intersection, along the cobbled road, turn left, following the sign for **Scavi-Ercolano** (excavations). Turn left at the traffic lights. You'll soon see a yellow sign **Parcheggio Turistico** to the right. Along this road there's a large **Polizia Urbana** sign; on your right is the parking lot. (Same hours as excavations. Admission: L1000 per hour.) Walk back to the main road and turn right. The entrance to the excavations is a few blocks up on the left, set back in a small square.*

NOTE: If you're coming from Naples, obtain brochures on Ercolano from the Naples Tourist Office in advance.

ERCOLANO (HERCULANEUM)

Open: Daily Jun 1–Aug 15 9am–7pm. Rest of year 9am–1 hr
  before sunset, except Nov 15–Dec 31 9am–2:45pm. Ticket
  office closes 1 hr before site.
Admission: L4,000 children under 12 free

Herculaneum (modern name Ercolano) was probably founded in
the fourth century BC. Like Pompeii, it was destroyed by the
eruption of Vesuvius in 79AD. This was not such an important town
as Pompeii, but was occupied by wealthy people who built elegant
villas. As the town here was buried by mud, and not lava (as
Pompeii), many of the wooden villas are remarkably well-
preserved. This gives you a real feel of how the place used to be
nearly 20 centuries ago. It's possible to see houses complete with
doors, window frames, beams, staircases and even furniture. The
mud solidified into an almost impenetrable shield many meters
thick, thus protecting the buried town from looters. It wasn't until
the 18th century that excavations began and they're still continuing.
  As you enter you have a view of the whole site, then you follow
a long path down to the site entrance. Not to be missed are: Casa
del Tramezzo di Legno (House of the Wooden Partition), an
elegant house with carved roof, on Cardo IV; Casa dell'Atrio a
Mosaico, further down on the left, where the lovely black and
white mosaic floor has been bizarrely deformed; and Casa
Sannitica (Samnite House) on the corner of Cardo IV and
Decumano Inferiore. Casa di Nettuno et Anfitrite has beautiful
mosaics; while Casa dei Cervi (House of the Deer) on Cardo V is
decorated with wallpaintings.

WHERE TO EAT IN ERCOLANO

(No name), Via IV Novembre 9, Ercolano   L
Tel: (081) 7390646
Open: Apr–Oct Tues–Sun 9am–midnight
Closed: Mon and Nov–Mar
No credit cards

Just up the road from the excavations this homely restaurant
without a name is ideal for an informal meal before setting off
again. The main room is a straw-covered verandah with bottles,
old lamps, even a ship's wheel hanging from the awning. There's
also an inner room – no smoking here – where the locals watch
TV. At lunchtime there's *pizza locale*: a pastry envelope (*calzone*)
with a filling of ham, mozzarella, ricotta and mushrooms. In the
evening there's real pizza (not served at lunchtime). The cooking
is home-style, mainly pasta and fish dishes. For something light,
have the *caprese*, a variation on the classic dish of tomato,

mozzarella and basil, with salad and oregano.

ERCOLANO TO POMPEII

Turn left out of the parking lot, then left again into Ercolano's main street, heading away from the excavations. After 1½kms you'll pass an Arab-style white church on your right; 500m after this the road divides around a small green piazza. Bear right, following the blue sign for Pompeii. There's another sign somewhat further on: turn sharp left – it's easy to miss this one. The road bears around to the right and you're now in a wider street with a white church on your right. Drive through the built-up area. After 5kms there's a sign to indicate you're leaving the Torre del Greco area with Pompeii 7kms ahead. At the blue sign (it's easy to miss) to Pompeii after about 1km, turn left. After 100m there's an arrow and a sign for Pompeii to your right. Turn here, and drive straight through the town. Drive over the railroad crossing, and pass under two bridges. Take the first left after the second bridge and there's a blue sign for Information on your right. You can park here, near the Tourist Office, Piazza Esedra. (Tel: (081) 8610913. Same hours as site.) The entrance to the excavations and the ticket office are also here.

POMPEII

Open: Daily Jun 1–Aug 15 9am–7pm. Rest of year 9am–1hr before sunset, except Nov 15–Dec 31 9am–2:45pm. Ticket office closes 1 hr before site.
Admission: L5,000, children under 12 free

Pompeii is the most famous of the towns buried by the eruption of Vesuvius in 79AD. Twenty-five thousand people were buried under the river of molten lava and cinders which swept over the town for a whole day. Some bodies can be seen, preserved by the lava, where they fell. There are temples, houses, covered theaters, amphitheaters, baths and grand villas to see, as well as numerous frescoes, mosaics and sculptures. Pompeii is an unforgettable place to visit, giving a profound insight into Roman life. In 63AD the town was damaged by an earthquake, and in 1980 an earthquake damaged the excavation site. Since the 18th century some 60% of the town has been uncovered.

Among the many interesting places to visit, the Casa dei Vettii is well-preserved, with remarkable frescoes. Note the roof construction similar to that of the Casa del Tramezzo in Ercolano. Phallus signs carved in the flagstones along the road point the way to the Casa del Lupanare (brothel). Inside are several chambers and above the entrances you can see faded murals illustrating the positions the girls offered. Inside the rooms are the stone beds upon which mattresses were laid. On the threshold of the House of the Tragic Poet is the famous mosaic of the chained dog with the inscription Cave Canem (Beware of the Dog). There are several lovely mosaic fountains, such as the one in the Casa del Orso Sorito. The Casa del Fauno has a copy of the original statue of the little dancing fawn set in a pretty courtyard (the original is in the Museo Nazionale in Naples).

Within the site there's a café and restaurant, and outside in the square a stall sells fresh squeezed lemon juice (L2,000).

A word of warning: if you visit Pompeii in mid-summer at midday, the broiling sun is extremely uncomfortable. The best time to visit is early in the morning, before the worst of the crowds arrive.

POMPEII TO TERME STABIANE NUOVE

From the parking lot retrace your route under the two bridges. After the second bridge turn left at the intersection and cross a small bridge. At the next intersection turn left following the sign for Castellammare–Amalfi. Watch out: it's easy to miss this sign, which is half-hidden over to the left. You now pass straight through the borough of Ponte Nuovo, with the sea on your right. After 3¹/₂kms you pass a white church on your right, then drive over a railroad crossing. Follow the road round and drive straight ahead (don't take the right fork). Follow the sign for Sorrento. The road becomes a divided highway and there's a yellow sign for Antiche Terme (right) and Sorrento and Nuove Terme (straight on). Drive straight on, and the road widens, becoming tree-lined and pleasant. There's a fork after 200m: take the right fork for Sorrento and pass under a bridge with Terme Stabiane written on it. Turn immediately right, signposted Hotel delle Terme. Ahead there's the entrance to the Terme where you can park and drink the waters. (On the other side of the bridge there's a center for more extensive treatments.)

CASTELLAMMARE DI STABIA/TERME STABIANE NUOVE

Castellammare has 28 mineral water springs, famous since Roman times. Here at the Nuove Terme Stabiane (New Spa) the waters are piped direct from the ancient spa to the modern one. Visitors come here to cure a wide variety of ailments, and to take advantage of the waters' reputedly beautifying properties. Visit the **Spa Drinking Fountains**. (Open: Apr–Nov 7am–1pm (gates close at 2pm). Admission: L7,000, children under 12 L1,000.) You can bring your own cup or buy a plastic one here for L200. You can't fill up bottles or bring in your dog. After filling your glass from the taps you can wander around the extensive grounds. There's a small pine wood and a swan lake. In summer there's a piano bar near the lake. To take the waters, you should sip several glassfuls, taking 15 minutes over each one.

TERME STABIANE NUOVE TO SORRENTO

Return to the main road and turn right in the direction of **Sorrento**. *The road now climbs steadily, passing through lush vegetation. After 1km there's an ancient castle, swiftly followed by glimpses of the sea on your right. About 1km further on you'll see two white factory towers ahead and a sign for* **Cast-di Stabia**.

If you'd like to make a detour to the **Antiche Terme** *(Ancient Spa), turn sharp left at the sign and follow the narrow road down under a gray stone arch to a small piazza. The entrance is on your right. (Open: Jun–Oct 7am–1pm. Admission: L7,000, children under 12 L1,000.) The grounds of the ancient spa are much smaller than the Terme Nuove, but the bonus is that you fill your glass from the original Roman drinking fountains. The different waters have various healing properties; Acqua Acidula is reputedly good for the digestion, Acqua Media (with a pleasant, light taste) for the liver; Acqua Ferrata (with a heavy, salty flavor) for the nervous system.*

Back on the main road continue towards Sorrento. After about 3kms you drive through a tunnel (open on the sea side), then another short tunnel past signs for **Vico Equense**. *Pass the right turn-off for Vico Equense and drive through another long tunnel (about 2kms). You're now on the Bay of Naples coastal road renowned for its fabulous scenery. Small belvederes, citrus trees and olive groves line the route. A few kilometers from the tunnel you pass through the towns of* **Meta** *and* **Sant Agnello**. *Keep following the signs for Sorrento, bearing right at the next fork. Drive under a bridge with Sorrento written on it, then turn right after ½km. At the end of the road there's a T-junction; turn right. Continue to the end of the road, then turn left, following the white sign for* **centro**. *The Grand Hotel Riviera lies ahead. At the end of the road turn right into* **Corso Italia**. *After 100m you come to the* **Piazza Sant'Antonino**, *with the church on your right. Park wherever you can near here. Walk down the street to the left of Ovest Tourist Office. A few yards up on the right, through the Circolo dei Forestieri (Foreigners' Club), is the* **Tourist Office**, *Via L. de Maio 35. (Tel: (081) 8782104. Open: Mon–Sat 9:30am–12.30pm, 4:30pm–8pm).*

The Circolo dei Forestieri has a pleasant garden, panoramic terrace and bar. You can buy English newspapers here. After 9pm there's live music. (Open: Summer daily 10am–2pm, 7pm–2am. Admission free.)

SORRENTO

"*Torna a Surriento*" goes the old song, and you'll surely want to come back to Sorrento. A lovely town, set amid citrus groves and lush bougainvillea, it stands on cliffs 50 meters above the Tyrrhenian Sea, with superlative views across the Bay of Naples. This popular seaside resort also makes an ideal base for touring the many sites in the area. From here there are boats and excursions to Capri, Ischia, Procida, the Galli Isles, Positano and Amalfi. Pompeii, Herculaneum and Vesuvius are also nearby.

The Greeks founded *Surrentum* in the fifth century BC. In the Middle Ages it was dominated by the Lombards. Torquato Tasso, (1544–95), the poet who wrote *Gerusalemme Liberata*, was born here. His epic romantic poem about the capture of Jerusalem was a favorite of Napoleon Bonaparte. You'll see his marble statue to one side of Piazza Tasso, the main square. Renowned for its huge walnuts and the lively Tarantella, Sorrento is also a town of legends. One such tells of a great bell which sounds from the depths of the sea off Punta Campanella, the very tip of the peninsula. In 1558 pirates stole the bell from the Basilica of Sant'Antonio, patron saint of Sorrento, but their ship capsized and the bell sank. At Punta Campanella, if you listen hard, you might hear the bell ringing with the sea currents – or so goes the legend.

WHAT TO SEE IN SORRENTO

Chiostro San Francesco, in the Duomo, Piazza Pargulio, Sorrento
Open: Daily dawn–sunset
Admission free

San Francesco's cloister is a 14th-century gem. Graceful white-stone columned arches enclose an exquisite courtyard abundant with flowering plants. Bougainvillea, vines and jasmine cover the old walls and add to the charm. On a summer's evening, in this ideal setting, you can listen to live classical music.

Via Pietà, Sorrento
Sorrento's main street is Corso Italia. Parallel to this, just off Piazza Tasso, to the right of the Tasso statue, is the quaint alley, Via Pietà. There are several medieval buildings to see as you stroll along here: the Palazzo Veniero, a short way down on the left, has a lovely facade with colored stonework. Further down is Palazzo Correale with bifor windows. There's a florist's shop at the beginning of this street with lovely mosaics on the far wall.

On the corner of Via Giuliani and Via Cesareo is the Sedile Dominova, a frescoed loggia with a 16th-century majolica dome. The majolica is bright orange, green and white and contrasts oddly with the old stone and faded fescoes. Local nobility used to meet here to discuss political issues and Sorrento's affairs. Now it's a working men's club (no admission to the public).

SHOPPING IN SORRENTO

Intarsia (wood mosaic) and embroidery are customary crafts here. Many shops sell beautiful inlaid wood in various forms from trays to sideboards. A couple of the more interesting shops include

Notturno, Via Fuorimura 33 (no credit cards). A bit of a walk will lead you to this shop/showroom/factory, where you'll find a wide variety of good quality products. If you want to see the craftsmen at work, the factory is open to visitors (weekdays, 7:30am–5pm).

A. E. Fiorentino, Via L. de Maio 28 (no credit cards) is unique. Mrs Fiorentino, now in her 80s, produces probably the finest handkerchiefs in Europe. These are made of the highest quality cotton and linen and are exquisitely embroidered and monogrammed by hand. There was a time when Mrs Fiorentino supplied the nobility all over the world, but demand for such a refined product has now all but disappeared. To interested enquirers, Mrs Fiorentino is happy to unwrap examples of the art and skill that made her so sought-after. Gift-wrapping and overseas deliveries are offered; prices for handkerchiefs from L15,000 to L500,000.

WHERE TO EAT IN SORRENTO

Grand Hotel Excelsior Vittoria, Piazza Tasso   LLL
Tel: (081) 8781900
Open: Daily 12:30pm–3pm 7pm–11pm
Credit cards: AE, DC, MC, V

Large windows overlook Capri on one side and the Bay of Naples on the other in this beautiful, frescoed room. First-class Italian and international cuisine is served. You can choose from the hotel menu of the day, fixed price, or à la carte, or you can mix the menus if you wish. Two popular à la carte dishes are ravioli Caruso-style (with truffles and cream), and *veal escalope Holstein* (veal cutlet in breadcrumbs topped with an egg and anchovies). Desserts include crêpes suzette flambées and ice-cream meringues.

Kursaal, Via Fuorimura 7, Sorrento   LLL
Tel: (081) 8781216
Open: Daily Sep–Jun noon–3pm 7pm–midnight/1am
Closed: Mon from Jul–Aug
Credit cards: AE, DC, MC, V

Dine in comfort and elegance in this Belle Epoque villa under ornate chandeliers, or on the glass-canopied verandah or shady, plant-filled terrace. There's a piano bar in the evenings, and an American bar. The restaurant offers Neapolitan and international cuisine and is also a pizzeria. From the long list of pasta and risotto dishes we recommend *pennette alla giorgetta* (short pasta with zucchini, onion, basil, Parmesan and cream), or *spaghetti alla posillipo* (with clams). For a main course, choose fresh fish, lobster, or a steak (*chateaubriand sauce Béarnaise*, or grilled *fiorentina*). If you prefer, try the *pizza Kursaal* with prawns and mushrooms. For dessert you'll be unable to resist the *delizia al limone* (a light sponge cake drenched in a delicious lemon sauce).

O'Parruchiano, Corso Italia 71–73, Sorrento   LL
Tel: (081) 8781321
Open: Daily Nov–May noon–4pm 7pm–11pm
Closed: Wed from Jun–Oct
Credit cards: v

From the unpretentious sidewalk entrance you climb to the top
level where you're surrounded by a semi-wild garden of bushes,
creepers, rockeries and strategic lighting. The owner, Signor Enzo
Maniello, is a keen gardener. Muted music from a nearby disco
adds to the atmosphere in the evening. The food is renowned for
its quality and your pocket doesn't suffer. The menu is in four
languages and there's plenty of choice. For a change from fish-
based pasta, try *gnocchi alla Sorrentina*: a plateful of piping hot
potato dumplings in a sauce of tomato, mozzarella and basil. The
homemade creme caramel is delicious, as is the excellent dry white
house wine from Signor Enzo's personal cellar.

Gelateria Davide, Via Giuliani 39, Sorrento   L
Open: Daily 9am–1am in summer   Closed Nov–Mar
No credit cards

For delicious homemade ice-cream, go to this ultra-modern café
set among the bougainvillea and oleander in a picturesque street.
There are about 40 flavors, including prickly pear, papaya, pina
colada, seven varieties of chocolate, all beautifully displayed and
decorated. There are *granitas* in summer, fat-free sorbets and over
50 different sundaes to choose from. Try the *cardinale*: seven
flavors of fruit ice-cream, solid fruit and strawberry mousse,
topped with fresh cream; or a banana split with profiteroles.
There's also a junior menu. For those who can resist one of Signor
Gugliemo Davide's ices there's a regular bar.

WHERE TO STAY IN SORRENTO

Grand Hotel Excelsior Vittoria, Piazza Tasso   LLL
Tel: (081) 8781900   Open: Year round
Amenities: ◘ ✕ ♀ ≳   Credit cards: AE, DC, MC, V

Just off Piazza Tasso, the hotel's three villas stand in superb
grounds. A central path, lined with rose bushes, leads through
thick groves of citrus trees and beautiful well-kept flowerbeds. The
park has yielded up ancient Roman stones, indicating that perhaps
there's an amphitheater underneath. The hotel dates from 1834
and its tone is one of refined elegance. In the older part, the
magnificent dining hall has a vaulted, frescoed ceiling, and
graceful, antique-furnished lounges with elaborate mouldings on
the walls and ceilings. There's a flower-filled, panoramic terrace
and a collection of old silver in the hall. The rooms are a sheer
delight, with snow-white linen, elegant furniture and marbled

bathrooms. If you prefer modern decor, there are luxury rooms in the newer villa. The 125 rooms have views of the Bay or grounds. For an unforgettable visit, book the Caruso Suite, named after the great Italian opera singer, who lived in this palatial apartment.

Hotel Bristol, Via del Capo 22, Sorrento   **LL**
Tel: (081) 8784522   Open: Year round
Amenities: **P** ✕ ♀ ≈   Credit cards: AE, DC, MC, V

This elegant, ultra-modern hotel offers many amenities: a splendid roof garden overlooking the Bay contains miniature golf, bowling, ping-pong and a climbing frame for children; plus a piano bar and disco. There are two pools (one for children) and bar, a sun terrace with sunbeds and bar; plus a fitness center where, for an extra charge, you can use the sauna, solarium and exercise equipment. The hotel also has private bathing huts down on the beach. There's air-conditioning in the dining room and 60% of rooms. The 132 good-sized rooms are airy and tastefully furnished. The hotel is on a busy road, so avoid the noisier lower floors.

Regina Hotel, Via Marina Grande 10, Sorrento   **L**
Tel: (081) 8782721   Closed: Nov–Mar 15
Amenities: **P** ✕ ♀   Credit cards: AE

A very pleasant, centrally located hotel with a pretty, peaceful garden containing a fountain. The dining room has a superb panorama of the Bay and an outside terrace for after-dinner coffee. Half-pension is obligatory from July 15–September 15, but the restaurant food is good and reasonably priced. Rooms are spacious and airy, with bright tiles on the floors and a view of the Bay or garden. Corner rooms are bigger, with balcony. No air-conditioning. There's a problem with parking in July and August so you'd do well to phone ahead so they can prepare a space for your car. The hotel is situated right opposite the splendid open-air night spot. Villa Pompeiana which you may consider a plus or a minus (open 10pm–2am, admission free).

SORRENTO TO POSITANO

*From **Piazza Tasso** turn right into **Corso Italia** which becomes the **Via del Capo**. Continue along Via del Capo, which curves right and then passes the Hotel Bristol on your left. After 3kms take the left fork for **Sant'Agata–Pasitano**. You're now following the ss145, crossing the toe of the peninsula, to join the ss163, the **Amalfi Drive**, one of the most panoramic routes in Europe. As you cross the peninsula you catch only glimpses of the sea, but the road is bordered with flowering plants. It's a narrow, twisting route with hairpin bends (in summer cars line the roadside and make traffic flow difficult).*

*Keep following signs for Sant'Agata. There's another fork just over 7kms from Sorrento: take the left for **Positano**, and soon there's a breathtaking glimpse of the sea. On your way down this road you'll find several cafés and pizzerias. Two kms from the fork you get your first view of the Amalfi coast and gulf of Salerno. Drive through the village of **Colli di Fontanelle** and you'll see an orange-and-white Saracen church on your right. After 1½kms there's a cluster of houses and a T-junction. Turn right for Positano. After 1½kms, you'll see a sign to indicate you're following the **Costiera Amalfitana** (Amalfi Coast). There are belvederes all along this route where you can stop and survey the scene. You'll see the three Galli islands in the bay. After 3kms you'll see Positano: a village clinging to the cliff and dominated by the gilded dome of Santa Maria Assunta church. A large road sign after 1km has a map giving the distances between the small towns along the coast. After 2kms there's a blue sign for **Positano**. Turn sharp right and drive down the steep, narrow lane. About 1km further you'll see the first of several parking lots along this one-way route which leads to Positano center. Park in one of these (L1,500 an hour). Parking is a nightmare in this resort so it's best to walk down into the center, where you'll find the **Tourist Office**, Via del Saracino 2. (Tel: (089) 875067. Open: Daily 9am–1pm, 4pm–6pm in season.)*

POSITANO

"Positano bites deep. It's a dream place that isn't quite real when you are there and becomes beckoningly real after you have gone." This oft-quoted observation by John Steinbeck after his visit in the early 1950s still holds true today. Positano is a popular resort, favored by artists, celebrities and tourists of every nationality, yet it remains largely unspoilt and quaint. Charming little houses and elegant villas cling to the steep hillside down to the beach. There's a single one-way narrow street encircling the village, and a small bus makes the journey in around 20 minutes. Otherwise, there's a network of steps and stairs cut into the cliff. No fun for the lethargic: you move about by climbing up and down. Positano is color: bougainvillea, geraniums and hibiscus crowd every terrace and multicolored garments are on display in the numerous boutiques of this important fashion center. The *Moda Positano* is renowned for its loose-fitting styles using soft materials in a variety of colors and patterns. The almost-forgotten crafts of lace-making and embroidery are plied with skill here. You'll find tablecloths, centerpieces and spreads which are both attractive and good value.

Historians believe Positano's origins are Phoenician. It became a Roman town which was destroyed by the eruption of Vesuvius in 79AD. It formed part of the maritime republic of Amalfi in early medieval times and became an important commercial center. Positano enjoyed a prosperous period in the 16th and 17th centuries, trading with the Middle East. Many of the town's elegant houses were built at this time. In the 19th century many Positanesi emigrated to America when the town began to decline as a commercial fishing center. Today its boats are fishing-smacks, not trading ships.

WHERE TO EAT IN POSITANO

Da Vincenzo, Via Pasitea 172–8, Positano   **L**
Tel: (089) 875128
Open: Daily 1pm–3:30pm 7pm–late   Closed: Winter Sun–Mon
No credit cards

Home cooking in a relaxed, cheery atmosphere, with brass pans and onions hanging on the walls. There's no menu; Vincenzo will tell you what there is. If you don't speak Italian, so much the better: the local custom is to let him decide for you. Have no qualms: Vincenzo and his wife Marcella prepare the dishes in full view in a spanking clean kitchen. You could begin with *panzerotti*: a sort of fried pastry envelope stuffed with ricotta, mozzarella, salami and ham. Follow with *spaghetti con lupini* (little clams) or pasta with eggplant, then savor a steak of fresh swordfish or local roast fish with mint. Finish with one of Marcella's homemade desserts. The tone is strictly informal and if it's too quiet, Vincenzo will ring a bell and shout a bit to liven things up. Then he'll go from table to table offering tasty tidbits on the house. If you're lucky you'll be able to sample Marcella's delicious candied orange-peel slices.

Chez Black, Spiaggia Grande, Positano   **LL–LLL**
Tel: (089) 875036
Open: Daily noon–4pm 6:30pm–late   Closed: Jan–Feb
Credit cards: AE, DC, MC, V

Situated on the beach, you can come here for lunch in your swimsuit, but be sure to dress for dinner as the clientele becomes more elegant in the evening. The large, semi-outdoor salon represents the inside of a galleon with wood beams and brass fittings. It's wise to book in advance, and if you want to sample the house's pride and joy – *spaghetti all'aragostai* (specially prepared spaghetti with lobster) – you'll have to order two days ahead, and only one table per night is allowed to eat it. Alternatively, there's *spaghetti alla Black* with a fish sauce. Salad fans will be happy: try the *insalata capricciosa*, a huge mixed salad. For dessert there's *awaiana di frutta* (large chunks of exotic fruit), or the *fior d'awai* (an ice-cream sundae with pineapple, cream and strega liqueur). In the evening, Chez Black is a pizzeria as well. The owner, Salvatore Russo, is also the proprietor of the restaurant next door,

Le Tre Sorel, and creater of Music on the Rocks nightclub. (Open: Apr–Sep 8pm–4am. Admission: L20,000.)

WHERE TO STAY IN POSITANO

Hotel Le Sirenuse, Via Cristoforo Columbo 30   LLL
Tel: (089) 875066   Closed: Nov–Dec 20
Amenities: ☎ 🅿 ✕ ⟨ ⟩   Credit cards: AE, DC, MC, V

Run by the Marquis Aldo Sersale, this lovely 19th-century villa with its vivid red exterior offers an ambience of refinement and five-star luxury. Greenery and antique furnishings provide the decor; a giant creeper entirely covers the ceiling of the reception hall. There's a spinet in the lounge and the bar has inlaid wood paneling. The 60 spacious rooms provide every comfort: double closets and sofas, plus hairdryer, phone and robes in the bathrooms. The rooms have a seaview balcony overlooking the church. If you prefer, there are deluxe rooms, complete with a separate sitting area and superb bathrooms with double basins and whirlpool tub. A green-tiled panoramic sun terrace runs the length of the hotel and leads to an outdoor heated pool. A private elevator takes you partway to the beach (not private) and 150 more steps lead you down to the sand.

Hotel Marincanto, Positano   LL
Tel: (089) 875130   Open: Year round
Amenities: ☎ 🅿 ⟨ ▮   Credit card: AE, DC, MC, V

The guidester's lot is at its most painful when we find a spot we are tempted to keep for ourselves. This hotel is a classic example for a variety of reasons. For openers it has parking in its own covered lot, a considerable bonus in traffic-clogged Positano. Then there's the location. It's central – just beyond the heart of town as the main road rises on its way out. Very importantly it's on the seaside of the road and thus both more scenic and less noisy. From the parking area you descend through three floors of rooms to the main lobby. All rooms are spacious and beautifully tiled with a combination of modern and antique furniture as well as enormous built-in wardrobes. All have pleasant balconies with excellent views of the water and Positano below and to the right. Off the lobby there is a spacious flower-lined terrace where you can take drinks and breakfast (the only meal served). One level down from this takes you to a further large terrace for sunbathing. From here steps lead to the beach. Prices are extremely reasonable, the staff a model of friendly efficiency.

POSITANO TO AMALFI

Leave the parking lot and drive down to the center. After about 1km *there's a small piazza with a sign left for **Amalfi**: turn here. The road now begins to climb. You'll see a sign 'Amalfi 15kms'. Drive straight on, bear to the right and you'll find yourself back on the **ss163**. After 2kms drive through a tunnel cut into the rock, then pass a cluster of houses and a Saracen-style church on the right. Shortly after, there's a sign indicating the popular resort of **Praiano**. You now drive through six more tunnels, and about 10kms from Positano there's a sign right for **Grotta dello Smeraldo**. Here you'll find a parking area and elevators leading down the cliff to the Grotto.*

Grotta dello Smeraldo, Conca dei Marini
Open: Daily Mar–May 9am–5pm, Jun–Sep 8:30am–6pm,
Oct–Feb 10am–4pm
Admission: L4,000 by elevator from Piazzale Grotta dello
Smeraldo. (You can also visit the grotto by boat from Amalfi)

This ancient cave is filled with stalactites and stalagmites reflected in brilliant green water in the filtering sunlight. The presence of stalagmites emerging from the sea indicates that, in the far-distant past, the grotto must have been on dry land.

WHERE TO EAT IN GROTTA DELLO SMERALDO

La Conca Azzurra, Piazzale Grotta dello Smeraldo   LL
Tel: (089) 831242/831271
Open: Daily noon–11pm   Closed: Nov–Mar
Credit cards: DC, MC, V

Sixty-six stone steps lead down the cliff from the café in the piazza to the restaurant. It's a particularly romantic spot on a summer evening with its intimate, plant-surrounded terrace jutting over the sea. Seated at one of the lamp-lit tables, you've the sensation of being on the water. As you wait for your meal, sip a "sunset", the house's aperitif concocted by head waiter, Signor Pietro. The menu features a number of delicacies of which the genial owner, Signor Salvatore Criscuolo, is justly proud. If you ask him, he'll tell you, in excellent English, of the birth of his speciality, *La Libecciata*: a pasta dish with a tasty, creamy sauce of seafood. One stormy evening, with *Il Lebeccio* (the local wild west wind) blowing hard, Salvatore and his friends went to the kitchen to prepare supper. They found an odd assortment of ingredients and, perhaps inspired by the crazy gale, combined these to create their *Libecciata*. In a corner of the terrace is the pizza oven; Salvatore's *pizza pirata* is recommended. This is a white pizza (no tomato) with mozzarella, hot peppers and pieces of squid and prawn.

*From the grotto, drive on for 2kms and you'll see **Amalfi** spread out before you. Just before entering the center of Amalfi you drive through two tunnels. Immediately after the second, drive under the* *stone arch straddling the road to **Piazza Flavio Gioia**, where you can park. In July and August the parking lot fills quickly, so it's best to get here early morning or late afternoon. A few blocks away on the left, you'll find the **Tourist Office**, Corso delle Republiche Marinare 25/27. (Tel: (089) 871107. Open: Daily 9am–12:30pm, 4pm–7pm in season.)*

AMALFI

> "Sweet the memory is to me
> Of a land beyond the sea,
> Where the waves and mountains meet,
> Where, amid her mulberry trees
> Sits Amalfi in the heat..."
>
> (*Longfellow*)

Amalfi is the pride of the Amalfi Coast, celebrated for its beauty, enviable setting and gentle climate. The town reached its zenith during the Middle Ages as the first Maritime Republic of Italy. Founded in the fourth century BC by Roman families fleeing the Barbarians. Amalfi became an independent republic in 893. For over 300 years it remained an important maritime, commercial and cultural center until its conquest in the 11th century by the Normans. A series of negative factors, including its size and remote geographical position, contributed to the town's subsequent gradual decline. Fittingly, Amalfi was the home town of Flavio Gioia, the reputed inventor of the compass.

From Amalfi you can reach Capri and Ischia by motorboat or ferry. There are also excursions to the Grotta dello Smeraldo at Conca dei Marini. (The Tourist Office provides details of times and prices.)

WHAT TO SEE IN AMALFI

Museo Civico, in the Municipio, Amalfi
Open: Mon–Sat 9am–8pm   Closed: Sun
Admission free

In this one large room you can see the Tavole Amalfitane which provided the code of maritime laws for Mediterranean navigation until the 16th century, and whose principles still form the basis of modern maritime law.

Duomo, Piazza Duomo, Amalfi
Open: Daily Jun–Sep 7:30am–1pm 3pm–7:30pm; Oct–May
   7:30am–noon 4pm–6pm
Admission free

Piazza Duomo is dominated by this lovely cathedral, with its facade of brilliant mosaics depicting Christ and the 12 apostles. A steep flight of stone steps leads up from the busy square to the sculpted bronze doors (the first in Italy) cast in Constantinople in the 11th century. The Duomo was constructed in the ninth century, and rebuilt in the 13th and 18th centuries. However, the belltower (1180–1276) is original. The interior is sumptuous, with richly colored marble intarsia and gold stucco.

Go down the stairs to the right of the altar, where you'll enter St Andrew's ached and richly frescoed crypt. His statue stands in the altarpiece, where his bones are conserved. At regular intervals, a special, miraculous liquid known as "manna" is observed. When this occurs, it's said also that droplets of blood form on the stone stained with St Gennaro's blood in Pozzuoli.

Chiostro del Paradiso, Piazza Duomo, Amalfi
Open: Daily Jun–Sep 9am–1:30pm 3pm–9pm; Oct–May until dusk
Admission: L1,000, small children free

By contrast with the adjacent Duomo, this 13th-century cloister is of the utmost simplicity with its many narrow, interlaced, Arab-style arches. Once it was the monks' burial place; now, in summer, piano concerts are held here in the evenings.

WHERE TO EAT IN AMALFI

Hotel Cappuccini, Via Annuziatella 46   LL–LLL
Tel: (089) 871008
Open: Daily 12:30pm–2:30pm 7pm–10:30pm
Credit cards: AE, DC, V

Dining out on the magnificent terrace would be reason enough to trek up here. The cuisine is also special, as Count Aielli offers many dishes prepared according to historic recipes, such as the octopus in tomato sauce taken from a 16th-century source. He prefers seasonal produce, so you won't always find the same goodies on the menu: there's mulberry sorbet in May and prickly pear sorbet in September. It's wise to book in advance.

Trattoria da Gemma, Salita Cavalieri di Malta, Amalfi   L
Tel: (089) 871345
Open: Daily Jun 16–Sep 14 12:30pm–3:30pm 7pm–11:30pm
Closed: Thur from Sep 15–Jun 15
Credit cards: AE, DC, MC, V

Signor Francesco Grimaldi is the first male cook in the kitchen since Gemma, his great-grandmother, founded the restaurant in 1872. Just up the road from the Duomo, this homely *trattoria* has a terrace which overlooks the narrow street below. The speciality, fish, is on display on beds of ice near the entrance, and an old-fashioned wine vat squats in a corner. It's customary to listen to the list of the day. Don't expect a wide variety of dishes: the emphasis is on quality, absolute freshness of local produce, and generous portions. Try the *spaghetti alla macinata* (a piping hot plate of pasta with a tangy sauce of tomato, caper, hot pepper and parsley). Not to be missed are the *profiteroles al limone* with egg custard inside and drenched in a light, delicate lemon sauce. Booking in advance is appreciated and highly recommended.

Bar Royal, Via d'Amalfi, Amalfi   **L**
Tel: (089) 871982
Open: Daily 9am–10pm
No credit cards

Just up from the Piazza Duomo, this café has delicious lemon cake slices, soft inside with a chewy, caramelized crust.

Pasticceria Andrea Pansa, Piazza Duomo, Amalfi   **L**
Tel: (089) 871065
Open Mon–Sat 9am–1pm 4pm–8pm
No credit cards

We couldn't resist a plug for this little café which has served homemade cakes since 1830.

WHERE TO STAY IN AMALFI

Hotel Cappuccini Convento, Via Annunziatella 46   **LL**
Tel: (089) 871008   Open: Year round
Amenities: ✕ ⵚ   Credit cards: AE, DC, V

High on the cliff, a 10-minute walk from the center, you'll find this converted 13th-century Cappuchin monastery with a lovely cloister. In this atmosphere of peace and austerity, Longfellow wrote his poem to Amalfi. A plaque on the wall commemorates this. The four-star hotel is reached by an elevator ascending the sheer cliff-face. White-walled, with a superb seaview and set in its own wood and garden, the hotel offers tranquility. The owners, the Aielli family, have lovingly preserved the ancient atmosphere. It's furnished with antiques, and you'll find no television or air-conditioning in the converted monks' cells (thick walls keep 39 rooms cool). Drinks in the bar are served on a grand piano, and old silver graces the armoires in the dining area. The dining room leads onto a magnificent terrace where diners can enjoy the splendid panorama. Distinguished guests include Roosevelt, Gladstone and Lady Hamilton. On March 31, 1893 no less than eight crowned heads slept here. Osbert Sitwell, after a two-month stay, was inspired to write: "He who has not seen the Cappuccini, has not seen Amalfi, he who has not seen Amalfi, has not seen Italy."

Hotel Miramalfi, Via Quasimodo 3, Amalfi   **LL**
Tel: (089) 871588   Open: Year round
Amenities: ▣ ✕ ⃒⃥ ⌂   Credit cards: AE, DC, MC, V

This modern hotel lies just up the road from the Cappuccini. It's comfortable and uncluttered with a friendly holiday atmosphere. The rooms have a seaview balcony and a view of the terraced garden which leads down by steps or elevator to the outdoor pool set against the cliff-face above the bay. More steps lead down to the private beach. The hotel has a glass-panelled dining room leading onto a panoramic terrace.

AMALFI TO RAVELLO

*From the parking lot, drive in the direction of **Salerno**, passing the Tourist Office on your left. Just up the road you'll pass the round stone tower of the Hotel Luna on your right, then drive through a tunnel. After ½km there's a sign left for **Ravello**. A few hundred meters after this, turn sharp left to climb steadily up the hillside on a twisting road. After 5kms you'll see an archway ahead: don't go under it. Just beforehand on the right is a parking lot: turn in here, as you can't park in the central square beyond the arch. Walk under the crumbling archway, and you'll be in **Piazza Duomo** (also known as **Piazza Vescovado**). To the left of the cathedral, you'll find the **Tourist Office**, Piazza Duomo 10. (Tel: (089) 857096. Open: Mon–Sat 9am–1pm, 4pm–7pm.)*

RAVELLO

The lovely town of Ravello sits on a balcony 350m above the sea. From this vantage point you have an unrivaled view of the Amalfi coast. Believed to have been founded by Roman refugees escaping the Barbarians, the town swiftly gained stature in the 10th century when it was a citadel defending the Republic of Amalfi. Its fortunes declined with those of Amalfi several centuries later.

WHAT TO SEE IN RAVELLO

Villa Rúfolo, Piazza Vescovado, Ravello
Open: Daily Jun–Sept 9:30am–pm 3pm–7pm; Oct–May
   9:30am–1pm 2pm–5pm
Admission: L1,000, children 6–12 yrs L300, free on Thur

This magnificent garden contains the ruins of the 12th-century Palazzo Rúfolo as well as trees from all over the world, with every species labeled. There are plants within and without the beautiful ruins, and the effect duly inspired Wagner's magical garden of Klingsor in his opera, *Parsifal*. Since 1953 the villa has held a festival of symphony music at the beginning of July.

Villa Cimbrone, Via Cimbrone, Ravello
Open: Daily dawn–sunset
Admission free

A wide, straight avenue leads through this lush garden to a belvedere offering one of the most famous and spectacular views in Italy. Built on the edge of a ridge, the villa looks down hundreds of meters of sheer rock to orange terraces and olive groves below and over a wide sweep of coast and sea. There's also a lovely courtyard with an ancient stone wall embellished with columns, coats-of-arms and a green-and-yellow tiled dome. Paths lead off the main avenue, winding among pines, eucalyptus and flowerbeds to gazebos and paved formal gardens. There's also a café and bar.

SHOPPING IN RAVELLO

Of all the shops to browse in, **Camo**, Piazza Duomo (no credit cards) is a must if you love coral and cameos. Signor Filocamo, a master craftsman, creates jewelry of superb quality at fair prices in his workshop. There's something for everyone on sale in the shop – from inexpensive bracelets to valuable antique brooches. Ask Signor Filocamo to show you his prized antique collection, which includes a beautiful 17th-century coral crucifix; a Louis XIV cameo snuffbox with elaborate scenes delicately carved on all sides; and a wonderful conch shell engraved with transparent cameos.

WHERE TO EAT IN RAVELLO

Hotel Caruso, Belvedere, Via Toro 50, Ravello   LL
Tel: (089) 857111
Open: Daily Apr–mid-Jan 12:30pm–3pm 7pm–10:30pm
Closed: mid-Jan–Mar
Credit cards: AE, DC, MC, V

This restaurant is well known for its view and the beauty of its architecture, not to mention its home-cooking. Particularly recommended is the delicious Vino Gran Caruso wine. Equally famed are the *crespolini* (cheese pancakes), and the chocolate-lemon soufflé. *Gourmet* magazine published some of the restaurant's recipes in 1972, but only the Caruso's chef seems able to make it like it is. Try Countess Caruso's refreshing lemon liqueur as a digestif.

Ristorante Salvatore, Via della Repubblica 2, Ravello   LL
Tel: (089) 857227
Open: Daily 12:30pm–3pm 7pm–10:30pm
No credit cards

Go through a tunnel to the right of the Duomo and you'll find the restaurant in front of you. Thirty-five steps lead down to a lovely garden on several levels with creeper-covered walls and a stone fountain. The dining room is large and airy, with one glass wall overlooking the bay. As if the romantic atmosphere isn't enough, the food is also superb. It's renowned for its fresh locally-caught fish, which is beautifully complemented by the crisp house wine. For dessert, try one of their mouthwatering ice-creams.

San Domingo Café, Piazza Duomo, Ravello   L
Tel: (089) 857142
Open: Daily 9am till late
No credit cards

Situated in the lovely cathedral square, with outside tables, this café has become famous since Jacqueline Kennedy made it one of her favorite haunts back in 1962. A photo of her, dedicated to the owner, hangs on the wall.

WHERE TO STAY IN RAVELLO

Hotel Caruso Belvedere, Via Toro 52, Ravello   LL
Tel: (089) 857111   Closed: mid-Jan–Mar
Amenities: ✕ ♀   Credit cards: AE, DC, MC, V

This lovely hotel, in an 11th-century villa, is a member of the Association of Italian Historic Buildings. Astonishingly good value for money, it offers gracious living combined with the warm hospitality of its host, Gino Caruso. The hotel provides all modern comforts yet the splendor and history of the building remain unspoilt. The hand-made, antique floor tiles come from Vietri: their superb quality is demonstrated by their excellent condition after 100 years of wear. Antique furniture and 19th-century paintings enchance the decor. The elegant lounge has a painted Renaissance ceiling. The 26 good-sized rooms are furnished in a pleasing combination of modern and antique pieces; and most have a panoramic verandah. There's a terrace dining area and a loggia to relax in. In the tranquil garden there's a long shaded walk that opens onto a little stone terrace with a glorious view of the valley and bay. Make your reservations now, as the hotel will probably be awarded four or five stars in the near future.

RAVELLO TO SALERNO

*Retrace your route down the hill, then rejoin the main road and turn left for **Salerno**. After about 3kms you come to the small town of **Minori** with its Roman villa, then another kilometer and you pass through the resort of **Maiori**. Drive straight on for Salerno for 7½kms, and pass through a tunnel. About 10kms from Maiori you reach the fishing port of **Cetara**: 5kms further on you come to **Vietri*** *sul Mare*. Famous for its ceramic art, Vietri marks the end of the glorious Amalfi Coast. As the road leads into this resort, you'll see the curbside lined with watermelon stalls in summer. Entering Vietri, follow the road straight ahead for **Salerno**. If you look to the right you'll see shop after shop selling ceramic tiles and pottery. After 200m you pass the freeway entrance: cross in front of it and turn right for Salerno. A little further on there's a peculiar tubular building of gold and green tiles on your left. A further ½km and you pass **Lloyd's Baia Hotel** on your right at the outskirts of Salerno. You now have the harbor on your right, as you drive into this rather seedy port.

Shortly after you enter Salerno, the road divides with a right turn-off for the autostrada. Continue straight ahead, passing under the freeway. Just ahead there's a red-brick building with a tower. As you pass it on your left you'll see that it's elaborately decorated with stone lions, arches and gargoyles. About 200m from here the road becomes a divided highway. In another 200m there's an intersection with a set of lights: drive straight across, and you'll see the municipal gardens on your left. Drive straight on, past the gardens, along **Lungomare Trieste**, and take the third left into **Via Porta di Mare**. (There's a yellow sign indicating Information.) Bear left again and you're in **Via Roma**. Immediately in front is **Piazza Amendola**, with a large parking lot on the left of the square. Opposite, you'll see "Azienda di Soggiorno e Turismo" written above the entrance to the **Tourist Office**, Piazza Amendola 8. (Tel: (089) 224774. Open: Mon–Fri, Sat am 9am–1pm, 4pm–7pm.)

SALERNO

This industrial city and port can't compete with the loveliness of the towns along the Amalfi Coast. In fact it's dirty, noisy and rather shabby: Naples scaled down. Yet it's a strategic point for the tourist – from here there are boat and hydrofoil services to Amalfi, Positano, Capri and Naples. Fifty kilometers south-east of the city is Paestum, important for its splendid Greek temples. Furthermore, Salerno boasts a number of attractions well worth visiting.

Salerno was once a great medical center, attracting scholars and would-be doctors from all over Europe. For this reason, in the Middle Ages it became known as the *Civitas Hippocratica* (City of Hippocrates) after the ancient Greek who is credited with founding medical ethics. Doctors to this day still take the Hippocratic Oath before they are permitted to practise. The Medical School in Salerno is generally reckoned to have been the oldest in Europe, and was certainly flourishing by the mid-12th century. It didn't close until nearly 700 years later.

More recently, Salerno was where the Allied armies first set foot on mainland Europe in September 1943. The Allied invasion was met by fierce resistance from the Germans and, in the ensuing battle, the ancient port area was largely destroyed. This quarter has now been completely rebuilt, with a pleasant promenade along the waterfront.

WHAT TO SEE IN SALERNO

Via dei Mercati, Salerno
This narrow street, full of character if rather dilapidated, is the main artery of Salerno's historic center. It was the hub of trade and commerce until the 19th century. A stroll up here brings you to Via Duomo and the cathedral.

Duomo di San Matteo, Via Duomo, Salerno
Open: Daily 8am–12:30pm 4pm–7:30pm
Admission free

In 1080, during the cathedral's construction, a discovery was made which gave a heightened significance to the undertaking: St Matthew's remains were found. The relics are now buried in the crypt. The cathedral was consecrated six years after construction began by Pope Gregory VII who was living in exile in Salerno. This consecration proved somewhat premature as the cathedral wasn't finally completed until the 12th century when the belltower was built. Pope Gregory's tomb is in the chapel to the right of the high altar. The cathedral has subsequently been restored several times.

Approaching the cathedral, you first cross a pretty courtyard with the simple facade at the far end. The bronze doors, cast in Constantinople in 1099, were a gift of a Salernitan citizen. He and his wife are depicted on the doors at the feet of St Matthew. The most impressive features of the cathedral are its mosaic detail, two ambos and an Easter candlestick. There's also the magnificent marble tomb (1412) of Margaret di Durazzo d'Anjou. The carved figures of the queen and her ladies-in-waiting are a fascinating visual document of the fashions of that period. Placards nearby explain (in Italian only) the restoration work carried out on the tomb, including a pictorial representation of the tomb's original colors. Now you can just make out some faded tints.

In the **Museo del Duomo** (temporarily closed for repairs), there are many historic relics. These include the 12th-century *Exultet* illuminated manuscript and a 12th-century ivory altar frontal. When the repairs are complete, the museum will be open daily 9:30am–2:30pm.

Museo Provinciale, Via San Benedetto, Salerno
Open: Daily 9:30am–1pm 5pm–8pm
Admission free

This medieval building contains a collection of local archeological finds, including a magnificent first-century BC bronze head of Apollo. The museum is housed in a building which was once the Abbey of San Benedetto.

Castello di Arechi, Salerno
Open: Daily 9am–1pm 3pm–1hr before sunset
Admission free

On the hill above Salerno is an ancient Byzantine castle, rebuilt by the Lombards and heavily fortified by the Normans. Recently restored, it houses a fine collection of pottery, some of it dating from the eight century. It's worth the 45-minute trek for the astounding view.

WHERE TO EAT IN SALERNO

La Brace, Lungomare Trieste 11, Salerno   LL
Tel: (089) 225159
Open: Mon–Sat 12:30pm–4:30pm 7:30pm–1am   Closed: Sun
Credit cards: AE, DC, MC, V

Don't be put off by the unprepossessing exterior: a neon sign pointing to a door below a dilapidated frontage. The interior consists of three pleasant rooms with an airy white-and-yellow color scheme and pine wood panelling. Dine at candlelit tables to the music of a piano bar in the evenings (no piano bar in August). The buffet is laden with inviting *antipasti*: spinach pie, thick Italian omelette, stuffed zucchini, roast peppers. The restaurant's speciality is fish, *alla brace* (grilled). It's also a pizzeria, and the speciality here is seafood pizza. Try the house wine, Gragnano: a red, aromatic wine, served *chilled*.

Nicola dei Principati, Corso Garibaldi 201, Salerno   LL
Tel: (089) 225435
Open: Tues–Sun noon–4:30pm 7:30pm–midnight
Credit cards: AE, DC, V

It's a real treat in itself to dine in such a splendid salon. Cool blue marbled wallpaper and white lacquered pillars contrast with warm wood detail. Glass panelling, a huge mosaic mirror, shiny black floor and clever lighting combine to create an elegant atmosphere. The food is attractively presented in generous portions. Since it's mainly a fish restaurant, why not start with *vermicelli ai frutti di mare* (pasta with a variety of shellfish, fresh mussels, clams, scallops and razor clams). Follow with *fritto di pesce misto* (lightly fried mixed small fish). Try the dessert speciality, *buchinotto*: a typical Salernitan cake with a tasty custard and amaretto filling. To finish, ask the charming owner, Signora Antonietta Violante, to let you sample her Amaro. This is concocted by her father, Nicola. There's a picture of him on the bottle label, dressed as Caesar with a crown of forks and spoons. On Saturday evenings there's a piano bar after 9pm.

WHERE TO STAY IN SALERNO

Lloyd's Baia, Via dei Marinis 2, Salerno LL
Tel: (089) 210145   Open: Year round
Amenities: ▣ ✕ ⚲ ⛵ Credit cards: AE, DC, MC, V

A superb modern hotel, situated between Vietri and Salerno (2kms from Salerno center). Spacious and airy, it offers every comfort, including two seawater pools (one for children) and private beach equipped with changing huts. There's an outdoor restaurant/bar, "Il Capanno", near the pools. This is informal by day but candlelit with piano bar at night. The decor of the large rooms is predominantly white with chrome fittings and azure carpeting. Ample balconies have seaviews. Rooms 233, 333 and 433 have an extra sitting area for the price of a regular double.

Jolly delle Palme, Lungomare Trieste 1, Salerno LL
Tel: (089) 225222   Open: Year round
Amenities: ▣ ✕ ⚲   Credit cards: AE, DC, MC, V

Modern and efficient, part of Italy's largest chain, this hotel is central (across the road from Piazza Amendola and on the seafront). The beach, however, looks grimy and the hotel's small paved garden backs onto a children's playground. There are 105 rooms; those on the corners have a double balcony and bigger bathroom. Some rooms are without balcony, but instead have an extra area for a third bed. Prices include an ample buffet breakfast: eggs, porridge and even a dieter's menu.

Plaza, Piazza Vittorio Veneto 42, Salerno L
Tel: (089) 224477   Open: Year round
Amenities: ▣   No credit cards

This central hotel (opposite the station and main Tourist Office) offers excellent value for money. An insignificant gray exterior belies a charming, fresh interior with white walls and arches and rust and brown furnishings. The pretty lounge has rather splendid glass chandeliers. The 42 rooms don't have a seaview, but front rooms overlook the piazza. Bathrooms are quite small but newly tiled. An interesting feature: some rooms have a head-to-head bed arrangement, affording a certain privacy within one room. Signor Guiseppe, the hotel secretary, speaks very good English and extends a warm welcome.

SALERNO TO CAVA DE' TIRRENI

*Go out of **Piazza Amendola** toward **Vietri**. You pass the strange house with the gargoyles again, this time on your right. Drive straight ahead, beneath the motorway and past **Lloyd's Baia Hotel** on your left. After 200m there's a blue sign to **Napoli**; bear right at the fork. Immediately after there's another fork: keep to the right for **Cava**. After you pass through the suburb of **Molina**, continue for another 1km to Cava. Keep on the road following signs for **Cava Centro** over the bridge. The road forks again; bear left, driving ¾ of the way around the green square and up the hill. Follow the white sign for **centro**. Turn left at a T-junction, then right following another sign for centro. You'll come to the **Piazza Roma**, where you can park. At the far right-hand corner of the piazza, you'll find the **Tourist Office**, Corso Umberto I 208. (Tel: (089) 841148. Open: Mon–Fri 8:30am–1:30pm 4:30pm–9pm.)*

CAVA DE' TIRRENI

Cava is a delightful place, set among green hills and mountains, 195m above sea level, and just a few kilometers from the Amalfi Coast. It was founded at the beginning of the 11th century, and originally developed around the monastery of Cava. The arcaded **Borgo Scacciaventi**, at the heart of the medieval village of Corpo di Cava, was begun in the 15th century. This was the trade and commerce center where artisans plied their crafts under the porches. Nowadays, you can stroll along under the original arcades and admire the handicrafts still sold there: leather goods, copper and wrought-iron articles, ceramics and local cakes.

The town bears the title of *Citta Sedelissima* (Town of Great Loyalty), an honor conferred in 1460 by the King of Naples and Aragon, Ferrante I. When the town's *Tromboniere* rescued the King from the Angevins, the monarch gave the township a parchment on which to write the reward they desired. But they requested nothing and the parchment remained white and unsullied: *La Pergamena Blanca*. Every year on the last Sunday in June the town celebrates the *Challenge of the Tromboniere*. Locals in full costume have a shooting match using their blunderbusses (*tromboni*).

A SIDETRIP FROM CAVA DE' TIRRENI

Abbazia della Trinità di Cava, Corpo di Cava
Open: Mon–Sat 9am–12:30pm, Sun 9am–10:30am
Admission free

*Directions: Drive halfway round **Piazza Roma**, and follow the blue sign for **Napoli**. Turn left at the end of this road, following the green* *sign for **Salerno–Napoli**. There's a sign left for the **Badia** then a yellow sign right for **Abbazia di San Benetino**. Drive up the hill, continue straight over a small intersection and follow the narrow, winding road. Bear left at the fork and follow the road. You can park in front of the abbey gates.*

The abbey was founded by St Alfiero in 1011, and was consecrated by Pope Urban II in 1092. Its facade was rebuilt in the 18th century. The elderly monk who conducts your guided tour speaks Italian and French but not English. Of particular interest is the grotto where the relics of St Alfiero are kept; magnificent 12th-century mosaicwork, similar to that in Salerno Cathedral; the 16th-century capitular hall with a lovely majolica floor (1771); the charming 13th-century cloister set under an overhanging rock which forms a roof (at present undergoing restoration); and the museum and picture gallery in a 13th-century hall.

The museum contains precious 16th-century illuminated manuscripts and a polyptych by Andrea of Salerno. There's a beautiful 11th-century casket and a 16th-century nautical map. Two small paintings, of the Perugino school, are of interest – especially the one on the right. The sarcophagus and legs of the recumbent figure in the painting point towards you; if you circle it, the figure and tomb seem to follow you round. As you leave the abbey, look over the balustrade of the front courtyard. This gives you an idea of the size of this large monastery.

WHERE TO EAT/WHERE TO STAY IN CAVA DE' TIRRENI

Hotel Scapolatiello, Badia de Cava de' Tirreni   **L–LL**
Tel: (089) 463911   Open: Year round
Amenities: ▣ ✕ ♀ ⌣   Credit cards: AE, DC, V

This four-star hotel, in the pretty village of Badia di Cava (Corpo di Cava), is set amid green hills and valleys nearly 500m above sea level. The decor is white, cool and uncluttered, and the elegant dining hall leads onto a wide terrace with a splendid view of the surrounding countryside. The rooms are tastefully decorated; some have a balcony, and others face the terrace. From June 1 to September 30 half-pension is obligatory.

The restaurant (**L–LL**) is also open to non-residents. The specialities here are substantial. Some tempting dishes include champagne risotto and *taglioline al limone* (with lemon and cream). Don't leave without sampling the barman's "Scapolatiello Cocktail": an amazing mixture of gin, vodka and tequila with lemon and coffee. A small glass is refreshing; a large one could knock you out. There's a piano bar in the evenings.

CAVA DE' TIRRENI TO AGNANO

Retrace your route to **Piazza Roma**, *then follow the blue sign for* **Napoli**. *Turn left, signosted* **Salerno–Napoli**, *then immediately right onto a divided highway with trees down the center. Take the second right, then turn left onto* **Corso Mazzini**. *Bear right at the fork. At the entrance to the autostrada on your left follow the signs for Napoli. The* **A3** *toll costs about* L1200 *upon entry and another* L500 *when you leave the highway. This fast road leads you past the urban sprawl of the Bay of Naples and continues to Agnano (see page 303).*

(If you wish to return to Naples, take the turn-off for the city center after 25kms, then continue for 4kms to busy **Piazza Garibaldi** *in front of the main railway station on your right.)*

After about 38kms on the **A3** *follow signs for* **Rome/Tangenziale**. *After 42½kms bear right for* **Casória**. *Several kms later follow signs for* **Napoli/Pozzuoli**. *Drive through a tunnel. Follow signs for* **Pozzuoli**. *At 51½kms go through another tunnel which is a little over 1km long. Drive through a third tunnel still following signs for Pozzuoli. Then get in the middle lane for* **Agnano Terme**. *Exit the highway, following signs for* **Agnano**. *(The whole trip is about 57½kms.) This road takes you back over the Tangenziale to the left turn for* **Agnano Terme**. *At the traffic lights turn left at the big yellow and blue sign for* **Terme di Agnano**. *The Terme is about 4kms from the highway toll booth. You can park on the left by the spa's large gray entrance gates.*

ROUTE J: AGNANO–POZZUOLI–GAETA–TERRACINA –CIRCEO–ANZIO–ROME

(Approx. 95kms)

AGNANO

Directions: see above.

Terme di Agnano (Open: Mon–Fri 7:30am–1pm, Sat 7:30am–11am. Admission varies.) The spa is situated in the Agnano valley: a huge volcanic crater about seven kms in circumference. The water from the two springs at Agnano has a temperature ranging from 63–75°C. The waters are undrinkable, but you can have a mud bath or inhale the vapors in one of several natural caves connected to the underground source. Treatments are allegedly beneficial for a wide range of ailments, including rheumatism, arthritis, obesity and fatigue. You can use the facilities for a morning or an afternoon, after a compulsory medical examination. If you want to stay longer, there's a modern hotel set in pleasant grounds.

AGNANO TO POZZUOLI

*Turn left out of **Agnano Terme**, pass the ancient stone gateway to the Terme on the left and go up the hill. When you reach the first intersection in about 300m, turn sharp right. After the blue sign for Pozzuoli, drive straight across an intersection with traffic lights. One kilometer later there's a sign to indicate you're entering Pozzuoli's outskirts. The **Accademia Aeronautica** and the sea lie to the left. After 1½km there's a yellow 'I' (information) sign indicating straight ahead. Go under the bridge. Bear right at the fork after 1km and you'll see a sign for the amphitheater. Bear left at the next fork, following signs for tourist information and in 100m you'll see the **Tourist Office**, Via Campi Flegrei 3. Drive through the gate and park in the small garden in front of the Tourist Office. (Tel: (081) 8672419. Open: Mon–Fri 9am–2pm 4pm–6pm Sat 9am–1pm.)*

POZZUOLI

Pozzuoli stands in the Phlegrean fields, an area of extinct volcanic craters; only Solfatara is semi-active. A geographical phenomenon called bradyseism (slow trembling) occurs in this zone. Although unnoticeable when it happens, it causes the land level to rise and fall. During the last 2,000 years it's mainly fallen, but in 1538 a sudden eruption caused the formation of Monte Nuovo.

 In the eighth century BC the Greeks first settled in Italy at Cumae (roughly 8kms from Pozzuoli). They were followed by the

Samnites then, in the fourth century BC, by the Romans. The port of *Puteoli* (Pozzuoli today) became a powerful and important center of commerce. Wealthy Romans built their holiday villas at nearby Baia and Cumae. Cicero had a house at Cumae; Seneca vacationed at Baia. Puteoli and Cumae later became Christian communities. In 61AD St Paul visited Puteoli and in 305AD St Gennaro was beheaded on Solfatara Hill.

WHAT TO SEE IN POZZUOLI

Flavian Amphitheater, off Via Solfatara, Pozzuoli
Open: Daily 9am–2 hrs before sunset
Admission: L2,000

This huge and imposing amphitheater is the third largest in Italy (149m × 116m). It held 40,000 people, but today only three tiers of seating remain. It has an amazing network of underground structures, including dens where wild animals were kept.

Serapeum, Via Roma, Pozzuoli
Open: Daily dawn–sunset
Admission free

The remains of the Serapis "Temple" – really the ruins of the Roman city market – stand in a pool of water and are floodlit at night. It's a spectacular place, now inhabited by seagulls who swim around the ruins and occupy the top of every truncated column. On the three main columns you can see clearly the discoloration and erosion caused by marine molluscs.

Solfatara Volcano
Open: Daily 7am–1 hr before sunset
Admission; L3,000

A wide path leads through woods of eucalyptus, oak and pine to a large, gravel-filled smoking crater which is the center of this semi-active volcano. Violent jets of steam shoot up and, though some of the holes are no larger than the size of a matchhead, they can scald if you get too close. Guides can be hired. (Tel: (081) 8672341 or ask at the Tourist Office.)

Convento di San Gennaro, Via Domiziana, Pozzuoli
Open: Daily 9am–7pm
Admission free

This convent is famous for its stone stained with the blood of St Gennaro, the patron saint of Naples, his birthplace. In 303 he was imprisoned in Miseon during the persecution of the Christians and in 305 he was beheaded on the site now occupied by the church. The stone is kept near the altar in the side chapel to the right.

Lago d'Averno

Situated to the west of the city center, this lake fills a volcanic crater and is ringed by green hills and cultivated vegetable gardens. Legend has it that this was the gateway to Hades. Nowadays, however, it presents a much less terrifying picture. There's a marvelous view of the ruined Temple of Apollo and the other lakes from the belvedere on nearby Via Domiziana.

Scavi di Cumae, 7kms north-west of Pozzuoli (ss7 Qu.)
Open: Daily 9am–2 hrs before sunset
Admission: L2,000

This archeological site contains an acropolis, ruined temples of Jupiter and Apollo and, especially worthy of note, the Sibyl's Cave. A strange trapezoid archway carved out of the rock leads into a high chamber. Here the Sibyl, a prophetess consulted in ancient times and mentioned in T. S. Eliot's *The Waste Land*, was believed to have lived.

Scavi di Baia, Parco Archeologico, Baia
Open: 9am–2 hrs before sunset
Admission: L2,000

Although much of the ancient spa here is now submerged due to bradyseism, you'll see the remains of the Terme Romani (Roman Baths).

BOAT TRIPS FROM POZZUOLI

Ferries leave Pozzuoli for the islands of Procida and Ischia every 30 minutes in summer from 5am to 8:30pm. The journey to Procida takes 30 minutes (price: L2,000 one way); to Ischia about 1¼ hours (price: L3,000 one way). For further details see page 275.

WHERE TO EAT IN POZZUOLI

Restaurant La Ninfea, Via Italia 1, Pozzuoli
Tel: (081) 8661326/8665308
Open: Daily 12:30pm–3:30pm 7:30pm–11pm
Credit cards: AE, DC, V

Situated on the shore of Lake Lucrino, this elegant restaurant is a converted fisherman's cottage. A room with very low ceiling and arches dates from the 18th century, and there are three other dining areas. In summer you can eat outside on a covered board-walk that rests on stilts in the lake. The menu is impressive and includes a selection of cheese dishes and *sfiziosi* (tasty treats) such as clam soup and mussels au gratin. Try the *linguine con scampi* (pasta with tomato sauce and clams, mussels and prawns). The *fritto misto di pesce* includes fried prawns, octopus, squid and various small fish.

WHERE TO STAY IN POZZUOLI

Hotel Solfatara, Via Solfatara, Pozzuoli   **LL**
Tel: (081) 8672666   Open: Year round
                        Credit cards: AE, DC, V
Amenities: ✕ ♀

A modern three-star hotel situated near the entrance to the Solfatara, just outside the city center. The rooms are decorated in beige, brown and apricot. Front rooms have a good-sized balcony with sea view; the back rooms look onto an ivy-covered wall.

POZZUOLI TO GAETA

*From the Tourist Office turn left onto **Via Domiziana** and follow the blue signs for **Roma/Formia**. After you go under two bridges (2½kms) you'll pass a belvedere with a vista of Lakes Lucrino, Averno and Fusaro on the left. When the road forks stay left to be near the coast. This single-lane road is flanked by bushes and canes, giving glimpses of the sea. After about 11kms the road widens and you pass **Lago di Patria**. The road bears to the right 2kms on and takes you up onto an overpass for about 350m. Follow signs for **Roma/Formia**. In just over 3kms you come to traffic lights. Continue straight ahead, signposted **Roma**. About 3kms after the lights bear right following the blue sign for **Roma**. You're now driving toward mountains with pretty fields on both sides. The overpass now widens. You travel along it for about 4kms, going over a river and through the outskirts of Mondragone. After 5kms, as you leave Mondragone, you'll see the town's last set of traffic lights. Follow signs for **Roma/Formia**. Cross the **River Garigliano** on a large white concrete bridge. Turn right and immediately left following signs for **Roma/Formia/Terracina**, onto an overpass. You're now on a divided highway with the gulf of Gaeta on your left. This good road lasts 9kms before becoming single lane again. Pass under four bridges and you're on the outskirts of **Formia**. After a while the road runs right along the seafront.*

*Follow the signs for **Roma/Terracina/Gaeta**. You'll find that Formia spills over into Gaeta. After 6kms bear left at the fork signposted **Gaeta Centro**. About 1½kms on drive across the traffic lights and after quite a distance, follow the sign for **Quartieri Medievale**. The road brings you down to the harbor. Bear left at the traffic island and after just under 1km you come to the **Piazza Caboto** on your right, where you can park. Behind this square is the **Tourist Office**, Piazza Traniello 19. (Tel: (0771) 462767. Open: Daily 8am–12:30pm.) There's another **Tourist Office** in the **Piazza XIX Maggio** in the newer section of town.*

GAETA

Gaeta is really two towns: the modern resort with sandy Serapo beach; and the medieval sector with its quaint, narrow streets such as Rampe Chiaromonte. There are two conjectures as to the origin of the city's name. Firstly, Virgil's *Aeneid* relates how Aeneas's nurse, Caieta, was buried here. Alternatively, the Greek historian Strabo suggested that the name derived from *kaiatas* (a cavity) and refers to the caves in the vicinity.

WHAT TO SEE IN GAETA

Duomo, Quartiere Medievale, Gaeta
Open: Daily dawn–sunset
Admission free

This pink cathedral has a magnificent 12th-century belltower decorated in the Moorish style. The huge 13th-century candelabrum inside is beautifully adorned with bas-reliefs depicting the lives of Christ and St Erasmus, patron saint of sailors.

Chiesa di Santissima Annunziata, Via Annunziata, Gaeta
Open: Daily dawn–sunset
Admission free

This 14th century church, rebuilt in the 17th century, is famous for its Chapel of the Immaculate Conception known as the Grotta d'Oro (Golden Cave). This name refers to the lavish gold ceiling and the gilded frames around 16th-century paintings by Pulzone and Criscuolo.

Mausoleum di Planco, Monte Orlando, Gaeta

You can drive part of the way up Monte Orlando, then you have to walk to the summit, where the mausoleum is situated. This circular tomb of Munatius Plancus, a Roman general, was erected in 22BC. It's an impressive monument and the location offers a sweeping view over the sea and mountains.

Santuário della Montagna Spaccata and **Grotto del Turco**, Strada della Trinità
Open: Daily 8am–noon (year round), 3pm–7pm (summer), 2:30pm–5pm (winter)
Admission: L2,000 (Grotto)

Three huge vertical chasms split the mountain where this Benedictine seminary is situated. It's said that the earth shook with such violence when Christ died that these giant fissures appeared in the mountain. A narrow staircase leads through one of the chasms onto a small, circular terrace which overlooks a steep gorge dropping to the sea below. In the first chasm there's an imprint of a large hand in the rock wall, said to be that of a *turco* (non-believer) who doubted the reason for the split mountain. Legend has it that the rock melted where his hand rested and left a print.

Nine ramps of steep, narrow stairs lead down to the cavernous Grotto del Turco, where waves crash against the rocks with a deafening roar.

BOAT TRIPS FROM GAETA

The Pontine Islands lie offshore and hydrofoil and ferry services link nearby Formia to the famous isles of Ponza and Ventotene (34 and 26 nautical miles away).

Ferry: Jun–Sep departs Gaeta 8am and 4:30pm, departs Ponza 3pm and 4:30pm; Oct–May one daily departure (time subject to variation: enquire at Tourist Office or on quay)
Cost: L56,000; car from L46–126,000 one way
Journey time: 2¼ hrs

Hydrofoil: Jun–Sep departs Gaeta 9:20am and 5:40pm, departs Ponza 4pm and 6pm; Oct–May one daily departure (time subject to variation: enquire at Tourist Office or on quay)
Cost: L53,000
Journey time: 1hr 10min

WHERE TO EAT IN GAETA

Caffe Ristorante Villa Fontania, Fontania Beach, Gaeta   LL
Open: Daily 12:30pm–3pm 7pm–11
No credit cards

The restaurant affords superb views of the bay, Monte Orlando, the Mausoleum di Planco, beaches and the remains of a Roman villa. Fontanina beach has a cave and flat rocks in the water, and the romantically-minded suggest this may be the submerged site of an amphitheater. An extensive menu includes *rigatoni alla mamma* (pasta with mozzarella, ricotta, mushrooms, peas and tomato), and linguine with prawns. For the sweet-toothed, there are delicious homemade desserts.

WHERE TO STAY IN GAETA

Hotel Summit, Via Flacca, Gaeta   L–LL
Tel: (0771) 463087   Closed: Nov–Feb
Amenities: ▣ ✕ ♀   No Credit cards

*Directions: See page 311 for directions from **Gaeta to Sperlonga**. The hotel is 3kms from the T-junction on the **Via Flacca** going toward **Terracina**.*

This ultra-modern, three-star hotel, 5kms from Gaeta center, is a great place to stay: there's a private beach, discotheque, fully-equipped gym, sauna, solarium, jacuzzis and many other amenities. The 83 large white, blue and beige rooms have balconies overlooking the bay or garden. Most bathrooms don't have a shower stall, but there are 14 rooms on the lower floors with shower stands. Half-pension is obligatory in August.

GAETA TO SPERLONGA

*From the Tourist Office drive along the **Lungomare Caboto** to the traffic island. Turn left into **Via Firenze** (don't go back into town), bearing right at the end onto Via Marina. This tree-lined highway, with well-kept pleasant houses, runs along the seafront. In just under 2kms the road begins to climb. After 1½kms there's a T-junction: turn left for **Terracina**. You're now on the **Via Flacca** (ss213), which gives a magnificent view of the bay. Drive through four tunnels and 2kms from the fourth one you'll see a sign, right for **Sperlonga**. Drive over a bridge, bearing automatically left to the T-junction. Turn right and instantly turn left and park. Continue on foot to the **Tourist Office**, Corso San Leone 22. (Tel: (0771) 54796. Open: May–Sep Mon–Fri 9am–noon 6pm–9pm, Sat to 10pm, Sun am only.)*

SPERLONGA

Sperlonga is a lovely, popular resort, crammed with holiday crowds in July and August. There's the modern part with its long stretch of beach; and the Old Town, on a clifftop, that's a honeycomb of narrow, whitewashed streets, curling around in apparently random directions. It was a favorite with the ancient Romans, as Tiberius's Grotto and the remains of his villa testify. As yet the town remains relatively unspoilt despite its popularity.

In prehistoric times there were hunters' settlements in the area: relics of this culture are kept in the Pigorini Ethnographical Museum in EUR, Rome. During the period of Roman domination, Sperlonga was a popular resort for wealthy Romans. The remains of their villas can be seen, most notably in the archeological area between Angolo beach and Tiberius's Villa and Grotto. After the Romans came the Barbarians. In 1534 Barbarossa (Redbeard) tried to abduct the young chatelaine of Sperlonga castle for Sultan Suleiman of Turkey. He failed, but plundered the town and took hundreds of captives as slaves.

On February 9, 1958, the panoramic coastal road, Via Flacca (ss213), was opened. This partly follows the ancient Roman road built in 184BC by Lucio Flacco, and covers 30 kilometers between Terracina and the Gulf of Gaeta. During its construction Tiberius's Grotto was used as a depot for tools and machinery. The chief engineer decided to investigate the possibility of

archeological remains, and pieces of ancient statuary were uncovered.

Tiberius's Villa and **Museum** are worth visiting. (Open: Tues–
Sun 9am–8pm (summer), 9am–5pm (winter). Admission: L2,000
(includes Grotto), children under 16 free.) The entrance is on the
road above Sperlonga, and it can also be reached from the beach.
This museum contains statues and other finds from Tiberius's Villa
and Grotto. From the museum a path winds through the sandy
dunes to the ruins of the Emperor's summer villa. You are left to
wander freely, past crumbled walls and fragments of mosaic
flooring, to the Grotto itself. The Emperor used this for orgies; the
naturally formed chambers off the main cave housed the beds and
couches. Lavish drapes once lined the walls and the pools outside
were stocked with alligators and man-eating fish. Slaves would be
plunged into the deadly waters to provide sadistic entertainment
for Tiberius and his guests.

WHERE TO EAT IN SPERLONGA

Laocoonte Da Rocco, Via C. Colombo 4, Sperlonga   LL
Tel: (0771) 54122/54421
Open: Tues–Sun 12:30pm–3pm 10pm–midnight   Closed: Mon
Credit cards: AE, V

A rustic atmosphere prevails in this excellent restaurant, with
white walls, wood beams and open fireplace. Draught beer is
drawn from an antique marble fountain set in the wall of the bar.
You can choose whether to eat at one of the pavement tables, or
inside if you want more privacy. Of the pasta dishes, opt for
fettuccine agli scampi (homemade pasta with prawn sauce).
Everything is cooked on the spot: there are no reheated dishes.
The restaurant specializes in fish, displayed on a pretty shell-
shaped font next to the buffet which bears a variety of side dishes.
The desserts are also special, prepared personally by the owners,
Rocco and Anna D'Arcangelo. Particularly recommended are the
coppa delizia with cream and chocolate, and the *semi-freddo
all'arancio* (ice-cream mousse with a divine marmalade sauce).

WHERE TO STAY IN SPERLONGA

Park Hotel Fiorelle, Localita Fiorelle, Sperlonga   LL
Tel: (0771) 54092   Open: Mar 16–Sep 30
Amenities: ⓟ ✕ ⓨ ⌂   No credit cards

The hotel is situated at the end of a side road, indicated by a small
sign on the gate. The owners don't encourage advertising; they
have a long list of regular guests and wish their hotel to remain
unspoilt and quiet. So if you want a restful stay in lovely
surroundings, book well in advance. The hotel has a cheerful and
friendly family atmosphere. Cats sun themselves in the rambling

garden and a path leads past vegetable plot and lawns to a private beach. The restaurant spreads onto a terrace overlooking the garden, pool and sea. Rooms, all with bath and balcony, are homely and very clean. There's no air-conditioning, so ask for a room on the lower floor, it's cooler. There's a piano in the lounge.

SPERLONGA TO TERRACINA

Come out the other end of the parking lot (opposite where you came in to park when you arrived in town). Head out of town, signposted **Roma***. Turn right at the piazza, passing the Ristorante Laocoonte and follow the road around, going out of town. Continue following signs for Roma. After the sign for Park Hotel Fiorelle on your right, turn immediate left, signposted* **Terracina***. Take care at the junction with the* **Via Flacca***: it's a nasty turning. Keep following signs for Terracina. After about 15kms on the Via Flacca the Terracina mountains loom ahead with the temple of Jupiter Anxur at the summit of the mountain rising above the town. A total of about 15½kms from Sperlonga brings you to the stone portal (***Porta Napolia***), the gate of the ancient town. Keep left of the portal and follow the yellow* **Information** *sign as the road bears right. Drive straight across* **Piazza della Repubblica** *into* **Via Roma***. At the traffic lights turn left into* **Via Derna***, which becomes* **Corso della Vittoria***, still following the yellow information sign to Piazza Mazzini. Turn right at the far end of the piazza, into a side street still following the tourist information sign. There's a parking lot on your right just in front of the* **Tourist Office***, Via G. Leopardi (Tel: (0773) 727759. Open: Mon–Sat Jul–Aug 9am–noon, 5pm–7pm; Sep–Jun 9am–noon).*

TERRACINA

The huge rock of Monte Sant'Angelo, with its ancient Temple of Jupiter Anxur, dominates this popular holiday resort renowned for its long beaches. The Etruscans erected the Cyclopean walls of the town, known as Anxur in Volscian times. It was renamed Terracina by the Romans who conquered it in 406BC, and the town grew in importance due to its position on the Appian Way.

At the heart of the medieval town is the Piazza del Municipio (no parking), with its lovely medieval Duomo and tower. The piazza is part of the ancient Roman forum and is paved with the original stones laid in the first century AD by Aulus Aemilius. His name can be seen clearly on some of the inscriptions. Remains of the old forum and part of its walls are preserved on the far left side of the Duomo. Next to the Duomo is the 14th-century Palazzo Venditti with its arch over the entrance to the piazza. On the other side are the ruins of the *capitolium*: a first-century BC temple to Jupiter, Juno and Minerva.

WHAT TO SEE IN TERRACINA

Museo Archeologico, Piazza del Municipio, Terracina
Open: Tues–Sun May–Sep 9am–1pm 5pm–7pm Oct–Apr
  8am–2pm
Closed: Mon, holidays and the day after a holiday
Admission free

This museum is housed in the 11th-century Torre Frumentaria
(Granary Tower). It's a small museum containing Greek and
Roman sculptures and many other artifacts found in Terracina and
the surrounding countryside.

Duomo, Piazza del Municipio, Terracina
Open: Daily dawn–sunset
Admission free

This impressive 11th-century cathedral is built on the site of a
pagan temple. Legend says that the Roman bath under the porch
on the right was used for the sacrifice of early Christians. The
belltower, with its white-pillared arcade and bright inset discs,
dates from the 13th century. The cathedral is dedicated to San
Cesareo, Terracina's patron saint. Note inside the lovely 13th-
century cosmatesque mosaic floor and the pulpit.

Tempio di Giove Anxur, Monte Sant'Angelo, Terracina
Open: Daily dawn–sunset
Admission free

A scenic 3kms drive along the Strada Panoramica leads to the
summit of Monte Sant'Angelo and the ruins of the Temple of
Jupiter Anxur. This temple, dating from the first century BC, is
Terracina's most important Roman monument. Look for a small
square base incorporating a large rock with a central hole. This is
what remains of the ancient oracle that was connected with one of
the underground rooms. The temple's arcaded base is still
magnificently intact, and from here you have a superb panoramic
view across the Bay with the great promontory Monte Circeo, the
island of Ponza and the mountains beyond.

BOAT TRIPS FROM TERRACINA

Ferries link Terracina to Ponza, the lovely island in the Pontine
archipelago. The journey takes 2½ hours. Departs Terracina Jul–
Aug 7:45am & 8.30pm, rest of year 8:15am; departs Ponza Jul–
Aug 4:30pm & 5:30pm, rest of year 4:30pm
Cost: L15,000 per person (return); cars L15,000–30,000 (one way)
– cars must be booked

WHERE TO EAT IN TERRACINA

Ristorante Grappolo d'Uva, Lungo Matteotti 1
Tel: (0773) 75251
Open: Daily 12:30pm–3:30pm 7:30pm–late
Closed: Wed from Jul–Aug, Jan
Credit cards: AE, DC, V

This is a pretty restaurant, set on the promenade above a beach. In summer you can sit on the roof terrace to sip an aperitif and listen to the waves and a piano bar. The irregular-shaped, white and red salon is filled with tall plants and has a sea view. The atmosphere is informal, yet the food is served elegantly. Fish is the speciality here, with a good selection of *antipasti*, including octopus salad and prawns in tomato sauce. Of the pasta dishes, *spaghetti alle vongole verace* (with large clams) is a tasty option, or try *risotto* or *linguine el nero di seppie* (with an inky cuttlefish sauce). For dessert the *tiramisu* (sponge cake, chocolate, cream and mascarpone cheese) is good, creamy, not too sweet and spiked with a dash of liqueur.

La Tartana Da Mario l'Ostricaro, Via Appia   LLL
Tel: (0773) 752461
Open: Daily 12:30pm–3:30pm 7:30pm–10:30pm
No credit cards

An informal yet high quality restaurant, elegantly decorated and offering a lovely sea view. This is a must for seafood lovers, with excellent food and service. The speciality here is *risotto alla pescatore*, but not to be missed are the *antipasti* of raw shellfish which include oysters, clams, mussels and a delicious tidbit called a sea-date.

WHERE TO STAY IN TERRACINA

Hotel River, Via Pontina, Terracina   LL
Tel: (0773) 730681/2/3   Open: Apr–Oct 15
                           Credit cards: AE
Amenities: ▣ ✕ ♀ ⍣

This new hotel is situated a few kilometers from the crush of the town center. The semi-private beach 100m away is equipped with changing huts, and there's a pleasant garden. All 92 rooms with bath are decorated in beige and cream and have a wide balcony overlooking the parking lot, gardens and trees. There are plans for a large discotheque adjacent to the hotel.

TERRACINA TO CIRCEO

*Turn left out of the parking lot, to **Piazza Mazzini**. Turn right into **Viale della Vittoria**. When you reach the water turn right at the T-*

junction into **Viale Circe**, a spacious shrub-lined street, running along the seafront. After 2kms make a sharp right turn into **Via Friuli Venezia Giulia** signposted **San Felice Circeo**. At the traffic island bear left, following the signs for **Latina/Roma**. In another 400m there's a complicated intersection. Drive over the main road following **Roma/Latina** signs. Pass the Hotel River on your left, go over a bridge and straight through a set of lights to the sign for **Circeo**. About 2½kms from the lights the road divides. Turn left over the traffic island and backtrack. Then take a right following signs for **Circeo**. After 2kms you'll drive over another bridge. Keep straight on this road for about 7kms, at the end of which you'll come to an intersection with the Ristorante Capreccio on the corner. Follow the yellow **Information** sign and cross the intersection into **Via de Gaspari**.

Keep around to the left, following the yellow information sign and then turn right. Pass the Hotel Circeo on your left. Turn right at the end of the road, following the yellow sign for **Centro Storico**. Take the right fork at **Via Cristoforo Colombo**, following the main road round and up the hill. Turn left at the T-junction and continue uphill, where old houses flank the road. After about 300m follow the road around to the left into **Via Roma** under an arch into **Piazza Vittorio Veneto**. Park here and walk through the arch on the right to the **Tourist Office**, Piazza Lanzuisi 4. (Tel: (0773) 52770. Open: May–Sep Mon pm, Tue–Sat 8am–1pm 5pm–8pm Sun am; Oct–Apr Mon–Sat 9am–noon.)

SAN FELICE CIRCEO

The coastline is dominated by the great rock with its famous profile like a huge head lying half-submerged in the water. Local legend has it that this is the enchantress *La Maga Circe* who has lain sleeping through the ages. The popular modern resort is spread in the lee of this fabled promontory, while the ancient village clings to the slopes of the hill, overlooking the boundary of the vast National Park.

Piazza Vittorio Veneto and the adjacent Piazza Lanzuisi are the two main squares of the charming historic center. They are overlooked by Torre dei Templari, a medieval stone tower. Piazza Lanzuisi is a lovely, quiet courtyard of cobblestones and palms, with classical music concerts in summer. In Piazza Veneto there's the pleasant Bar Petrucci, with shaded tables set out in the square.

A motorboat leaves Circeo at 8:30am for Ponza (passengers only). The journey takes 1¼ hours. Tel: Agency Gentur (0773) 528809. Cost: L14,000 (one way).

WHAT TO SEE IN CIRCEO

Grotta di Neanderthal and **Grotta delle Capre**, San Felice Circeo
Open: Enquire at the Hotel Neanderthal, Lungomare Circe 33
(Tel: (0773) 5280126) or at the Tourist Office for current details of
opening times and admission.

These two grottoes of prehistoric interest are well worth a visit. In
1939 a prehistoric skull was discovered in the Grotta di Neanderthal, offering evidence that man lived here around 50,000 years
ago. Both caves are pitted with marks and encrustations indicating
the movements of the earth over the centuries.

CIRCEO TO PARCO NAZIONALE DEL CIRCEO

*Reverse your direction turning right out of the arch from Piazza
Lanzuisi, back down the **Via Roma** for just a very short distance.
Then take the first left just before the iron cross. The road, **Via XXIV
Maggio**, travels steadily downhill, through several hairpin turns.
Two kms further at the T-junction turn left into the **Via Sabaudia**
entering the borough of Mezzomondo. After another 1km, turn
right at the ERG gas station following the blue sign for **Sabaudia**. In
another 6½kms from the ERG station you'll see yellow and brown
signs for the park. Turn left and within 300m you'll enter the park
on your left. You can't miss the huge yellow sign: **Parco Nazionale
del Circeo–Centro Visitatori**. Drive through the gateway on the left
into a clearing where you can park. An information booth is to the
left of the entrance.*

Parco Nazionale del Circeo, outside Circeo
Open: Daily 8am–8pm
Admission free
Enquiries to: Administration office of park, Via Carlo Alberto 6,
Sabaudia. (Tel: (0773) 57251/57252 weekdays 8am–2pm) or EPT
Office, Via Duca del Mare 19, Latina. (Tel: (0773) 498711.)

Reclaimed from swampland in 1934, this national park covers
thousands of hectares, including whole towns and stretches of
coastline. Although it's the smallest of the Italian nature reserves,
the variety of features it encompasses makes it especially interesting. These include three towns – Latina, Sabaudia and Circeo – 30
kilometers of beach, dunes, cliffs and caves, an island (Zannone),
two springs (hot water and mineral), four coastal lakes, an ancient
forest and archeological ruins. Many species of wild animals, birds
and vegetation can be seen here. There are signposted walks,
countless smaller paths along which you can wander freely, and
picnic areas. You can travel on foot, or by bicycle hired in nearby
Sabaudia.

National Park Museum, Parco Nazionale del Circeo
Open: Daily 8am–1pm 3:30pm–7pm
Closed: Mon (in winter sometimes Sun instead of Mon)
Admission: L1,000, children under 10 L500

Here you'll see an audio-visual display illustrating the wildlife of the national park, stuffed animals, the huge, gnarled roots of a centuries-old oak tree, a skull discovered in the Grotta di Neanderthal, plus displays of live snakes and an aquarium.

CIRCEO NATIONAL PARK TO NETTUNO

Turn right out of the park to the intersection. Turn left following signs for **Latina**. *After 5½kms you'll drive through a farming community called Sacramento. About 13kms from the park exit you'll encounter a built-up area with a mushroom-shaped stone water tower on your right. Turn left at the next intersection, following the sign for* **Capo Portieri**. *Drive 2½kms down this road to the sea. This area was part of the Anzio beachhead during World War II. You're now on the coast road, heading toward* **Foce Verde** *which is 6kms from the turn for Capo Portieri.*

Drive through the town of Foce Verde and now follow signs for **Nettuno**. *At the T-junction 8kms from Foce Verde, turn left signposted* **Nettuno**. *After another 6kms drive under the Nettuno town sign and into the center of town.*

Drive straight across the next intersection following a white sign for **Cimitero** *(cemetery). Turn right at the traffic lights (2½kms from the Nettuno town sign). Then cross the intersection with two sets of lights. The* **Piazza Kennedy** *and the* **American Cemetery** *are on your left. For Tourist Information apply at the office inside, and to the right of, the entrance. (Tel: (06) 9800396. Open: Mon–Sat 9am–1pm, 4pm–6pm.)*

NETTUNO

The ancient town of Nettuno was possibly of Saracen origin, and has a picturesque medieval quarter. The suburbs of Nettuno merge with those of Anzio. Both towns are chiefly remembered as the scene of the Allied invasion in World War II, when British and American troops landed on the beaches. British soldiers killed in the bloody battle that ensued lie in the British Military Cemetery near Anzio (see page 156); the American graves are to be found in the **American Military Cemetery**. (Open: Daily mid-May–mid-Sept 8am–6pm, rest of the year 8am–5pm.)

There are 7,862 graves, and in the chapel is a memorial to the 3,094 American servicemen and women who went missing in action or were buried at sea. The cemetery covers 70 acres and the graves are arranged in eight sections divided by avenues lined with cypresses, holm oaks and hedges. At the far end of the cemetery there are two lovely, formal gardens.

There's also a museum (open: same times as cemetery). A bronze-coloured table covered with a relief map of Italy dominates the center of this small museum, and shows the general outline of American military operations in Sicily and Italy during 1943–45. All the walls are covered with maps and text on the various battles waged during this campaign.

NETTUNO TO ANZIO

*Retrace your steps from the cemetery through the two sets of traffic lights, going straight ahead down the **Via Santa Maria**. At the next traffic lights turn right. There's another set of lights one block later where you drive straight ahead following signs for **Roma**. At the T-junction turn left signposted **Latina/Roma**. Drive straight ahead until you see a right turn for **Anzio/Roma**. Turn right following this coastal road which you meet in just under 2kms from the American Cemetery.*

*At the fork go right up the hill and you'll see the **Anzio** town sign on your left. After roughly 1km from this sign you turn left at the traffic lights. Go down the hill following **Porto** (Port) signs. At the bottom you'll see the **Information** sign which you follow and turn left into **Via Mimma Pollastrini**. Park in the piazza in front of you with the monument called **Anzio Aisuoicaduti**. Walk to the sea front. Turn right and you'll see the **Information Office**, Riviera Zanardelli 105 (Tel: (06) 98461190). For details of **Anzio** see **page 157**.*

*To continue your tour to **Rome** via **Ostia Antica** see directions beginning on **page 159**. If, however, you wish to go directly to **Leonardo da Vinci airport** at Fiumicino follow the directions below.*

ANZIO TO LEONARDO DA VINCI AIRPORT

*From the piazza near the Information Office, reverse your route back up to the traffic lights. Turn left following signs for **Roma/Ostia**. Then continue following signs for Ostia along the coastal road for about 37kms which will take you into **Ostia Lido**.*

*Drive through Ostia on this road until you see the **Viale della Mare** on the right. You'll know it because on the right corner of the road is a huge sign for **Gelateria Gran Café Miramare** and on the left corner is a sign for the **Albergo Belvedere**. Turn right onto the Viale della Mare. Drive down this road going straight ahead at the lights. Now get into the middle fast lane. Follow this road all the way out to the airport turnoff. After 2kms you'll see signs for **Fiumicino**. After 3½kms the signs you follow will read **Aeroporto/Fiumicino**.*

*A tip: If you're returning a rental car follow the signs for **International Arrivals** to the rent-a-car parking areas.*

INDEX

Note: Towns fully described on the tours are shown in **bold type**; towns and villages driven through are shown in *italics*; attractions, hotels and restaurants are shown in Roman type.

Abbazia della Trinità di Cava 302
Abbazia di San Galgano 190
accidents 16
Acquapendente 202
addresses, useful 19
Agnano 305
Albano 150
Altar of the Nation, Rome 65
Amalfi 292–5
American Military Cemetery, Nettuno 318
American War Cemetery 156
Amphitheater
  Montecassino 254
  Pozzuoli 306
  Santa Maria Capua Vetere 260
Anagni 250
Ancilia 160
Anguillara 171
Antiche Terme 283
Anzio 157–9
Appartamenti Storici
  Palazzo Reale, Naples 272
  Palazzo Reggia, Caserta 262
Appian Way 42
Ara Pacis, Rome 62
Aranova 162
Arch of Constantine 40, 58
Arch of Janus 59
Arch of Severus 56
Arch of Titus 56
Arco di Augusto, Perugia 210
Arco di Constantino 40, 58
Ardea 155
Ariccia 150
Assisi 216–22

Bagni di Tivoli 135
banks 9, 11
Barcaccia Fountain 60
Basilica of Constantine 57
Basilicas (Forum) 56
Baths of Caracalla 58, 69
Baths of Dioclethian, Rome 63
Beach Head War Cemetery 156
Bettolle 203
Boat trips
  from Gaeta 310
  from Naples 274
  from Pozzuoli 307
  from Terracina 314
Bocca della Verità 46
Bolsena 237
Borghesiana 247
Borgo Scacciaventi, Cava De'Tireni 302
Bracciano 168, 245
breakdowns 16
Bridge of the Four Heads, Rome 47
Build-a-Tour system 7
Buonconvento 202

Cafés/Bars (out of Rome):
Bar Enoteca Italica Permanente, Siena 199
Bar Enoteca Porrini Bar, Castiglione 188
Bar Marinella, Santa Marinella 180
Bar Montanucci, Orvieto 234
Bar Royal, Amalfi 294
Bon Caffè Bondolfi, Fregene 161
Caffè Enea, Pratica di Mare 155
Gelateria Davide, Sorrento 286

Gran Caffè Roma, Frascati 146
Gran Caffè Schenardi, Viterbo 244
Pasticceria Andrea Pansa, Amalfi 294
Rick's Bar, Monticiano 190
San Domino Café, Ravello 297
Campagnano 172
Campello 223
Il Campidoglio 41, 55
Campo dei Fiori, Rome 68
Campoleone Scalo 153
Camucia 203
Capena 174
Capitoline Hill 41, 55
Cappella Sistina 40
Capri 275
Capua 258
car rental 17, 38
Carceri Nuove, Rome 69
Casa dei Maestri Comacini, Assisi 217
Casa di Santa Caterina, Siena 194, 198
Cascata Grande, Caserta 262
Caserta 261
Caserta Vecchia 264
Cassino 254
Castel dell'Ovo, Naples 273
Castel Gandolfo 151
Castel Nuovo, Naples 273
Castel Sant'Angelo, Rome 70
Castellammare di Stabia 282
Castello degli Orsini-Odescalchi Bracciano 168
Castello di Arechi, Salerno 300
Castello Ducale, Fiano

Romano 175
Castello Odescalchi,
    Ladispoli 164
Castiglione della Pescaia
    188
Catacombs 42
Cathedrals:
  Amalfi 292
  Anagni 251
  Caserta Vecchia 265
  Ferentino 253
  Foligno 223
  Gaeta 309
  Naples 271
  Orvieto 232
  Palestrina (San Agapito)
      142
  Perugia 208
  Salerno (San Matteo)
      299
  Siena 193, 196
  Spoleto 225
  St Peter's (Basilica di San
      Pietro), Rome 40
  Terracina 314
  Todi 230
  Viterbo 241
Cava De'Tirreni 302
Cave 142
Cecchina 153
Certosa di San Martino,
    Naples 270
Cerveteri 166
Cesano 172
Cesario 248
Cetara 297
Chancellery, Rome 69
Churches:
  Abbey of Sant'Andrea in
      Fulmine, Ponzano
      Ramano 176
  Basilica di San
      Francesco, Assisi
      216, 218
  Cappella di Montesiepi,
      Monticiano 190
  Cappella di Piazza, Siena
      195
  Cappella Sanservero,
      Naples 271

Chiesa del Gesù, Rome
    66
Chiesa dell'Assunta 170
Chiesa Nuova and Casa
    Paterna di San
    Francesco, Assisi
    219
Chiostro del Paradiso,
    Amalfi 293
Cloister of Santa Chiara,
    Rome 66
Convent of Santa Maria
    della Verità,
    Viterbo 241
Convento di San
    Gennaro,
    Pozzuoli 306
Oratorio di San
    Bernardino,
    Perugia 211
Pieve di San Giovanni,
    Siena 197
San Domenico, Orvieto
    232
San Domenico, Siena
    194, 197
San Fortunato, Todi 229
San Francesco, Sorrento
    284
San Giovanni Battista,
    Morlupo 174
San Giovanni dei
    Fiorentini, Rome
    69
San Gregorio, Rome 58
San Luigi dei Francesi,
    Rome 67
San Nicolo, Ponzano
    Romano 176
San Pietro Apostolo,
    Segni 249
San Pietro in Carcero,
    Rome 57
San Pietro in Montorio,
    Rome 72
San Salvatore in Lauro,
    Rome 70
San Stefano, Fiano
    Romano 175
Sant'Agnese in Agone,

Rome 45
Sant'Andrea della Valle,
    Rome 68
Sant'Angelo, Viterbo
    240
Sant'Eufemia, Spoleto
    224
Santa Agnese, Rome 67
Santa Chiara, Assisi 219
Santa Chiara, Naples 273
Santa Cristina, Bolsena
    237
Santa Maria d'Aracoeli,
    Rome 55
Santa Maria degli
    Angeli, Assisi 218
Santa Maria dei
    Miracoli, Rome
    61
Santa Maria
    dell'Assunzione,
    Ariccia 150
Santa Maria della
    Consolazione 229
Santa Maria della
    Rotonda, Albano
    151
Santa Maria in
    Cosmedin, Rome
    46, 59
Santa Maria in Monte
    Santo, Rome 61
Santa Maria Infraportas,
    Foligno 223
Santa Maria sopra
    Minerva, Rome
    66
Santissima Annunziata,
    Gaeta 309
Santuario Santa
    Margherita,
    Cortona 205
SS Giovanni e Paolo,
    Rome 58
Trinita dei Monti, Rome
    60
Circolo dei Forestieri,
    Sorrento 283
Circus Maximus 58
Cisterna Roman, Segni 249

Civitavecchia 180
clothing charts 13
Colleferro 248
Colli di Fontanelle 288
Colonna 248
Colonna dell'Immacolata
    Concezione 60
Colonna di Marco Aurelio
    40
Colosseum 41, 58
Column of Immaculate
    Conception 60
Column of Marcus
    Aurelius 40, 62
Convento di San Damiano,
    Assisi 217
Cordonata 55
Cortona 203–7
Costalpino 191
credit cards 8, 9
cuisine 22
Cura 245
currency exchange and
    regulations 9
customs regulations, Italian
    and US 14

Domus Aurea 41

Ercolano 280
Eremo delle Carceri, Assisi
    217
Etruscan Necropolis,
    Tarquinia 183

Ferentino 252
Festival dei Due Mondi,
    Spoleto 224
Fiano Romano 175
Finocchio 247
Fiuggi 141
Foce Verde 318
Foligno 222
Fontana del Babuino,
    Rome 61
Fontana del Moro 67
Fontana del Tritone 44
Fontana dell'Acqua Felice
    63
Fontana delle Tartarughe

44
Fontana di Trevi 44, 62
Fontanella delle Api 44, 63
Fonte Gaia, Siena 195
Fonte Maggiore, Perguia
    210
Foreigners' Club, Sorrento
    283
Formia 308
Foro Romano 41, 56
Fortezza Medicea, Cortona
    205
Fortezza Medicea, Siena
    194
Forum Boarium 59
Forum
    Augustus's 57
    Caesar's 57
    Nerva's 57
    Roman 41, 56
Fountain of Joy, Siena 195
Fountain of Neptune 67
Fountain of the Baboon,
    Rome 61
Fountain of the Bees 44, 63
Fountain of the Four
    Rivers 67
Fountain of the Mask 69
Fountain of the Tortoises
    44
Frascati 146
Fregene 161
Frosine 191

Gaeta 309
Gallaria Umberto, Naples
    273
Genzano 149
Il Gianicolo 47
Giardino Zoologico, Rome
    48
La Giostra del Maialetto,
    Segni 249
Grosseto 187
Grotta delle Capre, San
    Felice Circeo 317
Grotta dello Smeraldo,
    near Amalfi 291
Grotta di Neanderthal, San
    Felice Circeo 317

Grottaferrata 147
Grotto del Turco, Gaeta
    309

Herculaneum 280
hotel codes 7
hotel dos and don'ts 8
hotel symbols 8
Hotels (out of Rome):
    Albergo San Luca,
        Cortona 207
    All'Antica Carsulae, San
        Gémini 228
    Aquila Bianca, Orvieto
        235
    Bassetto, Ferentino 253
    Bastiani Grand Hotel,
        Grosseto 187
    Bellavista, Frascati 147
    Boschetto, Fiuggi 142
    Bristol, Sorrento 287
    Brufani, Perugia 215
    Cappuccini Convento,
        Amalfi 294
    Caruso Belvedere,
        Ravello 297
    Castel Vecchio, Castel,
        Gondolfo 152
    Cavour, Naples 278
    Centrale, Caserta 264
    Chiusarelli, Siena 201
    Columbus, Bolsena
    La Conchiglia, Fregene
        161
    Continental, Siena 201
    Dei Duchi, Spoleto 227
    Feronia, Capena 175
    Fontebella, Assisi 221
    Forum Palace,
        Montecassino 257
    Gattapone, Spoleto 227
    Grand Hotel Dei Cesari,
        Anzio 158
    Grand Hotel Excelsior
        Vittoria, Sorrento
        286
    Jolly delle Palme,
        Salerno 301
    Jolly Hotel Excelsior,
        Siena 201

L'Approdo, Castiglione 189
Lloyds Baia, Salerno 301
Maitani, Orvieto 236
Marincanto, Positano 290
Millepini, near Tivoli 138
Miramalfi, Amalfi 295
Palace, Naples 278
Palazzo Ravizza, Siena 201
Park Hotel Fiorelle, Sperlonga 312
Plaza, Salerno 301
I Presidi, Orbetello 186
Reggia, Caserta 263
Regina, Sorrento 287
Rex, Naples 277
River, Terracina 315
Roma, Castiglione 189
La Rosetta, Perguia 215
Royal, Naples 278
Scapolatiello, Cava De'Tirreni 303
Signa, Perugia 215
Le Sirenuse, Positano 290
Solfatara, Pozzuoli 308
Summit, Gaeta 310
Sunbay Park, Civitavecchia 182
Tarconte, Tarquinia 184
Tuscia, Viterbo 244
Umbra, Assisi 221
Villa Fiorita, Fregene 161
Villa Luisa, Todi 230
Villa Margherita, Ladispoli 165
Villa Valentina, Trevignano Romano 171
Virgilio, Orvieto 236

insurance 10
Ischia 275
Isola Tiberina 44, 59, 71
Italián Senate Building, Rome 67

Janiculum 47, 72
Jewish Ghetto, Ancient 59

La Storta 171
Labico 248
Ladispoli 164
Legahetto 248
Lago d'Averno 307
Lago di Bracciano 169
Lago di Nemi 149
Lavinio 159
Lavinium 155
Lido di Ostia 159
Luna Park EUR 45

Maccarese 160
Maiori 297
Mamertine Prison, Rome 57
Marcellina 178
Marcellus Theater 42, 59
Marino 147
Il Mascherone 69
Mausoleo di Augusto, Rome 62
Mausoleum di Planco, Gaeta 309
menu translator 23–7
Meta 283
Minori 297
Miracle of Bolsena 237
Mithraeum, Santa Maria Capua Vetere 260
Monastery Convento di San Benedetto Subiaco 139
Monastery of Santa Scholastica, Subiaco 139
Monastery of St Martin, Naples 270
Mondragone 308
Monte Cavo 148
Monte Frumentario, Assisi 217
Monte Porzio 144
Montecassino Abbey 255
Montefiascone 238
Monterotondo Scala 177
Monticiano 190

Monumente Nazionale a Vittorio Emanuel II 45
Morlupo 174
motoring documentation 14
motorist's vocaculary 15
Museums (out of Rome):
    American Military Museum, Nettuno 319
    Collegio del Cambio, Perugia 211
    Galleria Nazionale dell'Umbria, Perugia 211
    Libreria Piccolomini, Siena 196
    Montecassino Abbey 256
    Museo Archaeologico Nazionale dell'Umbria, Perugia 212
    Museo Archaeologico Nazionale, Naples 272
    Museo Archaeologico, Montecassino 254
    Museo Archaelogico, Terracina 314
    Museo Campano, Capua 258
    Museo Civico, Amalfi 292
    Museo Civico, Civitavecchia 181
    Museo Civico, Orvieto 232
    Museo Civico, Viterbo 241
    Museo del Duomo, Salerno 299
    Museo dell'Accademia Etrusca, Cortona 204, 206
    Museo dell'Opera del Duomo, Orvieto 233
    Museo della Ceramica Duca di Martina, Naples 270

Museo Diocesano, Cortona 205
Museo Nazionale Archaeologico Prenestino and Tempio della Fortuna, Palestrina 143
Museo Nazionale Cerite (Archaeology), Cerveteri 166
Museo Nazionale Tarquiniese, Tarquinia 183
Museo Provinciale, Salerno 300
National Park Museum, Circeo 318
Pinacoteca, Siena 197
Pinoteca Comunale, Assisi 217
Raccolta Manzù, Ardea 156
Tiberius's Villa, Sperlonga 312

Naples 267–78
national holidays 18
Necropoli Etrusca, Cerveteri 167
Nero's Golden House 41
Nero's Villa, Subiaco 139
Nettuno 318
Nuova Florida 155

opening hours 11
Oratorio dei Pellegrini, Assisi 217
Orbetello 185
Oriolo Romano 245
Orvieto 202, 231–6
Ospedalicchio 216
Osteria Nuova 171
Ostia Antica 159
Ostia Lido 319
Ostia Nuova 245

Palace of the Falconieri Family, Rome 69
Palace of the Massimo Family, Rome 68
Palatine Hill (Il Palatino) 42, 57
Palazzo Altieri, Rome 66
Palazzo Borghese, Rome 62
Palazzo Casali, Cortona 204
Palazzo Chigi, Rome 62
Palazzo Comunale, Anagni 250
Palazzo Comunale, Siena 193, 195
Palazzo Comunale, Viterbo 240
Palazzo dei Consevatori and Museum, Rome 56
Palazzo dei Priori, Perugia 211
Palazzo del Comune, Cortona 204
Palazzo della Congregazione di Propaganda Fide, Rome 61
Palazzo di Bonfacio VIII, Anagni 250
Palazzo Doria Pamphili, Rome 67
Palazzo Farnese, Rome 69
Palazzo Gallenga Stuart, Perugia 210
Palazzo Madama, Rome 67
Palazzo Margherita, Rome 63
Palazzo Pretorio, Cortona 204
Palazzo Reale di Capodimonte, Naples 269
Palazzo Salimbeni, Siena 194
Palazzo Senatorio, Rome 56
Palazzo Soliano, Orvieto 232
Palazzo Tolomei, Siena 194
Palazzo Trinci, Foligno 223
Palazzo Venezia, Rome 65

Palestrina 142
Palidoro 163
Palio delle Contrade, Siena 193
Palombara 177
Pantheon, Rome 42, 67
Parco dei Mostri, Bomarzo 241
Parco di Palazzo Reale, Caserta 262
Parco Naturale di Maremma 186
Parco Nazionale del Circeo 317
Parliament Buildings, Rome 62
Passo Corese 177
passports 9
Perugia 208–15
   map of city center 209
Piazza Barberini, Rome 62
Piazza Barberini, Rome 63
Piazza Bocca della Verità, Rome 59
Piazza Colonna, Rome 62
Piazza del Campo, Siena 193, 195
Piazza del Colosseo, Rome 58
Piazza del Popolo, Rome 61, 64
Piazza della Repubblica, Rome 63
Piazza IV Novembre, Perugia 210
Piazza Navona, Rome 45, 67
Piazza San Bernardo, Rome 63
Piazza San Francesco d'Assisi, Rome 72
Piazza San Lorenzo, Viterbo 241
Piazza Santa Cecilia, Rome 71
Piazza Santa Maria in Trastevere, Rome 72
Piazza Trilussa, Rome 72
Piccola Farnesina 68

Pincio Gardens, Rome 47, 64
Pompeii 281
Ponte a Tressa 202
Ponte Cestio 71
Ponte delle Torri, Spoleto 225
Ponte Fabricio 47, 71
Ponte Milvio, Rome 47
Ponte Rotto 45, 71
Ponte Sant'Angelo, Rome, 47, 69
Ponza 157, 310, 314
Ponzano Romano 176
Porta Pinciana, Rome 64
Positano 288–90
postage 10
Pozzo Etrusco, Perugia 212
Pozzo San Patrizio, Orvieto 232, 233
Pozzuoli 305
Pratica di Mare 155
Procida 275
Punta Campanella, Sorrento 284

Raphael's House, Rome 70
Ravello 295
restaurant codes 8
restaurant, types of 27
Restaurants (out of Rome):
Agostino al Campanaccio, Morlupo 174
Alfredo di Geno e Toni, Tivoli 137
Antica Locanda Massa 1848, Caserta 263
Antico Ristorante Mastroangelo, Caserta Vecchia 266
Antico Ristorante Pagnanelli, Castel Gandolfo 152
Bar Daniele, Naples 277
La Bersagliera, Naples 275
Il Bersagliere, Tarquinia 184

La Brace, Salerno 300
Buca di San Francesco, Assisi 221
Le Campane, Siena 200
Casina del Lago, Bracciano 170
La Castellana, Caserta Vecchia 265
Cavour, Naples 276
Chez Black, Positano 289
Cielo e Mare (in Hotel Villa Margherita), Ladispoli 165
Il Cioceo, Tivoli 137
La Conca Azzurra, Grotta dello Smeraldo 291
d'Angelo, Naples 276
Da Righetto, Campagnano 172
Da Romolo, Castiglione 189
Da Titto, Genzano 150
Da Vincenzo, Positano 289
Del Gallo, Anagni 251
del Sole, Perugia 214
Enoteca Ombrone, Grosseto 187
Falchetto, Perugia 214
La Fontana da Carletto, Assisi 221
Forum Palace Hotel, Montecassino 257
Frantoio (in Hotel Fontebella), Assisi 220
Gambrinus, Naples 277
Giglio d'Oro, Orvieto 235
Gran Bar Nazionale, Ladispoli 165
Grand Hotel Excelsior Vittoria, Sorrento 285
Grappolo d'Uva, Terracina 315
La Grotta, Fiuggi 141
Guido, Siena 200
Hotel All'Antica

Carsulae, San Gémini 228
Hotel Bassetto, Ferentino 253
Hotel Cappuccini, Amalfi 293
Hotel Caruso Belvedere, Ravello 296
Hotel Scapolatiello, Cava De'Tirreni 303
Kursaal, Sorrento 285
Laocoonte Da Rocco, Sperlonga 312
La Loggetta, Cortona 207
Luccio d'Oro, Bracciano 170
Morino, Orvieto 235
Nello-La Taverna, Siena 200
Nicola dei Principati, Salerno 300
La Ninfea, Pozzuoli 307
O'Parruchiano, Sorrento 286
Osteria del Lupcante, Orbetello 186
Pentagramma, Spoleto 227
Porto Vecchio Fani, Ponzano Romano 176
Quattro Mori, Marino 148
Salvatore, Ravello 296
Scaletta, Viterbo 243
Sora Olga, Ladispoli 165
Stella, Palestrina 143
La Tartana Da Mario l'Ostricaro, Terracina 315
Il Tartufo, Spoleto 226
La Taverna, Perugia 214
Trattoria all Lupa, Civitavecchia 181
Trattoria Il Corazziere, Marino 148
Trattoria da Gemma, Amalfi 293

Trattoria da Pierino,
Anzio 158
Trattoria da Pino a
L'Oasi, Cerveteri
167
Trattoria O'Pescatore,
Civitavecchia 182
Tre Re, Viterbo 243
Il Turcotto, Anzio 158
Umbria, Todi 230
Unnamed Restaurant,
Ercolano 280
Villa Fontania, Gaeta
310
Rocca di Papa 149
Rocca Janula,
Montecassino 255
Rocca Paolina fortress,
Perugia 210
Rocca Paolina, Perugia 212
Rocca, Bolsena 237
Rocca, Orvieto 232
Rocca, Spoleto 225
Roccastrada 190
Rome
A Heritage of History 20
Rome 33–132 (maps *34, 36,
37*)
  Getting About
    Buses 35
    Trams 35
    Subway 35
    Taxis 35
    Rail 38
    Cars 38
    Car Rental 38
    Bicycles 38
    Scooters 38
    Horsedrawn Carriages
      8
    On Foot 38
    Guided Tours 39
  Top Sights 40–3
  Local Delights 44–6
  Bridges/Gardens/Parks
    47– 8
  Museums:
    Borghese Gallery 64
    Criminology Museum
      69

Galleria Doria-
  Pamphili 49
Galleria Nazionale
  d'Arte Antica
  49
Galleria Nazionale
  d'Arte
  Moderna 49, 64
Galleria Spada 49
Keats and Shelley
  Memorial
  House 50, 61
Museo Barracco 68
Museo Capitolino 50
Museo Capitolino 56
Museo Nazionale
  d'Arte
  Orientale 50
Museo Nazionale
  Etrusco 50
Museo Nazionale
  Romano 51
Museo Nazionale
  Romano 63
Palazzo dei
  Conservatori
  Museum 56
Vatican Museums 51–
  4
Villa Giulia 64
Roman Walking Tours
  55–72
Shopping:
  Department Stores
    73–4
  Markets 74–6
  Antiques 76–81
  Auctions 82
  Bookstores 82–6
  Food 86–8
  Gifts 88–95
  Jewelry 95–8
  Kids' Stuff 98–102
  Menswear 102–5
  Women's Fashion
    105–8
Restaurants:
  ABC 109
  Al Moro 109
  Al Vicario 109

Alfredo alla Scrofa 109
Andrea 109
Angelino ai Fori 110
Antico Falcone 110
Il Buco 112
La Campana 113
Il Cerchio e la Botte
  113
Charley's Saucière 110
Ciceruacchio 110
Coriolano 110
Da Amato 111
Da Mario 111
Da Pancrazio 68, 111
Dal Bolognese 111
El Toulà 116
La Fontanella 62
Galeone 111
George's 112
Giggetto 112
Giovanni 112
Hostaria dell'Orso
  112, 132
L'Eau Vive 114
Mandarin 114
Nihonbashi 114
Osteria
  dell'Antiquario
  70
Oteria Margutta 61
Otello all Concordia
  115
Polese 115
I Preistorici 113
Le Rallye 114
Ranieri 115
Re degli Amici 115
Regno di Re
  Ferdinando 115
La Rosetta 114
Sabatini 116
Santopadre 116
Spahetteria 116
Taverna Giulia 116
Il Tentativo 113
Vecchia Roma 117
Fast Food 117
Pizzerias 117
Cafés:
  Alemagna 118

Babington's Tea Rooms 118
Bar San Filippo 118
Berardo 62
Café de Paris 118
Caffè del Teatro 60
Caffè Greco 118
Canova 119
Doney's 63, 119
Giolitti 119
Rosati's 61, 65, 119
Tre Scalini 68, 120
Hotels:
Alexandra 121
Ambasciatori Palace 121
Atlante Star 121
Aventino 121
Bologna 121
Boston 122
Carriage 126
Cavalieri Hilton 122
Cicerone 122
Colonna Palace 122
Columbus 122
D'Inghilterra 123
De La Ville 122
Delta 123
Diplomatic 123
Eden 123
Esperia 123
Excelsior 124
Farnese 124
Fiorella 124
Flora 124
Fontana 126
Forum 57, 124
Genio 125
Giulio Cesare 125
Grand Hotel et de Rome 125
Gregoriana 125
Hassler-Villa Medici 125
Holiday Inn 126
Internazionale 126
Jolly 126
Londra e Cargill 127
Lord Byron 127
Orsini Residence 127

Pace Elvezia 127
Portoghesi 127
Quirinale 128
Raphael 128
La Residenza 127
Sant'Anna 128
Scalinata di Spagna 128
Sheraton Roma 128
Sicilia Daria 129
Siena 129
Sole al Pantheon 129
Suisse 129
Tiziano 129
Victoria 130
Villa Borghese 130
Villa San Pio 130
Nightspots:
Bella Blue 131
La Cabala 132
Il Dito al Naso 131
Easy Going 131
Folkstudio 131
Jackie-O 131
Much More 132
Piper '80' 132
Tartarughino 132
Rosia 191
Royal Apartments
Palazzo Reale, Naples 272
Palazzo Reggia, Caserta 262

Sacchetti Palace, Rome 69
Sacramento 318
Sacred Way 56
Salerno 298–301
San Cesareo 144
San Felice Circeo 316
San Gémini 228
San Lorenzo Nuovo 202
San Pellegrino, Viterbo 242
San Quirico d'Orcia 202
Sant Agnello 283
Santa Maria Capua Vetere 259
Santa Marinella 180
Santuario della Montagna Spaccata, Gaeta 309

Santuario di Santa Rosa, Viterbo 241
Scalinata della Trinità dei Monti 46, 60
Scavi di Baia, Pozzuoli 307
Scavi di Cumae, near Pozzuoli 307
Scavi di Ostia Antica 159
Segni 248
Senate of Ancient Roman Empire 56
Serapeum, Pozzuoli 306
Siena 191–202
map of city center 192
Sistine Chapel 40
size charts 13
Solfatara Volcano, Pozzuoli 306
Sorrento 283–7
Spanish Steps 46, 60
Sperlonga 311
Spoleto 224–7
Spring of San Gémini 228
St Peter's, Rome 40
Subiaco 139

Tabularium 56
Tarpeian Rock 60
Tarquinia 183
Teatro di Marcello, Rome 52, 59, 70
Teatro di Pompeii, Rome 68
Teatro San Carlo Naples 274
telephones 10
Tempio di Giove Anxur, Terracina 314
Temple of Aesculapius 64
Temple of Antonius and Faustina 56
Temple of Apollo 59
Temple of Manly Fortune 59
Temple of Saturn 56
Temple of Venus and Rome 57
Temple of Vesta 56, 59
Terme di Agnano 305
Terme Stabiane Nuove 282

Terme Taurine,
Civitavecchia 181
Terracina 313
Tiber Island 44, 59, 71
Tiberius's Villa and
Museum, Sperlonga
312
tipping 12
Tivoli 135
Todi 229
Tomb of Augustus, Rome
62
Tomb of C Publius Bibulus,
Rome 65
Tomb of the Horatti and
Curiatti, Albano 151
Torre del Mangia, Siena
193, 195
Torre Mancina 177
Torregaia 247
Torrita Tiberina 177
Tourist Offices 12
Tower of the Glutton,
Siena 193, 195
Trajan's Baths,
Civitavecchia 181
Trajan's Forum and

Column 57
Trastevere 71
Trevi Fountain 44, 62
Trevignano Romano 170
Triton Fountain 44, 62, 63

Valmontone 248
value added tax 13
Vatican Gardens 48
Vejano 245
Ventotene 310
Vetralla 245
Via Appia Antica 42
Via dei Cestari, Rome 66
Via dei Mercati, Salerno
299
Via Pietà, Sorrento 284
Via Veneto, Rome 63
Victor Emmanuel
Monument 45
Vietri sul Mare 297
Villa Ada, Rome 48
Villa Adriana, Tivoli 135
Villa Aldobrandini,
Frascati 146
Villa Borghese, Rome 48
Villa Celimontana, Rome

48
Villa Cimbrone, Ravello
296
Villa Comunale gardens,
Albano 151
Villa d'Este, Tivoli 136
Villa Farnesina, Rome 46,
72
Villa Floridiana gardens,
Naples 271
Villa Gregoriana, Tivoli
137
Villa Medici, Rome 60
Villa Rufolo, Ravello 295
visas 9
Viterbo 238–45
map of city center *239*
vocabulary
menus 23–7
motorist's 15

War Cemeteries,
Montecassino 257
weather 10

zoological gardens, Rome
48